Special Edition

USING
MICROSOFT®
POWERPOINT® 97

Special Edition

Using
Microsoft®
PowerPoint® 97

Written by Nancy Stevenson with

*Brian Reilly, Dave Johnson, Steve Rindsberg, Dorothy Burke,
Laura Monsen, Michael O'Mara, Todd White, Michael Desmond,
and Edward Willett*

Special Edition Using Microsoft® PowerPoint® 97

Credits

PRESIDENT
Roland Elgey

PUBLISHING DIRECTOR
David W. Solomon

TITLE MANAGER
Kathie-Jo Arnoff

EDITORIAL SERVICES DIRECTOR
Elizabeth Keaffaber

MANAGING EDITOR
Michael Cunningham

DIRECTOR OF MARKETING
Lynn E. Zingraf

ACQUISITIONS MANAGER
Elizabeth South

SENIOR PRODUCT DIRECTOR
Lisa D. Wagner

PRODUCT DIRECTOR
Dana S. Coe

PRODUCTION EDITOR
Lisa M. Gebken

EDITORS
Kate Givens
Thomas F. Hayes
Brian Sweeny
Nick Zafran

STRATEGIC MARKETING MANAGER
Barry Pruett

PRODUCT MARKETING MANAGER
Kris Ankney

ASSISTANT PRODUCT MARKETING MANAGERS
Karen Hagan
Christy M. Miller

TECHNICAL EDITORS
Nanci Jacobs
Nadeem Muhammed
Liz Reding

MEDIA DEVELOPMENT SPECIALIST
David Garratt

TECHNICAL SUPPORT SPECIALIST
Nadeem Muhammed

ACQUISITIONS COORDINATOR
Tracy C. Williams

SOFTWARE RELATIONS COORDINATORS
Patty Brooks
Susan Gallagher

EDITORIAL ASSISTANT
Virginia Stoller

BOOK DESIGNER
Ruth Harvey

COVER DESIGNER
Dan Armstrong

PRODUCTION TEAM
Michael Beaty
Julie Geeting
Kay Hoskin
Kaylene Riemen
Lisa Stumpf

INDEXER
Ginny Bess

Composed in *Century Old Style* and *Franklin Gothic* by Que Corporation.

To Liam Allard, the newest kid in town, for dusting off the definition of family and making it shine. And, as always, to Graham for putting up with it all.

Acknowledgments

This book represents an entirely new version of *Special Editon Using PowerPoint*, one that brought together an impressive team of authors with solid expertise in using PowerPoint in real-world settings. Elizabeth South, Que's able acquisitions representative, was responsible for assembling this group of experts and, along with acquisitions coordinator Tracy Williams, providing the support we needed to succeed.

The author team was also backed by an exceptional editorial group at Que, including Dana Coe who saw to it that we all organized and communicated our information effectively; Lisa Gebken, who juggled a myriad of details to see that the individual pieces became a book; and Nanci Jacobs, Nadeem Muhammed, and Liz Reding, who provided an excellent technical review. A special thanks to Ron Person who wrote Appendix B, "Glossary."

To all the authors and to Que and its excellent staff, thank you for the support needed to produce what I hope will prove to be an invaluable resource to all users of PowerPoint.

About the Authors

Nancy Stevenson is a freelance, writer, instructor, and consultant. She teaches technical writing at Purdue University in Indianapolis. Prior to going freelance, Nancy was a publishing manager at Que, and before that worked as a trainer, consultant, and product manager at Symantec Corporation in California.

Brian Reilly is a partner in Singer and Reilly Enterprise in New York City, which is a company that designs custom applications in corporate communication management. His background in consumer products management has convinced him of the need to be able to suppress unwanted information and graphically show only actionable information with instantly understandable graphics. Brian holds a B.A. in Communications from Fordham University, and an M.B.A. from Columbia University. An avid sailor in the Northeastern waters, he appreciates the difference between a datasheet and a spinnaker sheet. Brian can be reached on CompuServe at **75663,3456**.

Dave Johnson is a freelance writer and columnist for *Peak Computing* magazine. He has written *The Desktop Studio*, and contributed to *Platinum Edition Using Windows 95* as well as such magazines as *Computer Shopper* and *Digital Video*. Dave's years in the classroom and briefing room have hardened him into a PowerPoint warrior. He can be reached at **djohns@rmii.com**.

Steve Rindsberg is the owner of RDP, a slide imaging service bureau in Cincinnati, Ohio. In more than 20 years of slide and audiovisual production, he's never found an easier way of making slides than with PowerPoint. He hopes that your experience with it will be every bit as pleasant as his.

Dorothy Burke is an independent computer trainer and consultant, but she started out as a writer and magazine editor. A four-year apprenticeship in the magazine publishing industry gave her a set of skills she carried into computers, where she specializes in desktop publishing and graphics. Along the way, she sold medical equipment, wrote newsletters, prepared product catalogs, and trained company employees in business procedures, billing, and customer service. Her break into computers came during her years with a small management consulting firm, where her spreadsheet, word processing, and database skills were honed while she developed more efficient methods to analyze financial data and prepare promotional materials for her clients. Dorothy is a Certified Lotus Professional and a Certified Lotus Notes Instructor, and as such was a contributing author to the *10 Minute Guide to Lotus Notes Mail*. She can be reached through CompuServe at **71061,364**.

Laura Monsen is a senior instructor and consultant with Productivity Point International in San Antonio, Texas, where she teaches a variety of presentation graphic, spreadsheet, project management, and database applications. Laura has designed a diverse number of

PowerPoint presentations for her classes to graphically illustrate complex topics. Additionally, she frequently creates business presentations as part of PPI's consulting services. Laura contributed to Que's *Special Edition Using Microsoft Project for Windows 95*. She has a B.A. in Economics from the University of South, Sewanee.

Michael O'Mara is a freelance author and technical writer. Previously, he was a staff author with The Cobb Group where he wrote innumerable articles about leading computer software programs and served as editor-in-chief of several monthly software journals. He has co-authored or contributed to other Que books including *Using DOS*; *Using Windows 3.11*; *Special Edition Using CompuServe*; *Special Edition Using Windows 95*; *Special Edition Using Windows NT Workstation 3.51*; *10 Minute Guide to Freelance Graphics 96 for Windows 95*; and *Using Your PC*. He can be reached on CompuServe at **76376.3441**.

Todd White has spent the last year and a half working as the regional technology specialist for a Northern Michigan library cooperative. Specializing in Internet, PC networking, and Microsoft Office tools, Todd has developed and continues to conduct Internet training for librarians from nine Northern Lower Michigan counties. Todd also has the privilege of writing a bi-weekly column for a local newspaper, *Internet Coffee Talk*. Prior to the library co-op, Todd exclusively wrote and maintained a suite of documentation for a UNIX-based software corporation, a position Todd began while still attending Hope College in Holland, Michigan. During the past four years, Todd has also had the pleasure of working with a wide variety of people through independent contracts. His contractual experiences have allowed him many challenges ranging from documenting automotive manufacturing software to conducting Internet training for local groups including Air National Guard and Alpena Community College and educational school district staff and faculty. Todd can be reached via the Internet at **tmwhite@northland.lib.mi.us**.

Michael Desmond is senior news editor at *PC World* magazine, the world's largest computer publication. He is also vice-president of the Computer Press Association, an organization dedicated to promoting the computer press, its writers, and editors. In 1996, Michael earned the Jesse H. Neal Award from the American Business Press for runner-up in the best investigative article category. Previously executive editor at *Multimedia World* magazine, Michael has an M.S. in Journalism from Northwestern University's Medill School of Journalism, and a B.A. in Soviet Studies from Middlebury College in Vermont. Michael has also written for other publications, including *Working Woman* and *Video* magazines, and is a contributing author to Que's *Platinum Edition Using Windows 95*. A native of Cleveland, Ohio, Michael is an inveterate Cleveland Indians fan, and will never—ever—forgive Art Modell for moving the Cleveland Browns football team to Baltimore.

Edward Willett is a freelance writer in Regina, Saskatchewan, Canada. Born in New Mexico, he moved to Canada from Texas as a child but returned to the U.S. for college, graduating from Harding University in Searcy, Arkansas with a degree in journalism. He's worked as a newspaper reporter and editor and for a science center, which led to the weekly science column he now writes for several Canadian newspapers. Edward is also a singer and actor who has performed in numerous plays, musicals, and operas across Saskatchewan.

We'd Like to Hear from You!

As part of our continuing effort to produce books of the highest possible quality, Que would like to hear your comments. To stay competitive, we *really* want you, as a computer book reader and user, to let us know what you like or dislike most about this book or other Que products.

You can mail comments, ideas, or suggestions for improving future editions to the address below, or send us a fax at (317) 581-4663. For the online inclined, Macmillan Computer Publishing has a forum on CompuServe (type **GO QUEBOOKS** at any prompt) through which our staff and authors are available for questions and comments. The address of our Internet site is **http://www.mcp.com** (World Wide Web).

In addition to exploring our forum, please feel free to contact me personally to discuss your opinions of this book: I'm **73451,1220** on CompuServe, and I'm **dcoe@que. mcp.com** on the Internet.

Thanks in advance—your comments will help us to continue publishing the best books available on computer topics in today's market.

Dana Coe
Product Development Specialist
Que Corporation
201 W. 103rd Street
Indianapolis, Indiana 46290
USA

NOTE Although we cannot provide general technical support, we're happy to help you resolve problems you encounter related to our books, disks, or other products. If you need such assistance, please contact our Tech Support department at 800-545-5914 ext. 3833.

To order other Que or Macmillan Computer Publishing books or products, please call our Customer Service department at 800-835-3202 ext. 666. ▨

Contents at a Glance

Contents

VII | PowerPoint Charts and Tables

Introduction

by Nancy Stevenson

Welcome to *Special Edition Using Microsoft PowerPoint 97*, a collaborative effort by authors with unique experience and expertise with the most powerful presentation software available today.

Although computer books are sometimes simply updated to reflect changes in new software products, this book is entirely new. It has been written by a team of experts to cover all the exciting features in this new version of PowerPoint comprehensively, to offer a focus on real-world presentation examples, and to add value to your learning experience with special features such as Troubleshooting and Tips. ■

Why You Need PowerPoint

Presentation software such as PowerPoint is nothing new. However, recent advances in multimedia and online features are bringing presentations into a renaissance. With sound, animation, video, and even hyperlinks to World Wide Web sites, today's PowerPoint presentation has only a vague resemblance to the overhead transparency and slide-producing tool of years past.

In a media-savvy world, knowing how to produce professional, dynamic presentations to persuade, inform, or entertain is no longer a nice-to-have skill. Creating effective presentations is a way to survive and advance in a competitive world.

Who Should Use This Book?

Perhaps you work in a large corporation. On the other hand, you might run a home business, do marketing for a non-profit group, or need to organize the PTA's spring meeting. Whatever your presentation needs, the clear, logically organized information in this book will help you take advantage of all of PowerPoint's tools and features.

In this book, we have made the assumption that you are a competent user of Windows 95 and know the basics of file management and using a mouse. Perhaps you've never used PowerPoint or any presentation software. That's okay. Maybe you used an earlier version of PowerPoint, or count yourself proficient on another presentation software product. That's also okay. Whether you're new to presentation software or upgrading to the features of the PowerPoint 97 product, this book will provide added value.

Use this book to learn PowerPoint 97 and as a reference over the next year or two when a question arises. This book does address using PowerPoint with other software products. However, if you want to use PowerPoint extensively as part of the Microsoft Office suite of products, you might also want to own *Special Edition Using Microsoft Office 97*, also by Que.

How the Book is Organized

This book has been organized so that you can use it in two ways:

- You can use the book in a linear fashion, reading straight through from Chapter 1 to the last chapter. Using the book this way will build your knowledge of PowerPoint from more basic functions at the outset to more advanced features towards the end.

■ Because of handy features like cross-references, more advanced users can also just jump into the chapters that interest them. When a concept is discussed in more detail in another chapter, you are referred to that chapter so you can get more detail if you need it.

This book uses a combination of step-by-step procedures and easily understood conceptual information. *Special Edition Using Microsoft PowerPoint 97* helps you to not only practice keystrokes and mouse moves, but also to comprehend how mastering those processes can help you do your job in the real world. In fact, the last part of this book, "Building Presentation Applications," explores typical uses of PowerPoint presentations in a variety of business settings.

Special Edition Using Microsoft PowerPoint 97 is divided into eight parts.

Part I gets you acquainted with the PowerPoint interface by exploring its toolbars, menus, and different views in Chapter 1. In Chapter 2, you begin to build presentations and are introduced to PowerPoint templates, layouts, placeholders, and Master views.

Part II explores working with text in a presentation. Chapter 3 shows you how to add, edit, and format text, and use some of PowerPoint's proofing tools, such as AutoCorrect and Style Checker. Chapter 4 studies various features of the Outline view of PowerPoint, which is a powerful way to organize and structure the information contained in your presentation. Chapter 5 discusses Notes Pages and Handouts, two aids to understanding for the two key participants in any presentation: the speaker and his or her audience.

Part III is dedicated to visual elements of your presentation, such as drawing objects (covered in Chapter 6 and 7), ready-made artwork called clip art and text effects using WordArt (Chapter 8), and the exciting possibilities of adding animation and sound to your presentation elements (Chapter 9). In this part, you learn how to draw, insert graphics files, edit color and background patterns of objects, and use the text effects applet called WordArt to add sparkle to your slides.

Part IV discusses how to use charts and tables to visually represent data in your presentation. Here you learn how to build your own charts in Chapters 10 and 11, and create Word for Windows tables right within PowerPoint in Chapter 12. Chapter 13 teaches you how to take advantage of another built-in applet to create organizational charts quickly and easily.

Part V is where you take all the elements that you've learned to create on PowerPoint slides and bring them all together to make a presentation. Chapter 14 provides a valuable overview of presentation concepts that help you structure the most effective presentation possible. Chapters 15 and 16 give you details about rehearsing a presentation, by using features like Meeting Minder to take notes during a presentation and using the Pack and

Go Wizard to take your presentation on the road. Chapter 17 tells you how to print paper presentations and generate slides.

Part VI is where we've put some of the advances that link PowerPoint to the explosive growth of the Internet. Chapters 18 and 19 provide the information you need to publish your presentation on the Internet, while Chapter 20 looks at the benefits of distributing your presentations on a company intranet.

Part VII, "Advanced Topics," looks at topics you'll want to explore once you have become a proficient PowerPoint user. Chapter 21 and 22 look at customizing PowerPoint's interface and functionality to work best for you and automating functions with powerful macro technology. Chapter 23 explores all the ways you can link or embed information from other programs—even the World Wide Web—into your presentations. Chapter 24 deals with more advanced multimedia and electronic publishing topics such as video editing and use of various projection systems. The last two chapters enable you to put what you've learned to work building typical business presentations. This is where you get ideas for putting PowerPoint's features to use in your day-to-day activities.

Appendix A lists valuable resources such as slide bureaus to help you generate 35mm slide presentations, and online vendors of additional clip art, sound and video files that make your PowerPoint presentations truly unique. Appendix B contains a glossary of helpful Powerpoint terms.

Finally, the Index of Common Problems provides at-a-glance reminders of where you can find solutions to common problems and procedures to perform typical tasks in the book.

Conventions

This book uses certain conventions for representing computer procedures. In most cases you are provided with several methods for performing operations, including keyboard, tool and menu options. Underlined letters such as those in File, Save are called *hotkeys*. If you do not have or want to use a mouse to make a selection in a menu, you can hold down the Alt key while you type these letters to make your selection instead. These hotkeys are also found in various dialog boxes for making choices.

Terms that may be new to you are set in *italics* when they are first mentioned. If there is specific text that you are asked to enter during a step-by-step procedure, that text appears in **boldface**.

Menu selections are indicated by first listing the menu name, then the command to select from the menu, as in the following example: choose Edit, Cut to cut selected text from a document. Keystroke options are listed with any keys which must be pressed together connected by a "+" sign, as in "Press Ctrl+X."

Special Elements Used in This Book

We've provided certain special features to provide value-added information and to help you learn the various features of PowerPoint.

Each chapter begins with a *roadmap*, a brief description of the key skills and features you learn about in that chapter.

 When there is a PowerPoint tool button that can be used to execute an operation, it is shown in the margin of the book, next to the paragraph where its use is mentioned.

N O T E A note is a piece of additional information regarding a topic that might be of interest in using a particular feature. ■

ON THE WEB
We've highlighted related Internet sites that you might want to explore with a special On the Web icon. These notations include a complete Web site address so you can get to these helpful sites quickly and easily.

 A *tip* is a handy optional way to perform a mentioned procedure, or additional feature you might want to explore. In a tip, you might learn about often overlooked information, or pick up a shortcut to help you get things done more quickly.

CAUTION
Cautions warn you if performing a particular task carries possible risks, such as permanently losing information.

TROUBLESHOOTING
Troubleshooting boxes provide commonly asked questions about problems or challenges typically encountered by new users. These troubleshooting tips are presented in the form of a commonly asked question and its answer.

 Whenever a new feature in PowerPoint is mentioned, we've called attention to it with a special PowerPoint 97 icon.

Finally, you will occasionally see references in the margin to related or more in-depth information about a topic being discussed. These cross-references assist you in exploring all aspects of a topic, no matter how we have selected to organize that information in creating this book.

▶ **See** "Using 3-D Effects," **p. 215**

You also find an *Index of Common Problems*, a table that provides answers to many commonly encountered problems. ●

PowerPoint Basics

Getting Acquainted

by Nancy Stevenson

In today's media-driven world, the ability to create dynamic multimedia presentations is key to your success. Whether you are giving a simple presentation using a few bullet points on overhead transparencies, or going all out with animation, sound, and photographic images within an on-screen slide show, your presentation can be made more professional and more exciting by using the features available in PowerPoint.

This chapter provides an overview of all you can do with PowerPoint, and shows you why presentation software like PowerPoint is not only an essential tool, but an easy one to use as well. ■

Understanding the value of presentation software

Survey the many ways you can use presentation software, and specifically PowerPoint, to get your point across while helping your audience to retain more information.

Getting a first look at PowerPoint toolbars and menus

Take a first look at PowerPoint, along with a brief description of the tools and commands you need to build presentations.

Learning to navigate around PowerPoint's views

PowerPoint offers several ways to navigate around the program, among individual slides, and among different views of your presentation's content.

Overview of Presentations

Have you ever attended a lecture where there were no visual aids at all? The speaker droned on and on, and your eyes wandered everywhere around the auditorium. You probably wound up an hour later with only a vague idea of what the topic of the talk was and no recollection of key details.

Visual and audio elements in any presentation, whether a simple business sales presentation or a formal educational seminar, do more than just keep the viewer interested in what's going on. They dramatically aid in increasing exactly how much information audience members retain.

How Presentations Get Your Point Across

There are several elements of a typical presentation. First, there are the words the presenter speaks to deliver his or her message. Bulleted lists of key points from the presenter's message can be used on slides or overheads to help focus the audience's attention. Sometimes it helps to provide a visual depiction of a process or procedure, such as an organizational chart or flow chart. Sounds, such as a cheering crowd, can add emphasis or help build audience enthusiasm. And detailed statistics are often easier to envision when displayed on a bar chart or pie chart, showing trends or relationships among sets of data.

When you approach a presentation as an orchestration of all of these elements, you provide many more ways for your audience to understand and retain your message. That's where a software product like PowerPoint comes in. By using the power of the compatibility that Microsoft has built into the Office suite of products, you can generate charts in Excel or outlines in Word for Windows right from within PowerPoint (assuming, of course, that those other products are also on your computer or network). There are also mini-applications, called *applets*, which come with PowerPoint. These applets provide PowerPoint with the ability to perform tasks such as building organizational charts and creating elaborate text effects.

The Many Ways PowerPoint Can Deliver Your Message

PowerPoint allows you to create the contents of your presentation by typing in text, and inserting pictures, sounds, and animation. PowerPoint even provides galleries of images and sounds you can use for this purpose. You can then easily generate output of the presentation in print, slides, overhead transparencies, or as a computer file to present on a computer screen or projection system. PowerPoint makes the creation of any presentation simple by providing you with built-in professional design elements called AutoLayouts and

Presentation Templates. You can even publish PowerPoint presentations to the Internet, and establish links to Internet sites within your presentation. Once these links are established, either the presenter or viewers of an on-screen computer presentation in a location such as a trade show floor can access related World Wide Web sites by clicking an icon on the screen. You can also print Notes Pages or audience Handouts to assist the speaker and his or her audience in following along.

▶ **See** "Using Hyperlinks In Presentations," **p. 429**

One of the nice things about PowerPoint is that you create a presentation once, but when it's complete, you have the option of generating any or all of the types of output mentioned here. You can also create different versions of a presentation for different audiences, and build your contents in either a text-based outline view or a design-based slide view. Finally, PowerPoint offers ways for you to prepare for your presentation by allowing you to preview your show, add special effects to the way slides are displayed on-screen, and rehearse the timing of each slide.

Taking Your First Look at PowerPoint

If you've used PowerPoint in an earlier version, or if you've used any of the recent releases of other products in the Microsoft Office suite, such as Word for Windows, you'll find that many of elements you see on the PowerPoint screen look familiar. The major features you'll observe on first entering the program are menus, toolbars, the status bar, and on-screen measuring aides such as rulers and guides.

If you've never used PowerPoint, you'll find that the assistance PowerPoint offers—in the form of ScreenTips to help you learn tool names and functions, and a sophisticated help system—will make the transition to proficiency an easy one.

The PowerPoint Toolbars

Toolbars are simply collections of buttons that you can press to activate some of the most common commands in PowerPoint. All of these commands can also be activated through menus. In effect, tools are shortcuts to initiate these actions with a single mouse click.

PowerPoint has several toolbars on-screen by default when you first open the program. You can customize PowerPoint to display other toolbars, or even to add or delete tools from toolbars so that those you find most useful are readily available.

▶ **See** "Creating and Modifying Toolbars," **p. 470**

When you open a new or existing presentation in PowerPoint, you will see a screen displaying the toolbars shown in Figure 1.1.

FIG. 1.1

Several toolbars are displayed on your PowerPoint screen by default, with buttons representing the most common tasks you perform.

Lines to drag for floating toolbar

Standard toolbar

Formatting toolbar

Common Tasks toolbar

Drawing toolbar

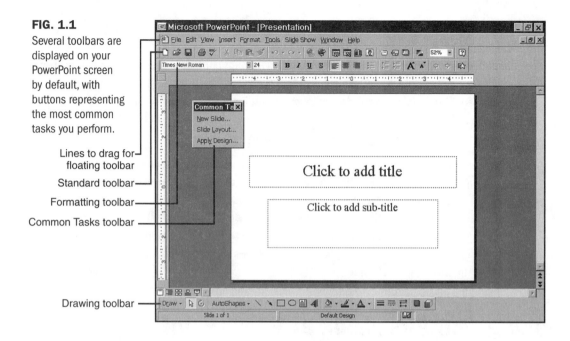

 N O T E Notice that the Common Tasks toolbar is a floating toolbar by default. *Floating toolbars* can be moved around your screen to be closer to the area where you are actually working on your presentation. You can make this toolbar a stationary toolbar by simply clicking its title bar, dragging it near a toolbar area, and releasing your mouse button. You can also make any stationary toolbar a floating toolbar by clicking the two pale gray lines at the left end of the toolbar and dragging it into the central display area of PowerPoint. ▧

T I P Whatever do all those buttons do? To get a quick hint, use PowerPoint's ScreenTips. Position your cursor over any button you want to know about and hold it still for a moment. PowerPoint pops up a brief explanation of what the button does.

If you'd like a little more information, choose Help, What's This? Or, press Shift+F1. The cursor changes to an arrow with a question mark. Click any button you want to know more about (or indeed, nearly *anything* in PowerPoint) and get a few more words of explanation.

If you're still not satisfied, it's time to turn to PowerPoint's Help feature.

The Standard Toolbar The Standard toolbar is the one nearest the top of the PowerPoint screen, just under the menu names. As you can see from Figure 1.2 and Table 1.1, the left side of this toolbar enables you to perform tasks common to many Windows-based programs, such as opening a new or existing file, saving or printing a file, cutting, copying and pasting text and objects, and undoing and redoing your most recent actions.

FIG. 1.2
The Standard toolbar offers many of the most common file management and editing tools.

The Standard toolbar ┘

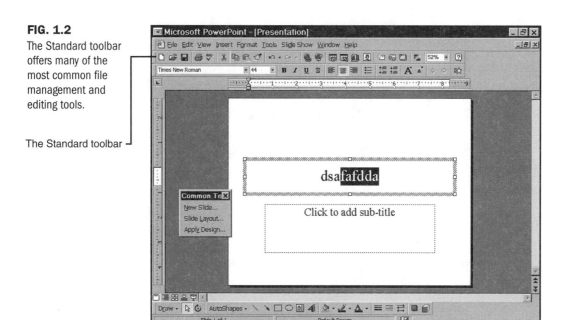

Table 1.1 reviews the name and function of each of the tools on the Standard toolbar.

Table 1.1 The Standard Toolbar

Name	Button	Function
New		Opens a new PowerPoint file.
Open		Opens a previously saved PowerPoint file.
Save		Saves the current file.
Print		Opens the Print dialog box.
Spelling		Initiates a spell checking function.
Cut		Places selected text or objects on the Windows Clipboard.
Copy		Places a copy of selected text or objects on the Windows Clipboard.

continues

Table 1.1 Continued

Name	Button	Function
Paste		Pastes the contents of the Clipboard on your slide.
Format Painter		Enables you to copy formatting from one object to another.
Undo		Undoes the last action.
Redo		Redoes the last undone action.
Insert Hyperlink		Inserts a link to a World Wide Web site on the slide.
Web Toolbar		Displays the Web toolbar.
Insert Microsoft Word Table		Inserts a Word table with Word tools available for editing.
Insert Microsoft Excel Worksheet		Inserts an Excel worksheet with Excel tools available for editing.
Insert Chart		Inserts a Graph 97 Chart.
Insert Clip Art		Opens a Clip Gallery to browse for clip art.
New Slide		Opens the New Slide dialog box.
Slide Layout		Allows you to select a different layout for your slide.
Apply Design		Allows you to change the design template the slide show is based on.
Black and White View		Displays the slide show in black and white.
Zoom	69%	Allows you to zoom in or out to view the slide larger or smaller.
Office Assistant		Opens the Office Assistant or Help.

Tool buttons are now somewhat smaller in appearance than they used to be in earlier versions of PowerPoint. To magnify them (particularly useful as you're learning to discern them), choose View, Toolbars, Customize. Select the Options tab, and click the Large Icons check box. When you close this dialog box, larger tool buttons appear on-screen.

 The right half of the Standard toolbar offers some functions more specific to PowerPoint presentations. These tools include:

■ Two tools related to connecting with the Internet and displaying another toolbar that allow you to move around the World Wide Web. These functions are new to this version of PowerPoint.

■ A series of tools for inserting objects into your presentation, such as a Word table or clip art.

■ Three tools which relate to creating and applying design elements to slides: New Slide, Slide Layout, and Apply Design. Notice that these are the same tools provided on the Common Tasks toolbar, which you'll see floating on your screen by default.

■ The Zoom feature to enlarge or reduce the display of your slide's contents on your screen.

■ The Black and White View tool, which you can use to remove color effects from your slide display. You might use this if you want to see how black and white printouts of your slides might appear.

 Finally, the Standard toolbar offers access to a new help feature in this version of PowerPoint—Office Assistant (see Figure 1.3). You learn more about this helpful little fellow later in this chapter in the section "Getting Help."

FIG. 1.3
This fellow shows up on your screen to answer questions and suggest what step you might want to take next.

The Formatting Toolbar   The second of three stationary toolbars displayed by default is the Formatting toolbar, shown in Figure 1.4. Many of the tools contained on this toolbar are also common to many Windows programs, and relate to formatting of text in your presentation as described in Table 1.2.

FIG. 1.4

The Formatting toolbar allows you to format text font, size, alignment, and effects at the click of a button.

The Formatting toolbar

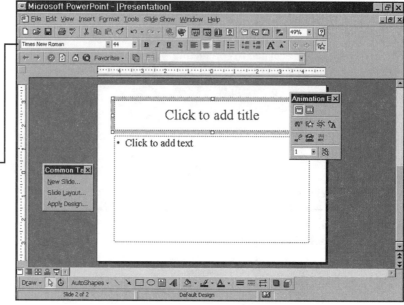

Table 1.2   The Formatting Toolbar

Name	Button	Function
Font	Arial	Opens a drop-down list so you can select a font.
Font Size	24	Allows you to enter a new size for selected type.
Bold	**B**	Toggles text from bold to unbold.
Italic	*I*	Toggles text from italic to non-italic.
Underline	<u>U</u>	Toggles text from underlined to non-underlined.

Name	Button	Function
Shadow		Applies a shadow effect to selected text.
Left Alignment		Aligns selected text to the left.
Center Alignment		Aligns selected text to the center.
Right Alignment		Aligns selected text to the right.
Bullets		Applies a bullet list format to selected text.
Increase Paragraph Spacing		Increases spacing between selected lines of text.
Decrease Paragraph Spacing		Decreases spacing between selected lines of text.
Increase Font Size		Increases font size for selected text.
Decrease Font Size		Decreases font size for selected text.
Promote		Moves selected text one level up in the outline hierarchy.
Demote		Moves selected text one level down in the outline hierarchy.
Animation Effects		Opens the Animation Effects dialog box.

The last three tools on the right of this toolbar are perhaps less familiar. These are the Promote, Demote, and Animation Effects tools. Promote and Demote are used to move text objects higher or lower in an outline structure that PowerPoint automatically applies to your presentation contents.

▶ **See** "Promoting and Demoting Text," **p. 88**

Finally, the Animation Effects tool displays a floating toolbar, shown in Figure 1.5. This toolbar is used to apply and manage the display of animation effects in your presentation.

▶ **See** "Adding Animation Effects," **p. 194**

FIG. 1.5

A variety of effects
to help animate
the elements on
your slides are
accessible through
this floating toolbar.

The Drawing Toolbar   The third stationary toolbar that appears by default in PowerPoint is the Drawing toolbar shown in Figure 1.6. Where the Formatting toolbar for the most part provides tools to format and manipulate text objects, the Drawing toolbar contains tools for formatting and manipulating drawn objects, such as shapes (circles and squares you draw on your slides, for example), as well as graphic objects you insert in your presentation, such as a clip art drawing.

The first object on the left end of the Drawing toolbar actually isn't a tool at all; it's the Draw menu. You'll hear more about this selection in the next section, "Menu Commands." Table 1.3 shows a quick rundown of the tools to the right of this menu on the Drawing toolbar.

Table 1.3   Drawing Toolbar Buttons

Button	Name	Description
	Select Objects	This tool is used to choose objects that you want to apply effects to.
	Free Rotate	You manipulate the orientation of shapes on your slide using this tool.
AutoShapes ▾	AutoShapes	The next several tools deal with drawing shapes: lines, rectangles, ovals and a variety of built-in shapes such as stars and flowcharts.
	Text Box and WordArt	These two tools create text objects outside of the normal text objects that are preset for you in PowerPoint. Text Box allows you to draw a text object, and WordArt is actually an applet that opens within PowerPoint so you can create graphically enhanced text objects.
	Fill Color, Line Color, and Font Color	You can add color to objects, lines, and text using drop-down palettes accessed from these three tools.

Button	Name	Description
	Line Style, Dash Style, and Arrow Style	There are three tools for modifying the width, dash, and arrow style applied to lines you draw on your slides.
	Shadow and 3-D	Finally, the last two buttons on this toolbar allow you to add shadows or three-dimensional effects to objects.

FIG. 1.6
You can use tools on the Drawing toolbar to draw objects on your slides and to format graphic elements in a variety of ways.

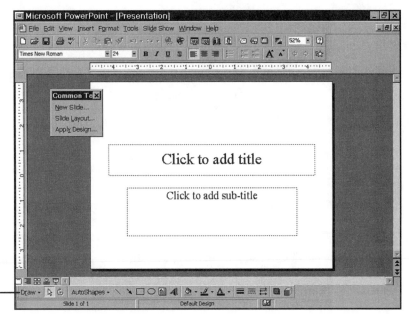

The Drawing toolbar

TROUBLESHOOTING

I can't locate the Drawing toolbar on my screen. Could I have deleted it? You can't delete a toolbar; you can only choose to stop displaying it. To see all the toolbars available to you and designate which should show on your screen, choose View, Toolbars. The cascading menu that appears lists all the available toolbars. Those with a check by them have been selected for display. If the one you want to see isn't checked, just click it so it appears on your screen again.

I used the previous version of PowerPoint and there was a Draw menu to perform all of these commands, but it's no longer there. Where did my Draw menu go? In this version of PowerPoint, the selection of Draw has been moved from the menu bar at the top of the screen down to the Drawing toolbar. Although it looks like a tool, it's actually a pop-up menu with many commands that you'll recognize from the previous version's Draw menu, plus a few new ones.

Menu Commands

The menus of PowerPoint are arrayed across the top of the screen. There are some, such as File and Edit, that you'll be familiar with from other software products. Others, such as Slide Show (see Figure 1.7), hold commands that are much more specific to PowerPoint and its features.

FIG. 1.7
The Slide Show menu provides several commands that help you control how your show will run.

T I P Notice in Figure 1.7 that the icon from the corresponding tool button is shown to the left of menu commands to help you learn to identify that tool as you learn to use PowerPoint. Although some of these tools don't appear on the default toolbars, they can be added to any toolbar by choosing View, Toolbars, Customize.

Table 1.4 provides a list of the menus, with the types of commands you'll find there.

Table 1.4 PowerPoint Menu Commands

Menu	Types of Commands
File	File management, including opening a new or existing file, printing, closing and saving files, and establishing page, printer, and file properties.
Edit	Editing functions such as undoing and redoing actions, cutting, copying, and pasting objects and text, duplicating and deleting, and finding and replacing text. In addition, you can manage links from this menu.
View	Managing how you view your presentation on-screen, including switching among the five main views of PowerPoint, accessing Masters, viewing slides in black and white or miniaturized, modifying toolbars, displaying rulers and guides, editing headers and footers, adding comments, and changing zoom level.

Menu	Types of Commands
Insert	Placing a variety of objects, files, slides, and information such as date and time in your presentation. This menu is also used to establish hyperlinks to the World Wide Web.
Format	Formatting objects and text, including font characteristics, bulleted list styles, alignment, and spacing. In addition, slide design, layout, and color are set, and you can modify drawing objects from this menu.
Tools	The tools you use to check text, such as spelling and AutoCorrect, manage presentations with features like Presentation Conference and Meeting Minder, and make global settings for how the program operates in the Options dialog box. Add-ins, macros, and AutoClipArt commands are also found here.
Slide Show	Commands for managing the timing, animation, narration, and transition effects of slide shows. You can also create play lists here to run custom slide shows.

▶ **See** "Taking Notes During a Presentation," **p. 368**

▶ **See** "Activating Hyperlinks to the Internet," **p. 435**

The Windows and Help menus hold typical Windows-based program commands for arranging multiple windows on-screen and accessing help features, respectively.

 Microsoft has enhanced the ways you can get information about its product through the World Wide Web. Check out the Microsoft on the Web command on the Help menu to search for answers through Microsoft's Web page, or get to the Web tutorial.

Rulers and Guides

PowerPoint AutoLayouts and Presentation Templates provide predetermined object placement; for example, a title slide will have a placeholder for both a title and subtitle placed on your slide in a way that balances with any design elements included in the template. However, you will often want to add elements to slides, or rearrange the preset objects to make your slides more readable or attractive. To place objects, both text and graphic, in precise positions in relation to each other or the edges of your slide, you can use two PowerPoint tools: rulers and guides.

Rulers are provided both across the top and along the left side of your screen in Slide view (which is the view in PowerPoint that you will use to arrange objects on individual slides). When you move your mouse around the screen, a small indicator appears on both rulers to show the cursor position.

Guides consist of two intersecting lines; these lines can be moved independently, and you can use the point at which they intersect to place an object on a specific spot on your slide. You can move a guide around your slide by clicking and dragging it. As you do, the corresponding ruler measurement is displayed numerically next to the guide line. Figure 1.8 shows a slide in Slide view with both rulers and guides displayed.

FIG. 1.8
Use rulers and the two intersecting lines of the guides to position elements on your slide precisely.

Horizontal ruler

Markers indicating mouse cursor position on rulers

Guides

Vertical ruler

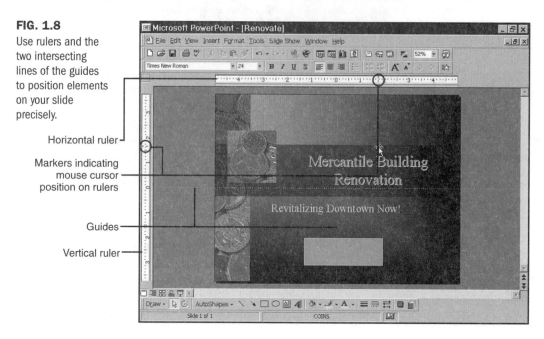

Rulers and Guides are displayed by using their respective toggle commands in the <u>V</u>iew menu. You can move the guides around your screen to place text and objects on your slide.

▶ **See** "Positioning Objects," **p. 144**

Checking the Status Bar

At the very bottom of the PowerPoint screen is the status bar (see Figure 1.9). This is also a feature frequently found in Windows-based software. In the case of PowerPoint, in the Slide and Notes view, the first item on the status bar tells you which slide is currently on-screen and how many slides there are in the whole presentation. The middle item on the status bar provides the name of the template that the presentation is based on. The final item is a tool for initiating a spelling check of your file.

FIG. 1.9

In any view but Slide view, Notes Pages view, and Slide Show view, the status bar tells you what view you are in.

Slide 2 of 2	COINS	
Which slide (or view) you are currently displaying	The design template currently applied	Spelling check

In the case of Outline and Slide Sorter views, the first item on the status bar is the name of the current view, rather than the slide number. The other two items are the same as in the Slide and Notes Page views.

The items on the status bar serve as a helpful reminder of which slide or view you are currently in, and the name of the currently applied template.

 Double-click the section of the status bar that identifies the current template to access the dialog box used to change templates for the presentation.

TROUBLESHOOTING

I started Slide Show view and can't find the status bar; where did it go? The status bar is removed from your screen when you enter Slide Show view. This view actually starts your slide presentation, and all toolbars, menus, and even the status bar disappear. You must leave the Slide Show view by pressing Esc to see the status bar again.

I drag the vertical guide to the right, but can't get it to go further than the measurement 10 inches. How do I make it go farther? The guides will only go as far as the farthest margin corresponding to the page size for the output you have selected for your presentation. Because any object you place beyond a margin will not print, there is no point in moving the guide further than PowerPoint allows you to.

Getting Help

When you choose Help, Contents and Index, PowerPoint provides a standard Windows help system, which you can search in several ways depending on which tab you select:

- *Contents* lets you search by a general topic.
- *Index* lets you search by a term or phrase in the predefined index.

■ *Find* enables you to search for words or phrases within help topics, even though they may not be in the index. The first time you choose Find, the help system creates an index of PowerPoint's help file. This can take some time and will use some of your hard drive space. How much of each will depend on the options you choose here. Unless you want to do some serious, "every word counts" searches of the help files, accept the default.

In addition to this main help system, you can select the What's This command in the Help menu. Your cursor changes to an arrow and question mark; you can then click an on-screen object to see a box with context-sensitive help for that item.

Microsoft on the Web is another command in the Help menu. It offers several choices for getting online support from Microsoft. If you have configured your computer to connect to the Internet, selecting any of the options shown on the menu in Figure 1.10 will connect you to the World Wide Web and take you to that specific page in Microsoft's Web site.

FIG. 1.10

More and more, Microsoft is providing its technical support through information it places on its Web site.

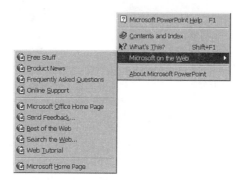

Finally, there is a help feature that is new to this version of PowerPoint called Office Assistant. You can display the Office Assistant by choosing Help, Microsoft PowerPoint Help. You can also use the Office Assistant tool on the Standard toolbar to make the animated feature shown in Figure 1.11 appear.

FIG. 1.11

The Office Assistant provides an intelligent interface to getting help with PowerPoint.

The Office Assistant allows you to type a statement of what you'd like to do, or a question. The Assistant then provides several options that will hopefully match or further clarify what you want to do next. Figure 1.12 shows the response to the statement "I want to format text." When you select one of these options, a help topic may be displayed, or you may be presented with the opportunity to watch a demonstration of that procedure.

 TIP Remember, Office Assistant is really just another searchable database of information. Keep your questions or statements straightforward and simple for the best chance of getting a useful answer. Complex sentences or non-standard computer or product terms may be difficult for Assistant to understand. For example, asking "How do I move an object" will work better than "I want to move this square over to the right of the page; how do I do it?"

Office Assistant will appear by default when you first open PowerPoint. Once it appears, you can remove the Office Assistant by clicking the close button in its upper-right hand corner.

FIG. 1.12
Office Assistant responds to your questions by finding matches to keywords in its special database.

NOTE You can modify the way Office Assistant works and when it appears by selecting the Options button on the Assistant main screen (shown in Figure 1.11). Here you can choose a different animated character to represent your Assistant (Einstein rather than the default Clippit character, for example), and determine how tips will appear and what kind of help Office Assistant will provide. ▦

Moving Around in PowerPoint

Although you'll begin to actually open a presentation and move around PowerPoint in Chapter 2, it's important that you understand at the outset the concept of how PowerPoint is organized. In this section, you get an overview of the different views available in PowerPoint, and what each is used for.

PowerPoint offers five views, and each can be used to gain a different perspective on your presentation. To help you understand the function of views, think of a piece of sculpture. To see the entire sculpture you would have to walk around it, viewing it from every angle. In the same way, a presentation which contains text, graphics, annotations, animation, and sound effects has different facets. To work on a particular element, you may want to isolate it so you aren't distracted by all the other elements. That's where PowerPoint views come in.

Moving from View to View

The five views in PowerPoint are Slide view, Outline view, Slide Sorter view, Notes Page view, and Slide Show view. You can move among the views in two ways:

- Use the view icons at the bottom left of the PowerPoint screen (the five tools above the Drawing toolbar).
- Select the View menu, then one of the top five commands to change views.

 Slide View   The view that shows by default when you open a new or existing presentation is Slide view. This is the view to use when working on the details of individual slides. Slide view shows a single slide, with placeholders for layout elements, such as a title or bulleted list, displayed. In addition, rulers are shown by default and guides can be displayed by selecting View, Guides. Figure 1.13 shows a new slide in Slide view.

FIG. 1.13
The Slide view is best used to view your individual slides, and add or arrange text and graphic objects.

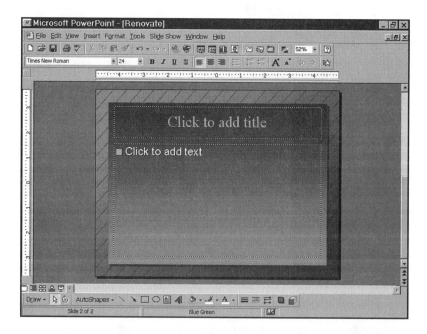

Slide view is the best place to appreciate and work with the overall design of each slide, ensuring that objects don't overlap each other, the arrangement of objects relative to each other is pleasing, and text is easily read.

You can move from slide to slide in Slide view by using the Page Down and Page Up keys on your keyboard or the scroll bar at the right of your screen. When you use the scroll bar, PowerPoint shows you the headline text and slide number of the slide the scroll bar is set to take you to when you release it. This makes for a very quick way to skip around in your presentation or find a particular slide in a hurry.

 Outline View   Outline view shows you the contents of your presentation in a way that helps you see the flow of ideas and information, rather than the arrangement of design elements. Outline view uses the traditional outline model to show major ideas with subordinate ideas indented beneath them. Although you can enter text in either Slide or Outline view, typing text into Outline view can be faster and help you focus on your presentation's ideas.

In addition, because the contents of all slides is shown in one long list in Outline view, you can appreciate how information is building as your presentation progresses from slide to slide (see Figure 1.14). By typing in a major topic heading, you enter text in a title place-holder. By typing subheadings, you enter text in a bulleted list placeholder. However, placeholders with no text entered will not appear in Outline view.

▶ **See** "Building Your Presentation in Outline View," **p. 87**

FIG. 1.14
Outline view has its own toolbar used to move items up or down in the outline hierarchy.

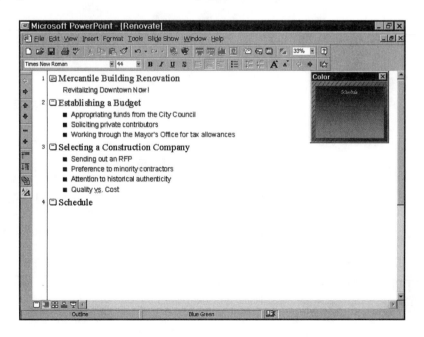

T I P When in Outline view, a small representation of the currently selected slide is shown in a window on-screen to help you get a quick glimpse of how text you enter here will appear on the individual slide.

Slide Sorter View Where Slide view lets you look at slide design details, and Outline view lets you see the flow of information in your presentation, Slide Sorter view lets you see the sequence of all the slides in your presentation in miniature, as shown in Figure 1.15. In Slide Sorter view, you can see how both the design and contents of each slide progress from one slide to the next.

FIG. 1.15
The slides in your presentation are displayed and numbered to indicate their sequence in Slide Sorter view.

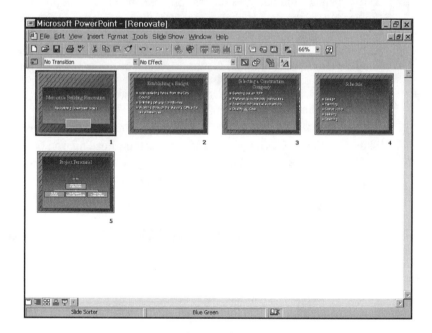

This is the view to use to check out the overall design consistency from slide to slide in your presentation. You can easily move slides around or duplicate them here. In addition, you can preview transition effects that will be used as you move between slides in a presentation. Transition effects are basically different patterns used to display the next slide in a presentation in an on-screen slide show. For example, a new slide may appear in a wipe from the top of the screen to the bottom, or it may appear to fly in from the side of the screen.

 T I P You can quickly move to a particular slide in Slide view by double-clicking on the miniature representation of that slide in Slide Sorter view.

▶ **See** "Organizing Your Presentation in Slide Sorter View," **p. 322**

▶ **See** "Transitions and Timing," **p. 331**

 Notes Page View PowerPoint enables you to create something called Notes Pages for your presentation. Notes Page is a representation of a slide's contents with associated notes. Notes Pages help the person making the presentation remember background information or key points to make at the point in a presentation when that slide is displayed. You can print out these notes and provide them to the speaker in hard copy.

To create Notes Pages, use Notes Page view, shown in Figure 1.16.

▶ **See** "Creating Notes Using Notes Pages," **p. 113**

FIG. 1.16
Place supporting facts or statistics and reminders to relate anecdotes or acknowledge contributions in Notes Pages.

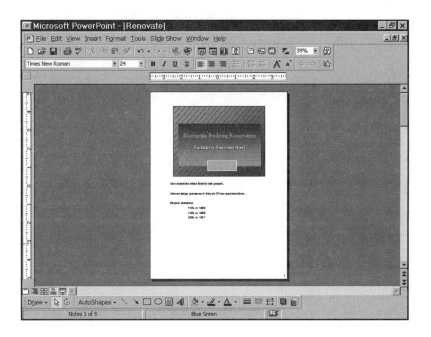

 Slide Show View The final view in PowerPoint is Slide Show view (see Figure 1.17). This view displays each slide in an on-screen slide show. In this view, all menus, toolbars, rulers, the status bar, scroll bars, and the Windows taskbar are removed from the screen. Slide Show view gives you the best idea of how your slides will appear to your audience during a presentation. This view is most often used towards the end of your presentation design process, to fine-tune design elements or rehearse your presentation.

▶ **See** "Previewing Your Presentation," **p. 330**

FIG. 1.17
Get rid of the clutter of
PowerPoint toolbars
and menus to see how
your slides will
actually appear in
Slide Show view.

Moving from Slide to Slide

The procedures used for navigating from one slide to another are also simple:

- In Slide view, you can use the scroll bar on the right side of your screen to move from slide to slide. You can drag the scroll bar, click just above or below it, or use the arrows at either end to move one slide at a time.

- You can use the set of double arrow icons at the bottom of the scroll bar to move to the previous or next slide.

- You can display Slide Sorter view and double-click the slide of your choice to display it in Slide view.

- You can collapse the outline of the presentation in Outline view and scroll quickly through just the titles of the slides to find the one you want.

CHAPTER 2

Starting Your Presentation

by Nancy Stevenson

You're about to be pleasantly surprised by how easy it is to build a simple PowerPoint presentation. Of course, PowerPoint offers a lot of bells and whistles that you can add to your basic presentation to make it very sophisticated, and you'll learn about those in later chapters. But the fact remains, the nuts and bolts of a basic presentation are really quite easy to master because of PowerPoint's built-in tools and design elements.

In this chapter, you learn how to start a presentation, use the placeholders PowerPoint provides to place content in your presentation, modify the look of your presentation, and save it.

You also learn some fundamentals about how PowerPoint assembles all the master, outline, notes and other elements into one coherent interlinked presentation. ▪

How to begin a new presentation

PowerPoint offers several methods of starting a new presentation, including a helpful AutoContent Wizard and built-in design templates.

Understanding placeholders

PowerPoint's layouts provide common presentation elements; all you do is click these placeholders and enter your content.

How PowerPoint Masters work

If you want to place content on every page in your presentation, Masters offer an easy shortcut.

Making simple changes to background and layout

Changing the look of your presentation is simple and easy with a variety of templates, layouts, and color schemes.

How to save a PowerPoint presentation

Now that you've done all that work, save your presentation for future use.

Creating a New Presentation

When you first start PowerPoint by selecting it from the Programs section of the Windows taskbar, a dialog box like the one in Figure 2.1 appears. This dialog box offers four options for opening a presentation:

- *AutoContent Wizard*. Walks you step-by-step through creating a new presentation. This is probably the best choice for those new to PowerPoint.

- *Template*. Opens a second dialog box which offers you a choice of built-in design templates to base a new presentation on.

- *Blank Presentation*. Opens a presentation with no elements or design background in place. This selection offers the most flexibility in creating your own presentation elements from scratch.

- *Open an Existing Presentation*. Opens a browse dialog box to locate a PowerPoint file that has previously been saved.

The Blank Presentation is selected by default. To select another option, click the radio button next to it. Only one choice can be selected at a time.

FIG. 2.1
Don't miss the helpful tip that shows in the right-hand corner of this startup dialog box!

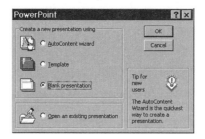

 You can customize the blank presentation to suit your own needs:

1. Back up the existing file called Blank Presentation.pot in your \MSOffice\Templates folder. You can simply rename it to something else if you like.

2. Open a presentation that looks the way you normally want your presentations to look, remove all the slides from it (it's easiest to do this in Slide Sorter view), then choose File, Save As.

3. Choose Presentation Templates (*.pot) from the Save as Type drop-down list box.

4. Save the file as Blank Presentation.pot in the \MSOffice\Templates folder.

The next time you start a new presentation and choose Blank Presentation, it begins life looking just the way you want it to, with all of your customized font and color selections, background choices, and even page setups intact.

Using AutoContent Wizard

If you select AutoContent Wizard, you see the opening window shown in Figure 2.2. On the left side of this window is a list that represents the various steps that the wizard will take you through. The first one, Start, is highlighted. Start is the screen you are on now. You can navigate through the items on the list by choosing the Next and Back buttons, or move directly to one of the items by clicking the box next to it in the list. You can always move back to Start by clicking it again in the list. Once you visit one of these windows, its check box becomes darkened to remind you that you've completed that step.

FIG. 2.2

Once you visit an item in this series, its check box is darkened, as is the Presentation Style item in this example.

To begin making settings for your new presentation, choose the Next button.

TROUBLESHOOTING

I'm working in PowerPoint and just closed a presentation. I want to start a new presentation using the AutoContent Wizard, but I can't figure out how. To use the AutoContent Wizard once PowerPoint is running, choose File, New or press Ctrl+N. In the New Presentation dialog box, choose the Presentations tab. Click the icon marked AutoContent Wizard.pwz, then choose OK. The AutoContent Wizard starts.

Whenever I start the AutoContent Wizard I get a warning message about macros and viruses. Is my computer infected with a virus? No, this is a PowerPoint feature that helps protect your computer against viruses. PowerPoint presentations can now include *macros*, small Visual Basic programs that perform useful functions. However, a macro might also contain code that could damage your system or files.

This warning message (see Figure 2.3) appears whenever you open a presentation that contains macros to remind you of the possible danger of opening the file. If you don't know and trust the person who sent you the presentation, you may not want to open a file that contains macros. On the other hand, if you don't feel that macros will be a problem, you can click the Always Ask Before Opening Documents with Macros check box. Clear the check mark from this box, and PowerPoint won't show you this warning again.

FIG. 2.3

This message warns you that the file or template you're opening contains macros.

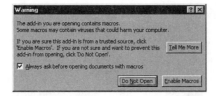

Selecting the Presentation Type   The Presentation Type window shown in Figure 2.4 appears, and the Presentation Type item is highlighted in the list of wizard items on the left.

In the middle of this window is a series of buttons. Use these to select categories of presentation types, such as Corporate or Personal. When you select a button by clicking it, the presentation types within that category are listed to the right of these buttons. You can scroll down this list using the scroll bar to the right. If you want to see all the presentation types in this list, choose the All button.

FIG. 2.4

Whether you're a corporate type or want to give a presentation to the local PTA, PowerPoint probably has a type of presentation that's right for you.

N O T E   You can add your own template to the AutoContent Wizard. Choose the category you want to add it to, then click Add. PowerPoint shows you a standard File Open dialog box. Choose the template you want to add, then click OK. Your template appears in the AutoContent Wizard's list of presentation types. You can also use the Remove button to delete items from this list. ▨

Once you've selected a presentation type, choose Next to proceed.

Designating Output Options   The window that follows (see Figure 2.5) offers two choices having to do with the way you will present your information:

- *Presentations, Informal Meetings, Handouts*. This is the choice to make if a speaker will guide an audience through a presentation.

- *Internet, Kiosk*. This option is best if you want to create a presentation that the viewer will move through independently. For example, an on-screen computer presentation that an attendee at a trade show can move through at an information booth would fit this category.

 TIP If you want to find out more about options offered in wizard windows, click the question mark help button at the bottom of the dialog box, and the Office Assistant appears with more details.

Make the appropriate choice for your presentation, then choose Next.

Part

I

Ch

2

FIG. 2.5

The AutoContent Wizard helps you pick the correct presentation options automatically.

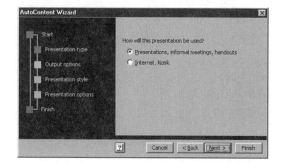

Choosing a Presentation Style   The next AutoContent Wizard window to appear is shown in Figure 2.6. Where the previous screen dealt with how the audience would interact with the presentation, this window allows you to designate the medium on which you will generate your presentation.

FIG. 2.6

The medium you select for your presentation may impact the size of the output, which affects the design of your slides.

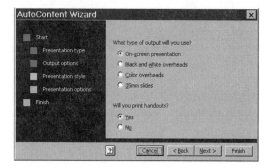

At the top of this window is a list of output types. Different output choices can impact the dimensions of each individual slide in your presentation. For example, 35mm Slides are constrained by their 3:2 proportion and (usually) landscape orientation, whereas an on-screen presentation matches the proportions of your computer monitor and a printed black and white or color overhead will have its own printed page parameters. Making this choice at the outset of your presentation can save you from having to rearrange elements on your slides at a later time.

CAUTION

If you intend to use this presentation with more than one output type—for example, to print both overheads and slides so you can use the presentation in different settings—you can make changes to output type. Choose File, Page Setup, and pick the appropriate option under Slides Sized For.

You can switch between On Screen presentation, Overheads, and Letter paper as often as you like, because PowerPoint uses the same size image for all of these. However, be careful when you switch to or from 35mm Slides. 35mm slides are more elongated than the other sizes, and PowerPoint may distort graphics, change line breaks in your text, and move elements around the page when it has to fit other size presentations to this different page proportion.

 TROUBLESHOOTING

I changed my presentation's Page Setup from On Screen Show to 35mm Slide, and now my graphics are distorted. First of all, choose File, Save As and give the presentation a new name so you don't accidentally overwrite your original.

Let's say your original presentation was named SCREEN.PPT and the newly saved version is called SLIDES.PPT. Without closing SLIDES, follow these steps:

1. Re-open SCREEN so you have both versions of the presentation open.

2. Choose Window, Arrange All so you can see them both at once.

3. Review the changes PowerPoint has made to SLIDES. Click its window to make it active, then press Page Down to view each slide in sequence. When you see one that looks suspicious, click the other window to activate SCREEN and Page Down to the same slide.

4. If there is indeed a problem with SLIDES, click it again, select the distorted graphics, then delete them.

5. Select the undistorted version of the graphic in SCREEN, then hold down the Ctrl key while you drag the graphic over to where you want it in SLIDES. You now have an undistorted copy of it in both presentations.

If you have a lot of graphics on a slide, it's quicker to select them all, then choose Edit, Copy (Ctrl+C). Click the other window and choose Edit, Paste (Ctrl+V). That copies all of the selected graphics at once. It also keeps their relative position on the slide the same, so you won't have to spend a lot of time dragging them into place individually.

Beneath the output type is a choice regarding printed handouts. You can generate hand-outs with several of your presentation slides on a printed page so that your audience members can follow along with the information you're presenting. If you think you might want to provide such handouts, click Yes, then choose Next to proceed.

▶ **See** "Creating Handouts," **p. 121**

Completing the AutoContent Wizard   The next wizard window allows you to enter some information for your presentation, including the presentation title and your name. Once you enter this information and choose <u>N</u>ext, you come to the final wizard window. This window tells you your presentation is complete. Choose <u>F</u>inish, to see what your wizard choices have created.

Part
I
Ch
2

As shown in Figure 2.7, you are placed in Outline view when you complete AutoContent Wizard, because this is the logical place to begin to enter the contents of your presentation. Notice in the Color preview of the selected slide that some design choices have been made for you. Depending on the choices you made throughout the wizard, what you see here will differ; however, the wizard is likely to have created several slides for your presentation. These choices are based on the Presentation Type you selected. In the case of Figure 2.5, that type was an Organizational Overview, and the slide titles reflect logical topics for such a presentation.

FIG. 2.7

The information entered in Auto-Content Wizard windows is placed on the title slide of your presentation and displayed in Outline view.

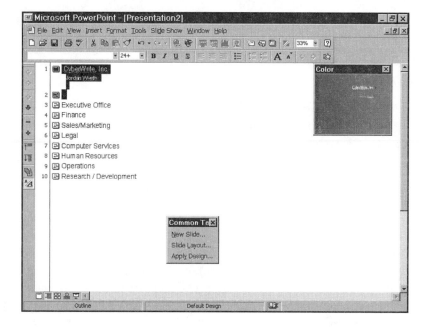

If you select one of the topic slides created by the wizard and move to Slide view, you see that logical information for that topic has already been entered. Often there are places designed for you to enter specific information, such as the names of specific positions in the Human Resources department of your organization, as shown in Figure 2.8.

FIG. 2.8
The AutoContent
Wizard provides a shell
with the types of infor-
mation that make
sense for your presen-
tation; you fill in the
blanks.

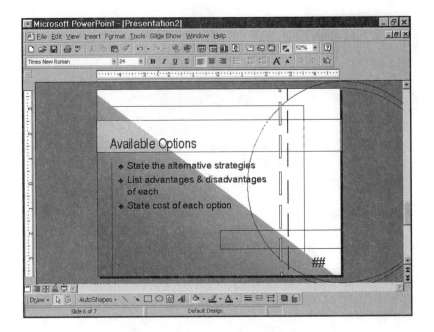

 TROUBLESHOOTING

I used the AutoContent wizard, but it created a couple of slides I can't use in my presentation. How do I get rid of them? Just because AutoContent Wizard has created some suggested slides and content, you don't have to use every element it creates. The easiest way to get rid of slides in a presentation is to switch to Slide Sorter view (choose View, Slide Sorter), click the slide to select it, and use the Cut button, choose Edit, Delete Slide, or press the Delete key. You can also delete the current slide in Slide view by choosing Edit, Delete Slide.

There are 15 First Name, Last Name items on one of the slides I created with the Organization Overview template, but there are only 10 people in that department in my company. What do I do with the rest of those names? Any text or graphic object placed on your slides by either AutoContent Wizard or a template can be removed from your slide. Just click the object, then press the Delete key. However, graphic design elements such as a border, line, or image that are part of a design template are on the Slide Master, so they cannot be deleted from individual slides. You would have to modify the Slide Master or change to a different design template to get rid of these.

Understanding PowerPoint Templates

If you select the Template option from the opening PowerPoint screen (refer to Figure 2.1), you have a bit more flexibility in determining the contents and look of your presentation than with AutoContent Wizard. However, you will still be able to take advantage of PowerPoint's built-in design and content elements.

If you select Template, you are presented with the New Presentation dialog box shown in Figure 2.9. The three buttons on the right of this screen can be used to display templates as icons, in a list, or as a list with details about the template files.

FIG. 2.9
Four tabs in this
dialog box offer
different ways of
determining the look
of your presentation.

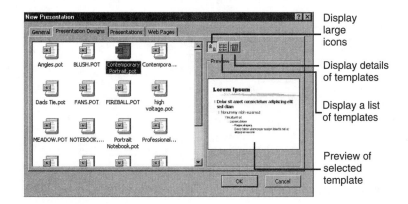

Display
large
icons

Display details
of templates

Display a list
of templates

Preview of
selected
template

To see a preview of any of these templates, click it once. Notice that there are four tabs to select from in this dialog box:

- *General*. Offers the option of creating a Blank Presentation or basing your presentation on any template file you've stored in the \Templates folder.

- *Presentation Designs*. Allows you to choose a set of design elements by a design name, such as Blue Diagonal or Professional. These choices will provide only design elements, such as a background, color scheme, and graphic elements.

- *Presentations*. Contains templates designated by a type of presentation, such as a Business Plan or Training presentation. These choices provide design elements, and may create one or more slides with suggested content elements in place.

- *Web Pages*. Contains templates for creating Web pages.

 T I P You can use Ctrl+Tab to move from tab to tab in PowerPoint's tabbed dialog boxes.

N O T E Remember, you could have chosen Blank Presentation from the PowerPoint opening screen shown in Figure 2.1 as well. However, this opening screen only appears when you first start PowerPoint. After working with a presentation in PowerPoint, you see the New Presentation dialog box when you start a new presentation. You would then need to use the Blank Presentation choice on the General tab to start a presentation with no design or content elements in it. ▨

If you select a Presentation template from the Presentations tab and choose OK, a new presentation will appear on-screen, complete with one or more slides already created. The items in the Presentations tab are *canned* presentations, complete with suggested topics and text. You simply customize them to suit your own circumstances.

If you select either a Blank Presentation from the General tab or a Presentation Design template, the New Slide dialog box appears, as in Figure 2.10.

FIG. 2.10
The name of the layout you select is shown in the lower-right corner, and reflects the elements your slide will contain.

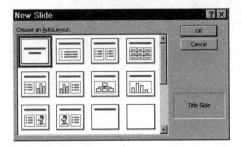

Selecting AutoLayouts

The New Slide dialog box allows you to select an AutoLayout for your initial slide. An AutoLayout (also called a layout) predetermines certain slide elements, such as a title or bulleted list. By selecting a particular layout, you put placeholders on your slide which you can use to more easily enter the content of your presentation. Each slide in your presentation can use a different layout. You can also change the layout for a particular slide any time you like.

When you select an AutoLayout icon, its name appears in the right hand side of the New Slide dialog box. You can use the scroll bar to see additional layouts in the list. You can usually tell from the layout icon what type of objects will be placed on your slide. For example, a bold gray line indicates either a title or subtitle element. A box with three bullets and squiggly gray lines indicates a bulleted list. A small picture in a box represents clip art, and so on.

 TIP If you don't want any presentation elements placed on your slide for you, select the Blank layout (it's in the lower-right corner of the layout icons).

Select the layout you want, then choose OK to see your first slide on screen. Depending on your layout choice, certain placeholders appear on your slide in Slide view, as in Figure 2.11. This figure shows the Clip Art & Text layout.

> **T I P** You can choose a layout more quickly if you double-click it rather than selecting it then choosing OK.

FIG. 2.11
Depending on the layout you've chosen, you may see place-holders for text, title, clip art, a chart, or even an animated movie.

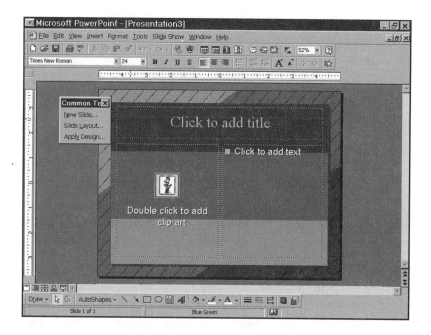

Changing a Presentation's Look

Just because you've chosen a template and layout providing a slide with a specific background and elements while creating the presentation, you're not limited to these choices. At any time you can easily change the template and layout, and even select from several built-in color schemes to modify the look.

Changing Your Page Layout

As you work with a slide you may decide that you need another element (for example a chart), in addition to the placeholders on the layout you've chosen. You can do two things:

- Add an object yourself, without using a placeholder (this option is discussed later in this chapter in the section "Adding Other Elements").

- Switch to a different layout that includes a placeholder for the additional element you want to add.

If you have selected a layout with more placeholders than you need, you don't have to change the layout; any placeholder which you have not placed anything in does not appear in your final presentation.

If you find unused placeholders distracting, simply select one and press the Delete key to banish it from your sight. To delete a text placeholder, the procedure is slightly different. Select it, press the Esc key, then the Delete key.

Switching to a different layout is simple, and can be done in one of three ways:

- Click the Slide Layout button on the Standard toolbar.
- Choose Format, Slide Layout.
- Right-click anywhere outside placeholders or other slide elements, then choose Slide Layout.

The Slide Layout dialog box appears. This is actually identical to the New Slide dialog box you saw in Figure 2.10; however, when you open this dialog box through the Slide Layout command, the title of it is different. Simply select another layout and choose the Apply button.

If you've modified the formatting or position of placeholders on the slide, you can use the same trick to revert to the original layout. The original layout has a square highlight around it in the Slide Layout dialog and the button is now Reapply rather than Apply. Choose it to revert to the original default formatting and position of the placeholders.

CAUTION

You should be aware that changing layouts after you have entered information or placed objects on a slide may rearrange those objects slightly to accommodate the new placeholder. If you don't like what a change to your layout does to your slide, choose Edit, Undo or press Ctrl+Z.

Changing Presentation Templates

Choosing a different template to base your slides on is also simple. Use the Apply Design button or choose Format, Apply Design. A browse window opens, allowing you to select and preview a template file. When you find one you like, choose the Apply button.

Remember, a template can change the background colors and pattern, add graphic elements such as borders, use a different font or font size. Also, you can have only one template for all the slides in your presentation, so changing the design while displaying one slide changes all of the slides.

Changing Color Schemes

Every design template is associated with a color scheme. There are seven color schemes in all, and each contains settings for background, text and lines, shadows, fills, accents, and hyperlinks. You can change the color scheme of a design template, or change the color schemes of charts, tables, or pictures you've added to slides.

You apply a new color scheme by choosing Format, Slide Color Scheme. In the dialog box that appears (see Figure 2.12), you can select one of the seven schemes shown there, then choose the Apply or Apply To All buttons to apply the scheme to the displayed slide or to all slides in the presentation, respectively.

FIG. 2.12

One of each of these seven built-in color schemes is used by each design template.

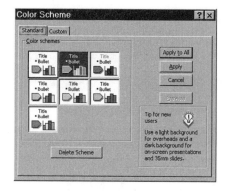

 TIP If you want to change the color scheme of just a few slides, simply select those slides in Slide Sorter view before choosing Format, Slide Color Scheme. When you make selections and choose Apply, any changes will apply only to those selected slides.

You can also create custom color schemes using the second tab of the Color Scheme dialog box (see Figure 2.13). To do so, simply select an element (Background, Text and Lines, Shadows, and so on), and choose Change Color. Select a new color from the palette that appears and choose OK. Repeat this for each element in the Scheme Colors list. If you like, you can choose the Add as Standard Scheme button to add this color scheme to the seven on the Standard tab of this dialog box. You can then apply the same scheme to other slides in your presentation.

▶ **See** "Using Color and Fill Effects," **p. 160**

FIG. 2.13
A preview of any changes you make to the custom color scheme appears in the bottom-right corner of this tab.

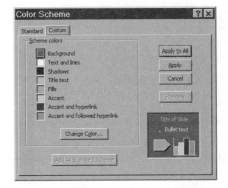

Using Placeholders

All the boxes with the words `Click To` shown in Figure 2.11 are placeholders. These placeholders make entering content easier. Placeholders are available for all kinds of presentation objects, including:

- Title
- Text (this is in the form of a bulleted list)
- Clip art
- Chart
- Organization chart
- Table
- Media clip (this can be sound, video, or animation)
- Objects (this would include a variety of objects generated within other software, such as Paintbrush, Word or Excel, multimedia clips, or even other PowerPoint slides or presentations)

Some placeholders, such as Title and Text, open up an editable text block when you click them, ready for you to enter text for your presentation (see Figure 2.14).

Other placeholders, such as Clip art and Media clip, open up a gallery of built-in artwork for you to insert on your slide. Still others, such as Table, Organization Chart, and Chart, start an applet running in a window within PowerPoint, so you can build an object, then insert it on your slide (see Figure 2.15).

FIG. 2.14
Clicking the Title placeholder in this slide opens it up for editing.

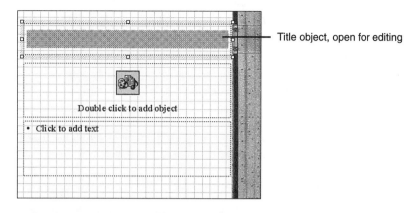

Title object, open for editing

FIG. 2.15
Double-click a chart placeholder, and a datasheet window appears, allowing you to enter your chart's data.

		A	B	C	D	E
		1st Qtr	2nd Qtr	3rd Qtr	4th Qtr	
1	East	20.4	27.4	90	20.4	
2	West	30.6	38.6	34.6	31.6	
3	North	45.9	46.9	45	43.9	

Presentation2 - Datasheet

If you double-click an Object placeholder, you see a dialog box like that in Figure 2.16, offering a list of possible applications you can open to create an object or select a file for insertion.

FIG. 2.16
A variety of applications, both those included with PowerPoint and others which you have installed on your computer, can be reached through this dialog box.

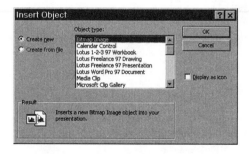

If you choose Create New, the program you picked starts with a new document open. Create whatever new material you like, then choose File, Close and Return to *<your presentation name>* (the exact wording and shortcut keys may vary from program to program). You may be asked if you want to update the object before returning. Unless you want to cancel the operation, choose Yes.

Some newer programs may behave a bit differently when you choose them as the source from which to insert an object; you may see a window appear in the middle of your slide and the available menu items may change to those of the program you chose (in place of PowerPoint's). This is called *in-place editing* because you can edit directly from within PowerPoint. In this case, once you're finished creating your new material, simply click outside the window to return control to PowerPoint.

The list of available programs is different on each computer, depending on what other software is installed, but you're almost sure to have Microsoft Paintbrush on your system. If you'd like to sample in-place editing in action, choose Insert, Object, select Paintbrush Picture, choose Create New, then OK.

If you've already created a file and want to insert it into your presentation, choose Create From File instead. You can then type in the drive, path, and file name of the file (if you know it) or choose Browse and use a standard Windows File Open dialog box to navigate to and choose the file you'd like to insert.

▶ **See** "Adding Clip Art," **p. 172**
▶ **See** "Creating WordArt Objects," **p. 182**
▶ **See** "Creating a Chart," **p. 201**
▶ **See** "Creating a Table," **p. 256**
▶ **See** "Creating an Organization Chart," **p. 269**

Adding Other Elements

The elements in the AutoLayouts are provided to make creation of typical presentation slides easier. However, you aren't constrained to adding elements in PowerPoint through placeholders; you can add new text boxes and insert all kinds of other objects anywhere on your page at any time.

To do so, you can use the Insert menu and its various commands, or some of the buttons you'll find on different toolbars in PowerPoint. Table 2.1 shows you some different ways to add objects to your slides.

Table 2.1   Inserting Items on Slides

Item	Menu command	Button
Clip art	Insert, Picture, Clip Art	🖼
Organization chart	Insert, Picture, Organization Chart	

Item	Menu command	Button
Microsoft Word Table	Insert, Picture, Microsoft Word Table	
Text box	Insert, Text Box	
Movie clip	Insert, Movies and Sounds, Movie from Gallery	
Sound file	Insert, Movies and Sounds, Sound from Gallery	
Chart	Insert, Chart	
Object	Insert, Object	

▶ **See** "Creating Text Outside a Placeholder," **p. 63**
▶ **See** "Adding Clip Art," **p. 172**
▶ **See** "Making Action Button Settings," **p. 191**
▶ **See** "Standard Charts and Their Uses," **p. 205**
▶ **See** "Creating a Table," **p. 256**
▶ **See** "Building an Organization Chart," **p. 270**
▶ **See** "Inserting Video Clips as Movies from the Clip Gallery," **p. 536**

In addition, you can insert Hyperlinks to World Wide Web sites (you learn more about this in Chapter 19), WordArt objects (see Chapter 6), and whole slides from the Insert menu.

▶ **See** "Creating WordArt Objects," **p. 182**
▶ **See** "Using Hyperlinks in Presentations," **p. 429**

Exploring Master Views

PowerPoint's masters are a tremendously powerful feature for customizing your presentations and giving them the consistency that's the hallmark of a real professional presenter. You can produce superb PowerPoint presentations without ever visiting the Master view, but knowing how to customize a master can save you hours of tedious, repetitive formatting work on your slides.

Later on in this chapter, you'll find a detailed explanation of how PowerPoint's masters, outlines, and layouts all dovetail to produce your slides, notes, and handouts. I save the theory for later, though. Let's look first at how you actually use PowerPoint's masters.

Part
I

Ch
2

Imagine that you have to produce a presentation for your company's annual meeting. The company president wants you to put the phrase `Acme TechToid Annual Meeting` and your company logo on each and every slide. You envision having to laboriously insert this phrase and graphic object on each page. That's where PowerPoint masters come in.

If you want to add an object to all slides—for example, a company logo or text box with the company name—you can do so by inserting that object on a master.

There are four kinds of masters:

- Slide
- Handout
- Title
- Notes

PowerPoint masters save you time, because you can place one or more objects on a master form once, and those objects will appear in all related slides, notes, or handouts, depending on which master you use.

Slide Master and Title Master affect the appearance of all slides in your actual presentation. If you add an object or change the settings for background, color, or size on either of these masters, those changes appear on all corresponding slides.

For example, let's say that one of PowerPoint's templates is perfect for your presentation, but you want to use a different typeface for all the headings. It's only a few seconds' work to change all the slides in your presentation.

Choose View, Masters, Slide Master (or Shift+click the slide icon in the lower-left corner) to get to the Slide Master. Select the headline text and change the font, then return to Slide view (click Close on the floating Master toolbar; choose View, Slide; or click the slide icon again without the Shift key). The heading text on all of your slides is now in the new typeface.

N O T E PowerPoint doesn't force you to make all of your slides fit the mold dictated by the placeholder formatting on the master. If you find that the placeholder settings aren't right for a particular slide, you can always change them. Select the item and make any formatting changes you like—size it up or down, or move it wherever you please.

Keep this in mind, though: PowerPoint also assumes that you mean business when you change a slide from the default Master settings. If you later apply a different template or change the Slide Master, those changes do not override any changes you've made to individual slides.

Using the same example again, let's say that you originally created 25 slides before you read this far in the chapter. Because you didn't know about Masters, you changed the color of each of the headlines from white to yellow the hard way: slide by slide. Now the boss wants the headlines changed to green. If you'd made the color change on the Master in the first place, you could change it there again and all of your slides would follow along. But because the change was applied slide by slide, and because PowerPoint won't override changes you made to individual slides, you have to go back and switch each headline to green the hard way: slide by slide.

There's one way out of this dilemma, though. You can re-apply the AutoLayout the slide is based on. Choose Format, Slide Layout or right-click off the slide and choose Slide Layout. The original AutoLayout is highlighted by a thick square. Choose Reapply and PowerPoint reverses anything you've done that changes the layout or formatting of the slide. This means all of the changes; you can't apply it selectively. If you've done a lot of reformatting on the slide, it's probably better to skip this technique. ■

T I P If you have formatting you'd like applied globally, for example to make all bullet list text 22 point, Arial font, you can change that formatting once on the Slide Master and it will apply to all bullet list text in your presentation.

Slide Master

Slide Master determines what will appear on all slides except slides with a Title layout applied. You can display the Slide Master form by choosing View, Master and selecting Slide Master. The form in Figure 2.17 appears.

FIG. 2.17
Dotted lines on a master indicate common objects found on slides which you can format universally.

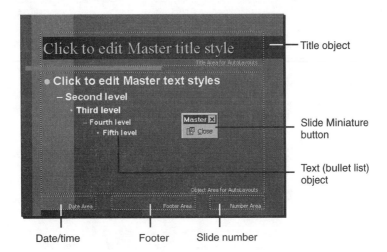

The Slide Master allows you to change the background, color, and size of all slides, with the exception of Title slides. You can also modify the text formatting for slide title text objects and text objects, add a footer, date and time, or slide number here.

▶ **See** "Formatting Text," **p. 69**

N O T E Notice that there is a little floating Master menu in Slide and Title Master views which consists of two items: a button called Slide Miniature and a <u>C</u>lose command. Sometimes it's difficult to see how changes on a master will really look with all of those dotted lines and placeholder text. When you click the Slide Miniature button, you get a floating window with a floating black and white representation of how a slide will look with the changes you're applying—without all the master guidelines. The Close command is a quick way to leave Master view. You can also leave by simply selecting any of the view buttons at the bottom of your screen. ▨

Title Master

Title Master is very similar to Slide Master, except that changes made here affect only slides with the Title AutoLayout applied to them. Figure 2.18 shows the Title Master, which you display by choosing <u>V</u>iew, <u>M</u>aster, <u>T</u>itle Master. If you're currently viewing a title slide in your presentation, you can also Shift+click the slide icon at the bottom left of your screen.

FIG. 2.18
This Master view has the slide miniature displayed in the upper-right hand corner.

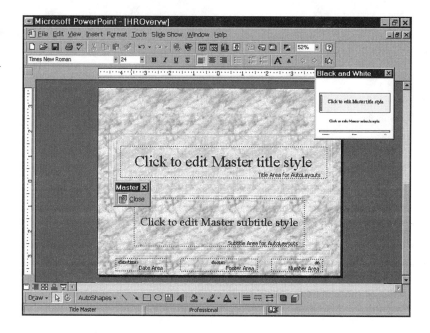

You can change background, color, size, and text object formatting for all title slides in Title Master. You can also add any additional objects you want to appear globally on title slides here.

Audience Handout Master

Handout Master has no effect on the appearance of the slides in your presentation. Rather, it controls the audience handouts you can print based on your presentation's content. These handouts contain miniature representations of your slides. You can distribute these to your audience so they can follow along with the presentation as you deliver it. One type of handout even includes space for them to take notes.

▶ **See** "Creating Handouts," **p. 121**

Display Handout Master by choosing View, Master, Handout Master. The form in Figure 2.19 appears.

Part

I

Ch

2

FIG. 2.19
Handout Master has its own floating menu which allows you to see different handout output choices.

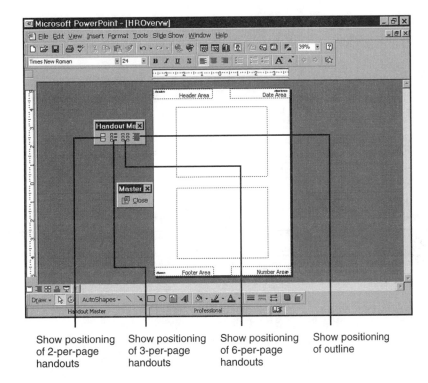

Show positioning of 2-per-page handouts

Show positioning of 3-per-page handouts

Show positioning of 6-per-page handouts

Show positioning of outline

Handouts can be printed with two, three, or six slide images per page. The floating menu that appears in this master view controls which of those output options is displayed. In addition, you can print the outline of your presentation, and that view can be selected by clicking the last of the four buttons on the Handout Master toolbar.

Notes Master

Finally, Notes Master controls Notes Pages. Notes Pages are used to provide a printout of each slide image with associated notes to assist a speaker in making a presentation. These notes can provide background, reminders, or details like statistics, that might help a speaker reinforce the points on the slide. Figure 2.20 shows the Notes Master, which you display by choosing View, Master, Notes Master.

▶ **See** "Creating a Note," **p. 113**

FIG. 2.20
Each speaker's note contains the image of one slide and an area for entering notes.

 The font size for a note is 12 points by default. During a presentation when you are often in a dimmed or poorly lit room, it's sometimes hard to read your own notes in this point size. For ease of reading during a presentation, consider changing the size of notes text in Notes Master to 16 or 18. In Notes Master view, select the Notes text placeholder (click a blank area in the placeholder, not on the text itself), then change the text size.

Once again, you can make changes to the background and color scheme of the Notes Master, but the default of black text on a white background works best for most purposes. You can also apply a new design template to the slide image if you like, but changes you make here will also apply to the actual slides. You can't apply one template for your notes and another for the actual slides.

You can also change text formatting and change the positions of the header, footer, date/timestamp, and slide number. Select them, then format and move wherever you like just as you would any other text in your presentation. The actual text on your individual Notes Pages follows suit.

To control whether or not these items print on your Notes Pages, you don't even need to be in Notes Master view. Choose View, Header and Footer. Choose the Slide tab or the Notes and Handouts tab, depending on which you'd like to set options for. You can choose to include Date and Time on each Notes Page; you can have the date Update Automatically, and choose the format you'd like it to have; or you can choose Fixed and enter any Time/Date information you like. It can actually be any text.

You can also choose to show a Header, Footer, and Page number on each Notes or Handouts page in your presentation.

TIP There's nothing forcing you to use the Notes pages as Microsoft intended them to be used. One slide service bureau owner I know never gives presentations himself but creates them for his clients. He uses Notes Pages to create proof printouts for them to approve before he does the final output of their slides or overheads.

Whenever he starts a new presentation, the first thing he does is switch to Notes Master view and delete the Notes Text placeholder. He selects the slide image and enlarges it considerably. He adds page numbers, of course, and makes sure that Notes Pages are set to print the current date and time, but he also puts the file name of the presentation in the header and his business name, phone, and fax numbers in the footer.

When it's time to proof print the slides, he picks Notes Pages in the Print dialog box rather than slides. By keeping all of his production information on the Notes, he makes sure his customers have all the information they need, but he doesn't have to remove it before printing the final slides or overheads; he just chooses Slides in the Print dialog box instead.

Saving Your Presentation

You can put many hours into building a polished presentation: typing in text, applying color and design elements, modifying text, and moving things around on your slides until each looks perfect. It's a good idea to save the changes you make frequently as you work.

 To save a PowerPoint file, click the Save button from the Standard toolbar, choose File, Save, or press Ctrl+S. If you have saved the file before, this will simply cause the latest version of the file to be saved. If you have not saved the file, the Save dialog box appears, as shown in Figure 2.21.

Most of the buttons and other options in the Save dialog box will be familiar to Windows 95 users, but PowerPoint 97 adds a few new ones (see Table 2.2).

FIG. 2.21
The Save dialog box allows you to browse around floppy, network, and hard drives.

Commands and Settings

Properties

Details

List

Create New Folder

Up One Level

Look in Favorites

Table 2.2 PowerPoint's New Save Dialog Box Options

Option	Description
Properties	Shows you the Properties information for the selected file (the info you entered when you saved the presentation or chose File, Properties).
Properties	Allows you to edit the properties of the selected files.
Sorting	Changes the order files are displayed in; you can sort by Name, Size, Type, or Modified date, in Ascending or Descending order.
Map Network Drive	Assigns a drive letter to a shared drive or directory on the network.
Add/Modify FTP Locations	Allows you to enter the details of FTP sites where you want to store/retrieve files. You must have access to an intranet or the Internet for this to work.

T I P You can save a file quickly by pressing Ctrl+S on your keyboard.

Select a location to save the file using the Save In drop-down list, or by moving up and down in your file hierarchy with the Up One Level button. Enter a file name in the File Name text box. By default, PowerPoint saves your file in PowerPoint 97 presentation format (PPT), but you can save in formats readable by earlier versions of PowerPoint (also PPT), a few special-purpose PowerPoint formats like Templates (POT) and Add-ins (PPA) and several common graphics file formats (WMF, JPG, GIF, and PNG).

When you've made your settings, choose Save to save the file.

Sometimes you'll create a presentation and save it, then you need to save it with another name so you can present a modified version of it for a different audience or occasion. For example, you might save one version with a conservative slide background for customers and another with a slightly snazzier background for employees. If you have previously saved a file but want to save it with a different name, choose File, Save As. The same Save As dialog box shown in Figure 2.21 appears. Simply give the file a new name, and save it.

How PowerPoint Pulls It All Together

So far in Chapters 1 and 2, you've seen most of the building blocks PowerPoint uses to build your presentations, and you'll be seeing a few more in the next few chapters. This seems as good a time as any to step back from the details and take a longer view of exactly how PowerPoint fits all the pieces together and how each of them affects your finished presentation.

I admit right up front that you don't really need to know how it works to create presentations in PowerPoint any more than you need to know how an internal combustion engine works to drive a car. But understanding a little bit of what goes on "under the hood" can help you learn PowerPoint sooner and to use it more efficiently.

Back when Walt Disney was making films like Snow White and Fantasia, cartoon animation was a long, slow process that required anywhere from six to 12 finished color drawings per second, or an average of something like 30,000 drawings for each hour of film. If each drawing had to be a complete rendering of the scene, Walt would probably never have finished Steamboat Willie, his first cartoon.

Instead of drawing each frame in total, animators use a single piece of art for the background and draw the characters—the only parts of the frame that move—on cels, thin sheets of plastic. They place these over the background and photograph them together. That saves huge amounts of time at the drawing table and makes it possible to re-film a scene on a different background (a different "location" if you will) should a plot change require it.

PowerPoint works much the same in many respects. Each PowerPoint slide you create is a cel sitting atop a background. The background is the Slide Master. Anything on the Slide Master appears on each of your slides. If you feel like a change of scene, you have only to apply a new template, which changes the graphics on the master. If you prefer, you can add your own graphics to an existing master, customize it extensively, or even create your own from scratch, but the fundamental rule is that anything on the master appears on all of your slides.

There's another layer that sits just atop the background, and in fact you can manipulate it at the same time; that's the *text placeholders*. While it may appear that the text placeholders are actually on the same level as the rest of the background graphics, PowerPoint has other ideas. For instance, if you draw a rectangle atop a text placeholder in the Slide Master, it appears that the rectangle will cover the text up, and in fact it does—on the master. Switch back to Slide view, enter some text into the placeholder, then try to send it behind the rectangle. It can't be done. PowerPoint assembles all the background elements on the slide first, then brings in the formatted text in placeholders.

continues

continued

The text placeholders act as a sort of filter. They take the text that you enter in Outline view or directly onto individual slides and apply formatting. They control the color, font, size, bullet, placement, line spacing, and other attributes. By default, all the formatting information the text placeholders apply is contained in PowerPoint's templates, but of course you can change any of it you like by altering it on the master.

Unlike the background graphics, which you can't even select when you're working on an individual slide, the text that bubbles up through the text placeholders is weakly glued in place. You're free to move it around, resize the text blocks, or change their formatting in any way you like. As mentioned before, though, once you break the bond, the text placeholders no longer control the formatting and placement of the text. Any placeholder formatting that you override on the individual slides can no longer be changed by altering the placeholders, unless you reapply the master; that tosses out any reformatting you've done and "re-glues" the connection to the placeholder formatting.

What About the Other Masters and Views?

As already mentioned, Outline view feeds text through the placeholders and into the individual slides (and receives the text you type into the placeholders on the slides).

Notes view provides a placeholder for a different type of text (which gets its formatting from the text placeholder on the Notes Master, just as the slide text placeholders get theirs from the Slide Master). Notes view also contains an image of the slide itself, which comes directly from the actual slide. You can't edit the slide in Notes view, but you can move the image around and resize it in the Notes Master.

The Handouts Master doesn't allow you to do anything with the slide images it displays, but you can add text or graphics that you want to have appear on each page of handouts. And there's no Handouts view comparable to the Slide and Notes Pages views. The Handouts "view" appears only on your printer when you print Handouts.

Using Text in Presentations

Working with Text

by Kathy Ivens

Virtually every slide in a presentation contains text of some kind, even if it's just a title. Entering and editing text in PowerPoint is similar to entering and editing text in any Office application. ■

Enter and edit text

Whether you enter text from the keyboard or import it, PowerPoint has all the editing functions you need to create an effective presentation.

Format text

Add special effects to your words to make them shout out their message or create a whimsical mood. Whatever you want to say can be enhanced when you learn how to change the way text looks.

Check your text

Make sure you're not embarrassed by spelling or grammatical errors with the tools provided in PowerPoint.

Adding Text to Your Slides

There are a variety of ways to add text messages to your PowerPoint presentation. The following sections describe how to enter the text content of your slides and how to edit the text when necessary.

Entering Text in a Placeholder

One method of entering slide text involves replacing the sample text in a slide *placeholder* with your own text. The slide shown in Figure 3.1 includes two placeholders for text—one that contains a sample title and one that contains a bulleted list. The third placeholder is for clip art. A faint, dotted line appears around each placeholder.

FIG. 3.1
This slide layout contains two place-holders for text and one placeholder for clip art.

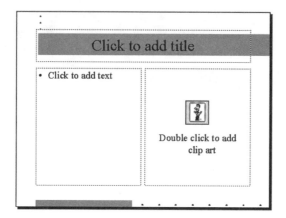

Click anywhere within a placeholder to select it. The faint outline is replaced by a wide hashed border (see Figure 3.2). This border indicates that the current placeholder is selected. The sample text disappears and an insertion point appears inside the place-holder, indicating that you can enter text. In a title or subtitle placeholder, the insertion point may be centered or left-aligned. In a bulleted-list placeholder, the sample text disap-pears and the bullet remains, with the insertion point positioned where the text will begin.

Type the actual text for your slide inside the selected placeholder. In the case of titles and subtitles, press Enter only when you want to begin a new centered line of text. In the case of bullets, press Enter only when you want to begin a new bulleted item. If your bulleted text is too long to fit on one line, PowerPoint automatically wraps the text to the next line and aligns the text appropriately.

FIG. 3.2
A selected text placeholder is indicated by a wide-hashed border.

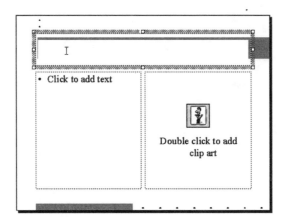

When you finish entering text, deselect the object by clicking a blank area of the slide or the gray border around the slide. Notice that the object is no longer enclosed by a line (see Figure 3.3). Now you have a more realistic idea of how the completed slide will look.

FIG. 3.3
Once you enter the text, get rid of the hashed border, lean back, and take a look at it the way it will look when you print it.

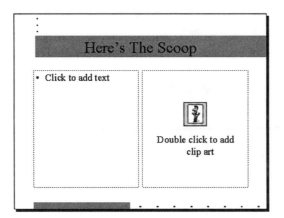

Adding to Existing Text

You may need to add a label or other text that is not part of a placeholder. Suppose your slide contains a title and a bulleted list and you want to add some plain text to your slide below the bulleted list.

The slide shown in Figure 3.4 has several bulleted items in addition to the title. Now suppose that you need to add a new sentence that's neither a title nor a bullet item.

FIG. 3.4
The slide needs some
additional text below
the bulleted list.

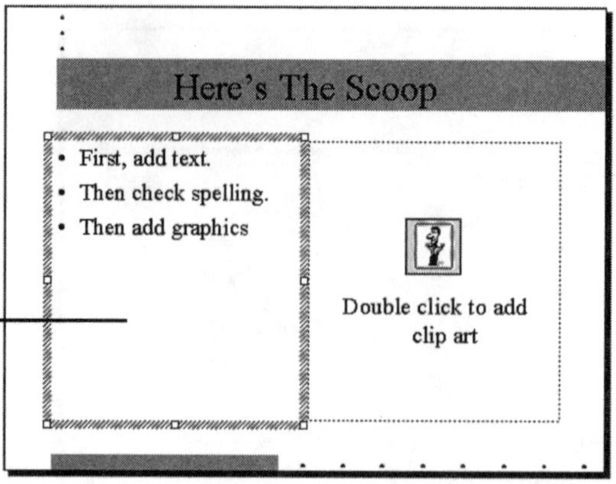

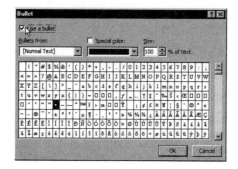

To add the text, follow these steps:

1. Select the placeholder (in this case, the bulleted list placeholder).

2. Place the insertion point below the bullet list.

3. Begin typing the text you want to add.

4. Select the new text to highlight it.

5. Choose Format, Bullet to see the Bullet dialog box (see Figure 3.5).

FIG. 3.5
The Bullet dialog box
offers various
characters for bullets
and a way to deselect
the use of bullets.

6. Click the Use A Bullet selection box to deselect the bullet feature for the highlighted text. Then choose OK to return to the slide.

7. Click outside the slide area to see the results of your work (see Figure 3.6).

FIG. 3.6

The additional text stands alone: it isn't part of the bullet list.

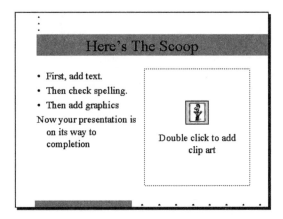

 TIP For a quick way to turn bullets off or on, click the Bullet button on the toolbar. It's a toggle and reverses the current state.

You can manipulate this new text a bit more if you want to change its placement or appearance. For instance, there probably should be more space between the last bullet item and the new text. It also should be centered instead of having a hanging left indent (which is the format for bullet items). To make these changes, follow these steps:

1. Click anywhere in the placeholder to make it active so you can edit its contents. The hashed placeholder border appears.

2. Place the insertion point to the left of the first word of the new text and press Enter to create space between it and the bullet items above it.

3. Select the text and choose an alignment scheme from the Formatting toolbar. You'll probably find that centered text looks best, so click the Center Alignment button.

4. Click outside the slide to see the final effect. You can continue to manipulate the text until you think it's right.

Creating Text Outside a Placeholder

You can place text anywhere on a slide without being restricted to using a text placeholder. To do this, you have to create a text object by taking the following steps:

1. On the Drawing toolbar, click Text Box.

2. Position your pointer at the place where you want to add text and click. A new text box appears (see Figure 3.7).

FIG. 3.7
When you use the Text
Box tool, a new text
box appears, with a
hashed border that
indicates it's active
and ready for editing.

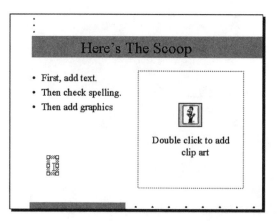

3. Enter the text you want to add. The text box expands to accommodate the new text.

> **T I P** You can also click the Text tool and drag the mouse to create a rectangle of any size in which the added text will go.

Importing Text from Other Applications

PowerPoint offers several menu items that help you import text from other applications into your presentation.

Import an Outline from MS Word   If you use Microsoft Word to prepare outlines for presentations or reports, you can import that outline into your PowerPoint presentation. What's even better is that when the outline is imported, it's brought in as slides. To accomplish this:

1. Choose Insert, Slides from Outline.

2. When the Insert Outline dialog box (which looks like a standard Windows Open File dialog box) appears, find the folder and file that has your Word outline.

3. Double-click the file's name.

Each top level of your outline becomes a slide. Move through the slides, editing or changing whatever seems necessary.

Import a Word Processing Document   You can also import documents into PowerPoint, and it's almost as simple as importing an outline. For instance, you can import a Microsoft Word document or a text document by following these steps:

1. Choose Insert, Object to bring up the Insert Object dialog box (see Figure 3.8).

FIG 3.8
Choose Browse to pick the file you want to import.

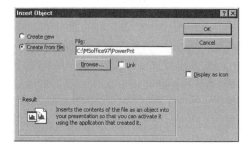

2. To import an existing file so that it becomes an object in your own presentation, select Create From File.

3. Enter the path and file name for the word processing document you want to import, or choose Browse to search your drive for it and select it when you find it. The text in the document becomes a slide.

4. If you want to edit the text you imported from Microsoft Word, double-click to bring up the Word tools you need right in your PowerPoint window (see Figure 3.9).

5. Edit, format, or otherwise manipulate the imported document as needed. Click anywhere outside the slide to leave the editing mode and see the results.

Part
II

Ch
3

FIG. 3.9
The Word menu bar and toolbar are displayed when you want to edit the imported document—if you click Help on the menu bar, you see Word Help.

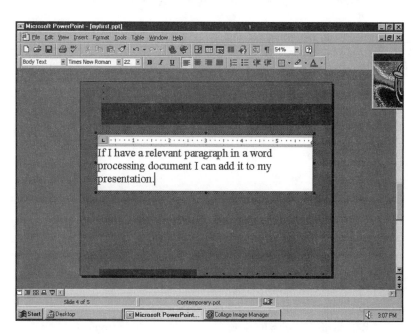

> **N O T E**   If you choose Create <u>N</u>ew in the Insert Object dialog box, you see the same editing
> window as in Figure 3.9, and you can use Microsoft Word tools to create the text for
> your slide from scratch. ■

Editing Text in a Slide

You can make changes to the text in any text object simply by clicking the object. An insertion point appears, indicating that the text is ready for editing. Then you can begin
making changes to the text.

Deleting Text

You can delete characters, words, or all the text in a text box. Use one of these methods:

- ■ The Delete key erases the character to the right of the cursor.
- ■ The Backspace key erases the character to the left of the cursor.

You can select characters or large sections of text, then press the Delete key. Table 3.1
shows the keystrokes for selecting text within a slide.

Table 3.1   Keystrokes for Selecting Text

Action	Result
Shift+left arrow	Selects the character to the left of the insertion point. Continue to use this key combination to select additional characters.
Shift+right arrow	Selects the character to the right of the insertion point. Continue to use this key combination to select additional characters.
Click and drag the mouse	Selects a string of characters.
Double-click a word	Selects the entire word.
Triple-click a line/paragraph	Selects the entire line (title) or paragraph (bullet item).
Ctrl+A	Selects all text in a selected text object.
Ctrl+click	Selects the sentence the insertion point is in.

 If you delete text accidentally, you can undo your action by clicking the Undo button on
the toolbar (you can also press Ctrl+Z or choose <u>E</u>dit, <u>U</u>ndo).

The fastest (and safest) way to use the Undo button is to click it immediately after you've
made an error. Don't enter any other keystrokes before you Undo your mistake. The

Undo button has the capacity to keep a list of your last actions however, so if you enter text or delete other text, you can ask Undo to correct the mistake you made a couple of keystrokes ago. Press the down arrow to the right of the Undo button to see a list of actions. Choose the ones you want to undo.

TIP By default, PowerPoint stores the last 20 actions in the Undo feature. You can change that by choosing Tools, Options and moving to the Edit tab of the Options dialog box. In the Maximum Number of Undos spin box, specify the number of actions you want to track for Undo. You can choose a number between 1 and 150.

Copying Text

You can copy text that appears in one place to another place, which can be a great time-saver. For instance, you may have a line of copy that you want to place in several slides. Instead of typing the same piece of text in each slide, you enter it once, copy it, and then place it everywhere you want it.

Copying text occurs with the assistance of the Windows Clipboard. The *Clipboard* is an area of your computer's memory that is used for holding data. As long as the data is on the Clipboard, you can place it anywhere in any Windows software application. The data stays on the Clipboard until you replace it with new data, or until you exit Windows.

To copy text to the Clipboard and duplicate it elsewhere in your presentation, follow these steps:

1. Select the text you want to copy.

2. When it is highlighted, click the Copy button on the toolbar (or press Ctrl+C, or choose Edit, Copy).

3. Move to the place in your presentation where you want to duplicate this text.

4. Click the Paste button on the toolbar (or press Ctrl+V).

Because the text is still on the Clipboard, you can move to another slide and paste it in again. In fact, you can keep doing this until every place this text should appear has received it.

Moving Text Around

If you think a particular block of text would be more effective in a different spot on a slide, you can easily move it. In fact, you can pick up text and put it down anywhere else you'd like, even on another slide.

In Figure 3.10, for example, it might be more effective to rearrange the items in the bullet list. Suppose that you want to move item number two so it comes *after* item three.

FIG. 3.10

When you change your mind, it's easy to move text around without retyping.

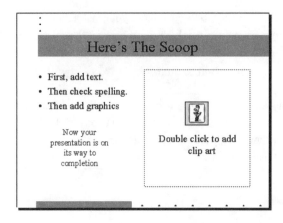

To move the text:

1. Click the text to put the text box into edit mode.

2. Select the text you want to move.

3. Place the mouse pointer anywhere within the highlighted text.

4. Press and hold the left mouse button down while you drag the text to its new location. Then release the mouse button.

There are a couple of other ways to accomplish the same thing:

   ▪ You can perform the steps described above, except use the right mouse button to drag the text. When you release the button, a menu appears (see Figure 3.11). Choose Move Here.

FIG. 3.11

It's sometimes easier and safer to use a right button drag because PowerPoint provides a menu of choices, and you won't accidentally move something you meant to copy.

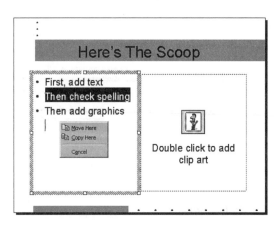

- You can select the text, then right-click and choose Cut. Move to the new location, right-click, and choose Paste.

- You can select the text and then click the Cut button on the toolbar (or press Ctrl+X). Move to the new location and click the Paste button (or press Ctrl+V).

Using Cut and Paste is the way to move text around between slides. Just select and cut the text, move to the appropriate slide, and paste it where you want it.

Formatting Text

Formatting means applying characteristics and effects to text in order to enhance its appearance. The formatting you apply to the text in a presentation is extremely important because it affects the way your words are received by your audience.

You can make some text more important than other text by applying formatting techniques that make it stand out. Perhaps bold or italic text will make a stronger impression, or a shadow effect will make everyone notice a word.

Part

II

Ch

3

Aligning Text in a Slide

Alignment is the way text is placed between the margins of a page or a text box on a slide. There are four alignment choices:

- *Left Align.* The left margin of each line is at the same place on the left, while the right edge of each line ends wherever appropriate (called a *ragged right edge*).
- *Right Align.* The right margin of each line is at the same place on the right. The left edge of each line falls in a different place, depending on the contents of the line (called a *ragged left edge*).
- *Center.* Each line is centered. The left and right edges of each line will differ, depending upon the number and size of characters in the line.
- *Justified.* Each line starts at the left margin and ends at the right margin. There are no ragged edges.

Justified alignment usually doesn't work very well if there are short lines such as titles. In order to make sure the first character of each line is at the left margin and the last character is at the right margin, there is frequently a great deal of empty space inserted between words. The effect can be pretty unsightly.

To align text, select it and then click the Left, Center, or Right Alignment button on the Formatting toolbar. There is no Justify button. To justify text, point to <u>A</u>lignment on the F<u>o</u>rmat menu, then choose <u>J</u>ustify from the submenu. Incidentally, the other alignment choices are on the same submenu.

Changing Fonts

Fonts—also called *typefaces* in computer programs—are groups of characters that share the same style or look. Fonts have personalities, and the personalities affect the text and its impact on the viewer. They can range from rigid to freeform, from serious to whimsical.

Fonts are divided into two sets of groups. The first group is defined by the way the characters are spaced—monospaced or proportionately spaced. The second group is defined by whether or not there is an extra little line at the edge of characters and the choices are serif and sans serif (the little line is called a *serif,* and *sans* is the French word for "without"). Figure 3.12 illustrates two fonts with opposite characteristics.

FIG. 3.12

These fonts are the same size but they certainly don't seem to be because the monospaced font doesn't nestle the characters together.

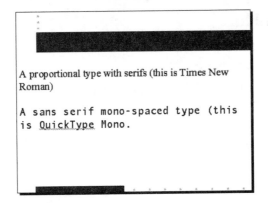

In a *monospaced* font, each character occupies exactly the same amount of space on a line. Picture a tiny box representing each character; if you're typing a five-character word, you have five little boxes of identical width lined up next to each other. Each character goes into the center of one of those boxes.

Proportionally spaced fonts use whatever amount of space that is required to accommodate that character's inherent width. Therefore, an *i* takes up less space than an *o*, and an *m* takes up more space than an *o*.

The characters in serif fonts generally take up a bit more width than those in sans-serif fonts (that little decorative line is the culprit, of course).

When you are choosing fonts for your presentation, there are a few guidelines to remember:

- Using too many fonts on the same slide looks unprofessional. It's OK to use one font for the headline and another for the rest of the copy (or even a third for bulleted items), but don't go overboard.

- Fancy fonts, such as ornate script, don't work well on slides, especially for headlines.

- Sans-serif fonts tend to have more of an authoritative and bold look.

- Proportional fonts work extremely well in body copy—they're more efficient because you can generally fit more characters on a line.

It's quite simple to change the font of any text in a slide:

1. Select the text you want to change.

2. Click the down arrow to the right of the Font box on the Formatting toolbar; a drop-down list of available fonts appears, as shown in Figure 3.13.

3. Click the font you want to use. The selected text changes immediately.

FIG. 3.13

PowerPoint provides plenty of fonts.

When you change the font for text in a slide, you're changing only that slide's appearance. If you want to change the font for all instances of text for the same type of slide element (for example a headline placeholder), you have to change the Master Slide.

Changing the Size of Text

Font size is measured in *points*, which is a height measurement. This is a printer's measure and each point is 1/72nd of an inch. Figure 3.14 gives you a sense of perspective about font sizes.

If you've used an older dot-matrix printer, you probably set print sizes by picking a measurement of cpi. This stands for "characters per inch," which is a measurement of width instead of height. Some printers (and fonts) use that measurement (although it's much rarer now). If you are used to cpi measurements, your dot-matrix printer output was probably the Courier typeface at 10 cpi. To help you use your visual memory as a guideline, that output was approximately a 12-point typeface.

FIG. 3.14
Gulliver was 72 points high, which amazed the 24-point high Lilliputians.

To change the size of text:

1. Select the text you want to change.

2. Click the arrow to the right of the Font Size box on the Formatting toolbar to see the list of available sizes.

3. Select the new size.

Different fonts may have different choices for sizes.

N O T E   Remember that when you change the size of your text, it may re-wrap. Even though points are a measurement of height, as you make characters larger or smaller, they change in width proportionately to the change in height (otherwise, they'd look awkwardly skinny when enlarged). ■

Creating Bullet Lists

Bullet lists are one of the most effective slide tools you can use. They provide a succinct way to get the important points of your subject matter to the audience (it's assumed that your speech will be less succinct).

The easiest way to enter a bullet list is to pick a slide format that has that format pre-designed in a text placeholder. The bullets are there, and every time you press Enter, the next line has a bullet ready for you.

You can, however, put any text into bullet list format:

 ■ If you have existing text, select it and press the Bullets button on the Formatting toolbar. Each paragraph (each section of text separated by an Enter key) will begin with a bullet.

■ If you are entering new text, click the Bullets button before you begin typing. A bullet appears before your first character and every time you press Enter to begin a new line; that line will have a bullet to the left. When you want to stop using bullets and begin typing regular text, just click the Bullets button again to turn it off.

You can change the character used for the bullet if you want something other than the standard filled circle. Choose Format, Bullet to see the Bullet dialog box (see Figure 3.15).

Press this down arrow to see the list of available fonts

Press this down arrow to see a color palette and select a color for your bullets

FIG. 3.15
The standard bullet is from the Normal Text collection of characters, and you can change the bullet character or look at a different collection of characters (which are really fonts).

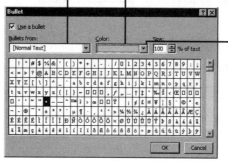

Select a size, which is measured in percentage of the size of the text you're using

If you change the font by picking a different one from the Bullets From text box, you'll see a different set of characters.

If you have several levels of bullets, you can change the bullet character for the additional levels:

1. Press the Tab key again to indent another level if you're creating a sublevel bullet.
2. Highlight the text and choose Format, Bullet.
3. Choose a font that has a character you'd like to use for this bullet level.
4. Select the character by double-clicking it.

The sublevel bullet text is indented and has its own bullet character (see Figure 3.16).

FIG. 3.16
Make a sublevel bullet stand out by changing the bullet character.

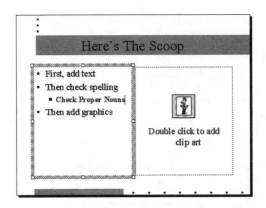

Here's The Scoop

- First, add text
- Then check spelling
  - Check Proper Nouns
- Then add graphics

Double click to add clip art

Adding Special Effects to Your Text

One of the easiest yet most effective ways to make text stand out is to add special formatting effects to characters, sentences, or paragraphs.

PowerPoint makes these tasks incredibly easy because the Formatting toolbar contains most of the necessary mechanisms. Just select the text you want to give special attention and click one of these buttons on the Formatting toolbar:

B
- *Bold*, which makes the text darker and usually makes it slightly larger (sometimes bolding text causes it to rewrap).

I
- *Italic*, which makes the text lean slightly to the right.

U
- *Underline*, which places an underscore beneath each character.

S
- *Shadow*, which places a gray line around the right and bottom side of each character, giving the effect of a shadow cast by a sun that is in the upper-left corner.

You can use multiple formatting effects on text, so that characters can be bold and underlined, or bold and italic, or any combination of any multiples of effects. To make text superscript, subscript or give it an embossed quality, choose Format, Font and select the appropriate effect.

Adding Symbols

There are times when you want to draw special attention to a word or phrase. If making the text bold or otherwise changing its formatting doesn't quite do it, you have to provide some eye-catching method for making sure the audience gets the importance of this item. You can solve this dilemma with the insertion of a symbol that draws attention.

Or, you may have a less dramatic reason to need a symbol in your text, such as a copyright or registration symbol to keep everything legal when you mention a brand name.

For either occasion (or anything in between), PowerPoint provides a full range of special symbol characters. To use a symbol in a slide, begin these steps after choosing the slide (and text box) that will receive the symbol:

1. Choose Insert, Symbol to see the Symbol dialog box (see Figure 3.17).

FIG. 3.17

The Symbol dialog box offers all sorts of interesting characters you can use when you need something special.

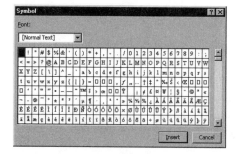

Part
II

Ch
3

2. By default, the Font box is set to Normal Text. Click the down arrow to see the choices for fonts, each of which provides a different set of symbols.

3. When you see a font with symbols you think might be just what you need, you can enlarge any symbol of interest by clicking it once (see Figure 3.18).

FIG. 3.18

Get a closer look at any symbol by clicking it.

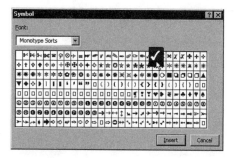

4. When you find the symbol you want to use, double-click it to place it on the slide (or select it and choose Insert).

5. Click Close to leave the Symbol dialog box and return to your slide.

My own particular favorites when I'm looking for symbols are the Wingdings and Monotype Sorts fonts, which are all symbols with no alphabetic characters.

Setting Tabs and Margins

PowerPoint's tab and margin settings give you some control over the way text aligns within a slide. Setting tabs, of course, controls the size of the indent when you start a new section or paragraph of text. You can also use tabs to set up columns, which is often an effective way to present information.

Using the Ruler

Tabs and margins are set with the ruler, which you can see if you choose View, Ruler. The ruler is actually two rulers, one that appears below the toolbar across the top of window, and another that appears on the left side of the screen (see Figure 3.19).

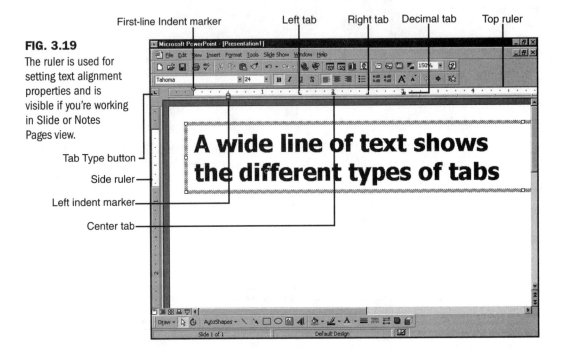

First-line Indent marker   Left tab   Right tab   Decimal tab   Top ruler

FIG. 3.19
The ruler is used for setting text alignment properties and is visible if you're working in Slide or Notes Pages view.

Tab Type button

Side ruler

Left indent marker

Center tab

Notice that the section of the ruler that is available for configuration matches the section of the slide you selected. In Figure 3.14, the left side of the slide (a text placeholder) is selected and the rulers match the selection.

Changing the Default Tabs

Default tabs are pre-determined left tabs that are always available. When you change the default tabs for a placeholder, you are changing the interval between the first and subsequent default tabs. To do this, display the ruler on the screen and follow these steps:

1. Put your insertion point in the placeholder you want to change the default tabs for.
2. Put your pointer on the first default tab marker and drag it to a new location on the ruler.
3. Release the mouse button to have all the other default tab markers move in order to keep the interval consistent with the new first default tab.

Setting Tabs

You can choose to set your own tabs instead of using the defaults. Besides giving you the opportunity to set tabs that aren't necessarily evenly spaced, this also provides a way to use tab types other than left. The available tab types are left, right, center, and decimal-aligned.

When you set a tab, any default tabs to the left of your new tab cease to exist (if you remove your tab, they return).

To place tabs on the ruler, make sure the ruler is displayed, then follow these steps:

1. Put the insertion point in the text you want to change.
2. Click the tab type button until the type you want to use is displayed (the types rotate as you click).
3. Click the ruler at the point where you want this tab.
4. If you want additional tabs of the same type, continue to click the ruler (the current tab type is inserted until you click the tab type button again to change the type).
5. If you want to move a tab you've inserted, drag it to the new location.
6. To delete a tab you've inserted, drag it past the edge of the ruler (dragging it off the ruler is like having it fall off the edge of the world—it disappears).

Setting Margins

When you work with margins in a PowerPoint placeholder, the effects are the same as working with margins in a word processor—text stays inside the margins.

Part
II

Ch
3

To change margins for a text placeholder:

1. Select the text placeholder you want to change.
2. Choose F̲ormat, Aut̲oShape to bring up the Format AutoShape dialog box.
3. Click the Text Box tab (see Figure 3.20).

FIG. 3.20
Use the Text Box tab to set margins and other text properties.

4. To change any margin specification, enter a new measurement (or use the incre- ment arrows to change the existing setting).
5. Click OK.

The text in the placeholder falls within the new margins.

Checking Text

PowerPoint, like your favorite word processor, provides a group of tools to help you make sure everything is just the way it should be. Spelling, punctuation, and writing style can be examined and corrected, if necessary.

Replacing Text

Suppose that you've completed a presentation about the new widget your company is going to manufacture, which the marketing department has named "grizby." This morn- ing the marketing department told you that as a result of research, they've decided that nobody would buy a widget called a grizby. Instead, they've named the new product "flibbick."

Don't go through the slides deleting *grizby* and typing *flibbick*—let PowerPoint do it for you. This process is called Replace (although many computer users tend to use the jargon expression "Search and Replace"). To invoke it:

1. Press Ctrl+H (or choose <u>E</u>dit, <u>R</u>eplace).

2. When the Replace dialog box appears (see Figure 3.21), enter the word or phrase you want to get rid of in the Fi<u>n</u>d What text box.

3. Enter the replacement word or phrase in the Re<u>p</u>lace With text box.

FIG. 3.21
Use Replace to search for and replace any word or phrase quickly and efficiently.

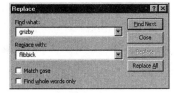

4. Select Match <u>C</u>ase if the case is the cause of the replacement (you'd changed the name to flibbick and now you found out that it should be treated as a proper noun, Flibbick).

5. Select Find <u>W</u>hole Words only if the word you entered could be part of other words you don't want to replace (for instance, if you wanted to replace *other* with *else*, you could end up with *melse*, *brelse*, *anelse*, and so on).

6. Click <u>F</u>ind Next (or press Enter) to see the first occurrence of the word that's going to be replaced. If you want to replace this instance, chose <u>R</u>eplace.

7. If you are sure that every time the word occurs you want to replace it, click Replace <u>A</u>ll. The Replace function zooms through your text, replacing every occurrence. Then it reports how many replacements it made.

8. When all the replacements have been made, click Close.

> **CAUTION**
> Before using Replace All, save your work. Then, because the Replace function goes through your document taking no prisoners, you can go back to the last saved version if you killed too much.

Using AutoCorrect

AutoCorrect is a feature that automatically corrects common typing errors. The corrections are made as you type, so you won't have to run the spelling checker to fix these common mistakes.

AutoCorrect arrives with lots of common errors already programmed for correction. For example, if you don't let go of the Shift key fast enough, it's a common error to capitalize the second letter of a word in addition to the first letter (which you wanted to capitalize). AutoCorrect changes the second letter to lowercase. The common typing errors involved in entering the word *the* (*teh*, for example) are automatically corrected.

In addition, you can use this feature to program automatic corrections of deliberate errors.

For instance, I frequently use the phrase `Press OK when you have finished configuring the dialog box`. I created an error, a misspelled word that I couldn't possibly use in a sentence. The word is *pok* (for `Press OK`). Every time I type that word, AutoCorrect changes it to the complete phrase as soon as I press the next space bar.

To personalize AutoCorrect so that it picks up phrases and words that you frequently misspell, follow these steps:

1. Choose Tools, AutoCorrect to bring up the AutoCorrect dialog box (see Figure 3.22).

FIG. 3.22

Configure the way AutoCorrect be- haves and add your own autocorrections using the AutoCorrect dialog box.

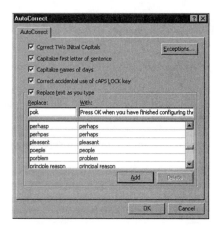

2. In the Replace text box, enter the characters you want to type in order to have AutoCorrect change them to a word or a phrase. Don't use any real words, just your codes (or your frequent misspellings if you're doing a real autocorrection).

3. In the With text box, enter the word or phrase you want to appear magically after you enter the word you invented.

4. Configure the way AutoCorrect works by selecting and deselecting the options.

5. Press OK when you have finished configuring the dialog box (see!!).

You can also delete any autocorrections if you find they get in your way, whether they are pre-loaded or entered by you. Select the characters in the Replace box and click Delete.

Using the Spelling Checker

Even if you think everything looks right, don't ever go public with a presentation that hasn't been checked for spelling errors.

The spelling checker in PowerPoint compares all the words in your document with a dictionary file, much the way any Microsoft Office application does. When the spelling checker finds a word that's not in the dictionary file, it highlights the word in your slide and displays the word in the Spelling dialog box, shown in Figure 3.23.

FIG. 3.23
If a word is unrecognized, you probably misspelled it. The Spelling dialog box displays unrecognized words.

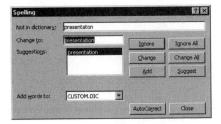

N O T E The spelling checker checks text in all objects in a presentation file except those objects that contain text imported from other applications. ▪

The spelling checker moves through your presentation one slide at a time, and then checks the Notes Pages (if any) before closing the Spelling dialog box. You can stop using the spelling checker at any time by clicking the Close button in the Spelling dialog box.

To check the spelling in a presentation file, follow these steps:

1. Choose Tools, Spelling or click the Spelling button on the Standard toolbar to display the Spelling dialog box. The spelling checker highlights the first unrecognized word in the presentation file and displays the word in the Not in Dictionary box.

2. Choose the appropriate command button, using these guidelines:

   - *Ignore.* Ignores this word and moves on.
   - *Ignore All.* Ignores this word every time you find it.
   - *Change.* Changes the original word by replacing it with the word in the Change To box.
   - *Change All.* Changes every occurrence of this word to the word in the Change To box.

- *Add*. Adds this word to the dictionary so the speller doesn't stop here any-more.

- *Suggest*. Searches the dictionary and displays possible replacement words (you choose the one that's correct).

3. The spelling checker takes the indicated action and then highlights the next unrecognized word.

4. Repeat step 2 until the spelling checker displays a message saying that the entire presentation has been checked.

5. Click OK.

You can configure the way the spelling checker works—for instance, telling PowerPoint not to check words under certain conditions—by choosing Tools, Options and moving to the Spelling tab (see Figure 3.24).

FIG. 3.24
Configure the Spelling
tool to behave in a
way that's comfortable
for you as you work.

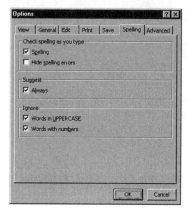

Using Style Checker

After you've finished your presentation, you should check it for style. That means a consis-tency in the way you handle the text elements. Do you want a period after the sentences that are slide titles (probably not)? Wouldn't you like to make sure that your title text is in a larger font than the body text (otherwise it wouldn't look very professional)?

The PowerPoint Style Checker can examine your presentation and correct anything that doesn't match the way you want it to be. Using the Style Checker is a two part process—first you set the options, then you check the presentation. Depending on the type of pre-sentation, it's possible that you'll want to change the options every time you use the Style Checker.

To begin, follow these steps:

1. Choose Tools, Style Checker to bring up the Style Checker dialog box (see Figure 3.25).

2. To configure the way the Style Checker works, choose Options.

FIG. 3.25

Check your work to make sure you've got the right tone, mood, and vocabulary level for this presentation.

Part

II

Ch

3

3. When the Options dialog box appears, the Case and End Punctuation tab is in the foreground (see Figure 3.26).

FIG. 3.26

For consistency in punctuation, you can have the Style Checker make changes to your presentation that match the style you want.

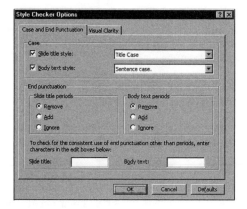

4. Go through the options and tell the Style Checker what to change in order to make each element consistent throughout all your slides.

5. Move to the Visual Clarity tab (see Figure 3.27) and go through the options to make sure they match the look you want for your presentation.

6. Press OK when you have finished configuring the dialog box. You return to the Style Checker dialog box.

7. Decide which styles you want to check (you should always check Visual Clarity and Case) and whether or not you want to check Spelling.

8. Click Start to begin checking the presentation.

FIG. 3.27
Keep your fonts, sizes, and other elements neat and tidy so you don't have a messy, unprofessional presentation.

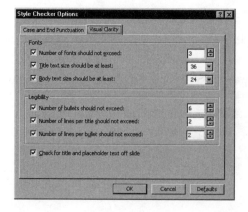

The Style Checker moves through every slide in the presentation, checking the contents against the configuration. When it finds something amiss, it shows you the problem in its dialog box (see Figure 3.28).

FIG. 3.28
When there's a problem on a slide, the Style Checker can fix it automatically and then move to all the other slides to fix any similar problems.

You can choose any of the following when the Style Checker finds a problem:

- Ignore to have the Style Checker leave this particular occurrence alone.
- Ignore All to leave all similar occurrences the way they are.
- Change to change this occurrence so it matches the configuration options for the Style Checker.
- Change All to change each similar occurrence to match the configuration options.
- Cancel to stop checking the presentation.

For some items, the Style Checker doesn't make changes—it just tells you about the problem. For instance, if you have too many bullets in a text placeholder, it will tell you which slide has the problem, but it takes no action. That's because it would be dangerous for the Style Checker to delete a couple of bullet items just because you'd over-run your configured allotment. If you decide to take action on the problem after the Style Checker tells you about it, you'll have to return to the slide and manually fix it. ●

CHAPTER 4

Working with Outline View

by Dorothy Burke

Outline view in PowerPoint allows you to plan and organize your presentation. You can begin your presentation in Outline view by typing the text portion, by importing the text from another source, or by starting your presentation with the AutoContent Wizard which fills in outline text for you.

The outline text becomes the slide titles or body text for your slides and automatically appears in the text placeholders in Slide view. Likewise, any text entered in a text placeholder in Slide view simultaneously appears in the outline. Even if you start the presentation from Slide view, the outline for the completed slides appears when you switch to Outline view, and then serves as an editing and organizing tool for the existing slides.

PowerPoint's Outline view gives you a tool to use in organizing first your thoughts and then your presentation as you develop it. It allows you to enter your ideas very quickly without having to give undue concern to what the presentation looks like during the early stages of creation. ∎

Create your presentation in Outline view

You encounter the "landscape" of Outline view and prepare to build your presentation there.

Set slide titles and bullet text

When entering text into the outline, you need to distinguish which lines are slide titles and which are bullet paragraphs. Discover the techniques that make this easy for you.

Import text from other sources into the outline

If you've already created the outline text elsewhere (such as in your word processing package), you can either import it or copy it through the Clipboard. Then you can organize it and separate it into slide titles and bullets.

Organize and refine existing presentations

Outline view gives you the ideal tools to edit and reorganize the presentation.

Print the outline

Use the printed copy of your outline to get approval on the presentation from your supervisor or to keep on track during the presentation. Learn how to print it out and how to export it for printing in Word.

Outline View

 To go to Outline view, click the Outline View button at the bottom of the screen, or choose View, Outline.

When you first open Outline view, you should see a slide miniature of the active slide in a floating window on-screen (see the slide miniature in Figure 4.1). If not, choose View, Slide Miniature. The slide miniature gives you a reference as you work with the text on that slide and saves you from switching to Slide view every time you want to see how your text changes will modify the slide. To remove the slide miniature, choose View, Slide Miniature, or click the X in the upper-right corner of the slide miniature. To move the miniature out of your way, drag it by the title bar at the top of the miniature window.

FIG. 4.1

The Microsoft PowerPoint Outline view shows slide titles and related body text.

Slide number ──

Slide icon ──

Slide miniature ──

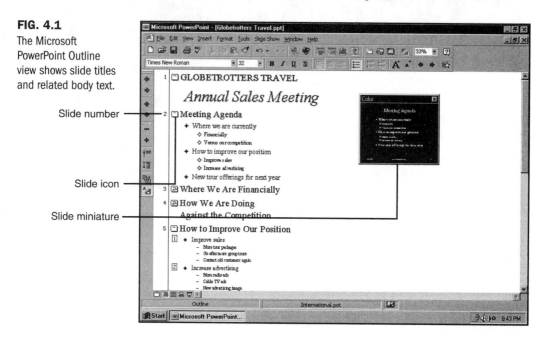

If you add text in the placeholders on the slides, that text is a part of the outline (text added outside the text placeholders does not appear in the outline). Click once on a line of text to position your cursor there, and that slide becomes the active slide.

Slide titles in Outline view have a slide number in the left margin of the slide followed by a slide icon (see the slide number and slide icon in Figure 4.2). By double-clicking the slide icon, you can quickly return to Slide view of that slide.

 You may also use the Slide View button to return to a slide, but make sure your insertion point is in the text of the slide you want before clicking the button.

FIG. 4.2
Like bulleted lists and title slides, the slide icons for text slides look different than slides that contain graphs, artwork, organization charts, or tables.

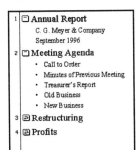

 T I P Any body text displayed on a slide—such as the subtitle on a title page or the bullet paragraphs from a bulleted list slide—appears below the title in Outline view. Slides that do not have body text may contain clip art, graphs, organization charts, tables, or graphics. The slide icons for these slides are different from the text slide icon. If you'd like more visible feedback about what's on each slide, turn on the slide miniature as described earlier.

Notice that a different toolbar appears on the left side of the screen (see Figure 4.3). The *Outlining toolbar* has specialized tools for controlling the indenting of text (promoting and demoting), moving text up and down in the outline, collapsing and expanding the slide text, changing the appearance of the text on-screen, and adding summary slides to the presentation. If you can't see the Outlining toolbar, choose View, Toolbars and select Outlining.

Part
II

Ch
4

FIG. 4.3
The Outlining toolbar has the special tools you need to edit and navigate within Outline view.

Building Your Presentation in Outline View

I know using an outline goes against your grain. I never did them until after I wrote my term papers in school, but I find them really helpful when I'm putting my presentations together.

In the average presentation, bulleted lists make up about 90 percent of the slides. For that reason, you may find it easier and a great deal faster to enter all your text at one time in Outline view. Even if text is scarce in your presentation, use the outline to set the order of your slides by entering all the slide titles. This is a great way to organize your thoughts as you assemble your presentation.

After completing the text portion of your presentation in the outline, go to Slide view to add the non-text items such as graphs, diagrams, organization charts, and clip art. By default, the first slide created in the outline is a Title slide; all the rest are bulleted lists, so you may need to change the slide layouts of some of the slides when you return to Slide view.

 TIP You can assign a slide layout from Outline view by clicking the Slide Layout button and picking the appropriate layout for the active slide.

When you start a new presentation without choosing the AutoContent Wizard, PowerPoint enables you to select the template for the presentation and the layout for the first slide. Once you do this, PowerPoint places you in Slide view of that first slide. At that point, you may enter the text in the placeholders on that slide, or you can switch to Outline view to begin building your presentation.

If you did not enter text on the first slide, there is no text in the outline for that slide. All you see is the number 1 in the margin and a slide icon. Your insertion point (cursor) is in position after the slide icon ready to receive your text input. Type the slide title and press Enter. A new slide title icon appears with the number 2 in the margin (see Figure 4.4). You are now ready to create your second slide. It's that easy.

FIG. 4.4
Your outline looks like this after you create your presentation's title slide.

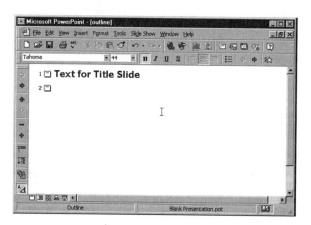

Promoting and Demoting Text

When you press Enter after a slide title, you automatically get a new slide title. If you want to change a slide title to body text for a slide, you must demote that paragraph one level. *Demoting* indents the paragraph one tab stop. Except where you have already assigned a slide layout that does not call for body text, the body text paragraph automatically displays a bullet. When you press Enter at the end of a bullet paragraph, another bullet paragraph appears (see Figure 4.5).

FIG. 4.5

After demoting text to bullet paragraph status, PowerPoint makes each new paragraph another bullet at the same indent level.

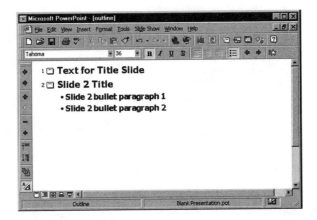

When you type the bullet paragraph, the text word wraps and automatically indents beneath the first letter of the first line of text. If you want two paragraphs of text following one bullet, press Shift+Enter at the end of the first line to start a new line without a bullet. Pressing Enter after that line begins a new bullet paragraph (see Figure 4.6).

FIG. 4.6

PowerPoint handles word wrap for you, and lets you add more than one paragraph of text per bullet point.

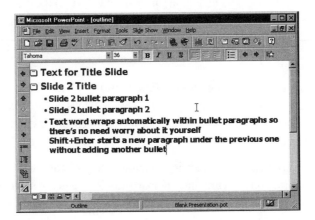

Part
II

Ch
4

If you've chosen the 2 Column Text layout for your slide, you see a small "1" icon next to the first line of text after the slide title. Enter the text for the first column, then press Ctrl+Enter to insert a column break. A "2" icon appears, meaning that any further text you enter will be in column two on your slide (see Figure 4.7).

FIG. 4.7

PowerPoint now lets
you enter and edit 2
Column Text slides
from Outline view.

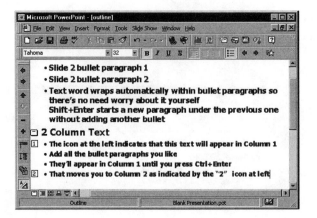

See Table 4.1 for a summary of Outline view keyboard shortcuts.

Table 4.1 Keyboard Shortcuts

Press:	To:
Enter	Add a new slide title or new bullet paragraph.
Shift+Enter	Add a new line within the current paragraph without adding a new bullet or slide title.
Tab	Demote (indent) a paragraph one level to the right.
Shift+Tab	Promote (unindent) a paragraph one level to the left.
Ctrl+Enter	Insert a column break in 2 Column Text layout slides.

You can create a subtopic by demoting (indenting) a paragraph, or a slide title by
promoting (unindenting) a paragraph. PowerPoint allows you to create up to five
indented levels (see Figure 4.8). As each level demotes, the text gets smaller in size
and the bullets change.

To demote a paragraph, click once in the paragraph you want to demote, and then choose
the Demote button on the Outlining toolbar (this button is the same as the Demote icon
on the Formatting toolbar). You can also press the Tab key to demote a paragraph.

To promote a paragraph, click once in the paragraph you want to promote, and then
choose the Promote button on the Outlining toolbar (this button is the same as the
Promote icon on the Formatting toolbar). You can also press Shift+Tab to promote
a paragraph.

FIG. 4.8

You can create up to five levels of bullet paragraph text. Don't use more than two levels if you want your text to be readable, though.

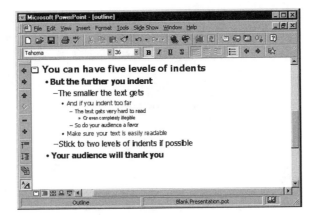

The most important thing to remember as you build your presentation is *keep it simple*. It's the one thing that I see most presenters doing incorrectly.

Breaking down your subjects to five levels (as shown in Figure 4.8) not only makes your slide hard to read but is really too detailed for presentations. Try to use no more than one or two levels of bullet paragraphs. If you have more detail to discuss, break down the topic into several slides. The audience will be able to read them clearly and remember your points better if you do.

Limit your bullet paragraphs to a few choice words, if you can. Bullet paragraphs should be like headlines in a newspaper—a few words to help the audience remember what the speaker says.

You should also limit the number of bullet paragraphs you put on one slide. Five or six is the recommended limit for a good presentation. When you have a large number of points to make about one subject, spread them over more than one slide.

> **N O T E** If this chapter were a presentation, here's the slide I would use to illustrate this section (see Figure 4.9):
>
> Keep It Simple!
>
> - Use two text levels or less
> - Keep points short
> - Include key words, not sentences
> - Use five bullet points or less
> - Know your subject!
>
> Your audience will be better able to follow what you mean if you ensure that your bullet points are "parallel." In other words, if one is written as Verb-Object, they all should be. ■

Part

II

Ch

4

FIG. 4.9
Slides should highlight and summarize your points, not deliver your speech for you.

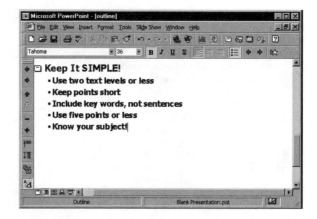

Too many people use their slides as crutches because they're really not comfortable standing and talking before a group or because they want to impress the group with all they know. Presentation pros call this the *Anxious Parade of Knowledge* or *APK syndrome*, and it inevitably leads to slides crammed full of details.

A crowded slide is an illegible slide, and an illegible slide is a boring slide. The point of a presentation is to inform and entertain your audience, *not* to put them to sleep. If you want to impress people, know your subject well enough to do it without the slides. Slides are an enhancement, but they are not a substitute for a well-rehearsed speaker. So if you have lots of material you want to include in your presentation, hand it out; don't put it on the screen.

Importing an Outline

There are times when you have already prepared the text or outline for your presentation in another application, such as Microsoft Word. There is no need to retype the text in PowerPoint. You can import it instead. My motto is, "Never do work twice."

PowerPoint formats the outline based on the styles used in your word processing document. Heading 1 becomes a slide title, Heading 2 the first level bullet, Heading 3 the second level bullet, and so on. If you didn't use styles in the original document, PowerPoint uses the paragraph indents or tabs at the beginning of the paragraph to set levels. The further indented the paragraph is (or the more tabs at the beginning of the paragraph), the lower the level of bullet paragraph.

PowerPoint can import text files that you've saved as rich text format (RTF) or plain text (TXT) format. You can start a new presentation based on an imported outline, or import outline text into an existing presentation.

To start a new presentation by importing an outline, follow these steps:

1. Choose File, Open.

2. In the Open dialog box that appears, select All Outlines from the Files of Type list box (see Figure 4.10).

FIG. 4.10
PowerPoint lets you import many different types of text and outline files into Outline view.

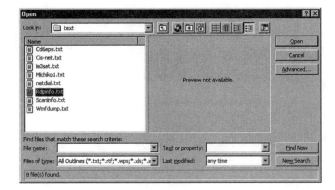

3. Select the drive and folder where you originally stored the file you'd like to import.

4. Select the file you want to use.

5. Choose Open to open the outline. The text from the imported file appears in Outline view. All you have to do is format and edit the text, select slide layouts, and choose a template.

To add text to an existing presentation, position the text insertion cursor where you want to insert the imported text, then follow these steps:

1. Choose Insert, Slides From Outline.

2. In the Open dialog box that appears, select All Outlines from the Files of Type list box (see Figure 4.10).

3. Select the drive and folder where you originally stored the file you'd like to import.

4. Select the file you want to use.

5. Choose Open to open the outline. The text from the imported file appears in Outline view at the insertion point. All the newly added slides will take on the same template as the presentation you've inserted them into.

N O T E Some of the outline file types PowerPoint imports don't really have an outline structure (TXT files, for instance). In cases like this, PowerPoint adds a new slide for each line of text in the file you import (see Figure 4.11).

Part
II

Ch
4

continues

continued

If you run into this, simply start at the original insertion point and use the cursor keys or mouse to move down the outline, pressing the Tab key to indent each line to where you want it (see Figure 4.12). The cursor can be anywhere in the text; there's no need to position it at the start of each line. ■

FIG. 4.11

Inserting a plain text file into the outline produces too many slides.

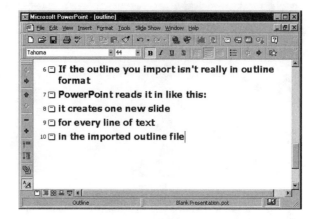

FIG. 4.12

A few seconds' work with the cursor and Tab keys fixes it right up.

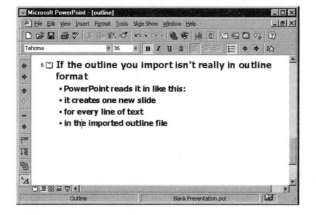

If you don't need the entire outline file, you can copy and paste text from word processing documents into PowerPoint's Outline view. Select the text in the word processing application, and choose Edit, Copy. Then switch to the PowerPoint Outline view, position your insertion point where you want the text to appear, and choose Edit, Paste.

N O T E   Microsoft Word has a special feature that automatically exports a Word outline to PowerPoint. The feature depends on the PRESENT7.DOT template file, which has to be loaded as a global template (when you install Microsoft Office, the Setup program installs

PRESENT7.DOT in the Startup folder inside the Word Program folder, so Word should auto-matically load it as a global template). The Present It button appears on the Microsoft toolbar. Clicking this button activates a macro that copies the active Word document and creates a PowerPoint presentation from it. ▪

Working with Existing Presentations in Outline View

When you open an existing presentation, the outline is already in place. It acts like a table of contents for the presentation, which is especially helpful when you're dealing with longer presentations or presentations prepared by someone else. Although you can page down or scroll down through the outline to find a topic, it's much faster to take advantage of PowerPoint's Find feature.

To quickly find a topic in a PowerPoint outline, follow these steps:

1. Choose Edit, Find or press Ctrl+F.

2. In the Find What box that appears, enter the text (search string) for which you are looking (see Figure 4.13).

FIG. 4.13
Enter the text you are looking for in the Find What box.

3. If the text appears in uppercase or mixed case and you want to find it exactly that way, check Match Case. When you select this option, PowerPoint does not locate Microsoft if you enter **MICROSOFT** as your search string.

4. If you are not interested in locating words that contain your search string, check Find Whole Words Only. By selecting this option, you are asking PowerPoint to ignore words like *worked*, *working*, or *worker* when you enter **work** as your search string.

5. Choose Find Next or press Alt+F.

6. Repeat step 5 until you find the reference you want.

7. When your search is complete, choose Close to close the Find dialog box.

Refer to Chapter 3, "Working with Text," to get a complete description of PowerPoint's Find and Replace features.

Part
II

Ch
4

Once you've given a presentation or had your coworkers review it, use the outline to re-work it. Edit your wording, rearrange your bullet paragraphs, delete unnecessary slides, add new ones, and change the slide order. This is especially important for presentations you use periodically for purposes such as monthly or quarterly reports, morning staff meetings, annual reports to the board, or annual sales meetings. Refresh these old presentations with new material or a new outlook.

Expanding and Collapsing Levels

When you can see all of the text in an outline, it is fully expanded. It's difficult to find a particular slide when you have to read through all this text. Instead, *collapse* the outline so all you see are the slide titles, then scan through the outline for the slide you want (refer to Figure 4.7). When all you can see is the slide title, it's also easier to manipulate slides and indented bullet paragraphs. In PowerPoint, you can collapse all the slides to their titles or collapse just the active slide. To see all the paragraphs again, you *expand* the entire outline; if you prefer, you can expand just the paragraphs in the active slide.

FIG. 4.14

It's easier to find a slide title when the outline text is fully collapsed.

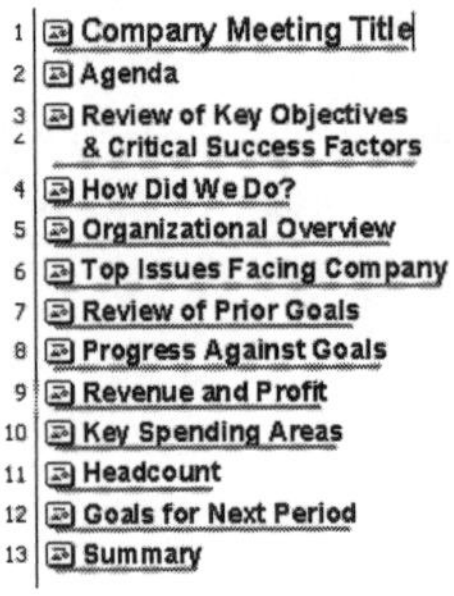

```
 1  Company Meeting Title
 2  Agenda
 3  Review of Key Objectives
       & Critical Success Factors
 4  How Did We Do?
 5  Organizational Overview
 6  Top Issues Facing Company
 7  Review of Prior Goals
 8  Progress Against Goals
 9  Revenue and Profit
10  Key Spending Areas
11  Headcount
12  Goals for Next Period
13  Summary
```

When you collapse an outline or part of an outline, PowerPoint underlines the title text in gray to indicate that there is hidden text below it (see Figure 4.14). If there's no body text on the slide, PowerPoint doesn't underline the title.

To collapse the entire outline so all you can see are the slide titles, click the Collapse All button on the Outlining toolbar.

To expand the collapsed paragraphs so you can see all the text in the outline, click the Expand All button on the Outlining toolbar.

To collapse only the text in a particular slide, position your cursor in the slide title and click the Collapse button on the Outlining toolbar.

To expand just one slide's text, position your cursor in that slide title and click the Expand button on the Outlining toolbar. The rest of the slide text appears.

Moving Text

When you are working with your presentation, you may decide that you need to move slides, paragraphs, words, or phrases to different locations. This is especially true after you have given a presentation the first time, and you want to fine-tune it for the next occasion.

CAUTION

Before you move anything, always save your file as a precaution. You wouldn't be the first person interrupted by a phone call or visit who forgets to paste out the text in the Clipboard before copying or cutting something else. Or maybe you're one of those users who drags a file to the wrong location and then forgets where you originally got it. If you save the file first, you always have a good copy to fall back on.

To move words or phrases, you must first select the text. You can perform one of four actions:

- Double-click a word to select it.
- Drag across the text you want to select.
- Click once at the beginning of the text you want to select, hold down Shift, and then click once at the end of the text.
- Triple-click anywhere in the line to select the whole line (or the whole bullet paragraph if it's more than one line).

Once the text is selected, point in the middle of the selected text and drag it to a new location. As you drag, the mouse pointer becomes an arrow with a box around the tail (see Figure 4.15), and a thick gray vertical line appears at the point of the arrow. Just position that thick gray line where you want the text to fall, and release the mouse button. This method is called *drag-and-drop*.

TROUBLESHOOTING

Why does my text move around when I try to select it? Drag-and-drop can be dangerous for some users, especially if you're not really comfortable with the mouse. But even experienced "mousers" can accidentally drop text where they don't mean to. If you have problems with this, stick to cut and paste: it always works.

If you keep moving text accidentally when you want to select it, you're letting go of your mouse and then trying to drag the text again. Drag-and-drop is activated, and away goes your text to who knows where. Watch out for that drag-and-drop mouse pointer, and remember to use the Undo feature. Or, if this is a real problem for you, disable drag-and-drop; choose Tools, Options, select the Edit tab, and remove the check mark from Drag-and-Drop Text Editing, then choose OK.

Part
II
Ch
4

FIG. 4.15

If you see a vertical bar or a two-headed arrow cursor, STOP. That means you're demoting/promoting text, not moving it.

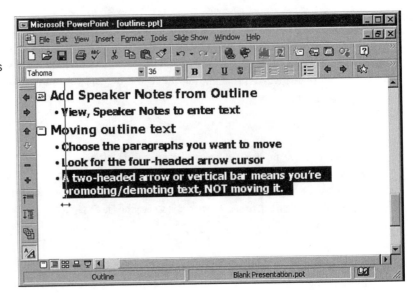

Whether you've disabled drag-and-drop editing or not, you can always use standard Windows editing commands. Once you've selected the text you want, choosing Edit, Copy or Ctrl+C copies it to the Clipboard; Edit, Cut or Ctrl+X deletes it; and Edit, Paste or Ctrl+V puts a copy of whatever's on the Clipboard at the insertion point. You can also Cut, Copy, and Paste using the right mouse button. Right-click the selected text and choose the option you want from the pop-up menu.

To move body text paragraphs or entire slides, select the text you want to move by clicking the bullet or slide icon to the left of the paragraph (hold down Shift and click additional paragraphs if you want more than one, or drag through all the paragraphs you want to move).

Selecting a slide title or bullet paragraph with indented bullets under it also selects the text under it, which is why it's easier to collapse slides or bullets before you move them. Placing the insertion point in a particular title or bullet paragraph selects that line without selecting the indented paragraphs attached to it.

Choose one of the following methods to move paragraphs or slides:

■ Position the mouse pointer over the bullet or slide icon in front of the text you want to move. When you hold down the left mouse button, the mouse pointer becomes a four-headed arrow (see Figure 4.16). Drag the text up or down until you see a horizontal line appear where you want the text to go. When the horizontal line is where you want it, release the mouse button.

CAUTION

If you accidentally drag left or right, you're demoting or promoting the paragraph, not moving it. If you see the cursor turn into a two-headed arrow or you see a vertical line appear, you're promoting or demoting the text. Keep the mouse button down and move the cursor until the vertical line disappears, indicating that you've put the text back where it came from, then release the mouse button.

FIG. 4.16

The mouse pointer becomes a four-headed arrow when you move it over a bullet or slide icon, which is a sign that you are in position to move that slide or paragraph.

Part

II

Ch

4

- Use the Move Up or Move Down buttons on the Outlining toolbar to move the selected text up or down in the outline. Each time you choose one of these buttons, the selected text moves up or down one line in the outline.

- Choose Edit, Cut (choose Edit, Copy if you only want to make a duplicate of the text). Position your cursor where you want the text to go, and then choose Edit, Paste.

Editing Text

Editing text in Outline view is very similar to working in a word processor. Use the Backspace key to remove characters to the left of your insertion point; use the Delete key to remove characters to the right of your insertion point. You may also select text, paragraphs, or slides, and then press Backspace or Delete, or choose Edit, Clear to delete the selection.

To add text to the outline, position your insertion point where you want to put the new text and begin typing. To replace existing text, select it and then type the new text. To copy text, select it and then choose Edit, Copy. Position your cursor where you want the duplicate text to go, and then choose Edit, Paste.

If you accidentally change or delete something, you can choose Edit, Undo, click the Undo button on the Standard toolbar or press Ctrl+Z. In PowerPoint, you may undo 20 steps for the default (you set the number of steps it will allow you to undo by choosing Tools, Options, Edit). Just continue selecting Undo until you return to the desired point in your editing process. If you undo one too many steps, you can choose the Redo button, choose Edit, Redo, or press Ctrl+Y.

The text in the outline reflects the text attributes that you assigned it on the slides or the standard formatting applied by the slide template. You may change the font, font size, and font style (bold, italic, underline) in the outline as you do in Slide view (refer to Chapter 3, "Working with Text," for instructions on formatting text). The text on the slide is modified automatically. The only attribute you won't see in the outline is color. Switch to Slide view to see the color attribute.

▶ **See** "Exploring Master Views," **p. 47**

▶ **See** "Formatting Text," **p. 69**

N O T E If you plan to make overall adjustments to your presentation's text using the Slide Master, it's best not to change the formatting in either Outline view or Slide view until after you've changed the Master. ■

 If you don't want to see any text attributes in the outline, click the Show Formatting button on the Outlining toolbar. The outline text changes to a uniform font, size, and style. Click the Show Formatting button again to recall the text attributes.

Where you have bulleted text in the outline, the bullets have the same appearance as they do on the slide except for the color. This means you can change the appearance of the bullets as you would in Slide view by choosing Format, Bullet.

If you forget to release the Caps Lock key or need to capitalize a phrase, you can change the case easily in PowerPoint. Select the text involved and choose Format, Change Case. Pick from the list of possible corrections, as shown in Table 4.2.

Table 4.2 Case Corrections

Correction	Example
Sentence Case	The first letter of each sentence is capitalized.
Lowercase	the whole selection becomes lowercase.
Uppercase	THE WHOLE SELECTION BECOMES UPPERCASE
Title case	The First Letter of Each Word in the Selection Becomes Uppercase (Except Words Like *in*, *the*, and *of*.)
Toggle Case	"The Quick Brown Fox" becomes "tHE qUICK bROWN fOX."

As explained in Chapter 3, "Working with Text," PowerPoint has a spell checker to catch typing errors and misspellings. You don't need to expand the outline first. PowerPoint expands it for you wherever it finds a spelling error so you can see the word in context.

▶ **See** "Checking Text," **p. 78**

PowerPoint also has a feature called AutoCorrect that automatically corrects some misspellings as you type. If you type two capital letters at the beginning of a word or forget to capitalize the first letter of days of the week, AutoCorrect automatically corrects these mistakes. To access AutoCorrect, choose Tools, AutoCorrect (see Figure 4.17).

▶ **See** "Using AutoCorrect," **p. 79**

FIG. 4.17
PowerPoint's
AutoCorrect can fix
spelling errors
automatically and
can save you lots of
typing.

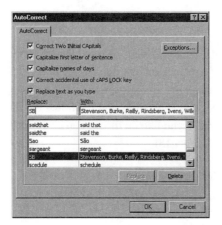

AutoCorrect has a list of common misspellings and shortcuts that it automatically replaces with the correct text. You can even add your own by typing your common error or shortcut in the Replace box and then entering the correct text in the With box. Click Add to add them to the list of corrections, and then choose OK to exit the dialog box. When you're typing, the correction will occur when you press the spacebar after the incorrect text.

You can also use AutoCorrect as a kind of typing macro or shorthand program.

Say you work for a law firm called Stevenson, Burke, Reilly, Rindsberg, Ivens, Willett, Johnson, Monsen, O'Mara, White, and Desmond. You dread coming to work each morning, knowing full well that you'll have to type that name dozens of times.

Dread no more, put AutoCorrect to work for you instead. Pick an abbreviation you'd like to use in place of the firm's full name (but don't choose anything that's a real word). Let's use SB, for example.

Choose Tools, AutoCorrect. In the box marked Replace, type the abbreviation you've chosen. Type the full name of the firm in the box marked With. Choose OK, but first note the table of existing corrections below. Yours will be added to that list, and you'll be able to choose it from the list in

continues

Part

II

Ch

4

continued

the future if you ever need to edit the AutoCorrect abbreviation you've just set up (for instance, if Reilly gets disbarred and thrown out of the firm).

From now on, all you have to do is type **SB** and PowerPoint will spring to the rescue and fill in the full name of the firm for you.

Adding Speaker Notes from Outline View

 You can add text to your Notes Pages as you work in Outline view. Position your insertion point in the text of the slide for which you need notes. Choose View, Speaker Notes, and PowerPoint gives you an edit box to enter your notes into. As you switch from slide to slide in Outline view, the box updates to show you the notes for each slide. You can move the Speaker Notes box anywhere you like on the screen or dismiss it by clicking the X in its upper-right corner (see Figure 4.18).

FIG. 4.18
PowerPoint now lets you add Speaker Notes text directly from Outline view.

 If you want more control over the formatting of your Notes text, choose View, Notes Page or click the Notes Page View button. Click in the Notes box (you may want to zoom in to see what you are typing), and type the notes you want for that slide (see Chapter 5, "Notes Pages and Handouts," for more information on using Notes Pages). Choose View, Outline or click the Outline View button to return to Outline view.

▶ **See** "Creating a Note," **p. 113**

Making One of Many Slides or Many from One

 A new feature of PowerPoint provides you with the capability to automatically make a Summary Slide of all the main topics in your presentation. You can do this from Outline or Slide Sorter view.

To make a summary slide, follow these steps:

1. Select the slides that you want to include on the summary slide (hold down Shift and click each slide icon).

2. Click the Summary Slide button on the Outlining toolbar. A new slide appears before the first selected slide. The bullets on the new slide are the slide titles of the selected slides.

Also new to PowerPoint 97 is the capability to make many slides from one slide. If you have a slide with several bullet topics, you can turn each bullet into a slide title. You can do this from Outline or Slide Sorter view.

To create many slides from one slide, follow these steps:

1. Select the slide you want to expand into many slides.

2. Choose Tools, Expand Slide. Several new slides appear after the selected slide; each bullet paragraph on the original slide becomes the title of a newly added slide.

Printing Outlines

When you print the outline, it appears exactly as it does in Outline view. Before you begin printing, you may want to select options to change how the printed outline will look. For example, if you only want to print the slide titles, you should click the Collapse All button. To print the outline without all the text formatting, click the Show Formatting button to turn off the formatting. Changing the percentage in the Zoom Control also increases or decreases the type size of your printed outline.

The outline prints in a portrait orientation because that is the default page setup. If you want to change the default, choose File, Page Setup and click Landscape under Notes, Handouts & Outline, then choose OK.

To show headers and footers on your printed outline, follow these steps:

1. Choose View, Header and Footer.

2. Select the Notes and Handouts tab (see Figure 4.19). Although strictly speaking, the outline is not a Handout; the Handout Master also controls the headers and footers on the outline.

FIG. 4.19
The Header and Footer
dialog box enables
you to add header,
footer, and page num-
bers to the outline
pages you print.

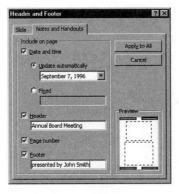

3. Under Include on Page, check the options you would like to have on your outline pages:

   - *Date and Time*. When you select this option, the date and time appears in the upper-left corner of the outline page. Select Update Automatically to display the current date and time the outline prints. From the list box, select how you want the date or time to appear. Select Fixed to print the date, time, or whatever other text you type into the text box every time the outline is printed.

   - *Header*. The header appears in the top right corner of the outline page. Enter the text for the header in the box below the option.

   - *Page Number*. The page numbers appears as numerals only and in the lower-right corner of the page. Numbering is automatic once you turn on this option.

   - *Footer*. The footer appears in the lower-left corner of the outline page. Enter the text for the footer in the box below the option.

4. Choose Apply to All. PowerPoint applies the headers and footers (including time, date, and page number options) to your Outline printouts.

To print the outline, follow these steps:

1. Choose File, Print.

2. If you use a different printer for your handouts, notes, and outlines than you use for your slides, select the correct printer from the Name box in the Printer section of the Print dialog box (see Figure 4.20).

3. From the Print What list box, select Outline View.

4. Set the Number of Copies you want to print.

5. Choose OK.

▶ **See** "Modifying Handouts," **p. 122**
▶ **See** "A Guided Tour of PowerPoint's Print Dialog Box," **p. 391**

FIG. 4.20
Select Outline View from the Print What box of the Print dialog box.

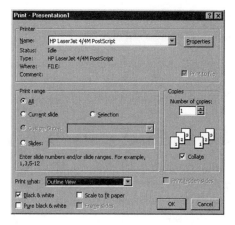

If you have Microsoft Word, consider using PowerPoint's Write-Up feature to send your outline to Word for further formatting. Write-Up can send the outline text, slides, and notes from PowerPoint into Word, where you have a great deal of control over how your printouts are formatted (see Figure 4.21).

Choose File, Send To, Microsoft Word to open a Word document containing the text from the outline. Select Outline Only, and then choose OK. By using Word's tools, you can edit and enhance the text and print it from Word.

FIG. 4.21
Use the Write-Up dialog box to select any of several formats for printing PowerPoint information in Word, including the outline.

Putting Together a Typical Presentation in PowerPoint

As a way of summarizing what you've learned in this chapter and showing you how you can put it to use, I'd like to show you how I go about putting together a typical

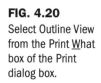

presentation in PowerPoint. After having produced thousands of PowerPoint slides and hundreds of presentations, this is the method that gets the job done fastest and with the least wasted motion…for me. Feel free to adapt it to your own work habits and needs.

The general rule is to start at the "lowest layer" of the presentation and do as much of the text entry and formatting there as possible; the text entry is done in Outline view, and the formatting in Slide Master view:

1. Start PowerPoint and pick an appropriate template from the opening dialog.

2. Switch to Outline view (turn Show Formatting off if working on a slow computer).

3. Enter the titles and bullet paragraph text for all slides in the presentation. For slides that will include charts, tables, or other objects, enter just the titles. For slides that will be based on the Blank layout (have no title), enter a reminder title of some sort, like **Insert photo of the Chairman here**.

4. Double-click the icon next to the first slides title to switch to Slide view, positioned at the first slide.

5. Use the Page Down key to look quickly at each slide in the presentation; specifically look for slides with more text than will fit comfortably, long headlines that run off the slide, and so forth.

6. Keeping any of these problem slides in mind, switch to Slide Master and make any needed adjustments to the text placeholders. Adjustments here will affect the placeholder text in every slide in the presentation.

7. Switch back to Slide view and re-check the problem slides; also check to see that placeholder adjustments haven't caused text formatting problems on other slides.

8. Inevitably, there will be a few slides that just don't "fit the mold." If you adjusted the Slide Master placeholders to accommodate them, all the rest of the slides would suffer. Instead, adjust the text size and positioning on the slide itself.

9. Make another pass through the presentation, this time adding graphs, tables, and clip art—all the elements you can add using the facilities built into PowerPoint or the associated applets like Graph, WordArt, and Clip Gallery. At the same time, bring in other data and images that are already stored on disk in some other form. For instance, photos (such as the picture of the Chairman), linked data from Excel spreadsheets, and so on.

10. During the final pass through the presentation, do any remaining "tweaks" to text formatting, add any needed drawing elements, and generally fine-tune the presentation's appearance.

CHAPTER 5

Notes Pages and Handouts

by Dorothy Burke

Notes Pages and Handouts are two of PowerPoint's more powerful, helpful features, yet most PowerPoint users gloss over or ignore them altogether. Learning to use these features can make your presentations go more smoothly and make them much more worthwhile for your audience.

Most people would rather die than get up and talk in front of other people. You'd think they'd jump on anything that would make it easier to deliver a smooth, professional presentation. PowerPoint's Notes Pages do just that. It's surprising how few presenters use them.

PowerPoint's Notes Pages help you pull together all the pieces that make up the oral portion of your presentation, so you can rehearse and prepare yourself to handle questions from the audience. Some people spend hours making the slide show portion of their presentation look good, but fail to allow enough preparation time to bring all their facts and supporting arguments together and rehearse their talk. If you slap something together, that's what it will look like *and* that's what it will sound like. Know your stuff, organize it well, rehearse it thoroughly and your talk can't fail.

Make the best use of Notes Pages and Handouts

Use Notes Pages to script your presentation and to rehearse your talk. Print Handouts for your audience to take notes on or refer to later.

Create your notes while you build your slides

As you add slides to your presentation in either Slide or Outline view, you can add notes as well. Write down the important thoughts you want to share with your audience.

Produce useful handouts

Make the materials you pass out during your presentation worth holding on to. Leave space for your audience to make notes, or give them Notes Pages.

Print your Notes Pages and Handouts

You can print Notes Pages and Handouts from PowerPoint, or you can copy your presentation information to Microsoft Word, refine the formatting, and print it from there.

A good presentation doesn't end with the applause when you finish speaking, either. Once you've given your "unforgettable" presentation, make *sure* your audience can't forget it. People in business today spend about 60 percent of their time in meetings, so you're competing for their attention with every word. When your audience goes back to the office, make sure they take your words with them in the form of PowerPoint's Handouts. You can make those Handouts meaningful with more than just the pictures of the slides. ■

What are Notes Pages and Handouts?

Notes Pages are usually portrait oriented. Each Note Page includes an image of the associated slide, about 3 3/4 × 5 inches in size. Below that, there's an area where you can enter any text you'd like to have handy when you get to that slide in your presentation (see Figure 5.1).

FIG. 5.1
Notes Page printouts include a picture of the slide at the top and your notes written below.

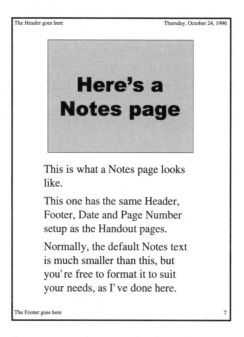

At least that's what you get when you simply create your presentation, add notes to your Notes Pages, and print them. If you don't like the standard Notes Pages, you can customize them in any number of ways:

- Change the orientation to Landscape.

- Change the size and position of the slide image.

- Add page numbers, dates, headers or footers.

- Add any other text and graphics to individual Notes Pages or to the Notes Master, so they appear on each Notes Page.

You learn how to customize Notes Pages later in this chapter, but see Figure 5.2 for a taste of what's possible.

FIG. 5.2
You can customize your Notes Pages in many ways.

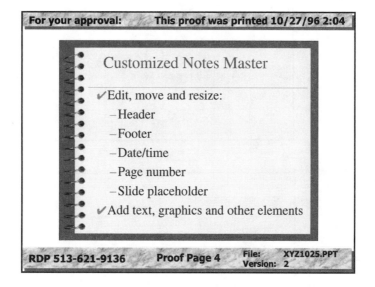

Part

II

Ch

5

Every slide in your PowerPoint presentations has a Notes Page "attached" to it, whether you choose to use it or not. You can add text notes to each slide's Notes Page or not. The choice is always yours.

Handouts are also portrait-oriented. Each Handout includes two, three, or six small images of the slides in your presentation (see Figures 5.3, 5.4, and 5.5). You choose the number you want when you print them. You can apply many, though not all, of the same customizations to Handouts that you can to Notes Pages.

FIG. 5.3
Handouts printed with two slides per page give you nice, large, legible slide images.

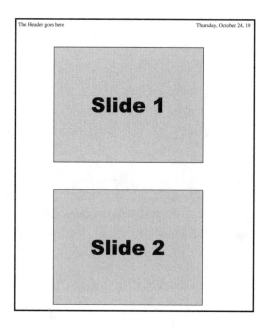

FIG. 5.4
If you print Handouts with three slides per page, you leave your audience more room for note-taking.

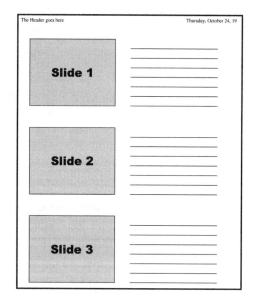

FIG. 5.5
Six-slides-per-page
Handouts save paper
and make a handy file
reference copy of your
presentations.

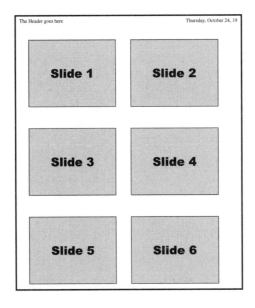

Using Notes Pages Effectively

Let your Notes Pages act as a script for your presentation. You can write out the information you want to include about each of the slides. Not only will this help you formulate your thoughts, but by writing the notes out you are making your first step in rehearsing what you are going to say. Although your outline (and the slides that are generated by it) sets up the organization of your talk, there will be only a few key points per slide (see Chapter 4, "Working with Outline View"). Your Notes Pages can hold as much text as you can fit on one page (see Figure 5.6).

▶ **See** "Building Your Presentation in Outline View," **p. 87**

N O T E As you're scripting your presentation, include short case histories or anecdotes that support your recommendations or arguments. Sharing your own experiences in similar situations makes what you're saying more real and more interesting.

Use quotations (if they're short and to the point). Try out Mark Twain and Will Rogers. They spoke on a wide variety of subjects and can serve as a source of humor for your presentation. Humor adds a useful transition, but only apply it where applicable and in good taste.

If you have to present often, you may want to start a collection of clippings from business and industry publications that you can use to reinforce your points. ▨

FIG. 5.6

Notes Page view shows you how your Notes Pages will appear, with a picture of the slide at the top and your notes written below.

If you're preparing a presentation that will be delivered by more than one person, Notes Pages can help each presenter stay on track and deliver the same material in the same way. One company I worked with prepared a sales presentation to be used by all their field sales personnel. In order to make sure all the salespeople gave essentially the same presentation, they gave a copy of the Notes Pages to each salesperson to rehearse with.

 Don't let your Notes Pages become a crutch. Reading them verbatim is a sure way to put your audience to sleep. I sometimes prepare two sets of notes. The first set is a relatively complete script of what I plan to say. I use this version as I learn and rehearse my talk.

Then I make a copy of the presentation file and reduce the text in its Notes Pages to a few key points that will help me remember what to say. This is the set I use in front of the audience. The Notes Pages contain just enough information to keep me on track and remind me to share important information, but don't include so much detail that I lose my place while I'm speaking.

Because there's not a lot of text in the Notes Pages, I can increase the size of the text enough to make it easily readable, even in a darkened room. And because I don't have my complete speech written out, I'm never tempted to read it to the audience.

Using Handouts Effectively

When you print Handouts, you can print two, three, or six slide pictures per page. The two-per-page Handouts have much larger pictures, but there is no space for the users to take notes. On the three-per-page Handouts, one column prints with lines for user notes. The six-per-page Handouts also lack room for notes. The type of Handout you choose to print depends on how much information you want to leave with your audience and how you want them to use the materials you give them.

A speaker once told me that he never gives printouts of any sort to the audience until after his presentation because he doesn't want them rustling papers during his speech. He also doesn't want his audience to read ahead of him, and thus miss what he was saying. I prefer to give handouts with room for the audience to write notes, because I believe people remember what is said better if they write it down.

Some trainers and other speakers who give rather long talks adopt a compromise approach. They hand out materials as they summarize what they've already talked about. This gives the audience a chance to jot down important points as they review them. The change of pace also creates a kind of break that audiences find refreshing.

NOTE The cardinal rule in presentations is "Say more than you show and hand out more than you say." Based on this rule, the materials you pass out (either before or after your presentation) should be more than just pictures of your slides. Include supporting articles, spreadsheets, or data. That also helps you forestall the person in the audience who always wants to know where you got that figure or detail. Don't delay (and thus bore) the rest of your audience while you explain tiresome details; that only distracts you and the rest of the audience from the mainstream of your talk. Instead, include the details on paper and just point out where the interested party can find the answer, or tell the person you will discuss the details after your talk. ▨

Creating a Note

Part
II

Ch
5

There are two approaches to creating Notes Pages. You can prepare them all after you've finished making the slides, or you can create each one as you're working on each individual slide.

The first approach has the advantage of allowing you to carefully script the entire presentation, planning the flow from one slide to another. However, the second approach lets you track your thoughts while you're making the slide so you don't forget the important points you intend to make.

You may want to combine the approaches. Write some of the notes as you go and then go back through all the Notes Pages and script the presentation incorporating the thoughts you "jotted down" as you went.

Creating Notes Using Notes Pages

 When you want to create notes, switch to Notes Page view by clicking the Notes Page View button or by choosing View, Notes Page.

In Notes Page view, you see the entire Notes Page as it will later print. There is a picture of the slide at the top and a text placeholder at the bottom. Click the placeholder to begin entering the text for your note (refer to Figure 5.6).

You use the same text formatting tools in Notes Page view that you use on your slides (see Chapter 3, "Working with Text," if you need help in using these tools). You can increase the size of the text or make it bold, and probably should. Remember, you have to be able to read this text while in a darkened room, so make it as clear and easy to see as possible (see Figure 5.7). If you plan to hand out your Notes Pages, make sure you use the Spell Checker.

▶ **See** "Entering Text in a Placeholder," **p. 60**

▶ **See** "Creating Text Outside of a Placeholder," **p. 63**

▶ **See** "Editing Text in a Slide," **p. 66**

▶ **See** "Formatting Text," **p. 69**

FIG. 5.7

Make your notes easy to read by enlarging the text or using bold to add emphasis.

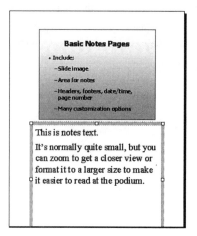

Use Page Up, Page Down, or the scroll bar to move through the Notes Pages for each slide in your presentation.

PowerPoint saves Notes Pages along with your slides whenever you save your presentation.

T I P Unless you have superior eyesight, you'll find it difficult to read the text in Notes Page view. Change the magnification of the view by clicking the Zoom button. Pick any of the standard magnifications or type any percentage you like into the text box. You can also choose View, Zoom, pick the magnification percentage you want, then choose OK.

> **CAUTION**
>
> Because Notes Pages are "attached" to each slide, when you delete a slide, you also delete its Notes Page. If you use Notes Pages extensively to organize and script your presentation, check the Notes Page before you delete a slide. That way, you won't accidentally delete any important information.
>
> Another thing to watch out for: if you move information from one slide to another, remember to move the relevant notes as well. To move text from one Notes Page to another, select the text, choose Edit, Cut or press Ctrl+X, switch to the other Notes Page, click where you want to put the text, and choose Edit, Paste or press Ctrl+V.

Creating Notes Without Changing Views

 When you want to create notes on-the-fly, you don't need to change views in PowerPoint. From Slide, Outline, or Slide Sorter view, you can add notes by choosing View, Speaker Notes and entering your text in the Speaker Notes window that appears (see Figure 5.8).

FIG. 5.8
With the Speaker Notes window open, you can enter notes text without leaving the current view.

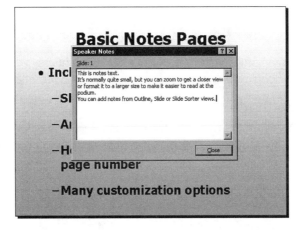

Part
II

Ch
5

 If you open and close the Speaker Notes window often, you can save time by adding a Speaker Notes button to one of PowerPoint's toolbars. To learn how, see the instructions for adding Black and White buttons in Chapter 17. Scroll down below the Black and White buttons, and you'll find a button for Speaker Notes that you can add in the same way.

▶ **See** "Previewing Your Presentation," **p. 386**

You can leave this window open as you switch from slide to slide. When you change to a slide with no notes text, you see a blank window in which to enter new notes. Otherwise, you see the notes you've already entered for the slide. The window even stays open as you add new slides. To move it out of your way when you don't need it, drag it by the title bar.

Once your notes are complete, choose Close to close the window. When you check Notes Page view, you see that all the text you entered is now part of the Notes Pages for the presentation.

The advantage of entering notes as you work on your slides is that you can write down your thoughts as you go. The disadvantage is that you can't format the text in the Speaker Note window. You have to go to Notes Page view to format your notes text. You should return to Notes Page view in any case to check what you've written and see that it makes sense.

PowerPoint's spelling checker (choose Tools, Spelling or press F7) now checks *all* of the text in your presentation, whether it's in the Outline, in text blocks on individual slides, or in your notes.

Adding Date, Time, and Page Numbers

You can add date and time, headers, footers, and page numbers to each of your Notes Pages and Handouts. To add one or more of these items, follow these steps:

1. Choose View, Header and Footer.
2. Choose the Notes and Handouts tab from the Header and Footer dialog box (see Figure 5.9). In this and any other "tabbed" dialog box, you can use Ctrl+Tab to move from one tab to another.
3. Check the items you want to include on each page. As you do, the Preview window highlights the box where the item appears on the page:
    - *Date and Time.* When you select this option, the date and time appear in the upper-right corner of the page. Select Update Automatically if you want PowerPoint to print the actual date and time the printouts are made. Use the list box to select the format you'd like the date and time to appear in. Choose Fixed to have PowerPoint print the literal text you type in the text box, whenever you print Notes Pages or Handouts.
    - *Header.* The header appears on the top-left corner of the page. Enter the text for the header in the box below the option.

- *Page Number.* The page numbers display as numerals only and appear in the lower-right corner of the page. Numbering is automatic once you turn on this option.

- *Footer.* The footer appears in the lower-left corner of the page. Enter the text for the footer in the box below the option.

4. Choose Apply to All.

FIG. 5.9
You can add the date and time, headers, footers, or page numbers to your Notes Pages and Handouts.

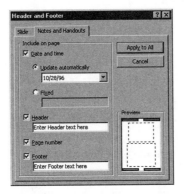

Using the Notes Master

The Header and Footer dialog box is a quick and easy way to add the items above to all of your printouts, but it doesn't give you much control over the formatting of the various items or where they appear on your printouts. If you want to move the date, header, footer, and page number, or if you'd like to make other formatting changes to your Notes Pages, it's simple to do. All you have to do is change the Notes Master (refer to Figure 5.6) and your individual Notes Pages will follow. The Notes Master is the template for your Notes Pages just as the Slide Master is the template for your slides.

If you want to print Landscape rather than Portrait Notes Pages, it's best to change orientation before starting to customize the Notes Master. Choose File, Page Setup to open the Page Setup dialog box (see Figure 5.10). Then select Landscape in the Notes, Handouts & Outline area. Choose OK.

FIG. 5.10
You can change the orientation of Notes Pages in the Page Setup dialog box.

To see the notes master, choose <u>V</u>iew, <u>M</u>aster, <u>N</u>otes Master, shown in Figure 5.11.

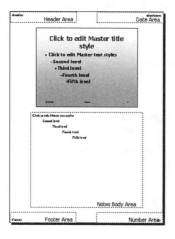

When you look at the Notes Master, you may see text objects where you'd expect the header, footer, date/time, and page number to be. These contain placeholders that PowerPoint inserts when you use the Header and Footer dialog box. Each placeholder represents a specific item that you entered in this dialog, as follows:

Placeholder Text	Represents
`<header>`	Header text as you typed it in the dialog box.
`<date/time>`	Date and time, formatted as called for in the dialog box.
`<footer>`	Footer text as you typed it in the dialog box.
`<#>`	Page number.

Each of these placeholders is linked to the text you typed into the Header and Footer dialog box. When you print Notes Pages, PowerPoint substitutes your text for the placeholder.

You can add additional text before and after the placeholders if you like. For instance, you could click the page number placeholder and change it from `<#>` to **Page `<#>` of 20**, which would print as `Page 1 of 20`, `Page 2 of 20`, and so on when you print Notes Pages.

You can delete the placeholder text and replace it with your own. It's simpler to apply and edit your headers and footers from the Header and Footer dialog box, but if you want to format your text extensively, you can't tell exactly what it will look like in Notes Master view. All you see is the placeholder.

Switching back and forth between Notes Master and Notes Page views would show you the effect of your formatting changes, but there's an easier way. Select the placeholder text, delete it, then type in your actual text and format it to taste. You'll be able to see the exact effect of your formatting changes as you make them.

Apart from the presence of placeholders, Notes Master header, footer, date/time, and page number text is just like any other text in PowerPoint. You can select it, move it anywhere you'd like it to appear on the Master, change the font, color, size, or any other attribute, just as you would any other text in PowerPoint.

▶ **See** "Adding Text to Your Slides," **p. 60**

▶ **See** "Editing Text in a Slide," **p. 66**

▶ **See** "Formatting Text," **p. 69**

TROUBLESHOOTING

I deleted one of the placeholders and now I've changed my mind and want it back. How can I do that? You can recover deleted placeholders, or you can insert placeholders wherever you like (see Table 5.1).

Table 5.1 Working with Placeholders

To Get This Item	Do This
Header text block	Choose Format, Notes Master Layout, choose Header, then OK.
Footer text block	Choose Format, Notes Master Layout, choose Footer, then OK.
Date/Time text block	Choose Format, Notes Master Layout, choose Date, then OK.
Date/Time placeholder	Choose Insert, Date and Time.
Page Number text block	Choose Format, Notes Master Layout, choose Page Number.
Page Number placeholder	Choose Insert, Page Number.
Slide image placeholder	Choose Format, Notes Master Layout, choose Slide Image, then OK.
Body text placeholder	Choose Format, Notes Master Layout, choose Body, then OK.

Part
II

Ch
5

You can also format the notes text placeholder on the Notes Master. This placeholder dictates the formatting for the notes text that you enter on individual Notes Pages, just as the Slide Master's text placeholder supplies the format for text on your slides. See Chapter 2 to learn how to work with text placeholders and Chapter 3 to learn more about formatting text.

▶ **See** "Using Placeholders," **p. 44**

You can change the position and size of the slide image on the Notes Master. Click it and drag any of the four corner handles while holding down the Shift key to resize it without distortion, or click it, then drag it anywhere on the Notes Master you'd like it.

If you want to add a logo or a photo that will appear on every Notes Pages printout, cut and paste it from another application into the Notes Master or choose Insert, Picture, From File to import a picture file (see Chapter 8, "Adding Ready-Made Art to Your Presentation," if you want to bring in clip art or graphics from the Internet). Then in the Insert Picture dialog box, specify the location and file name of the picture you want to import. Choose Insert. When the graphic appears on the page, size it and move it to the correct position. For more information on moving and sizing graphics, refer to Chapter 6, "Creating Drawing Objects."

▶ **See** "Moving Objects," **p. 139**
▶ **See** "Adding Clip Art," **p. 172**

Save the presentation file to save any changes you made to the Notes Master.

 T I P   Changes to the Notes Master affect only the presentation you're currently working on. If you find yourself changing the Notes Master every time you start a new presentation, you can save time by creating a new template that incorporates all the changes you normally make to the Notes Master. Here's how:

1. Start a new presentation based on the template you'd like to use, but don't add any slides to it.

2. Modify the Notes Master to suit your needs using the techniques explained in this chapter.

3. Save the presentation as a new template. Choose File, Save As, type in a name for the file, choose Presentation Template from the Save as Type list, and choose OK. It's easiest to use the new template if you save it to the Templates folder in the folder where you installed PowerPoint 97.

4. To use the new template, choose File, New and pick the template you just saved. It should appear in the General tab of the New Presentation dialog box.

Your new presentation will automatically include the formatting changes you made to the template. If you customize the Handouts Master at the same time as you do the Notes Master, you'll be able to save changes to it into your new template also.

Printing Notes

One of the many choices you have in printing your presentation is to print Notes Pages. To do this:

1. Choose File, Print.
2. In the Print dialog box that appears (see Figure 5.12), choose Notes Pages from the Print What list box.
3. Choose which Slides you want to print.
4. Specify the Number of Copies you want to make.
5. Choose the other printing options you'd like to use.
6. Choose OK.

See Chapter 17, "Selecting and Generating Output," for a more detailed explanation of the various Print dialog box options.

▶ **See** "A Guided Tour of PowerPoint's Print Dialog Box," **p. 391**

FIG. 5.12
In the Print dialog box, choose Notes Pages as the item you want to print.

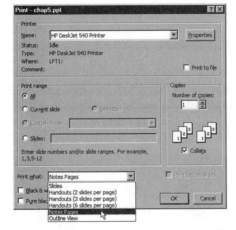

Part
II

Ch
5

Creating Handouts

You can handle PowerPoint Handouts in two ways:

- Print them using PowerPoint's standard formats: two, three, or six to a page as in Figures 5.3, 5.4, and 5.5 earlier in the chapter.
- Customize the handout master to make your own handout format.

Using Handouts Without Changes

PowerPoint uses the slides you've created, shrinks them in size, and prints them several to a page when you choose Handouts in the Print dialog box. If you don't want to change the standard Handout formats, then you only have to select how many slides you want to print on a page when you print Handouts.

Handouts normally print in Portrait orientation. If you prefer Landscape, choose File, Page Setup to open the Page Setup dialog box (refer to Figure 5.10). Then choose Landscape in the Notes, Handouts & Outline area. Choose OK.

You can also add headers, footers, page numbers, and/or the date to each Handout page you print. If you have set up any of these items for your Notes Pages, PowerPoint also applies them to your Handouts (see the section in this chapter "Adding Date, Time, and Page Numbers"). Change your choices in the Header and Footer dialog box before you print Handouts if you want them to have different headers, footers, page numbers, or dates from your Notes Pages.

Modifying Handouts

To modify your Handouts , you need to change the Handout Master (see Figure 5.13). Choose View, Master, Handout Master to work on the Handout Master.

Once you're in Handout Master view, select the format of the master you want to change. In the Handout Master toolbar, select two slides per page, three slides per page, or six slides per page (see Figure 5.13). The Handout Master toolbar should be on your screen. If it is not, choose View, Toolbars, Handout Master.

FIG. 5.13

From the Handout Master toolbar, select the two slides per page, three slides per page, or six slides per page format.

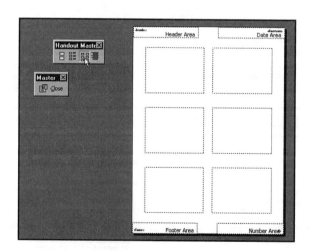

All of the same techniques you learned earlier in the section "Using the Notes Master" apply here as well, with two exceptions:

- There is no notes text placeholder to work with on the Handouts Master.
- You cannot change the position of the slide images on the Handouts Master.

Apart from that, you use exactly the same methods to modify the Handouts Master as you would the Notes Master.

Printing Handouts

Once you finish customizing your handouts, you'll want to print them. To print handouts (with your customizations or in default PowerPoint format):

1. Choose File, Print.
2. In the Print dialog box (refer to Figure 5.12), choose Handouts (2 slides per page), Handouts (3 slides per page), or Handouts (6 slides per page) from the Print What list box.
3. Choose which slides you want to print.
4. Specify the Number of Copies you want to make.
5. Choose other printing options as appropriate.
6. Choose OK.

   ▶ **See** "A Guided Tour of PowerPoint's Print Dialog Box," **p. 391**

Part

II

Ch

5

TROUBLESHOOTING

When I print Handouts, it's hard to see the edges of the individual slides clearly. Is there anything I can do to improve the printouts? If your slides have a lot of white area in the background (especially when you print them in black and white), they may not appear defined when you print the handouts. Choose Frame Slides in the Print dialog box when you print Handouts. This puts a black line around each of your slides on the Handout page.

Using Microsoft Word Write-Up

PowerPoint can send your presentation information to Microsoft Word and automatically create a document that you can edit, format, and enhance using Word tools. Using Write-Up gives you a great deal more control over your Handouts than PowerPoint alone does.

Five layouts are available:

- Two slides on a page with the Notes next to the slides
- Two slides on a page with blank lines next to the slides
- A single slide per page with the Notes beneath the slides
- A single slide on a page with blank lines beneath the slide
- The outline (see Chapter 4, "Working with Outline View")

It's best to wait until your presentation is substantially complete before using Write-Up. If you add new slides to your presentation afterward, they won't be linked to the Word document that Write-Up created, so won't appear there.

To use Write-Up, first save your file, then follow these steps:

1. Choose File, Send To, Microsoft Word.
2. Choose a page layout from the Write-Up dialog box (see Figure 5.14).
3. Pick a method for adding the slides to the Microsoft Word document: Paste or Paste Link. If you select the latter, the Word document is automatically updated whenever you modify the presentation.
4. Choose OK.

FIG. 5.14

In the Write-Up dialog box, select a page layout for the Microsoft Word document into which you're going to paste your slides.

 For best results, Microsoft recommends that you switch your PowerPoint presentation to the Black and White view before performing this operation (choose View, Black and White or click the Black and White View button).

Using Notes Pages and Handouts Creatively

Don't be hemmed in by the terms *Notes Pages* and *Handouts*. Because they're so customizable, you can use both types of printouts for other purposes. Here are a few tricks other PowerPoint users have come up with:

- Some presenters use their Notes Pages as handouts. The audience members get a copy of each slide *and* any additional information the speaker wants them to have.

- A designer prints two sets of handouts of each presentation she creates for her clients. She customizes them to include the date, customer name, and the file name on each page. One set goes to the client along with the bill; the other goes in a notebook. Clients love it because they can see exactly what they're being billed for; the designer loves it because when the client calls six months later for revisions to "that presentation you did for us last June," she can find the handouts (and from them the name and location of the presentation file) in just a few seconds.

- An administrative assistant creates presentations for his boss who always seems to be at a meeting in another city, so he faxes proofs for her approval. Rather than just fax slide printouts, he customizes the Notes Page Master and sends Notes Page printouts. He changes the orientation to Landscape, enlarges the slide image on the Master, removes the notes text placeholder, then adds text that identifies the presentation name and version. If necessary, he adds confidentiality warnings and any other notes as well. Finally, he makes sure that the date is set to update automatically and that the printout includes the slide number, then prints the Notes Pages to the fax card in his computer with Print dialog box options set to Pure Black and White and Frame Slides. His boss receives clear, easy-to-read faxes, and when she calls back with questions or corrections, there's never any confusion over what version or slide they're discussing.

Part

II

Ch

5

Adding Visual Elements to a Presentation

CHAPTER 6

Creating Drawing Objects

by Nancy Stevenson

Although many presentations rely strongly on text to get their point across, the ability to demonstrate things visually is always a powerful tool. Drawing features in PowerPoint allow you to easily draw shapes such as rectangles, squares, circles, and even stars on a slide. In addition, several tools for creating and modifying lines and connectors allow you to use lines to show visual relationships between objects on your slide. ■

Draw a variety of shapes

PowerPoint offers tools to draw simple rectangles, ovals, and lines, as well as a feature called AutoShapes, which allows you to easily draw objects like stars and banners.

Learn how to modify drawings, clip art and imported graphics

Once you create or import a drawing, you can move it, resize it, and duplicate it easily.

Position drawing objects on a slide

Several features such as rulers, guides, and grids allow you to place and position drawings accurately on any slide.

Drawing Objects

There is a great reliance in desktop design these days on both text and ready-made artwork, called *clip art*. Still, there are many times when all you need is a simple circle or line. Although you could build elaborate artwork with the drawing tools PowerPoint provides, you don't have to be a great artist to create drawings like the one in Figure 6.1. Most drawing tools simply require that you be able to click and drag across your slide.

FIG. 6.1
This simple drawing of a computer was created with just a few easy-to-place objects.

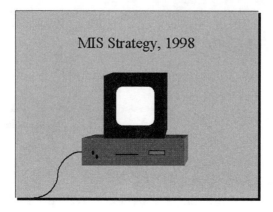

Anything you draw on your page is a drawing object. Once created, these objects can be manipulated in several ways:

- Resize objects to become larger or smaller.
- Move objects around your slide.
- Group objects together to become one larger drawing object (you learn more about this in Chapter 7).
- Format the line that delineates a drawing object to use different thicknesses or dash line styles.
- Fill objects with color and patterns.
- Add shadows and create 3-D effects.
- Rotate objects in exact increments.

The key to performing all these actions is the Drawing toolbar.

The Drawing Toolbar

On the bottom of the PowerPoint screen is the Drawing toolbar (see Figure 6.2), which also contains a button that reveals the Drawing menu.

FIG. 6.2
The Drawing toolbar
contains several tools
that provide click and
drag drawing ease.

The Select Objects tool is used to select a drawing object so that you can perform various editing and formatting tasks on it. The Free Rotate tool allows you to turn an object on your slide so that you can place it at any angle you please.

The next set of drawing tools is used to draw objects: lines, lines with arrows, rectangles, ovals, and text boxes. You see how to use these shortly.

The WordArt button actually opens up an applet, or small application, that allows you to create unusual effects with text, such as the curved text shown in Figure 6.3.

When you select any of the next three buttons, which enable you to work with color, they reveal pop-up dialog boxes. You can use these to apply color to the inside of objects, lines, and text. The Object Fill Color tool also allows you to apply patterns, textures, and even gradient effects to the inside of objects.

There are three tools for working with the style of lines. They allow you to change the thickness of a line, work with dashed line styles, and apply different styles to lines with arrows, respectively.

The final two buttons on the Drawing toolbar are used to apply shadow effects or 3-D effects to objects.

▶ **See** "Creating WordArt Objects," **p. 182**

Part
III

Ch
6

FIG. 6.3
Applying a curved effect to text with WordArt can give more impact to your message.

Drawing Rectangles and Ovals

Creating drawing objects in PowerPoint is very simple, although it does work a little differently for different types of objects.

 Rectangles and ovals are drawn in exactly the same way. Select one of these buttons, then place your mouse cursor on the slide where you want the drawing object to begin. Drag your cursor in any direction, as far as you'd like. As you drag, you see an outline of the object (see Figure 6.4).

When the object is the size and shape you want, release the mouse button and the shape appears on your slide. By default, the drawing object will have a fill color already applied to it.

FIG. 6.4
Your mouse cursor changes to a crosshair shape, and the outline of your object indicates what it will look like when you release the mouse.

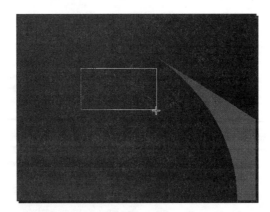

 The Rectangle and Oval tools allow you to draw objects from one edge outward in the direction you drag. To make the point where you initially click your mouse as the center of the object, and draw the object outward from there, press the Ctrl key before you begin to draw the object and hold it down as you drag across your slide.

Hold down the Shift key while you drag, and PowerPoint draws a perfect square or circle.

Hold down both Shift and Ctrl keys to combine the two actions; PowerPoint draws a perfect square or rectangle with its center where you first clicked.

Drawing Lines and Arrows

 The Line tool in PowerPoint allows you to draw a straight line of any length and place it at any angle on your page. To draw a line, select the Line tool. Click anywhere on your slide where you want the line to begin. Drag across your page. As you do, a line appears, stretching from your starting point to the location of your cursor. You can move the end point of the line anywhere around the page. When you're satisfied with the line's length and direction, release your mouse cursor.

Drawing Text Boxes

PowerPoint AutoLayouts provide text placeholders for common text such as a slide title or bulleted list. Most of the time these text placeholders will satisfy your text needs. However, you may occasionally want to add more text elements to a page. Or, if you're the type who wants the most flexibility in designing your own slides, you can use a blank layout and create all the text objects yourself.

 Drawing a text box is very much like drawing a rectangle, except that when you finish drawing it, you have a box where you can enter and edit text (see Figure 6.5). Select the Text Box tool, then click your slide where you want to place the object. Drag your cursor until you have a text box of the proper length.

All the drawing tools behave a little differently if you hold down "modifier" keys while you draw:

If You Hold Down...	While You Draw...	PowerPoint Does This...
Control	Oval, Rectangle, Line, Arrow	Draws from the center rather than the corner.
Shift	Oval, Rectangle	Constrains to a circle or square.
	Line, Arrow	Constrains to 15-degree angles.

continues

If You Hold Down...	While You Draw...	PowerPoint Does This...
Ctrl+Shift	Any object	Combines the effects of Shift and Ctrl keys.
Alt	Any object	Temporarily turns off Snap To Grid.

FIG. 6.5
When selected, a text box is surrounded by a dashed gray line, and your cursor appears ready for you to enter text.

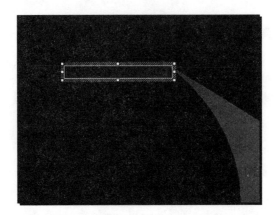

N O T E   Once you have drawn a text box, you can select it and type text in it. If you enter more text than can fit in the box, it will expand downward to accommodate the text. However, the box will not expand side to side unless you change the Text Box settings from PowerPoint's defaults or resize it manually, which you'll learn to do later in this chapter. ▦

TROUBLESHOOTING

I created a text box, and now I don't want it anymore. When I click it and press Delete, nothing happens. The Cut command doesn't seem available on the Edit menu, either. How do I get rid of a text box? Have you ever heard the expression, "That's not a bug; it's a feature"? This is a classic example of that. It really *is* a feature. PowerPoint assumes that if you click a text box, you want to edit the text, which is exactly what you want to do, usually. This saves a lot of time compared to selecting the text first, then switching to a special text editing mode.

The downside—and it's really a minor one—is that if you really do want to select the entire text box in order to delete it (or change the font, text size, color, or text box fill/outline), you have to let PowerPoint know that's what you want to do.

How? Once you've clicked the text box and see a text insertion cursor, do one of the following:

- Press the Esc key.
- Point at the outline of the text box; when the cursor changes to a two- or four-headed arrow, click the mouse button.

The outline of the text box changes from a pattern of diagonal hash marks to a dot pattern to let you know the whole box is selected. Now you can work with the attributes of all the text in the box, change the attributes of the box itself, or press the Delete key to get rid of it altogether.

If you want to format the text box rather than delete it, click the box, then right-click and choose Format Text Box. Note that if you right-click a word that PowerPoint has underlined in red (that is, a word that it thinks is misspelled), you see a menu of spell checker choices instead of the usual menu.

 I still get a line outlining my text box on-screen, even though it's not selected and I have no text in it. Why? You can apply a line style outlining the text box. You must have done this at some point by selecting the text box and then choosing a line style in the Line Style button pop-up. If you don't want to see the text box anymore, select the Line Color button and choose No Line from the pop-up dialog box.

Using AutoShapes

 In addition to the rectangle, oval, text box, and line tools, a treasure-trove of other less commonly used drawing tools appears when you select the AutoShapes tool. These fall into eight categories:

 ■ *Lines*. Contains six tools, including the Line, Arrow, and Double-Arrow tools. Three new tools in PowerPoint 97—Curve, Freeform, and Scribble—are used to draw irregular shapes and lines that have no constraints as to shape or angle. In effect, using these tools is like drawing with a pencil, with any jags or shifts in your mouse movement reflected in the line.

 ■ *Connectors*. Consists of nine special line tools you can use to draw connecting lines between other objects on a slide. These come in handy for tasks such as building a process description or organizational chart where the relationship between several objects must be shown visually. They automatically "snap" to connecting points on other objects, and once connected, stay connected even though you later move the object elsewhere on the slide (see Figures 6.6 and 6.7).

■ *Basic Shapes* contains 32 shapes, ranging from the simple rectangle and oval to cubes, smiley faces, and heart shapes, as shown in the side menu in Figure 6.8.

■ *Block Arrows*. Provides 28 arrow shapes, including the examples shown in Figure 6.9. These are also useful for showing the flow of activity or relationships with a little more graphic punch than connector lines have.

Part
III

Ch
6

FIG. 6.6

Setting up a simple flow chart is a piece of cake with PowerPoint's new Connector tool.

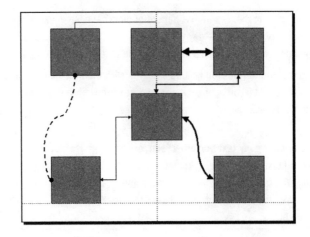

FIG. 6.7

And when you move the connected shapes, the connector lines follow along.

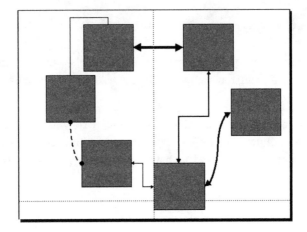

FIG. 6.8

Drawing valentines, rainbows, or even no-smoking signs becomes a snap with some of these built-in shapes and a little imagination.

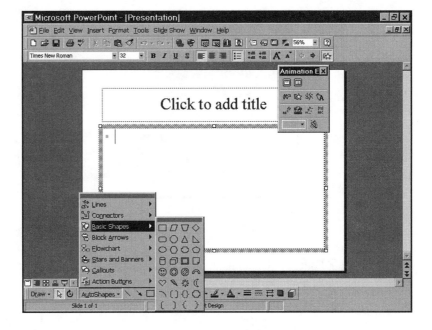

FIG. 6.9

The flow of a process of material can be shown using a variety of block arrow shapes; three different examples are used here.

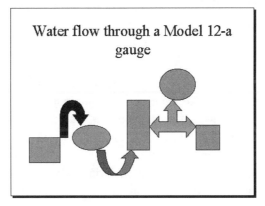

Water flow through a Model 12-a gauge

■ *Flowchart*. Offers 28 shapes that you can use to build the elements of a process flow or organizational chart. Several of these shapes are useful for equipment diagrams or cross sections, such as the cylinder or crosshair in a circle. Used in combination with connectors or block arrows, these can allow you to build very detailed and effective illustrations.

■ *Stars and Banners*. A selection of 12 AutoShapes that provide you with stars and banner shapes of various designs. These can be effective on slides that contain product announcements or an exciting bit of news, as shown in Figure 6.10.

Part
III

Ch
6

FIG. 6.10

A starburst and banner, combined with a WordArt effect and text box, make an announcement much more dynamic.

■ *Callouts.* Consist of 20 tools that allow you to draw text annotations in forms that range from simple lines to cartoon-like bubble captions. If you choose the Rectangular, Rounded Rectangular, Oval, or Cloud callouts, you then draw them just as you would a rectangle or ellipse. Click where you want the upper-left corner of the callout to appear, then drag to make it the size you want. To use the Line Style callouts, choose the one you want, place your mouse on the object where you want the callout to point to, then drag your mouse. When you release your mouse button, the callout object offers you a text box area to enter the callout text. Once you've placed the callout, you can use the yellow diamond-shaped handles to modify the callout lines.

■ *Action Buttons.* Twelve button shapes you can place on a PowerPoint slide, with common symbols like a question mark for help or a small speaker to represent a sound file. Choose the button you want, then click your slide where you want the upper-left corner of the button to appear. PowerPoint draws the button in its default size, and then opens the Action Settings dialog box so you can specify what should happen when you click the button during a show. You can associate an Action Button with a sound or movie file, a hyperlink to a World Wide Web site, or have it run a program on your system. See Chapter 9 for more on animation and action settings.

Like the other AutoShapes, Action Buttons have a yellow diamond-shaped handle in addition to the usual selection handles. Drag it to change the 3-D "depth" of the button or use the regular selection handles to resize the button.

▶ **See** "Using Action Buttons," **p. 189**

▶ **See** "Adding Animation Effects," **p. 194**

▶ **See** "Creating Internet Hyperlinks," **p. 430**

Working with Drawing Objects

Once you have created a drawing object, you aren't stuck with the shape that appears. PowerPoint offers a great deal of flexibility in moving, resizing, reshaping, and repositioning drawing objects. To do any of these actions, however, you first have to select an object.

Selecting Objects

You've already selected text objects such as text placeholders in previous chapters. When you selected those objects by clicking them, a dashed gray line and eight handles appeared and the text was available for editing. You also select a drawing object by clicking it. Although no line surrounds a drawing object when selected, the same eight handles do appear forming the selection rectangle. These are called *sizing handles* and you'll see how they're used to change the size or shape of your object shortly.

To select more than one object, you can click the first one, then hold down the Shift key and click another object. You can do this with as many objects as you like.

If you select an object by accident while you're selecting several, there's no need to start over. Click a selected object with the Shift key held down, and it becomes unselected again.

You can select several objects at one time by clicking and then dragging with the pointer. PowerPoint shows you a dashed rectangle to indicate the area you're enclosing and selects any objects that fall completely within it. To select all the objects on your slide, choose Edit, Select All, or press Ctrl+A. Once you've selected multiple objects, any action you take will be applied to all.

Moving Objects

When you select a drawing object and move your mouse over the middle of it, your cursor changes to a bold, four-directional arrow. This cursor is used to move objects around your slide. When this cursor, shown in Figure 6.11, appears, you can click your object and drag it anywhere you like on the page. As you drag, an outline of the object appears to help you position it. When you release your mouse button, the object has been moved.

Part
III

Ch
6

Duplicating Objects

Drawing an object isn't a precise science, in that you are unlikely to drag and draw two rectangles with exactly the same dimensions. For that reason, it's sometimes better to duplicate an existing object rather than try to draw another, assuming you want the objects to be identical. In addition to making the size of the two objects consistent, any formatting you've applied to one object is also duplicated, saving you the effort of formatting the second object all over again.

FIG. 6.11
The outline of
this object shows
you where it would
appear if you released
the mouse button
at this point.

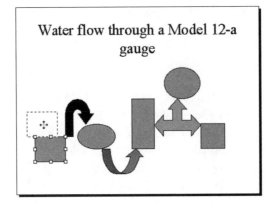

Water flow through a Model 12-a gauge

To duplicate an object, select it, then choose <u>E</u>dit, Dupl<u>i</u>cate. You can also use the keystroke combination Ctrl+D. A copy of the object appears, overlapping the first. It will always be exactly two grid units to the right and two grid units down from the original. To line them up perfectly, press the up arrow key twice, then press the left arrow key twice.

You can also make a duplicate by holding down the Ctrl key while you drag the object to the place where you'd like it duplicated.

Still another way is to right-click and drag the object to where you want the duplicate. PowerPoint gives you a choice of duplicating it or moving it there.

T I P There is another way to make sure two drawing objects are exactly the same size. Select each object and choose F<u>o</u>rmat, Drawing <u>O</u>bject. In the Format AutoShape dialog box, select the Size tab. Here you can enter specific dimensions for each object so that they match exactly.

Deleting Objects

Deleting objects is also simple. Select the object and do one of four tasks:

- Press the Delete key.
- Press the Backspace key.
- Choose <u>E</u>dit, Cu<u>t</u> (or press Ctrl+X) to place the object on the Windows Clipboard.
- Choose <u>E</u>dit, Cle<u>a</u>r to remove the object. In this case, the object will not be stored on the Windows Clipboard.

If you want to delete multiple objects, select them all while holding down the Shift key. When you use any of these methods, all the objects that have been selected are deleted from your slide.

 TIP If you want to delete every object on your slide you can use the Select All command on the Edit menu prior to deleting your selection. This will delete any object you have inserted on your slide, including text in placeholders from the applied AutoLayout. It normally leaves the placeholders themselves, but will also delete any blank placeholders.

Resizing Objects

When it comes to resizing drawing objects, there are basically three categories of objects:

- Two-dimensional objects drawn with an AutoShape tool, such as a square, block arrow, cube, or star.
- One-dimensional lines, including connectors and lines with arrows.
- Objects drawn with the Freeform or Scribble AutoShape tools.

Resizing Two-Dimensional Drawing Objects To resize any two-dimensional object such as a square, circle, or star shape, follow these steps:

1. Select the object. Eight square sizing handles appear around it, as shown in Figure 6.12.

FIG. 6.12
The square handles form the selection rectangle, indicating the parameters of the object.

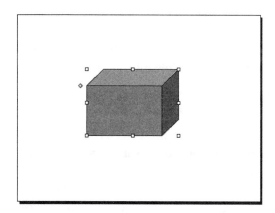

Part
III

Ch
6

2. To resize an object to make it wider, click either of the handles on the right or left side of the object. When you place the cursor over one of these handles, it changes to a two-headed arrow. Drag the sizing handle to the right or left. The object will expand or shrink in the direction in which you drag.

3. To resize an object to make it taller, click either of the handles on the top or bottom of the object and drag it up or down. The object will grow longer or shorter in the direction in which you drag.

CAUTION

If you resize an object using either of the side or the top or bottom handles, the object will not stay in proportion. A circle becomes an oval if stretched from the top, a square becomes a rectangle if you drag on its side handle, and so on.

---

4. To keep the proportions of the object, but change its overall dimensions, you can use one of four methods:

- To resize proportionally from the object's corner, press Shift and drag a corner handle. The cursor becomes a four-headed arrow when it's over a corner handle.

- To resize vertically, horizontally, or on a diagonal from the center of the object out, press Ctrl and drag any handle. The object resizes equally about its center point.

- To resize proportionally from the center out press Ctrl+Shift and drag a corner handle.

- If you want to resize without being restricted by any grid or guide settings, press Alt and drag any handle.

5. 3-D AutoShapes have one or more yellow diamond shaped handles that you can drag. The cursor becomes an arrowhead when you're over one of these handles. Each shape has its own unique behavior when you drag these handles, but a little experimenting will familiarize you with how each of them works.

Resizing Lines and Connectors   When you select a line, sizing handles appear on each end. You can use these handles in several ways:

■ Click one handle; your mouse cursor changes to a two-directional arrow. Drag towards the center of the line to make it shorter and away from the center to lengthen it in the direction of the handle you have selected. As you do, a dashed line appears, indicating the new path and length of the line. Notice that as you drag these handles, you can also change the direction of the line on the slide.

■ Hold down the Ctrl key as you drag to make the line resize symmetrically around its center point. This effect is shown on two selected objects—a line and connector line—in Figure 6.13.

FIG. 6.13

These objects are being stretched from their centers; their new lengths and positions are indicated by the dashed line.

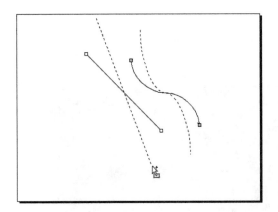

- Hold down the Shift key and drag to lengthen or shorten the line without changing its angle.

- When you select an AutoShape connector (other than the straight connector), an additional yellow diamond-shaped handle appears in the center of the line. Click this handle and drag it to change the place where the line "breaks" or to alter the curvature of a curved connector line, as shown in Figure 6.14.

FIG. 6.14

To make connector lines flow properly between objects and fit on your slide, it is sometimes necessary to adjust their angles.

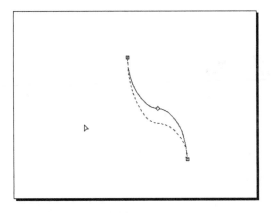

Resizing Freeform Objects   You can use these same sizing methods with Curve, Freeform, or Scribble tool objects, but you have an additional option. These objects are made up of points and straight or curved line segments connecting the points. In addition to sizing these objects, you can also adjust the individual points that control their shapes.

To reshape a selected Curve, Freeform, or Scribble object, choose Draw, Edit Points or right-click the object and choose Edit Points. As you can see in Figure 6.15, the hat-shaped Freeform object now shows a sizing handle for each point on the object. These additional handles enable you to fix small errors you may have made while drawing this object, or change its appearance with much more flexibility.

FIG. 6.15
A freeform object can have many more sides and angles than its more geometric sym-metrical counterparts such as squares and circles.

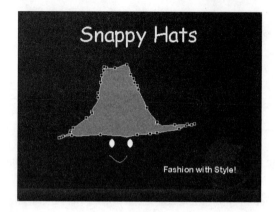

To reshape a Curve, Freeform, or Scribble object, click any of these points and drag in any direction. The selected point and the lines extending out from it on either side move, changing the overall shape of the object. Use this method to smooth out irregular bumps or ridges in this type of object.

Positioning Objects

Once you've drawn an object and have sized it to your liking, it's important that it be placed on your slide in a way that balances with the other elements. To do this you can take advantage of PowerPoint features that allow you to change the angle of an object, and position it more exactly in relation to the edges of the slide and other objects.

Rotating Objects

At times it's necessary to rotate the angle at which an object is placed on your slide. This is useful to create new shapes, for example by rotating a square to become a diamond, or to fit shapes within the constraints of the edges of your slide. Look at the drawings in Figure 6.16. Being able to rotate these AutoShapes adds variety to the slide.

 To rotate an object, select it, then choose the Free Rotate tool from the Drawing toolbar. When you do, the four round green handles, like the ones displayed in Figure 6.16, ap-pear. Click any of these handles and drag to spin the object. A ghost image of the object, shifted to its new position, appears as you turn. When the object is in a position you like, release the mouse button. The object appears in its new, rotated position.

FIG. 6.16
The same shape, rotated slightly, gives a feeling of movement and variety to this slide.

Making Morale
a Priority

You can also use commands on the Drawing menu to rotate or flip an object. Flipping causes an object to turn 180 degrees, either horizontally or vertically. Select the object, then choose D*r*aw, Rotate or Fli*p*. A submenu offers you these commands:

- *Free Rotate*. The equivalent of selecting the Free Rotate button on the Drawing toolbar.

- *Rotate Left*. Rotates the selected object 90 degrees to the left.

- *Rotate Right*. Rotates the selected object 90 degrees to the right.

- *Flip Horizontal*. Mirrors the object left to right (the right side becomes the left side and vice versa).

- *Flip Vertical*. Rotates the object 180 degrees top to bottom (the bottom becomes the top and vice versa).

You can rotate any kind of object, including text objects, drawing objects, and objects inserted from other programs, as well as any placeholders included in an AutoLayout.

Part

III

Ch

6

 You can use most of PowerPoint's object modification tools to move, resize, and re-color any object. This includes AutoShapes and 3-D objects to some extent, but you can't modify the individual objects that make up these special objects.

That is, you can't unless you do the following:

1. Select the object.

2. Choose E*d*it, Cu*t* or press Ctrl+X.

3. Choose E*d*it, Paste S*p*ecial and select Picture or Picture (Enhanced Metafile) from the next dialog box.

The AutoShape reappears, but actually it's not an AutoShape any longer. You can ungroup it and change any of the component objects using all of the normal PowerPoint drawing tools, but remember that it won't behave like an AutoShape any longer.

Using Rulers

By now you've noticed the two rulers on your PowerPoint Slide view screen. One, the horizontal ruler, runs along the top of Slide view and the other, the vertical ruler, runs along the left hand side of Slide view. These same rulers appear when you are in any of the Master views.

The ends of these rulers represent the edges of your printable page. The measurements on these rulers differ depending on the type of object you have selected:

- Normally, the ruler numbers increase to the left and right of 0, which is at the center point of your slide. This helps you center objects on the page.

- When you click an insertion cursor in a text box, the starting point of the ruler is at the left. This is because PowerPoint measures tab settings from the left edge of the text.

If you click the text you've typed into a text box, the ruler also shows you any indent markers and tabs for the text, as shown in Figure 6.17. Note also that the two rulers now reflect the width and height of the text box, not the dimensions of the entire slide.

FIG. 6.17
Notice the origin of the ruler on the left when text is selected, and the tab marks at regular intervals.

Tab marker

Horizontal ruler

Vertical ruler

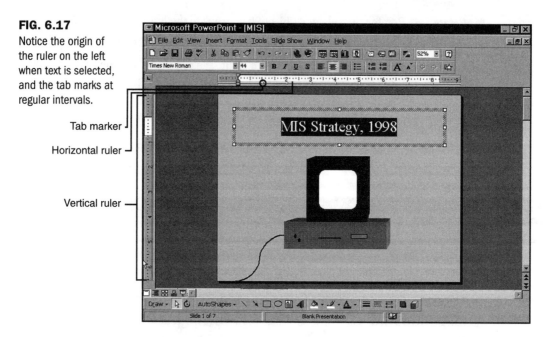

▶ **See** "Setting Tabs and Margins," **p. 76**

These rulers measure in inches. If you move your mouse around the screen, you will notice a little line on each ruler; these lines mark the location of your cursor on the slide. By using these markers, you can line up an object at a precise location on your slide.

Rulers can be displayed or hidden from your screen by checking or unchecking the Ruler command on the View menu.

N O T E You can also position an object precisely on your page by using the Format AutoShape dialog box. Double-click the object, or select the object and choose Format, Drawing Object. When the Format AutoShapes dialog box appears, select the Position tab. Enter a specific measurement for both horizontal and vertical placement relative to either the top left corner or center of the slide. When you choose OK, your object is precisely repositioned.

By default, you enter measurements in inches. If you prefer, you can enter dimensions in other units by entering an abbreviation for the units you want after the measurement. For instance, type **72pt** to enter 72 points, or **25mm** to enter 25 millimeters. ▪

Using Guides

In addition to rulers, PowerPoint offers a feature called *Guides* to assist you in placing objects precisely. Guides are two intersecting lines—one horizontal and one vertical—that you can choose to display in Slide view. These two lines can be moved on your slide to locate a precise point at their intersection.

To display Guides, choose View, Guides. Two faint dotted lines appear. To move a guide, click it and drag it to another location: the horizontal guide can be moved up and down and the vertical guide can be moved from side to side. As you move a guide, its distance from the center of the slide is displayed numerically, as shown in Figure 6.18. The horizontal guide measurement corresponds to the horizontal ruler, and the vertical guide measurement corresponds to the vertical ruler.

 You can also use the guides to measure the distance between any two points on your slide. Drag the guide to the first point. This becomes the zero point for the measurement. Then hold down the Shift key as you drag the ruler to the other point. The numerical read-out gives you the distance between the points.

 TROUBLESHOOTING

I can't move the guide past the 10-inch point on the right of my slide. Why? Guides cannot be moved beyond the printable area of the slide, which is determined by the settings you have made for printing output, such as landscape or portrait orientation, or handouts versus slides.

continues

continued

I resized a picture and want to get it back to exactly the size it was originally. I can't use Undo, because I've saved, closed, and then opened the file since I resized the object. Is there a way to do this? Select the shape, then choose Format, Picture (you can also right-click an object and choose Format Picture to bring up the same dialog box). In the dialog box, select the Size tab. At the bottom of this dialog box is a Reset button. Click it so the object returns to its originally drawn size.

FIG. 6.18
The two faint dotted lines are guides. As you move one, its position is displayed numerically.

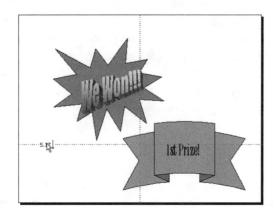

Snapping Objects to Align Them

When you have created several objects on a page, you might want to arrange them so their edges line up exactly with each other. Objects snap to the guides, and that's one way of getting the job done, but PowerPoint has a few more tricks up its sleeve. It's sometimes more efficient to use the Snap To setting in the Drawing menu.

Snapping uses an invisible grid to align selected objects precisely as you move them. For example, say you created several objects and you want to line them up near the left side of your page. If you turn on the Snap To Grid feature, objects only move in *grid increments*. That is, they "snap to" the grid as they move. With Snap To turned off, you can position objects anywhere you like. They won't snap to the grid.

Two types of snapping commands are available. You can Snap To Grid, which lines up the corners of objects on this invisible matrix of lines. Or, new in PowerPoint 97, you can Snap To Shape, which causes objects you're moving to snap to the edges of the other objects on your slide when they get close.

Both Snap features are saved when you save your PowerPoint presentation. You can toggle these features on and off by choosing Draw, Snap and clicking either To Grid or To Shape.

Nudging Objects

Another useful tool in the Draw menu is Nudge. Sometimes it's difficult to be precise when you want to move an object in very tiny increments on your slide. You can nudge an object in any direction in one grid unit increments (a *grid unit* is approximately .08 inch). There are two ways to do this:

■ Select the object, then choose D<u>r</u>aw, <u>N</u>udge. Select a direction (<u>U</u>p, <u>D</u>own, <u>L</u>eft, or <u>R</u>ight) from the submenu that appears, and the object is nudged one grid unit in that direction.

■ Select the object, then use the arrow keys on your keyboard to move in the direction of the arrow key in one grid unit increments. Hold down the Ctrl key for quadrupled precision. PowerPoint then nudges the object in .02 inch units.

 You can temporarily override Snap To Grid by pressing the Alt key while nudging objects.

Part
III

Ch
6

Modifying Drawing Objects

by Nancy Stevenson

In the previous chapter, you learned about creating drawing objects ranging from simple lines to more complex AutoShapes. You also saw how to move, duplicate, resize, and position those objects.

In this chapter, you learn how to refine the look of objects you've drawn in your presentation. By adding color, patterns, shadows, and line styles, you can make objects more attractive. And by learning to group and order objects in relation to text and each other, you can build more complex drawings to help get your message across. ∎

Change line styles

Once you've created drawings, you can modify the outline styles of drawing objects in a variety of ways.

Add shadows and 3-D effects to objects

Shadows and 3-D styles can provide depth and perspective to your drawings.

Use color with drawings

You can fill drawing objects with a large selection of built-in color choices, create custom colors, or even fill objects with realistic textures like marble or wood.

Work with several objects

Drawing objects can be grouped together so you can work with the collection as though it were a single object; or change the stacking order of objects on your slide to give a sense of perspective.

Working with Drawing Objects

Whether curved or straight, simple or more complex, nearly all drawing objects have fills and outlines. PowerPoint offers you the ability to apply various fill and outline styles and shadows to drawing objects so that you can create drawings like those shown in Figure 7.1.

FIG. 7.1
Textures, patterns, shadows, and various line styles make this simple collection of drawings come alive.

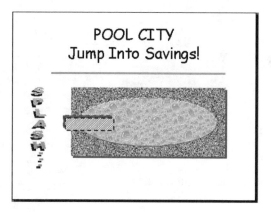

Changing Lines

You can format the outlines of your drawing objects with various line styles. By using several line tools, you can create:

- Lines of varying thickness
- Single or double lines
- Dashed or solid lines
- Lines with no arrows, an arrowhead, or arrows at both ends

Look at the cylindrical AutoShape in Figure 7.2. The single lines that form this object are of a certain weight (3/4 point), are solid, and have no arrow styles applied. There is also a line object drawn across the cylinder. It too has weight, is solid, and has no arrows.

Four tools on the Drawing toolbar enable you to modify lines:

Button	Name
	Line Color
	Line Style

Button	Name
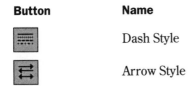	Dash Style
	Arrow Style

N O T E Even though there is both a Line and Arrow tool for drawing lines and arrows respectively, you can draw an object as a line and later use the Arrow tool to add arrows to the ends of the line. ■

 All four of these tools work similarly. Each becomes available once you've selected a drawing object, and each offers a pop-up palette of choices (see Figures 7.3, 7.4, and 7.5). To change the style of the selected object, just select a new style from the palette of choices. The Line Color tool shows you the current default color beneath the paintbrush icon. If this is the color you want, simply click the icon. To choose a different color, click the arrow to the right of the icon to see more choices.

FIG. 7.2
A simple AutoShape is made up of solid, narrow lines by default.

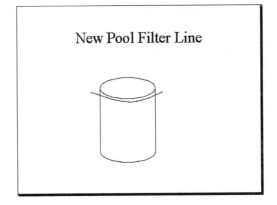

New Pool Filter Line

FIG. 7.3
The Line Style button reveals 13 styles to chose from.

FIG. 7.4
The Dash Style button offers eight dashed line styles.

FIG. 7.5
The Arrow Style button opens up to 11 arrow styles, some of which aren't really arrows at all.

The Line Styles palette has an option of More Lines, and the Arrow Style palette has an option of More Arrows; these options take you to the Format AutoShape dialog box where you can control several aspects of line formatting (see Figure 7.6).

FIG. 7.6
The Format Auto-Shapes dialog box opens to the Colors and Lines tab when you get there through the Line Style or Arrow Style buttons.

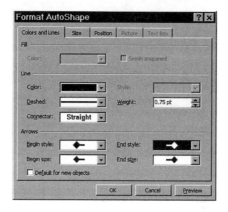

 TIP You can also get to the Format AutoShapes dialog box by double-clicking a drawing object, right-clicking it and selecting Format Drawing Object from the shortcut menu that appears, or by choosing Format, Drawing Object.

The Colors and Lines tab of the Format AutoShape dialog box includes sections for both Line and Arrow styles. Within the Line section, you can choose line color, make dashed line selections, set the line weight, and even add patterns to your lines.

Modifying Line Styles   The first option in the Line section of this tab deals with the color of the line. Clicking Color opens a drop-down palette of color choices, one of which is an option to create custom colors through the More Colors option. The final choice here,

Patterned Lines, opens the Patterned Lines dialog box shown in Figure 7.7. Pattern fills apply a pattern to the full width of the line you've selected, and don't display very well with narrower line styles.

FIG. 7.7
Patterns work best on thicker line styles.

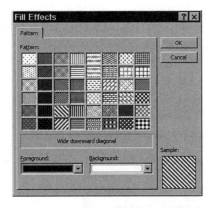

 When you first open the Patterned Lines dialog box, you see a wide variety of patterns to choose from. Each is drawn in a Foreground color (which you can change) against a Background color (also yours to control). As you click each sample pattern, you see its name below. PowerPoint shows you a larger sample of the pattern in the area at the lower right of the dialog box. Click OK when you're satisfied with your choices.

The Dashed setting in the Format AutoShape dialog box opens to offer the same dash line styles available through the Dash Style button on the Drawing toolbar.

If you have selected a connector object before opening this dialog box, the Connector option is available to you. The drop-down menu of choices here has three options: Straight, Elbow, and Curved. The three effects are shown in Figure 7.8.

FIG. 7.8
Straight, Elbow, and Curved shaped connectors give you flexibility in drawing relations among other objects.

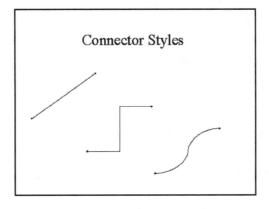

Part
III

Ch
7

The Style drop-down list box lets you choose from several preset line weights and different types of double- and triple-line styles.

New to PowerPoint 97, you can choose any thickness you like rather than being restricted to a limited selection of line weights. Use the arrows in the Weight field, or type a new value. This weight is set in points by default, but you can override the units of measure by typing **in** for inches, **mm** for millimeters, and so forth.

Making Changes to Arrows   You can add arrows to one or both ends of any line with two end points. This includes objects drawn with the Line, Arrow, or Connector tools and the Arc tool from Basic AutoShapes.

Arrows have four settings in the Format AutoShape dialog box:

- *Begin Style*. Offers six styles of arrow you can apply to the point where you began, as shown in the drop-down palette in Figure 7.9.

FIG. 7.9

From no arrow to a diamond shape, you can choose among these six options in the Begin Style list.

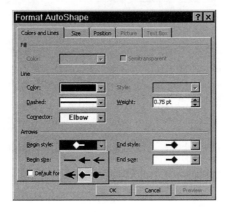

- *Begin Size*. Allows you to choose from among nine sizes of the style you've selected for the beginning arrow.
- *End Style*. Offers the same six choices of arrow styles to apply to the point where you ended of the selected line.
- *End Size*. Allows you to choose the size of the arrow on the end point of the line.

Settings for Begin Style and Size and End Style and Size can all be used independently.

If you would like to set a new default for any line objects, you can use the Default For New Objects check box. Any settings you have made in this dialog box become the default for any new object you draw.

Adding Shadows and 3-D Effects

A good way to add some depth or perspective to drawing objects is to use the Shadow and 3-D buttons on the Drawing toolbar. Each offers a pop-up palette of choices you can click to apply, as shown in Figures 7.10 and 7.11.

FIG. 7.10
Twenty Shadow settings, plus the choices of No Shadow or Shadow Settings, appear when you click the Shadow button.

FIG. 7.11
3-D effects can give a simple drawing object depth.

Shadow and 3-D effects give you a wide range of results. For example, look at the simple line drawing that was displayed in Figure 7.2. Figure 7.12 shows how a 3-D effect added to the line and a shadow effect added to the cylinder have changed it.

FIG. 7.12
Shadows and 3-D effects have changed this simple line drawing.

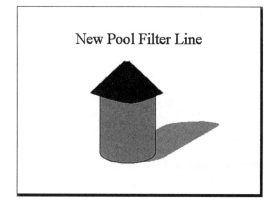

New Pool Filter Line

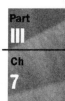
Part
III

Ch
7

Believe it or not, that black cone-like shape is actually the simple curved line from Figure 7.2 with a 3-D (Style 20) effect applied. The cylinder object has had a fill color added (which I cover shortly) and a shadow applied.

Working with Shadow Settings   Besides selecting a shadow shape from the pop-up palette, you can also display a shadow toolbar that allows you to modify shadow effects. To see it, choose <u>S</u>hadow Settings from the pop-up palette (see Figure 7.13).

From left to right, the buttons on this toolbar enable you to do the following:

- Shadow On/Off allows you to toggle shadow effects for selected objects on and off.

- Nudge Shadow Up pushes the shadow offset from the object up slightly.

- Nudge Shadow Down pushes the shadow offset from the object down slightly.

- Nudge Shadow Left moves the shadow slightly further to the left of the object.

- Nudge Shadow Right moves the shadow slightly further to the right of the object.

- Shadow Color is a drop-down palette of color choices for the shadow itself. You can also choose to make a shadow semitransparent from this palette. The shadow in Figure 7.13, for example, has a shadow filled with a pale gray color.

FIG. 7.13
The Shadow Settings toolbar can also be displayed by choosing <u>V</u>iew, <u>T</u>oolbars, Customize, then choosing Shadow Settings.

Working with 3-D Settings   When you select the 3-D button on the Drawing toolbar and choose <u>3</u>-D Settings, the 3-D Settings toolbar shown in Figure 7.14 appears.

FIG. 7.14
You can manipulate 3-D settings in a variety of ways from this toolbar.

The tools in this toolbar allow you to do the following:

■ 3-D On/Off toggles the 3-D effects on and off.

 ■ Tilt Down deepens the 3-D effect.

 ■ Tilt Up makes the 3-D effect more shallow.

 ■ Tilt Left shifts the 3-D effect to the left.

 ■ Tilt Right shifts the 3-D effect to the right.

 ■ Depth allows you to select a setting for how deep the 3-D effect is; Infinity makes the end point of the object appear to disappear in space, and the lowest setting provides only a slight 3-D effect.

 ■ Direction allows you to choose to have the 3-D effect appear to the left, right, or behind the object and at various angles away from it.

 ■ Lighting applies a slight gradient effect to the 3-D effect from whichever direction you choose in this drop-down palette.

 ■ Surface gives you a choice of materials so that you can make your 3-D object look like plastic, metal, matte, or a wire frame.

 ■ 3-D Color provides a drop-down palette of colors to fill your 3-D effect with.

Figure 7.15 shows a variety of these 3-D effects applied to exactly the same AutoShape.

You can experiment with both Shadows and 3-D effects to produce a variety of results.

FIG. 7.15
Three of these are filled with a blue color; notice how the three surface effects change the darkness of the color slightly.

Metal surface, lighting from underneath, 288 point Depth

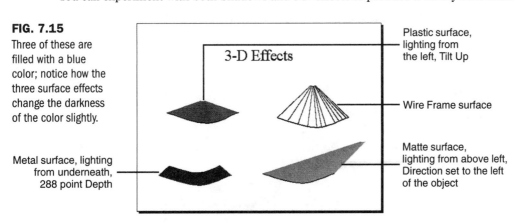

Plastic surface, lighting from the left, Tilt Up

Wire Frame surface

Matte surface, lighting from above left, Direction set to the left of the object

Using Color and Fill Effects

If you are giving your presentation as 35mm slides, an on-screen computer show, or in any other medium that supports color, you have a powerful tool at your command. Color can do more to enliven a presentation than almost any other effect.

Remember that you already have a color scheme built into your slides if you have applied a design template. However, you may want to add color or a pattern to drawing objects to make them match or even contrast with the pre-selected scheme colors. The area inside a drawing object's outline is called its *fill*.

You can modify your drawing objects' fills simply to add visual interest. But there are also times when adding color or a fill pattern to an object helps you differentiate among objects or helps your audience see them more clearly. For example, look at the three drawing objects in Figure 7.16. Then see how fill color and pattern has modified them in Figure 7.17.

FIG. 7.16
Simple line drawings can be effective, but these become hard to differentiate without any fill color added.

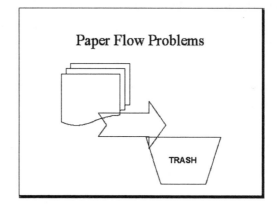

FIG. 7.17
A pattern and two different color fills add interest as well as clarity to this series of drawings.

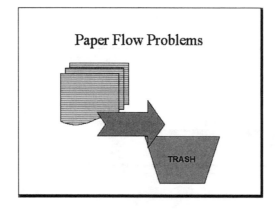

Adding Color Fills

To change an object's fill color, follow these steps:

1. Select the object.

2. Choose the arrow on the right of the Fill Color button on the Drawing toolbar. (You can also reach this palette in a dialog box by choosing F_ormat, Colors and Li_nes or by double-clicking the object.) The pop-up palette shown in Figure 7.18 appears.

 TIP To modify the color of the object's outline rather than the fill, use the Line Color button on the Drawing toolbar. This works in exactly the same way as the Fill Color button, but it changes the object's outline rather than its fill.

FIG. 7.18
You can choose from the eight color squares here or display many more colors with the M_ore Fill Colors choice.

3. Choose from three areas of this palette:

- *No Fill*. Makes the center of the object clear. You can see through the object to whatever's underneath it.

- *Automatic*. Fills the object with a default color based on the color scheme used by the design template you have selected. With a blank template, this color is a deep turquoise.

- *Eight color squares across the middle of this palette*. The scheme colors and will vary depending on the design template you have selected.

You can select M_ore Fill Colors to see the Color dialog box shown in Figure 7.19.

FIG. 7.19
You can choose from dozens of standard colors or create your own custom color from this dialog box.

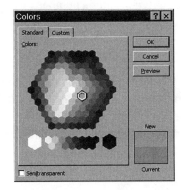

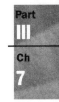
Part
III

Ch
7

When you select a color in the Colors dialog box by clicking it, the object's current color and the new color you've selected are displayed for you in the bottom-right corner.

Choosing the Preview button temporarily changes the object to the selected color so you can see how it looks on your slide.

Clicking the Semitransparent check box makes the color sheer, so you can see other objects through it.

To create a custom color, select the Custom tab of the Color dialog box (see Figure 7.20).

FIG. 7.20
Thousands of colors can be generated by mixing and matching the choices in this tab of the Color dialog box.

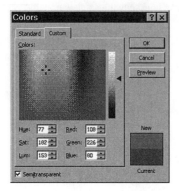

There are many so-called "models" for describing colors. PowerPoint uses two of them—HSL or RGB—and you can work with whichever one you prefer. The HSL color model describes color in terms of its Hue, Saturation, and Luminance. If you're more an artist than a technician, you'll probably prefer HSL over RGB.

Here's what the settings on this tab control:

- Hue is the color. Enter a number from 0 to 255, or drag the crosshair cursor on the Colors block to pick a color. As you move the cursor from left to right, the color changes across the spectrum.

- Saturation is the color's intensity. Again, enter a number from 0 to 255 in this setting, or drag the crosshair control vertically on the Colors block. The higher the number, the more intense the color. As you drag the crosshair downwards or enter a lower value in the number box, the color becomes grayer.

- Luminance controls the color's brightness. Again, the numbers range from 0 to 255; the higher the number, the brighter (or more nearly white) the color. You can also adjust Luminance using the vertical slider to the right of the Colors block. Move the triangle pointer up to lighten the color, down to darken it.

If you're more technically inclined, you might prefer the RGB color model over HSL. These controls allow you to enter the proportions of Red, Green, and Blue you want to use for your color; settings range from 0 to 255, with 0 producing the darkest value, 255 the lightest.

You can use the crosshair cursor in the Colors block and the triangle on the vertical slider as well. Any adjustment you make here or to the numbers in either the HSL or RGB models is reflected in the other settings. In fact, there's no reason why you couldn't use the Colors block to get a rough approximation of the color you want, switch to entering HSL numbers to fine-tune the color, then finally tweak the RGB values "to add just a little more red."

TIP Once you have selected a color for an object, the Fill Color button provides a shortcut: the most recent color you selected becomes its default. Click the button itself, rather than the arrow on its side, to apply the default color to other objects.

Adding Fill Effects

Sometimes a solid color isn't quite what you need. There are times that a pattern or gradient lighting effect might enhance an object more appropriately. For example, if you've drawn a rectangle to represent a piece of writing paper, a horizontal line pattern is the perfect fill to add the detail of a lined piece of paper.

When you select a drawing object, then click the Fill Color button on the Drawing toolbar, one of the options is Fill Effects. Selecting this displays the Fill Effects dialog box shown in Figure 7.21.

FIG. 7.21
Four tabs in this dialog box provide a wealth of fill effects for your objects.

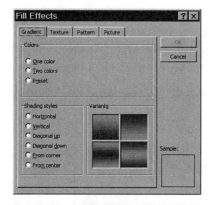

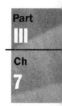

Part
III

Ch
7

N O T E You can also get to the Fill Effects dialog box by selecting the Fill Effects option from the Fill Color drop-down palette in the Format AutoShape dialog box. ■

The four tabs available in this dialog box are:

- *Gradient.* An effect that seems to illuminate the an object as if light were being shined on it from a selected direction. Choose the direction in the Shading Styles section, and Qne or Two colors (or one of the Preset combinations) to get just the shading effect you want.

- *Texture.* Offers backgrounds such as marble, canvas, water drops, or wood grain. On this tab, you simply click a texture effect to select it. You can also experiment with creating your own textures. The Qther Texture button lets you pick an image file to use as a texture.

- *Pattern.* Offers the variety of patterns shown in Figure 7.22. You can choose to have different colors for the foreground and background. If you leave the background white and make the foreground black, you will have a pattern of black lines filling your object.

FIG. 7.22
Choose a pale gray foreground for a more subtle patterned effect.

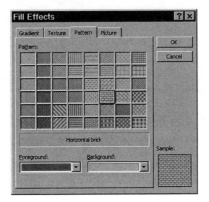

- *Picture.* Allows you to use a picture to fill an object. The Select Picture button on this tab opens a Select Picture dialog box (very similar to the Open File dialog box) where you can choose an image file to fill your object with.

When you've selected the effect to fill your object, choose OK to apply it. Figure 7.23 shows various fill effects applied to objects.

> **CAUTION**
>
> Patterned, Semi-Transparent, and Texture fills and lines may not reproduce the way you expect them to on some printers, or they may print agonizingly slowly. Before using them extensively, test a few examples on the printer you'll use to output your presentation. If you send your presentations to a service bureau for output, check with them to learn what works and what doesn't.

FIG. 7.23
The heart has a gradient for depth; the window has a picture of clouds and a pattern in its shutters. The log uses a wood texture.

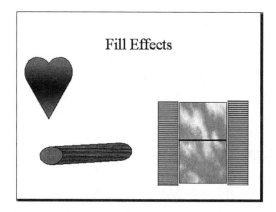

Adding Backgrounds

Besides adding the various colors and fill effects to your objects, you can add these same styles to the background of your entire slide.

Here's how this works. If you have used a design template and change the background, the new background pattern or effect will replace the background of the template, but other template elements, such as bars or graphic objects, color scheme and typeface remain. The slide background is really just a rectangle that completely fills the page you set by choosing File, Page Setup. You can apply all the same formatting styles to the background that you can apply to any other drawing object.

You change the background by choosing Format, Background. The Background dialog box in Figure 7.24 appears.

FIG. 7.24
The color scheme displayed here is taken from the template the file was based on.

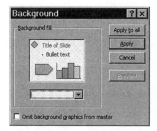

When you open this dialog box a color scheme based on the current design template appears. To select a new background color, open the drop-down field in the Background Fill area.

T I P If you want to omit background elements from a particular slide, choose Format, Background, then click Omit Background Graphics From Master. Choose Apply, and PowerPoint leaves the background graphics off the slide you're working with. Don't choose Apply To All unless you want background graphics removed from all of your slides.

If you only want to remove some of the background graphics from the slide, it's a little trickier, but you can still do it. Follow the previous instructions to remove the background graphics, then follow these steps:

1. Choose View, Masters, Slide Master and pick the graphics that you want on your slide.

2. Choose Edit, Copy or press Ctrl+C, then choose View, Slide. You're back where you started, looking at your original slide, with no background graphics.

3. Choose Edit, Paste or press Ctrl+V to put a copy of the chosen background graphics on your slide.

4. From the Drawing toolbar, choose Draw, Order, Send to Back, which puts the new graphics back behind all the other objects on your slide.

This provides exactly the same palette as you saw when you choose backgrounds for drawing objects in the previous section of this chapter, with a selection of color squares, More Colors for creating custom color settings, and Fill Effects to display the Fill Effects dialog box. By using the settings on this palette, you can apply colors, gradients, patterns, pictures, and textures as the background to your entire slide.

When you've finished making these settings, you have a choice of applying them to all slides by choosing Apply To All, or only to the currently displayed slide by choosing Apply. Figures 7.25 and 7.26 show the same slide with the Rules template and the Rules template with the waterdrop background applied, respectively.

FIG. 7.25
Templates have their own background setting...

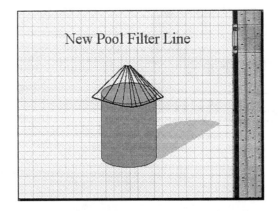

FIG. 7.26
...but you can override that setting with a new background. All other elements remain, such as the ruler and graph lines.

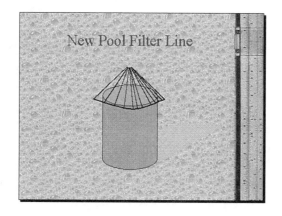

▶ See "Design Issues," **p. 310**

TROUBLESHOOTING

I drew a new object on my slide and now I can't see it. What happened? Check the default colors for the object's fill and line. These are shown under the paint bucket and paintbrush icons on the Drawing toolbar. If they're set to the same color as the background or object behind the object you drew, it will seem to be invisible. Select the object and apply a different fill or line color to make it visible again.

I changed the background of the Risk template on my slide to marble, but I don't like it. How do I get back the original background? To return the background of slides to the one dictated by the design template, choose Format, Background. In the Background dialog box, select Automatic from the drop-down field, then choose either Apply To All or Apply.

 I added a fill effect to an object, but now I can't read the text in the text box I placed there. You may need to change the text color to stand out against any new object fill. Select the text, then choose the Font Color tool on the Drawing toolbar. Select a different color. If your fill effect is very dark, try white or gray for your letters. If the fill in your object is lighter, black or dark gray letters might be best. If you can represent color in your presentation output, a bright yellow or red can sometimes do the trick.

Working with Several Objects

When you are working with several objects , you may want to apply effects to more than one at once to save time. In addition, you may sometimes have to reorganize the order of objects in relation to one another, so that one appears in the front and others appear to fall behind it. The two PowerPoint features that enable you to manipulate objects this way are called Group and Order.

Part
III

Ch

7

Grouping Objects

You can group as many objects as you like together. Once grouped, the objects behave as though they were a single object; anything you do to that group of objects—moving, resizing, formatting with different line styles and fill colors, or any other modification—applies to all the objects in the group.

To group objects, select the first object, then hold down the Shift key while you click each successive object you want to add to the group. When you've chosen all the objects you want, choose Draw, Group. The many sets of resizing handles that appeared when all the objects were selected are gone, replaced by a single set of resizing handles surrounding the grouped object.

To ungroup the objects again so you can work with them individually, select the group, then choose Draw, Ungroup.

Changing the Order of Objects

To understand the concept of drawing order in PowerPoint, it helps to think of drawing objects as though they were pieces of sticky-back paper in various shapes and colors. If you put one of them on top of another, it covers it up wherever there's overlap between the two. The difference between drawing with "stickies" and drawing with PowerPoint is that PowerPoint lets you change the order of drawing objects quite easily. Figure 7.27 shows the same group of objects in two different drawing orders.

FIG. 7.27
Both the object and text box within it disappear behind the star when the order is reversed.

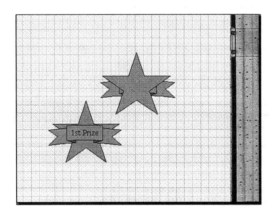

To change the order of an object, select it, then choose Draw, Order. A side menu offers four choices:

- *Bring to Front*. Brings the object to the top of the "stack" of objects on the slide. It draws atop all the other objects and covers up any that are beneath it.

- *Send to Back*. Sends the object to the bottom of the stack, putting it behind all the other objects on the slide. Any other object that overlaps it covers it up partially or fully.

- *Bring Forward*. Moves an object up one place in the stack. If you have only two objects overlapping, this places the object on top; however, if you have several objects on top of each other, this moves the selected object only one place forward in that stack.

- *Send Backward*. Sends an object back one place in the stack of objects.

These commands works on all kinds of objects, including text, drawings, and inserted objects like clip art.

▶ **See** "Adding Clip Art," **p. 172**

TROUBLESHOOTING

I accidentally moved a large object on top of a smaller one. I'd like to change their order, but when I click it, it just selects the larger object that's in front. How do I select an object that's behind another one? Use the Tab key. If you start with no objects selected, the Tab key successively selects each object in your slide, starting with the one furthest down in the stack. Each time you press Tab, the next object is selected. If it's a complex drawing and you don't want to take the time to work through the entire stack, select an object you know is behind the one you're after, then use the Tab key. It then starts with the object you've selected, rather than the bottommost object on the stack.

If you hold down the Shift key while you press Tab, PowerPoint moves downward through the stack rather than upward. In other words, you could select the large object that's in front of the object you want to select, then Shift+Tab until PowerPoint selects the object you want.

I have two objects and I don't want one to block the other; I want the text beneath to show through the top object somehow. How would I do that? Select a semitransparent fill effect for the top object. That would create a sheer effect that would allow the viewer to make out text in the object in back.

Part
III

Ch
7

Adding Ready-Made Art to Your Presentation

by Nancy Stevenson

Through two features, Clip Gallery and WordArt, Microsoft has built the ability to add a lot of visual impact into PowerPoint. These two features offer you already designed artwork and text effects that can make a slide really stand out. And the bonus is, they're both incredibly easy to use. ■

Add clip art to your slides

Clip art provides ready-made, professionally designed artwork for use in your presentation to make a point or add visual interest.

Import graphics files

You can import images stored in many common graphics file formats. If you find yourself using a particular graphic often, you can add your own graphics files to the Microsoft Clip Gallery, building your own storehouse of visual images.

Find additional clip art on the World Wide Web

By using Microsoft's online gallery of clip art, you can import additional images directly from the World Wide Web.

Use WordArt to create enhanced text effects

WordArt is a Microsoft applet built into PowerPoint that allows you to manipulate and enhance text to curve it, slant it, and even make it run vertically on a slide.

Adding Clip Art

Clip art is something that started out years ago as a service for graphic design companies. Designers would pay a yearly fee and receive a huge book of designs they could literally clip out and copy or paste into advertising or promotional designs.

With the prevalence of computer design programs, clip art has turned into a term for collections of graphics files that you can use as you please, once you've paid for the collection itself. Microsoft has built a gallery of clip art images into Clip Gallery, so you have your own collection of artwork already available. Using this artwork in selected slides in your presentation can help you make a point, add humor, or simply make your presentation more visually interesting to your viewers.

N O T E   You can purchase additional collections of clip art from a variety of companies. These collections are always being updated and added to. Because Microsoft's clip art is free, you'll notice a lot of it around you—on club newsletters and school handouts, for example. If you want a unique look for your presentation, you might consider investing in a second collection. Browse through any desktop publishing magazine to find ads for these. You can also find clip art collections at most large computer stores or mail-order computer retailers.

New to PowerPoint 97 is the capability to browse the World Wide Web for clip art directly from PowerPoint. It can even take you right to a Web page where Microsoft makes updated clips available for you to download. ▪

Adding a Clip Art Object

You can add clip art in two ways:

- ■ If you select a page layout with a clip art placeholder, you can simply double-click that placeholder to open the Clip Gallery.

- ■ If you are using a layout without a clip art placeholder, you can insert clip art anywhere by using the Insert Clip Art button on the toolbar, or by choosing Insert Picture, Clip Art.

The Clip Gallery, shown in Figure 8.1, appears.

This dialog box has only a few basic choices to make:

- ■ On the left side, you can choose a category of clip art such as Animals or Sports & Leisure. If you're not sure which category you need, select All Categories.

■ You can edit categories to delete them, rename them, or add new categories by clicking the Edit Categories button. When you do, the dialog box shown in Figure 8.2 appears.

FIG. 8.1

The Clip Gallery contains not only clip art but sounds, pictures, and videos as well.

Categories

Preview of clips in selected category

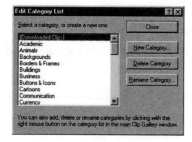

Connect to the Web for additional clips

Import Clips

FIG. 8.2

The choices here are simple: create a New Category, Delete a Category, or Rename it.

 T I P You can also perform these functions from the Clip Gallery; right-click any category name in the category list and select the Add, Delete, or Rename commands from the shortcut menu that appears.

■ In the middle of the Clip Gallery dialog box is a preview of all the clip art in the selected category. You can use the scroll bar here to see more choices. The currently selected item is surrounded by a box.

■ You can modify the Clip Gallery using the Import Clips or Connect to Web for Additional Clips buttons.

■ You can view details about each clip by choosing the Clip Properties button. This displays the dialog box shown in Figure 8.3.

FIG. 8.3
Find out about the file type, size, location, and category in the Clip Properties dialog box.

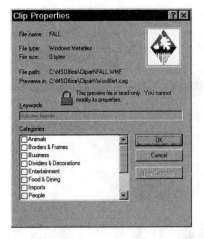

N O T E Notice that the clip shown in the preceding figure—and in fact, any clips that run from your CD—are read-only. That means that you can't change their categories or keywords. However, if you place your own clips in the gallery or install additional clip art onto your disk, you can use this dialog box to modify their properties by adding a keyword or changing their category. ▨

To place a clip art file on your slide, select it in the preview area of the Clip Gallery, then choose Insert. The image appears on your slide as in Figure 8.4 and it becomes part of your presentation file.

FIG. 8.4
A clip art image can help your viewer remember a key point.

Using AutoClipArt

As if using the Clip Gallery isn't easy enough, Microsoft has also built in a feature called AutoClipArt. AutoClipArt searches the text of your presentation to find matches to clip art files and categories. It then suggests appropriate art to add to your presentation. You can assign keywords to your clips in the Clip Properties dialog box shown in Figure 8.3 to make the AutoClipArt search even more customized.

N O T E   If there is no match to the concepts and terms in your presentation, you get a dialog box telling you so and suggesting you browse through the Clip Gallery to find an appropriate image. ■

You start the AutoClipArt feature by choosing Tools, AutoClipArt. PowerPoint runs a match to concepts and words in your presentation. If it finds a match, it displays the dialog box shown in Figure 8.5.

FIG. 8.5
Suggestions of appropriate clip art help you focus on the best clip art files for your uses.

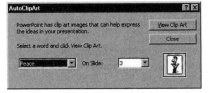

Editing Clip Art

Once you've placed a clip art image into a presentation, it is almost exactly the same as a group of drawing objects. You can move it, resize it, recolor it, and format it. The only difference is that it remembers it came from the Clip Gallery. If you double-click it, you return to the gallery, where you can choose a different image if you like.

Ungroup the clip art, and it becomes just like any group of drawing objects that you can manipulate using any of PowerPoint's tools. Just remember that ungrouping a clip art object breaks the link to the Clip Gallery. And in case you forget, PowerPoint shows you a warning message when you ungroup a clip art object. If you mistakenly ungroup a clip art object, immediately choose Edit, Undo, Ungroup Object or press Ctrl+Z.

▶ See "Editing Clip Art," **p. 175**

To edit a clip art object, select it. Then, use any of the following procedures:

- ■ To resize the object, drag on any of the eight resizing handles that surround it.
- ■ To convert the clip art into separate drawing objects so you can manipulate them individually, choose Draw, Ungroup.

■ To copy a clip art object, choose Edit, Copy, click the Copy button on the toolbar, or Ctrl+drag the object to where you want the copy to appear.

■ If you want to place the clip art in front of or behind other objects on your page, use the selections in the side menu of the Order command on the Draw menu or right-click the object, choose Order, then pick one of the Send To or Bring To options from the submenu.

 ■ To recolor the clip art, click the Recolor Picture button on the Picture toolbar.

When you select a clip art image, you also see a Picture toolbar, shown in Figure 8.6, that provides tools for modifying the format of the picture.

FIG. 8.6
You can use the same tools to manipulate clip art or ordinary PowerPoint drawings.

▶ **See** "Working with Drawing Objects," **p. 152**
▶ **See** "Using Color and Fill Effects," **p. 160**

The buttons on this toolbar have the functions described in Table 8.1.

Table 8.1 Picture Toolbar Functions

Button	Name	Function
	Insert Picture from File	Opens the insert Picture dialog box.
	Image Control	Contains settings for grayscale, B&W, and a Watermark effect.
	More Contrast	Adds contrast between colors in the image.
	Less Contrast	Lessens contrast between colors in the image.
	More Brightness	Lightens colors in the image.
	Less Brightness	Darkens colors in the image.
	Crop	Provides a tool to crop the picture.

Button	Name	Function
	Line Style	Provides menu of line styles for a border.
	Recolor Picture	Opens the Recolor Picture dialog box, allowing you to edit colors of fills and outlines.
	Format Picture	Opens the Format Picture dialog box where you can change fill color, line style, size, position, cropping, and image control centrally.
	Set Transparent Color	Allows you to make colors transparent in bitmap images.
	Reset Picture	Returns picture to original settings.

The Format Object button on this toolbar is only one way to get to the multi-purpose Format Picture dialog box shown in Figure 8.7. You can also choose Format, Picture or right-click the picture and select Format Picture from the shortcut menu that appears. The settings you can use on these tabs are identical to those discussed for drawing objects in Chapter 6.

FIG. 8.7
You can determine attributes like fill color, line, arrows, size, and position all from this central location.

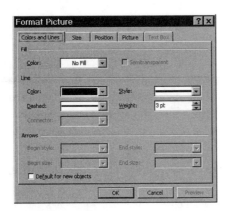

▶ **See** "Postioning Objects," **p. 144**
▶ **See** "Editing Clip Art," **p. 175**

Some of these picture effects are shown in Figure 8.8.

FIG. 8.8
A variety of effects can subtly change clip and other art images.

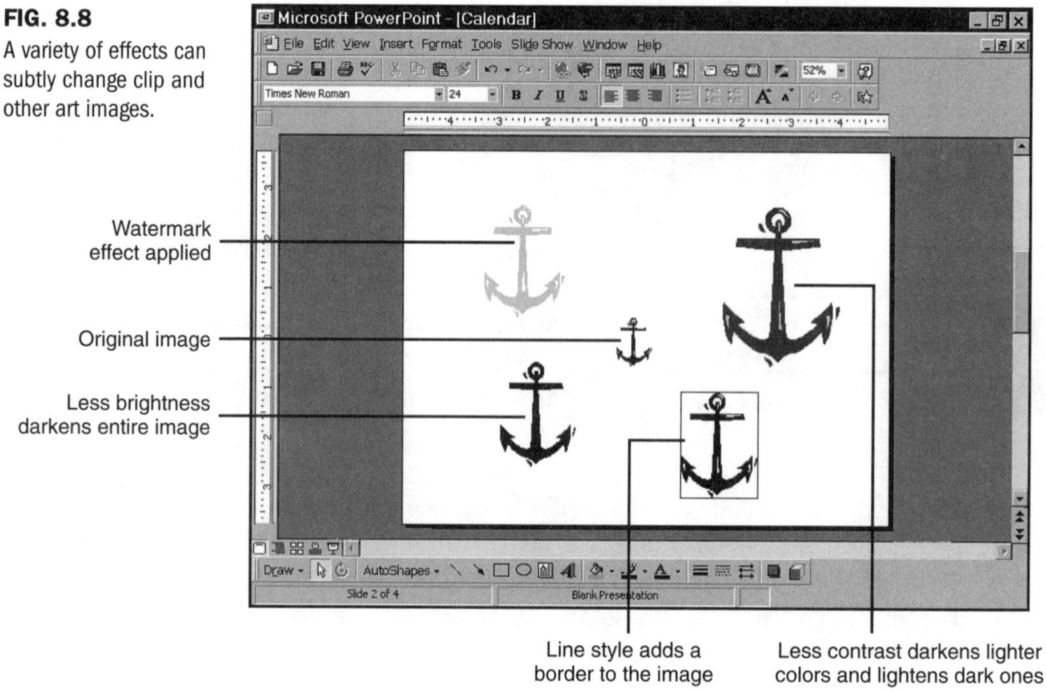

Watermark effect applied

Original image

Less brightness darkens entire image

Line style adds a border to the image

Less contrast darkens lighter colors and lightens dark ones

 TROUBLESHOOTING

I applied the watermark style to my clip art, but it blocks the text I put it near. Watermark is a style that produces a faint image of your artwork, much like the watermark that appears on fine writing paper. This style is typically used as a background element. However, even though it's pale, a watermark is still solid, so it will block other objects on your slide. Select it, then choose D**r**aw, **O**rder, and select Send to Bac**k**.

 I placed a clip art animal object on my slide, because it's our school mascot. Now I want to put the name of our school on it. How would I do that? You can use the Text Box tool on the Drawing toolbar to add text to any clip art object. Simply choose the tool and place your cursor anywhere over the clip art and click. The text box opens, ready for you to enter text. Hint—if you want to keep the text and clip art object together, don't forget to use the Group feature on the Drawing toolbar to make them one object.

Modifying the Clip Gallery

You can add images to the Clip Gallery, create new categories of images, and move images among categories. You can place almost any graphics file in the gallery because

Microsoft has provided filters to support a variety of graphics file formats. You can even import graphics files from the Internet.

▶ **See** "A Word About Animation," **p. 188**

▶ **See** "Adding Animation Effects," **p. 194**

Part

III

Ch

8

Adding Graphics to the Clip Gallery

The Clip Gallery comes loaded with files you can use in your presentations. However, it's likely that, as you use PowerPoint more and more, you will want to add other graphics files. You can add files such as a company logo to your Clip Gallery by simply opening them from within the gallery itself.

Follow these steps to place a file in the Clip Gallery:

1. Open the Clip Gallery by choosing the Insert Clip Gallery button, or by choosing Insert, Picture, Clip Art.

2. Click the Import Clips button. The dialog box in Figure 8.9 appears.

FIG. 8.9
Use this dialog box to browse for files to add to the Clip Gallery.

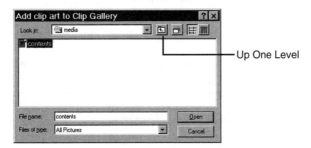

Up One Level

3. Use the Look In field, in combination with the Up One Level button to locate the file you want to import.

4. Make sure you've selected the specific type of graphics file format for the file you are importing in the Files of Type field.

You can also select All Pictures in the Files of Type field to display all graphics file formats that PowerPoint accommodates. Microsoft has built-in filters for most graphics file formats, such as JPEG, EPS, GIF, and so on. You can see the list of available formats in the Files of Type list.

If you want to import an entire package of Microsoft clip art from a CD or disk, select Clip Gallery Packages from the Files of Type list.

5. When you've located the file you want to import, choose Open. A message appears for a moment telling you the file is being imported.

6. The Clip Properties dialog box (see Figure 8.10) appears.

FIG. 8.10
This dialog box tells you the file type, size, and path name.

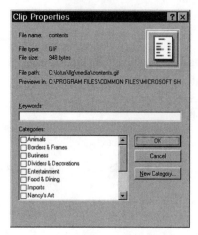

7. You can select as many categories as you like in which to place the image's preview.

 You can also create a category of your own by clicking the New Category button, which opens a small dialog box with a single field where you type the name of the category.

8. You can type Keywords which can help you search for the clip in the future.

9. When you've selected a category or categories and entered any keywords, choose OK.

You return to the Clip Gallery dialog box, where a preview of the newly imported art will be available in the category or categories you designated.

 The Clip Gallery will sometimes import files that PowerPoint itself won't. If PowerPoint won't import a graphics file when you choose Insert, Picture, From File, try bringing it through Clip Gallery.

Importing a Graphics File from the Internet

Microsoft has also provided an online source of additional clip art on the World Wide Web called Clip Gallery Live.

To access Clip Gallery Live, you need two things:

- Access to the Internet
- A Web browser

If you don't have either of these in place, they are built into Windows 95 in the form of The Microsoft Network (MSN) online service and Internet Explorer browser. If you decide to use MSN, and you don't already have an MSN account, you have to sign up for one. Whether you use MSN or another method of connecting to the Internet, you must still set up Internet Explorer to use the appropriate account if you want to use it. From within Internet Explorer (represented by an Internet icon on your Windows desktop), choose View, Options to make these settings.

Once you have set up an online account and a browser, you're ready to access Clip Gallery Live. To import a file from Clip Gallery Live:

1. Open the Clip Gallery. Notice there is a button in the lower-right hand corner called Connect to Web for Additional Clips. When you click this button, you see a message telling you that if you have access to the World Wide Web, you can import clips from there. Simply choose OK to proceed.

CAUTION

Depending on your Web browser and how you have it configured, you may need to manually connect to the Internet before you click OK. Not all configurations will automatically dial and connect for you.

2. PowerPoint opens up your browser, and connects to the gallery. Once you're there, read the agreement, then click Accept. The gallery then shows you several buttons that let you choose the type of clip you'd like to add.

3. Use the list box below to pick the category you want.

4. Click Go, and a list of available clips appears on the left side of your browser, complete with previews.

5. Click the file name beneath the clip you want; it is immediately downloaded and added to your own Clip Gallery category—keywords and all.

 You can use the Clip Gallery to insert graphics, sounds, and media into nearly any Windows program. You're not limited to using it with PowerPoint and the other Office programs. Choose Insert, Object or Edit, Insert Object in your other programs, then choose Microsoft Clip Gallery. From that point, you can use the Gallery just as you would from within PowerPoint. The same is true of the other applets (Graph, Word Art, and so on).

Creating WordArt Objects

WordArt is a small application (or applet) that comes with several Microsoft products, including PowerPoint. WordArt is one of the easiest to use features of PowerPoint, but it allows you to add exciting special effects to the text in your presentation. These effects include styles such as curved or vertically oriented text. WordArt styles work very well on headings or words in your presentation that require strong emphasis, such as the word "Free" in a product offer.

Choosing a WordArt Style

You can open up WordArt in one of two ways:

- Select Insert, Picture, WordArt
- Choose the WordArt button on the Drawing toolbar

The WordArt Gallery dialog box shown in Figure 8.11 appears, offering you a choice of WordArt styles.

FIG. 8.11
Each style choice is previewed for you in the WordArt Gallery.

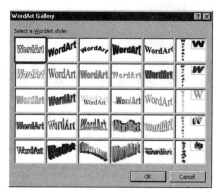

All the choices in the far right column are vertical choices. Any of these will display your text from top to bottom of your slide, using the text style shown in the representative letter "W" in these previews. Other choices add effects ranging from curved text to text with shadow or gradient effects.

Entering Text

Click a style to select it, then choose OK. The Edit WordArt Text dialog box in Figure 8.12 appears, allowing you to enter the text you want to format in the selected WordArt style.

FIG. 8.12
Whatever text you enter here is formatted in the WordArt style you chose in the previous dialog box.

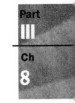

Type the text you want to use as WordArt. Although each WordArt style has a certain font, font size, and effects like Bold or Italic applied to it already, you can use the drop-down lists and buttons in this dialog box to change those settings, if you like. When you've added your settings, choose OK to see the WordArt object on your slide.

The WordArt toolbar

The WordArt object has resizing handles around it, just as drawing objects and clip art objects do (see Figure 8.13). Also, a WordArt toolbar appears whenever the WordArt object is selected.

FIG. 8.13
Use WordArt styles to add punch to important points in your presentation.

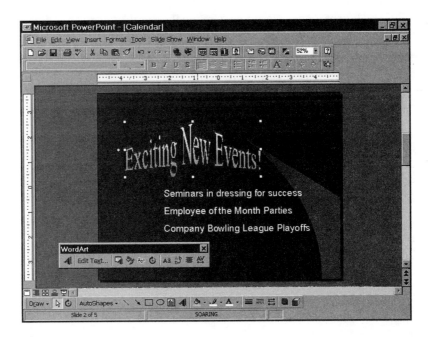

▶ **See** "Working with Drawing Objects," **p. 139**

The WordArt toolbar contains the following buttons:

  ■ Inserts a new WordArt object.

  ■ Edit Text opens the Edit WordArt Text dialog box.

  ■ WordArt Gallery opens the WordArt Gallery.

  ■ Format WordArt opens the Format WordArt dialog box so you can edit colors, lines, size, and position of the object.

  ■ WordArt Shape opens the pop-up collection of styles shown in Figure 8.14 so you can select a new shape for the object.

FIG. 8.14
Change shapes of your WordArt easily at any time using this pop-up palette of shapes.

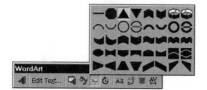

  ■ Free Rotate allows you to rotate the WordArt object 360 degrees on your slide.

  ■ WordArt Same Letter Heights makes all the letters in the object proportionally the same (see Figure 8.15).

  ■ WordArt Vertical Text converts any WordArt style so that it runs vertically down your slide.

  ■ WordArt Alignment offers a pop-up menu so you can align the object left, center, right or justified, and so forth.

■ WordArt Character Spacing produces a pop-up menu of choices for adjusting spacing between the letters of your WordArt object from very tight to very loose. The two extremes of spacing are shown in Figure 8.15. If you click Kern Character Pairs, WordArt improves the appearance of character pairs like "AV" and "WA" by removing a little of the excess space between them.

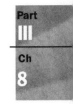

FIG. 8.15
The same WordArt appears with different effects applied.

Very tight character spacing

Very loose character spacing

WordArt Same Letter Heights applied

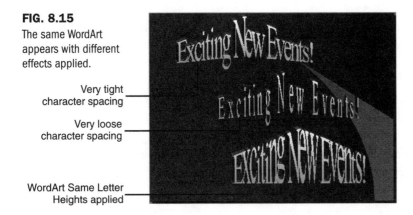

Editing WordArt

 The Format Object button on the WordArt toolbar opens the dialog box shown in Figure 8.16. Here you can make a variety of formatting changes to the object.

FIG. 8.16
Three of the tabs in this Format dialog box are available for WordArt objects.

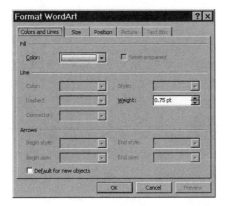

 T I P You can also open this dialog box by choosing Format, WordArt, or by right-clicking the object and selecting Format WordArt from the shortcut menu that appears.

A few of the options on the tabs of this dialog box are accessible through other means, but the additional settings here allow you to be more precise:

- To rotate WordArt, you can use the Free Rotate tool on the toolbar or select the Size tab of the Format WordArt dialog box to enter a specific angle of rotation.

■ You can move a WordArt object by clicking and dragging it with your mouse, or you can enter an exact location by entering that location relative to the edges or center of the slide on the Position tab of the Format WordArt dialog box.

■ You can use resizing handles to change the size of the WordArt object by dragging a handle inward or outward, or you can use the Height and Width settings on the Size tab of the Format WordArt dialog box.

 If you want to resize an object and not retain its original proportions, you can drag on a top or side resizing handle or change the Scale of the object on the Size tab of the Format WordArt dialog box.

The Format WordArt dialog box is the only place where you can adjust the fill color for objects. You do this by selecting a new color in the drop-down palette in Fill section of the Colors and Lines tab. ●

CHAPTER 9

Adding Animation and Sound

by Nancy Stevenson

In this age of multimedia, PowerPoint has kept pace by adding exciting and easy-to-use features for animating objects in your presentation. With these features, you can control special effects that occur when objects appear during an on-screen slide show. You can add sound and animation effects that run when you click an object, or place Action Buttons in your presentation that can take your viewer onto the Internet with a single click.

These capabilities allow a speaker to add interest to a presentation, but they really shine in an interactive setting, such as a trade show booth presentation, where viewers themselves can cause sounds to play, run animations, and navigate to related information. ■

Add action buttons to presentations

Action buttons add instant animation to your presentation and are an invaluable aid to interactive presentations.

Use Action Settings

Action Settings can be associated with any object in your presentation, allowing you to play sounds, run movies, and even jump to another presentation with the click of a mouse.

Assign animation effects

The Animation Effects toolbar allows you to instantly add animation effects to the way objects appear on screen in a slide show.

A Word About Animation

This version of PowerPoint features four principal kinds of animation effects:

- *Action Objects.* Active regions of the screen which perform some kind of action when "activated." This is a completely new feature and is the focus of this chapter.

- *Animation Effects.* Motion effects that cause screen objects like buttons, text, and clip art to move on and off the screen. These effects are discussed in this chapter as well.

- *Transitions.* Effects to text and slides that occur on cue, such as when going to a new slide. This is discussed in Chapter 15.

- *Video Clips.* Played within a PowerPoint slide on cue. This is discussed in Chapter 23.

All these animation possibilities bring up the question of general guidelines on using animation in a presentation.

As with other effects, such as WordArt, clip art, and fancy font and text stylings, you can easily go overboard. Animations are fun to watch, and sounds can be clever and elicit a laugh from your viewers. But beware: the same sound clip that made people laugh on first occurrence causes only a smile the second time, and on the third playing, becomes an annoyance. The animation that so brilliantly reinforces your point when you preview it on your networked desktop computer may play slowly and prove distracting on the stand-alone PC at the trade show.

The bottom line is that you should use animation and sound sparingly; use these effects to make a special point, not every point. You should be alert to whether these effects run slowly because of hardware limitations. You also need to be aware of the timing that these effects have, so that you can pace your presentation to accommodate them.

▶ **See** "Transitions and Timing," **p. 331**

With those guidelines stated, let's take a look at some of the features of PowerPoint that you'll have the most fun with: Action Buttons, Action Settings, and Animation Effects.

N O T E   All the settings described in this chapter only work with on-screen presentations; if you want sounds or animation to play with a 35mm slide show or overhead version of the presentation, you have to dig out your tape recorder and hand puppets! ◼

Using Action Buttons

Action buttons are objects you can place on a slide for the express purpose of providing an action that the speaker or viewer may take. For example, a right-facing arrow button can be clicked to move to the next slide in your presentation. An action button with a house symbol on it can be placed on a slide; when you or a viewer clicks it, it can take you to your corporate home page on the World Wide Web.

▶ **See** "Creating Presentations Destined for the Internet," **p. 414**

There are two steps necessary to create an action button: add a button to the slide from the menu, and apply action settings to give it life.

Creating an Action Button

The essence of an action button is to perform some service—such as play a sound, start an application, move to another slide, or enter the Internet—while inside PowerPoint and viewing a presentation. The possible actions include:

- Moving to another location, such as another slide in the presentation, another presentation, a World Wide Web site, or another file.
- Running a different program; for example, you might want to open up Microsoft Outlook to look at a detailed schedule while discussing a project timeline.
- Executing a macro you've created with PowerPoint's Macro Recorder.
- Opening, playing, or editing an object that's embedded in your presentation.
- Playing a sound file. You might, for example, want to play a sound clip of applause when one of your viewers correctly answers a question you've posed.

▶ **See** "Linking Data with OLE," **p. 218**
▶ **See** "Using the Macro Recorder," **p. 488**

Twelve action button styles are available for you to choose from. You get to these by choosing Slide Show, Action Buttons. The side menu shown in Figure 9.1 appears.

 TIP If you plan to add many action buttons to a presentation, you can detach it from the menu and leave it out for later use. Drag the Action Button submenu by its title bar and place it elsewhere on the screen.

These buttons act like drawing tools. When you click one, your cursor turns into a crosshair. You can then simply click anywhere on your slide to place the button at default size, or click and drag to draw your button on your slide.

FIG. 9.1
Eleven button designs
and one blank custom
button are offered in
this side menu.

Formatting Action Buttons Action buttons can be formatted just like ordinary drawing
objects. Click on an action button, and the Format Picture toolbar becomes available.
Click the Format AutoShape tool, and you have several options available:

- Change the color and background of the button. You can render a picture or texture
  behind the button, for instance, or click the Semitransparent button to make the
  button more subtle.

- Change the outline of the button to thicker or dotted lines.

- Change the size or position of a button precisely.

▶ **See** "Working with Drawing Objects," **p. 152**

In addition to the format controls offered by the Format Picture toolbar, you can change
the appearance of action buttons in one other important way. Each of the buttons has a
configurable bevel style. To change the appearance of this bevel, add a button to the
screen and follow these steps:

1. Click the action button to select it. Drag boxes appear around it, and a small yellow
   diamond appears at the top left of the button.

2. Click the diamond and hold the mouse button. Drag the diamond to the left or right.

3. As you drag the diamond, notice that the outline of the bevel changes. Release the
   mouse when you have achieved the degree of bevel you want. Note that the intensity of bevel varies between none (a rectangle) and 50 percent of the total button
   size.

When you have drawn the action button, an Action Settings dialog box appears automatically, allowing you to associate a specific action with the button.

Making Action Button Settings

The Action Settings dialog box, shown in Figure 9.2, has two tabs with identical options:

- *Mouse Click*. Actions assigned via this tab occur when a user clicks directly on the button.

- *Mouse Over*. Actions assigned via this tab occur when the mouse pointer moves over the button—no mouse click is required.

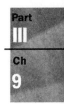

Part

III

Ch

9

FIG. 9.2
Make settings for action buttons on one or both of these tabs.

You can configure each of these tabs separately so that you could perform two independent actions using one action button: one that occurs when you pass your mouse over it, and one that occurs when you click the mouse.

The settings in each tab are the same. They are:

- If you want no action associated with the button, choose the None radio button. It prevents any of the actions except sounds from occurring; you can still play a sound via the button with this option selected.

- To associate a location to the button, click the Hyperlink To radio button and select one of the options in the drop-down list, shown in Figure 9.3. When the action button is clicked during the presentation, you move to the location selected from the Hyperlink To drop-down list.

T I P

To avoid getting "stranded" in a hyperlinked location, it is a good idea to place a complementary button in the new location so you can easily return to where you started.

FIG. 9.3

The choices for places to "jump" to using a hyperlink are many.

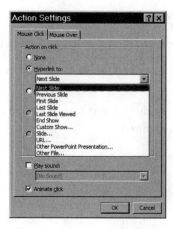

- To run a program other than PowerPoint from within your presentation, click the Run Program radio button and use the Browse button to locate the program's executable file.

- To run a macro, choose the Run Macro radio button and select a macro from the drop-down list.

- To associate an object action with your object, check the Object Action radio button and select an appropriate action from the drop-down list.

- If you'd like the button to play a sound clip, choose the Play Sound check box. Several sound files such as applause, ricochet, and screeching brakes are already available to you in the drop-down list. You can also use this option to stop a sound that is already playing. If you want to use a sound clip of your own or search the Web for a clip, select Other Sound from this list to get to an Add Sound dialog box (see Figure 9.4).

 Each button can only perform one action per click or mouse over. One button, for instance, cannot simultaneously launch a macro and jump to a hyperlink. Sounds, however, can be combined with any of those actions as desired.

 Large sound files can cause the effect to pause as it loads from disk. You can avoid that delay by clicking the buttons before the presentation, which loads the sounds into memory. The next time they're played, they load much more quickly.

- Choosing the Highlight Click check box at the bottom of the Mouse Click sheet or Highlight When Mouse Over on the Mouse Over tab makes the action button appear depressed when activated, like a button you push on a keypad.

FIG. 9.4
Office has many new
sound clips built in, or
you can locate any
sound file you like
from this dialog box.

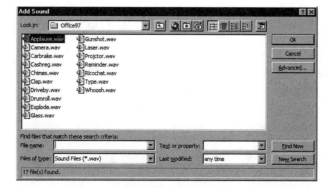

When you're finished adjusting settings to one or both tabs, choose OK to apply them to the action button.

If you want to edit these settings at a later time, select the action button, then choose Slide Show, Action Settings to display this dialog box again.

TROUBLESHOOTING

The option to run a macro from the action button is ghosted. Why? You must have at least one PowerPoint macro already created for this option to be available. If it isn't, choose Tools, Macro to create a macro script, and then try the Action Button dialog box again.

The option to associate an object action is ghosted. Why? This option only works on OLE objects that you have added to a presentation. In this way, for instance, you can click an embedded Excel spreadsheet to launch Excel and edit the data. You must first insert an appropriate OLE object and use this option on it; it will always be ghosted for action buttons.

I had associated a link to a file with an action button, but it doesn't seem to work anymore. What would cause that? The file you associated with the button may have been deleted, renamed, or moved to another location. Review the action settings for the object to make sure the path for the file is correct. If you are taking the presentation on the road, don't forget to load any programs or files you've associated with action buttons onto the presentation computer.

 You can reach the Action Settings dialog box by clicking the right mouse button over the desired button object.

 To see how the action button works, enter the slide show by choosing Slide Show, View Show. Navigate to the slide where the button is located, and either click the button or pass your mouse over it to test its action.

Assigning Action Settings to Other Objects

You can use the same settings from the Action Settings dialog box discussed in the previous section on any object in your presentation. Simply select the object (such as a piece of clip art or even title text) and choose Slide Show, Action Settings. The Action Settings dialog box appears. Again, you can associate two actions per object: one that occurs when you pass your mouse over the object, and one that occurs when you click the object.

> **CAUTION**
>
> Be careful when assigning Mouse Over actions. Several on a page could trigger unwanted actions at your slightest movement and make you lose control of the effects. It's also a good idea to create a play sheet for yourself so you can remember what objects perform which actions, and when. This is especially important when you are preparing an on-screen show that someone else may present.

Frequently, you may need to set up an autonomous, interactive presentation, such as at a trade show or kiosk. If you have such a show that will be running without the benefit of a presenter, there are a few things to keep in mind:

- It is more intuitive for the viewer if you associate actions with action buttons. They are more recognizable as event triggers than clip art, text, or other common objects.
- Mouse Over actions are less discoverable and can surprise the viewer, so use them sparingly and only when necessary.
- Ensure the purpose of your buttons are understandable to a novice viewer before they are clicked. Graphical buttons may look attractive but don't convey the object's intent without a caption or explanatory text.

Adding Animation Effects

One final multimedia setting you can make to objects in your slide show is an animation effect. An *animation effect* is a motion effect that determines how an element appears on your slide during a presentation. Objects can appear to fly on-screen, to drop in from the top of the screen, or to seem to be typed on the page as with a typewriter.

These effects can be used in combination with Action Settings, so that you can cause the title of a slide to fly on from the side of the screen, while a screeching brake sound clip plays. This ability to combine actions and animation effects can make for a very dynamic presentation.

The Animation Effects Toolbar

 To add animation effects, select an object on your slide, then choose Slide Show, Preset Animation. Alternately, you can click the Animation Effects button on the toolbar. The floating toolbar shown in Figure 9.5 appears.

TIP You can also display the Animation toolbar by choosing View, Toolbar, Animation Effects.

Part

III

Ch

9

FIG. 9.5
The Animation Effects toolbar lets you select animation effects and order in which it occurs on-screen.

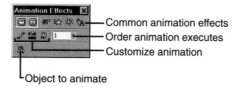

Common animation effects

Order animation executes

Customize animation

Object to animate

TROUBLESHOOTING

I selected a clip art object and the Animation Effects toolbar I get looks different from the one you show. Why? This toolbar will be somewhat different depending on the type of object you have selected. That's because some of these tools work only with text objects, so if a non-text object is selected, those tools aren't available.

Table 9.1 describes the functions of the various tools in the Animation Effects toolbar.

Table 9.1   Animation Effects Tools

Button	Function
	Animate title
	Animate slide text
	Drive-in
	Flying
	Camera

continues

Table 9.1   Continued

Button	Function
	Flash Once
	Laser Text
	Typewriter Text
	Reverse Text Order
	Drop-In
	Animation Order
	Custom Animation

The name of each of the Animation Effects tools is descriptive of the effect itself. Because these can't be demonstrated in a book, give each one a try for yourself to see exactly how they work. The Animation Order drop-down list tool in the Animation Effects toolbar shows the number of animated objects on the currently displayed slide, and the order in which they appear on your screen. The Custom Animation tool takes you to the Custom Animation dialog box, where you can change the order of animation effects and make more refined settings for how your slides display.

▶ **See** "Working with Text Preset Animation," **p. 340**

Applying Animation Effects

To apply one of the effects in the Animation Effects toolbar to the object you have selected, simply click the effect tool you prefer. You can select different objects on your slide with the Animation Effects toolbar displayed and make settings to as many as you like. The objects are animated in the order in which you have applied the effects, but that can be changed in the Custom Animation dialog box (discussed in detail in Chapter 15).

Switch to Slide Show view and click with the left mouse button anywhere on the screen. The first animated object appears. With bulleted lists, each mouse click adds another bullet point. When all objects have appeared, your next mouse click displays the next slide in sequence.

> **N O T E** Once again, it's important to find a method to keep track of all of these effects, so you don't click and move to another slide when you thought there was one more item to display on the current slide. ■

To remove an animation effect from an object, select the object, then choose Slide Show, Custom Animation. In the dialog box that appears (see Figure 9.6), select the Effects tab from the lower half of the box. In the drop-down list of available titles for Entry Animation and Sound, select No Effect.

> **N O T E** The Preset Animations only scratch the surface of what is possible with motion animation effects. Significantly more flexible is the Custom Animation controls discussed in detail in Chapter 15. You can find the custom animation dialog box by selecting an object and choosing Slide Show, Custom Animation. This dialog box lets you affect such characteristics as:
>
> • *Timing.* The objects can animate on mouse clicks or after a specified period of time.
>
> • *Effects.* Choose from a variety of effects (Dissolve, Blinds, Fly-ins, and more) and accompanying sounds.
>
> • *Chart Effects.* Specify the way a chart appears, such as one bar at a time. ■

FIG. 9.6
The Custom Animation dialog box provides greater control over animation settings.

P A R T

IV

PowerPoint Charts and Tables

CHAPTER 10

Creating a Chart

by Edward Willett

There's nothing more intimidating for someone viewing a presentation than endless lists of figures. One or two slides like that, and eyes start to glaze over or stray to wristwatches. The best way to keep all eyes on your presentation is to turn those numbers into a chart. Not only will you keep your viewers' interest, but you'll also heighten their understanding and your own of the relationships among those numbers. Charts bring dull data to life. ■

Create a chart

PowerPoint lets you create many different types of charts, ensuring that you can always find the perfect way to present complex data in an informative, graphical style.

Create a datasheet

A chart is only as good as the information it contains. Learn how to enter your data into a chart and import and link to data from other applications.

Edit data

Things change. Fortunately, so will your chart, easily and automatically, as you edit the data in your datasheet.

How Charts Work

Charts are visual metaphors. In words, you might say, "Think of our total expenditures as a giant pie. The largest slice of the pie is salaries…" A pie chart makes that metaphor visible and, in the process, makes it more easily understood. This is demonstrated in Figures 10.1 and 10.2.

FIG. 10.1

Data presented solely with text tends to be dull and not immediately understandable to the viewer.

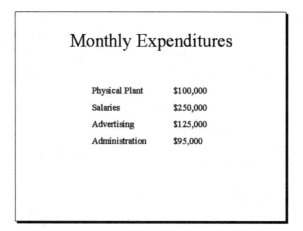

Monthly Expenditures

Physical Plant	$100,000
Salaries	$250,000
Advertising	$125,000
Administration	$95,000

FIG. 10.2

Using a chart to present data helps to illustrate data relationships and is also more visually appealing.

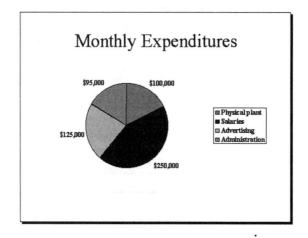

Monthly Expenditures

In order to make effective use of charts, though, you need to have a firm grasp on the data you want to present, and why you are presenting it.

Visualizing Data

Carefully consider your data. Different types of data call for different types of charts. For instance:

- Do the figures represent percentages? In that case, a pie chart might be the best bet.

- Do you want to demonstrate a trend in the data? Perhaps a line chart should be your first choice.

- Do you want to show how one set of figures compares to another over a period of time? For that, you'd probably turn to a bar chart.

Charts are such powerful visual metaphors that choosing the wrong type to display your data will only confuse your viewers and muddle your message.

Part
IV

Ch
10

Creating a Chart

 To add a chart to your presentation, choose <u>N</u>ew Slide from the Common Tasks toolbar, or click the New Slide button on the Standard toolbar, then choose an <u>A</u>utoLayout that contains a chart from the New Slide dialog box. This will give you a slide with a placeholder where the chart will be placed (see Figure 10.3). The placeholder shows an Insert Chart icon and the words `Double click to add chart`.

FIG. 10.3
If you choose an AutoLayout format that contains a chart, you'll see this placeholder. Just double-click the icon to add a chart to the slide.

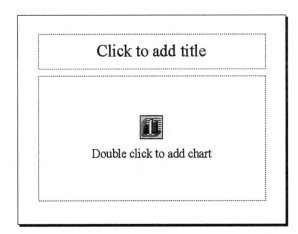

Double-clicking the Insert Chart icon activates Microsoft Graph, a special chart-creating applet (a small program separate from PowerPoint dedicated to one particular task). You will notice two items—a sample bar chart and a datasheet (which looks like a miniature spreadsheet) containing the data the bar chart illustrates (see Figure 10.4).

FIG. 10.4
This chart and datasheet, complete with sample information, appears any time you insert a chart into PowerPoint.

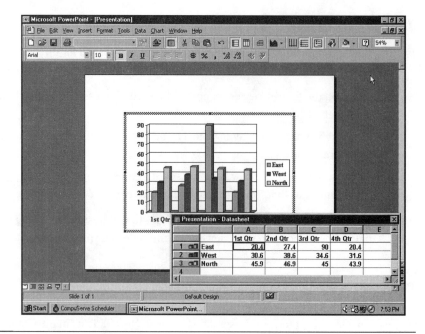

 TIP   If you want to add a chart to an existing slide, just click the Insert Chart button. This inserts the same sample bar chart and data sheet that appears when you select an AutoLayout slide that contains a chart.

Selecting a Chart Type

To immediately change the sample chart you've just inserted to another type:

1. Choose Chart, Chart Type. You are presented with the Chart Type dialog box in Figure 10.5.

2. Select the type of chart you want from the Chart Type list on the left. The available variants of the selected type appear in the Chart Sub-Type area on the right.

3. Select the variant you want. A chart sub-type name and sometimes additional information about it appears in the message area below the variants.

4. To see what your chart looks like with the new chart type applied, click Press and Hold to View Sample.

5. If you would like PowerPoint to automatically create this new chart type whenever you insert a chart, click Set As Default Chart.

6. If you're satisfied with your selection, click OK. Your chart changes to the new type.

FIG. 10.5
The Chart Type dialog box presents you with all of the various charts PowerPoint makes available to users.

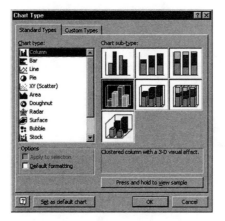

N O T E   Even though the new chart may look completely different from the old, it still uses the same data. No matter how many times you change the format of the chart, your data remains safely unchanged—so experiment at will! ■

You enter data differently into the datasheet to create different types of charts. The next section lists the standard types of charts that PowerPoint provides and indicates how data should be arranged in the datasheet to create them.

Standard Charts and Their Uses

PowerPoint provides 14 standard chart types to choose from. Each type of chart has several sub-types. In the order PowerPoint presents them, with an accompanying sample of each (all using the same data), they are:

Column   *Column charts* are particularly useful for comparing items or showing how values change over time—for example, comparing sales at three different stores over a one-year period. Categories (quarterly sales periods) are listed along the bottom and values (sales figures) along the side, as in Figure 10.6. One of the sub-types you can choose—the final one listed—is a three-axis, 3-D column chart, shown in Figure 10.7. The third axis is called the series axis, and allows you to add another set of identifying labels—store location, for instance.

To create either of these charts, you would label the columns in your datasheet with the names of the categories (the four quarters) and the rows with the names of the data series (the three stores: East, West, and North). Then you would enter the appropriate values (sales figures) for each store for each quarter in the corresponding cells.

FIG. 10.6
This clustered column chart with a 3-D visual effect is the default chart PowerPoint creates whenever you insert a chart.

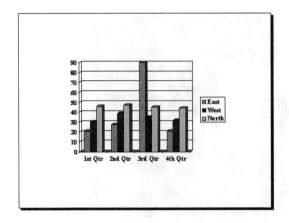

FIG. 10.7
The 3-D column chart adds an extra axis, the series axis, with an additional set of data labels.

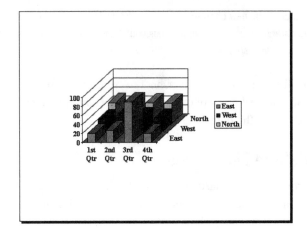

Bar A *bar chart* is similar to a column chart, but with the axes switched. It reads data from the data sheet the same way—rows are data series, columns are data categories—but in a bar chart, the categories appear along the side and the values at the bottom. If the chart shows changes over time, this places less emphasis on time and more on values.

Both column and bar charts can be stacked charts, such as the stacked bar chart in Figure 10.8 with 3-D visual effects. Stacked charts show how individual items relate to a larger whole. In this figure, for example, you can see how large a percentage of total company sales each store contributed.

FIG. 10.8
A 100 percent stacked bar chart with a 3-D visual effect shows the relationship of individual items to the whole.

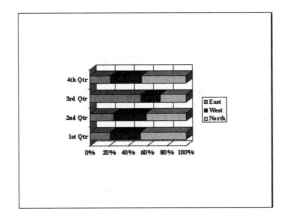

Part

IV

Ch

10

Line A *line chart*, such as the one in Figure 10.9, is usually used to show how values change over time. It's a good way to illustrate and emphasize trends— a trend toward lower or higher sales, for example. Like the column chart, it can be either two-dimensional, with only categories and values as the axes, or, by choosing the last sub-type offered, you can create a 3-D line chart, which includes a series axis.

The line chart, like the bar and column charts, reads columns on the datasheet as categories and rows as series.

FIG. 10.9
This line chart is well-suited to displaying a trend over time or categories.

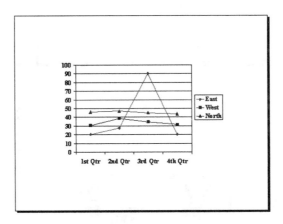

Pie A *pie chart* shows how much of the whole various items account for. It's a good way to emphasize one particular figure, because whichever item makes up the largest piece of the pie is the one people will notice. It's frequently used to illustrate "where your tax dollar is going" and similar information.

A pie chart displays less data than a bar, column, or line chart. It shows only categories and values for a single data series; so in Figure 10.10, although the same datasheet is being used as was used for the previous charts, the only values displayed are those that appeared in the first row. You would need an additional pie chart for each data series—each row of values in the datasheet—you wanted to display.

Two interesting sub-types of pie charts are the pie of pie and bar of pie charts; a pie of pie chart is shown in Figure 10.11. The pie of pie chart allows you to break down one slice of your pie into an additional pie chart. In this instance, it has used the first two values in the data series to represent the first two slices of the larger pie, then broken down the remaining portion of the pie into a small pie chart based on the remaining two values in the series.

FIG. 10.10

A pie chart is ideal for showing how various elements contribute to a whole.

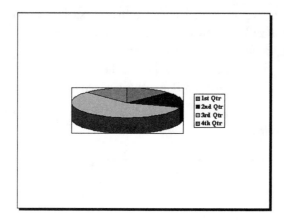

FIG. 10.11

A pie of pie chart allows you to show more detailed information about a particular interesting portion of your pie chart.

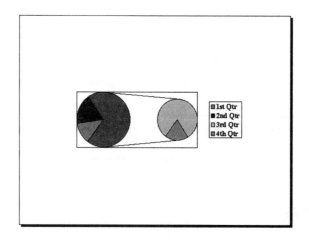

XY (Scatter)   An *XY (scatter) chart* (see Figure 10.12) is commonly used to plot scientific data—temperature and humidity readings, for example. Each point of data has two values: one assigned to the X, or horizontal, axis, and one assigned to the Y, or vertical, axis. The points may or may not be connected by lines.

Figure 10.12 graphically demonstrates the importance of using the right type of chart to best illustrate your data. The scatter chart reads the datasheet differently than any of the charts I've looked at so far. The top row, in which your category labels have been entered up until now, is where the XY chart looks for its X values. Because I'm using PowerPoint's default data in this chart, what it finds in that top row is 1st Qtr, 2nd Qtr, and so on. It's only looking for numbers, so it has changed those to values, 1, 2, 3, 4, and so on, which appear along the bottom, X axis. The values for each data series provide the Y values. In other words, the data you have in your datasheet at this point is totally unsuited to an XY (scatter) chart. Make sure you always use the right chart for the right task.

FIG. 10.12

The basic XY (scatter) chart shows only values as individual points. Other available Chart Sub-Types in the Chart Type dialog box connect the points in each data series with lines.

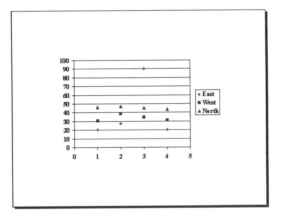

Area   The standard *area chart* is like a line chart with the area under the line filled in with a solid color, as you can see in Figure 10.13. Unlike a line chart, however, but like a bar or column chart, an area chart can be stacked, showing how several data series change over time and how they relate to each other and to a whole.

The area chart reads the datasheet the same way a line chart does; rows are data series and columns are categories.

FIG. 10.13

An area chart is similar to a line chart, but with the area under the line filled in. Like many of the other charts, it comes both with and without 3-D special effects.

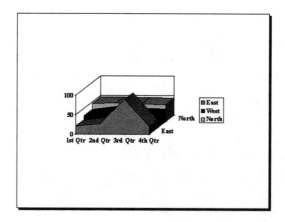

Doughnut A *doughnut chart*, like a pie chart, shows how the values of various categories of data relate to the total value of the whole data series. Unlike a pie chart, however, it can illustrate more than one data series at a time. The doughnut chart in Figure 10.14, unlike the pie chart in Figure 10.10, can show how large a portion of the total annual sales for each store was achieved in each quarter. Each doughnut represents a different store (although, in the default doughnut chart, the different "doughnuts" are not labeled), with each quarter's sales illustrated as a different-colored section of the doughnut.

Like column, bar, and pie charts, the doughnut chart reads datasheet columns as data categories and rows as data series. The doughnut chart's cousin, the pie chart, also offers an "exploded" sub-type, seen in Figure 10.15.

FIG. 10.14

This is an exploded doughnut chart (you can also explode a pie chart). The exploded doughnut chart sub-type can make it easier to identify particular values.

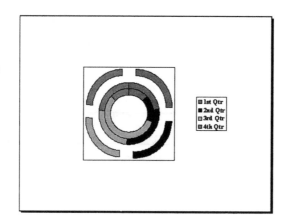

FIG. 10.15
Despite its name, an exploded pie chart doesn't leave a mess on the walls of your kitchen; instead, it makes the data values you want to emphasize more immediately apparent to your viewers.

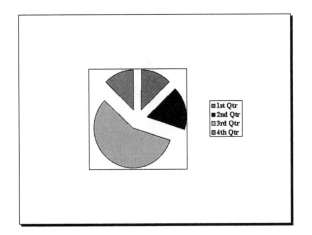

Radar   In a *radar chart*, each category of data (each column in the datasheet) is represented by an axis radiating out from the center—in Figure 10.16, therefore, there are four axes, one for each quarter. The values of each data series (each row of the datasheet, quarterly sales in this example) are plotted along these axes, and then lines are drawn from axis to axis. The data series that encloses the largest area has the highest overall value. In this instance, the store with the highest annual sales, although this is another chart you wouldn't normally use to present this kind of data. Like the XY (scatter) chart, the radar chart is probably most useful for scientific data—relative amounts of basic nutrients in a breakfast cereal, for example.

FIG. 10.16
A radar chart is a good way to analyze data that includes several different values for each category.

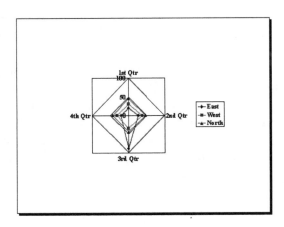

Surface A *surface chart* lets you combine two sets of data and find out where together they produce the greatest overall value—what combination of temperature and humidity makes for the best fishing, for example. Figure 10.17 shows where, once again, the default data has been used, and the combination of time of year and store location that produced the best sales. It illustrates the result as a kind of topographic map of hills and valleys, where areas of the same color and pattern indicate similar values.

FIG. 10.17
The 2-D version of this 3-D surface chart shows the same thing from directly above, eliminating one of the axes.

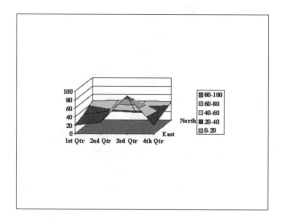

Bubble A *bubble chart* is like an XY (scatter) chart, with a third variable added. Two of the variables determine the bubble's position on the chart; the third variable determines the size of the bubble. You can plot temperature, humidity, and number of fish caught using this kind of chart, as well.

The bubble chart reads the datasheet differently than any of the other charts. Because it requires three values, it reads the top row, not as the labels of the categories, but as the values determining the horizontal position of the bubbles, which is why "1st Qtr," "2nd Qtr," and so on, have been turned into 1, 2, 3 along the bottom of the chart in Figure 10.18. Then it takes the first row of the datasheet as the set of values determining the vertical position of the bubbles. Finally, it reads the second row of the datasheet as the set of values determining the size of the bubbles. Because in the default datasheet, there are only three rows, only one set of bubbles appears in the chart, labeled with the name of the first row in the datasheet, "East." Because there is no fourth row of data in the datasheet, the third row, "North," has horizontal and vertical positions on the chart but no indicated size for the bubbles; its tiny bubbles are therefore completely hidden by the "East" bubbles.

FIG. 10.18
The bubble chart lets you compare three values at once. Two values determine the position of the bubble on the chart and the third determines the size.

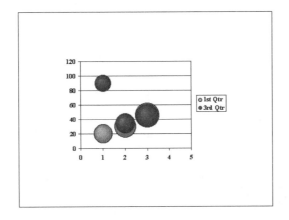

Stock   This is a specialized kind of chart most often used to illustrate stock prices. A *high-low-close stock chart* shows where a value was at the beginning of a time period, where it finished, and how much it fluctuated. Volume of trading can also be indicated by the addition of a bar chart underlying the high-low-close chart.

The stock chart in Figure 10.19 is the only chart in this series of examples where I've changed the default datasheet, just so the chart would look better. That's because the stock chart looks for its values in a particular order. Unlike most charts, it sees each column to be a data series, instead of each row. The high-low-close chart in Figure 10.19 then looks for values across each row, expecting the first row to be the highest values each stock reached during the period's trading, the second row to contain the lowest values reached, and the third row to contain the closing values.

FIG. 10.19
The high-low-close chart is the simplest form of stock chart. The more complicated forms require four or five series of values because of all the information they convey.

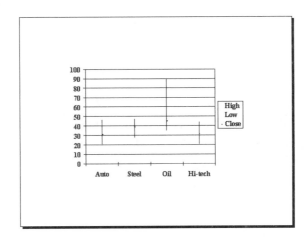

For the more complicated stock charts, additional rows of values are required, in a particular order. The open-high-low-close chart looks for the opening values of the stocks in the first row, then the high, low, and closing values, requiring four rows. The volume-high-low-close chart takes the first row of values as representing the volume of trading. And the volume-open-high-low-close chart, of course, requires five rows of values.

Cone, Cylinder, and Pyramid   These are just variations of the bar and column charts, using shapes other than the standard rectangular ones, such as the pyramids in Figure 10.20.

FIG. 10.20
Bored with rectangular shapes? Choose a cone, cylinder, or pyramid variation on the standard column and bar charts.

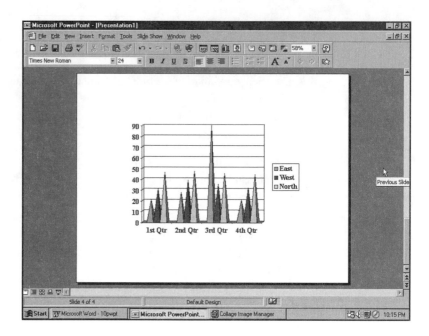

Custom Charts

In addition to the standard charts listed in the previous section, PowerPoint provides many different pre-formatted custom charts, which combine one or more of the standard charts with various combinations of colors, patterns, gridlines, and more. You can also create and save your own custom chart.

To browse through the custom charts, choose the Custom Types tab in the Chart Type dialog box.

▶ **See** "Formatting a Chart," **p. 225**

Using 3-D Effects

You'll notice that most of the chart types have both two- and three-dimensional variants. There are two kinds of 3-D charts. In most of the supposed 3-D charts, the third dimension is just a visual effect. In some, however, the third dimension is "real," in that it allows for a third axis—called the Series axis. You can tell which is which in the Chart Sub-Type menu: the names of graphs using the 3-D appearance simply as a visual effect include the words with a 3-D visual effect, which means, "Clustered column with a 3-D visual effect," while the true 3-D column chart is simply called 3-D column.

N O T E   Although 3-D effects are eye-catching, it's important to remember the most important rule of designing a presentation—clear communication. There's no point in creating a flashy graph if your viewers are more confused than enlightened by it. ■

▶ **See** "Modifying a Chart," **p. 252**

Editing Datasheets

A chart is only as good as the data it contains. You can't adjust the height of bars or the size of the pieces of pie in a pie chart by clicking them; instead, you have to alter the data that is being used to create the chart. To do that, you use the datasheet, which opens automatically when you create a chart. You can also access it whenever you have a chart selected by choosing View, Datasheet (choosing it again will close it) or clicking the View Datasheet button on the Charting toolbar.

What is a Datasheet?

A *datasheet* (see Figure 10.21) looks a little like a spreadsheet. Information is entered in cells, which are formed by the intersection of rows and columns. For most types of charts—with the exceptions noted in the list of standard chart types I provided earlier—each column represents a category of data, while each row is a data series, and is marked with a symbol—for example, a small 3-D bar—to indicate what type of chart you're creating.

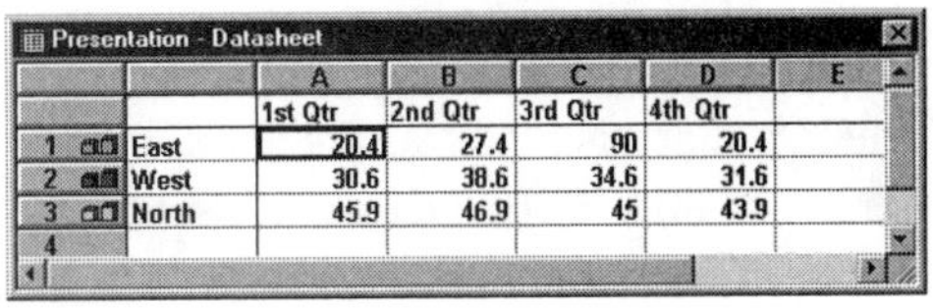

FIG. 10.21
Your chart is only as useful and accurate as the data you enter into the datasheet.

		A	B	C	D	E
		1st Qtr	2nd Qtr	3rd Qtr	4th Qtr	
1	East	20.4	27.4	90	20.4	
2	West	30.6	38.6	34.6	31.6	
3	North	45.9	46.9	45	43.9	
4						

Adding Data to a Datasheet

There are two ways to add data to a datasheet: enter it in PowerPoint, or import it from another application.

TROUBLESHOOTING

I'm trying to create my own chart, but the sample data PowerPoint entered in the datasheet is confusing me. How do I get rid of it? To completely clear the datasheet, click the blank button in the upper-left corner of the Presentation-Datasheet window. This highlights all cells in the datasheet. Now choose E̲dit, Cle̲ar, A̲ll. Both the data in the chart and the chart itself disappears, clearing the way for your work. You can achieve the same effect by highlighting the entire datasheet and pressing Delete.

To enter data in the blank datasheet:

1. Click the top cell in the column labeled A. Enter your category labels across the top row. You can move from column to column by pressing the Tab key, or by using the cursor control keys.

2. Each row represents a data series. Enter the names of the data series down the length of the first column, beginning in the first cell in the row labeled 1.

3. Enter the values for each category in each cell of each series. Notice that as you add data, your chart is constructed piece by piece, changing as each new bit of data is added. The chart automatically adjusts its size to reflect the range of data you have entered.

CAUTION

Remember that some charts, such as bubble charts and XY (scatter) charts, use data differently than standard bar, column, and pie charts. If you're using a 3-D chart, experiment with it carefully to make sure it's showing what you want it to show.

Importing Chart Data

Often you may want to create a chart using data from another application—typically, a spreadsheet. PowerPoint allows you to import data that's saved in an Excel file, as text files, as Lotus 1-2-3 files, or as SYLK (symbolic link) files.

To import data into a datasheet:

1. Open the datasheet, then select the cell where you want the data to begin appearing.

2. Choose Edit, Import File.

3. Locate the file, then click Open.

4. What happens next depends on what kind of file you are importing. If you're importing a text file, the Text Import Wizard opens and leads you through the process of deciding how the text data should appear on the datasheet. If you're importing an Excel file, you'll see the Import Data Options dialog box in Figure 10.22.

FIG. 10.22

Here you can determine which Excel spreadsheet—and how much of it—you want imported to your chart.

5. In the Select Sheet From Workbook list, select which spreadsheet you want to import from the Excel workbook you've opened.

6. Next, click one of the radio buttons in the Import area to either import the Entire Sheet, or a Range (which can be expressed either by coordinates—A1:D4, for instance—or by a name, if you've named the range in Excel).

7. Decide if you want to Overwrite Existing Cells. If this box is checked, your imported data erases any data already in the cells it fills. If this box is left blank, your imported data is simply inserted, and the datasheet (and chart) expands to accommodate it.

8. Click OK. The datasheet and chart immediately change to reflect the imported data.

If you have another application that uses a version of the Microsoft Graph applet to create charts, as Excel does, you can create the entire chart in the other program and then simply copy and paste it into PowerPoint.

TROUBLESHOOTING

I don't have Excel; I have another Windows-based spreadsheet program that PowerPoint doesn't seem to recognize. How can I use it to create a chart? Using the tools in your spreadsheet program, copy the spreadsheet cells to the Clipboard, then enter PowerPoint and paste them into the datasheet. You should be able to do the same thing from most other Windows applications.

Linking Data with OLE

OLE stands for *Object Linking and Embedding*. If the program in which the chart data originates supports OLE, you can link the chart to it, so that any changes made to the data in the originating program is automatically reflected in your PowerPoint presentation. This is a valuable feature if you are bringing in data from many different sources and want to ensure that your presentation always reflects the latest figures.

An embedded object is a little bit different. It is fully part of your PowerPoint presentation, so the data in it does not change when you input new data. Clicking an embedded object, however, calls up the originating program, making the object easier to edit.

You can't simply create a chart in PowerPoint and then create a link to another program. Instead, the chart must be created in the other application first, then inserted into PowerPoint.

To create a linked chart:

1. Create the chart you want to link to in its own application—for example, Excel.

2. In PowerPoint, go to the slide where you want to insert the chart, and choose Insert, Object. This brings up the Insert Object dialog box. Click Create From file to give you the dialog box shown in Figure 10.23.

3. Enter the location of the file or click Browse to go find it.

4. Check Link, and click OK.

Your chart appears in PowerPoint just as it did in the original application. In the future, whenever you're working in the originating application and change any of the data used to create the chart, you'll find the chart has automatically updated itself whenever you return to PowerPoint.

FIG. 10.23

From this dialog box, you can create links to charts created in other applications, such as Excel, to ensure that any changes made in the original application are reflected in your presentation.

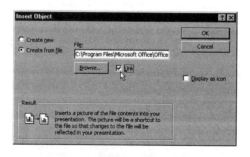

Once you have a linked object in place, new commands become available. Choose Edit, Links, and the Links dialog box in Figure 10.24 appears, listing all of the linked objects in PowerPoint. For each linked object, you have more options:

- *Update Now.* Click this button, and the linked chart retrieves the latest data from its originating application, and updates accordingly.

- *Open Source.* This opens the chart's originating application.

- *Change Source.* This lets you specify a different source file for the link. You could replace a linked Excel chart with a linked Works chart, for instance, or replace it with some other type of object altogether.

- *Break Link.* Choose this, and the chart remains in your presentation, but will no longer be linked to its original application (and no longer reflect any changes made there).

- *Update: Automatic.* If this radio button is selected, your chart will be updated with the latest information from the originating application whenever you open the presentation or change the source file.

- *Update: Manual.* Select this, and the chart is updated only when you click the Update Now button.

FIG. 10.24
You can edit the attributes of all the linked objects in your presentation from this dialog box.

Three other link-related commands also become active when you have a linked object in your presentation. Choose Edit, Linked (type of object) Object, and a small pop-up menu offers Edit, Open, and Convert options.

Edit and Open both let you change formatting and other attributes. The difference is that Edit simply opens up the controls from the source program while keeping you in PowerPoint, and Open opens the source program itself. Convert, which allows you to convert one form of chart to another—say Microsoft Excel to Microsoft Works—can only be done within the source program, so you have to open the linked object first.

Editing Data

If you're able to input errorless data into a datasheet on your first attempt, then you're one of a kind. Most people find they have to make changes—sometimes a lot of changes. Fortunately, the datasheet in PowerPoint makes editing data easy.

Working with Cells

The basic unit of the datasheet is the *cell*. To edit a cell, you first have to activate it or highlight it. A cell is activated when it has a dark border around it; it's highlighted when it appears in colors reverse to those around it (both are visible in Figure 10.25):

- To activate a single cell, simply click inside it. Start typing, and what you type will replace what's already inside the cell.

- To highlight a row of cells, click the numbered button to the left of the row; all the cells in the row will be highlighted.

- To highlight a column of cells, click the lettered button on the top of the column.

- To highlight a range of cells, click and hold down the mouse button while moving the mouse pointer from the upper-left corner of the range to the lower-right corner.

Once cells are highlighted, you can cut, copy, or delete the information in them using the usual <u>E</u>dit tools.

N O T E   When you highlight more than one cell, the first cell in the row, column, or range remains active; if you begin typing, that's the only cell where information will appear. However, you can cut, copy, or format the information in all the highlighted cells. ■

FIG. 10.25

In this datasheet, a range of cells have been highlighted. The cell in the upper-left corner of the range is activated.

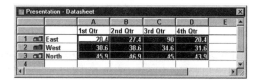

	A	B	C	D	E
	1st Qtr	2nd Qtr	3rd Qtr	4th Qtr	
1 East	20.4	27.4	90	20.4	
2 West	30.6	38.6	34.6	31.6	
3 North	45.9	46.9	45	43.9	
4					

 If you find the default cells are a little too small, you can easily adjust their size. Just aim your mouse pointer at the intersection of the column or row buttons along the top and left edges of the datasheet. Your pointer changes to a two-headed arrow. Click, hold, and move the pointer in either of the indicated directions to expand or shrink the column or row.

To set editing options, choose <u>T</u>ools, <u>O</u>ptions while the datasheet is open. This brings up the Graph Options dialog box. The default tab, called Datasheet Options, offers two check boxes:

- *Move Selection After Enter.* If you check this box, pressing Enter when you've finished entering data in one cell will automatically activate the next cell down. (You can use Shift+Enter to move back up.)
- *Cell <u>D</u>rag And Drop.* This enables you to move cells by highlighting them, then holding down the mouse button and dragging them to a new location on the datasheet.

The Graph Options dialog box also contains a Chart tab, which you can use to choose how empty cells in the datasheet will be plotted.

If you click <u>N</u>ot Plotted (Leave Gaps), the default choice, then blank cells will not be plotted at all. In a column chart, this means a column would be missing; in a line chart, it would mean a break in the line.

If you click <u>Z</u>ero, empty cells are plotted as if they had zeroes in them.

If you click Interpolated, Microsoft Graph fills in the empty cell with what it calculates to be the most likely value, based on the values of the other cells in the series.

The other choices in the Chart tab are two Chart Tips options. If you check the S<u>h</u>ow Names box, Microsoft Graph shows the names of the data series when you place the mouse pointer on them. If you check the S<u>h</u>ow Values box, it also shows the value.

Editing Within Cells

To make changes within a cell without completely retyping it, double-click the cell. This places your cursor inside the cell. You can then position it wherever you like within the entry and change a single character at a time. Double-clicking again will select the whole cell and enable you to change fonts or perform other formatting functions, discussed in the next chapter.

Copying and Moving Data

To copy a cell or range of cells, highlight them and choose <u>E</u>dit, <u>C</u>opy.

To move data from one cell to another, highlight the original cell, then choose <u>E</u>dit, Cu<u>t</u>. Next, highlight the cell that you want to move the data to, and choose <u>E</u>dit, <u>P</u>aste. The data from the original cell will appear in the new cell, replacing any data that is already present.

Working with Rows and Columns

Each cell in a datasheet is formed at the intersection of a row and column. In general, each row is a data series, while each column is a category.

Adding Rows and Columns

You can have as many rows and columns in your datasheet as you want. Scroll right or down, and you'll notice that when you get to what appears to be the limits of the datasheet, it just keeps scrolling. If you scroll right, once you run out of letters the rows start appearing with two-letter combination labels: AA, AB, AC, and so on.

Sometimes, though, you don't want more columns at the bottom or to the right of the datasheet: all you want is to insert a single row or column between two existing ones.

To insert a row or column to your datasheet:

1. Highlight the row or column that is currently located where you want the new row or column to appear.

2. Choose Insert, Cells. A new, highlighted row or column appears. The row or column you originally highlighted moves below or to the right of the new row or column.

Clearing and Deleting Rows and Columns

To clear a row or column or an entire range of cells, highlight them and choose Edit, Clear. This offers three options in a pop-up menu: All, Contents, or Formats. Selecting All removes all of the information from the selected cells, plus all formatting information. Selecting Contents leaves format information, but removes all data. Selecting Formats leaves the data, but removes any formatting information.

To delete cells entirely, choose Edit, Delete. This opens the dialog box in Figure 10.26, which offers you four choices:

- *Shift Cells Left*. Any cells to the right of those you delete shift left to replace them.
- *Shift Cells Up*. Any cells below those you delete shift up to replace them.
- *Entire Row*. All rows that include any highlighted cells are deleted, whether the entire row is highlighted or not.
- *Entire Column*. Az ll columns that include any highlighted cells are deleted, whether the entire column is highlighted or not.

FIG 10.26

This dialog box gives you a choice of options as to how you want cells, rows, and columns cleared or deleted.

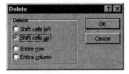

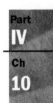

CHAPTER 11

Formatting a Chart

by Edward C. Willett

As you saw in Chapter 10, PowerPoint (via the Microsoft Graph applet) provides an extensive variety of charts you can use to present your data in an eye-catching and informative manner. But if you limit yourself to the Standard chart types that PowerPoint offers, or even the Custom types, you're not making good use of the program's capabilities.

By using the powerful formatting commands discussed in this chapter, you can customize any chart—Standard or Custom—by adding fills, shading, borders, or pictures, or even combining two or more types of graphs, until it perfectly suits your data and makes the points you want to make. The possibilities are almost endless! ■

Edit a chart

Change the fonts, titles, and colors used in your chart, or apply snazzy patterns and fills to make your chart unique.

Change labels and axes

Make the chart fit your needs by changing the labels or switching the axes around.

Modify your chart

Resize your chart, move it around, even add graphics to it. PowerPoint lets you do whatever you need to do to make your chart sing.

Save your chart

Odds are, once you've created a chart you like, you'll want to use it again. PowerPoint lets you build your own library of custom charts.

Editing a Chart

Before you start changing your chart, you need to know how to select the various chart elements, starting with the chart as a whole.

Clicking the chart will bring up a frame and handles (see Figure 11.1). This allows you to move the chart and resize it, but nothing more.

FIG. 11.1
This chart has been selected with a single click.

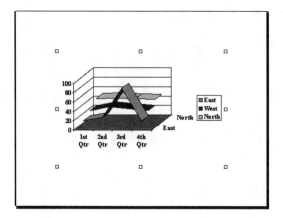

Before you can make any changes to the chart, you have to double-click it. This also opens the chart's related datasheet. You'll know you've successfully selected the chart because it will have a shaded border around it, as shown in Figure 11.2.

TROUBLESHOOTING

I've used previous versions of PowerPoint, but now I'm confused. What happened to AutoFormat? AutoFormat let you choose from a series of custom graphs with advanced formatting already applied. In PowerPoint 97, AutoFormat has been replaced by the Custom Types tab in the Chart Type dialog box. The effect is the same: PowerPoint still provides you with several pre-designed charts offering more variety in appearance than the Standard Charts. But whether you use a Standard Chart or a Custom Chart, you can still change the format to your heart's content once you've entered your data.

▶ **See** "Standard Charts and Their Uses," **p. 205**
▶ **See** "Custom Charts," **p. 214**

FIG. 11.2
This chart has been selected by double-clicking, and is now ready to be formatted.

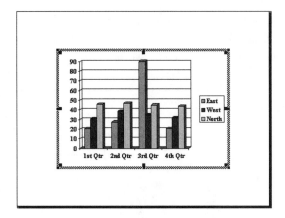

Elements of a Chart

Each chart consists of several distinct parts, called *chart objects*. The major chart objects, labeled in Figure 11.3, are:

- *Chart Area.* The entire area inside the shaded gray line.
- *Plot Area.* The area immediately surrounding the graph itself, but excluding the legend and title.
- *Floor and Walls.* Elements of the partial "box" surrounding charts that use 3-D effects. The floor is what the 3-D display elements stand on, while the walls are the planes on which gridlines are drawn.
- *Corners.* On a graph that uses 3-D effects, the bottom and top corners of the walls. You can manipulate them to change the angle of the 3-D effects.
- *Legend.* The box that identifies each category by color or pattern.
- *Axes.* The base reference lines against which the chart is plotted. There are three of them: the *category* and *values* axes appear in almost all charts, while the *series* axis appears only in certain 3-D charts. The series axis is labeled with the names of the data series being plotted, such as the store locations. The category axis is labeled with the names of the categories of data, such as the four quarters of the fiscal year. Finally, the values that appear in the cells of the datasheet are plotted against the value axis.
- *Gridlines.* These are lines drawn on the walls and floor to make it easier to relate the display to the various axes.
- *Data table.* A table that displays the numerical data from the datasheet on which the chart is based.

To select one of these chart objects for formatting, use the Chart Objects pull-down menu that appears in the Chart toolbar. Then, to access the formatting commands for that particular object, choose F<u>o</u>rmat, S<u>e</u>lected Chart Area.

FIG. 11.3

Each chart is made up of a number of different elements, called *chart objects*. Each of these objects can be formatted individually, which makes it easy to fine-tune your chart just the way you want it.

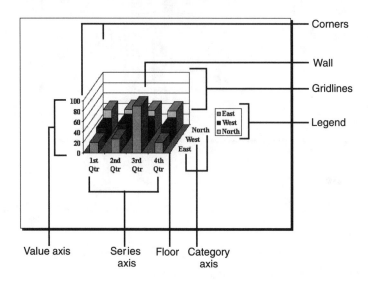

TROUBLESHOOTING

I just double-clicked my chart, and I can't access the Chart Objects pull-down menu. What's going on? You cannot access the Chart Objects pull-down menu while the datasheet window is active. Either close the datasheet or click the chart again to render the datasheet inactive.

T I P Once the chart as a whole is selected, the fastest way to access the formatting commands for the various elements of the chart is to double-click the element you want to format. Almost as fast is to right-click it; this opens a pop-up menu with several useful commands on it that vary from object to object.

Be aware, however, that both of these methods can be a problem when your chart has a lot of elements; sometimes it can be hard to click the right one. If that's the case, try zooming in to reduce the confusion.

The Chart Toolbar

The Chart Objects pull-down menu is only one of several new tools at your command on the toolbar. These tools are outlined in Table 11.1.

Table 11.1   The Chart Toolbar

Button	Name	Description
	Format	Provides instant access to the formatting tools of whatever is selected in the Chart Objects pull-down menu.
	Import File	A one-button way to bring in data from an outside application.
	View Datasheet	Toggles display of the datasheet on and off.
	By Row	Switches the axes of the chart to the default, where each row in the datasheet represents a data series.
	By Column	Switches the axes of the chart so that each column in the datasheet represents a data series.
	Data Table	Places a table containing the data from the datasheet right in the chart.
	Chart Type	Provides quick, one-click access to some of the most common standard charts.
	Category Axis Gridlines	Toggles the category axis gridlines on and off.
	Value Axis Gridlines	Toggles the value axis gridlines on and off.
	Legend	Toggles the legend on and off.
	Drawing	Makes the Drawing toolbar available so you can add drawing objects to your chart.
	Fill Color	Provides quick access to the color palette for selecting fills, patterns, and backgrounds. It also remembers the last color chosen, so that with a single click, it can fill the selected chart object with the last color used.
	Currency Style	Converts any numbers in the selected chart object—usually the numbers along the values axis—into currency figures.
	Percent Style	Converts number in the selected chart object into percentage figures.
	Comma Style	Converts decimals in decimal numbers into commas instead of periods.

Part

IV

Ch

11

continues

Button	Name	Description
Table 11.1	**Continued**	
Button	Name	Description
	Increase Decimal	Adds a decimal place to any numbers in the selected chart object.
	Decrease Decimal	Removes a decimal place from any numbers in the selected chart object.
	Angle Text Downward	Angles any labels in the selected chart object downward at a 45-degree angle.
	Angle Text Upward	Angles any labels in the selected chart object upward at a 45-degree angle.

Formatting Fonts

Although some types of formatting commands are peculiar to a chart object, others are common to several. Formatting fonts is common to all chart objects that contain text; it's also one of the most important. Choosing the right font is vital. An Old West font will look laughably out of place in a slick presentation on high-tech computer equipment, while a sleek futuristic font would not be appropriate for a presentation about a historical site.

Something else to consider is whether your presentation will be printed or shown on the computer. There's not much point in using colored fonts, for instance, if you're going to be printing your presentation on a black-and-white printer; on the other hand, you're missing an opportunity to spruce up your presentation if you stick to black fonts on a white background for a computer-based presentation.

Fortunately, PowerPoint gives you great flexibility in formatting fonts. You can format fonts for the whole chart or for individual elements.

To format all the fonts in your chart at once:

1. Choose Chart Area from the Chart Objects pull-down menu, and click the Format button just to the right of the menu on the Charting toolbar.

   This brings up the Format Chart Area dialog box, which has two tabs: Patterns and Font. (I get to the Patterns tab later in the chapter in the section "Adding Patterns to Your Chart.")

2. Click the Font tab, and the property sheet in Figure 11.4 appears. This property sheet gives you several options:

   - *Font.* Shows all the fonts available on your system. Choose the one you want. You don't even have to remember what they look like, because a sample is shown in the Preview area.

FIG. 11.4

This property sheet is available any time you are formatting a chart object that includes text.

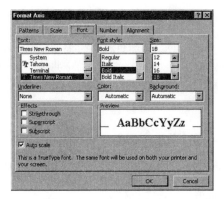

- *Font style.* Choose Regular, Italic, Bold, or Bold Italic.

- *Size.* Select the size you want the fonts to be, in points.

- *Underline.* There are three choices: None, Single, and Double.

- *Color.* Choose the color you want the font to be. The Automatic choice is black; you can choose a different color from the palette provided.

- *Background.* You have three choices: Opaque, Transparent, or automatically determined by Microsoft Graph. If you choose Opaque, the small text box containing the text hides whatever is behind it. If you choose Transparent, it won't. And if you choose Automatic, Microsoft Graph decides for you (usually it's transparent).

- *Strikethrough, Superscript and Subscript.* Strikethrough puts a horizontal line through the middle of each letter, as though it had been crossed out with a pen. Superscript is most commonly used for mathematical equations: it makes text smaller and prints it above the baseline of the normal font, as in $E=mc^2$. Subscript also makes text smaller and prints it below the baseline of the normal font. It's most commonly seen in chemical formulas, such as CO_2.

- *Auto Scale.* If selected, ensures that your fonts automatically change size as your chart is resized, so you don't end up with too-large fonts in a too-small chart, or vice versa.

3. Click OK, and all the fonts in the chart will change to match your new selections.

To change fonts selectively in your chart, simply select the individual chart objects whose fonts you want to change: Category Axis, for example, or Legend. By selecting objects individually, you can have as many fonts in your chart as you want.

Part
IV

Ch
11

> **CAUTION**
>
> Be careful when mixing fonts; too many fonts spoil the chart, making it look cluttered and amateurish. You're better off sticking with just one or two good, legible fonts, with only the occasional foray into something more exotic for extra impact.

Titling Your Charts and Labeling Axes

Odds are, if you've created a chart, you're going to want to give it a title. You may also want to label the axes. You could do this by inserting a special text box elsewhere on the slide, but that's not necessary. To add a title and/or axes labels:

1. Select the chart by double-clicking it.

2. Choose Chart, Chart Options. The Chart Options dialog box opens, displaying six tabs; choose the first one, Titles (see Figure 11.5).

FIG. 11.5
Attach an overall title and labels to all axes to make your chart communicate better.

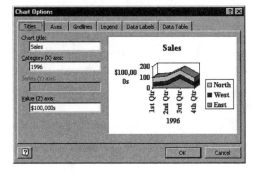

3. Type the overall name of the chart in the Chart Title blank.

4. Type the name of the category and value axis in their respective blanks. Notice that the chart preview changes to include each title as you type it.

5. Click OK.

TROUBLESHOOTING

When I add titles, the chart preview gets muddled. It shows all the titles I've added, but the chart itself becomes very small and the elements seem to be overlapping each other. Is this a problem? No. PowerPoint does this so that you can see that all your titles have been added, and where they appear. The titles appear normally on the slide itself (see Figure 11.6).

FIG. 11.6
Although your titles may have looked a little peculiar in the preview on the Titles tab, once you click OK they appear fine on the slide.

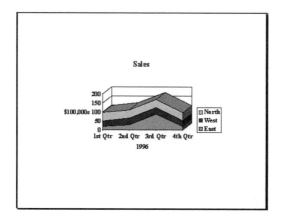

Once you've clicked OK, you see your titles on the slide. Note that the last title you entered has a box around it. You can grab this box and drag it—and the title—anywhere you want it to go. You can also click any of the other titles you've just entered and reposition them.

Notice, too, that these titles are now included in the list of items you can select using the Chart Objects pull-down menu—which means you can format each one individually, if you want. To do so, select it from the Chart Objects pull-down menu and click the Format button.

The Format Chart Title dialog box that comes up contains the Font tab you've already seen, the Patterns tab (which you learn about in the section "Adding Patterns to Your Chart") and an Alignment tab. Click the Alignment tab to bring up the property sheet shown in Figure 11.7.

FIG. 11.7
Your text isn't restricted to being horizontal in your PowerPoint chart, thanks to this property sheet.

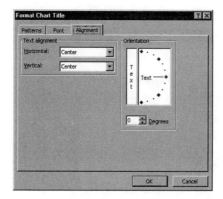

Part
IV

Ch
11

There are two sets of controls here: Text alignment and Orientation.

Text alignment refers to the alignment of the title within its own text box. Your choices are Left, Center, Right, and Justify in the Horizontal box, and Top, Center, Bottom, and Justify in the Vertical box. Because the text box for your title is the same size as the title, you won't notice much effect.

However, you'll notice a great deal of effect when you use the Orientation controls. If you click the box on the left with Text written in it vertically, your title assumes the same position. Or you can tilt your text up or down by using the other control. Click and drag the red diamond either way along the graduated semicircle to change the text angle, or enter the precise angle at which you want text tilted in the Degrees box at the bottom. (Positive numbers tilt the text up, while negative numbers tilt it down.) Slanting your text can add interest to your chart and also save you valuable space.

Using Borders, Patterns, and Fills

Besides fonts, the other most common formatting option you'll see, no matter which Chart Object you've selected, is Patterns. Clicking the Patterns tab, which has already come up twice this chapter, opens up several new formatting possibilities. By using the additional tabs available under Patterns, you can set off various elements with plain or fancy borders and fill the entire chart area, the chart walls and floor, or the data series displays with patterns, gradients, pictures, or any color you want.

These colorful options can take your slide from mundane to beautiful, if you use them wisely.

Whichever part of the chart you've selected—in this case, Chart Area—click the Format button, then select the Patterns tab, and you'll see the property sheet shown in Figure 11.8.

FIG. 11.8
When the Patterns tab appears in your formatting dialog box, you've got a whole new world of options to play with.

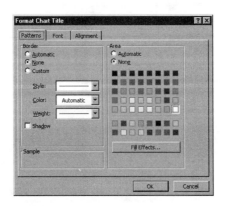

Borders

On the left of the Patterns tab, you can select a border for the part you're formatting. You're offered seven options:

- *Automatic*. Allows PowerPoint to draw a standard black line.
- *None*. Not only is no border drawn, but if the chart object has a border, it's erased.
- *Custom*. Enables you to move on to the next three options: Style, Color, and Weight.
- *Style*. Offers you a small selection of solid, dashed, and shaded borders.
- *Color*. Opens up the same color menu as you see to the right of this property sheet.
- *Weight*. Allows you to choose from four different weights of line, from light to heavy.
- *Shadow*. Adds a shadow to the bottom and right sides of the selected chart object.

By way of example, here's how you'd add a custom border to the entire chart. Notice that as you select each option, it's previewed for you in the Sample box at the bottom of the tab:

1. Select Chart Area from the Chart Objects pull-down menu.
2. Click the Format button.
3. In the Format Chart Area dialog box, click the Patterns tab, which gives you what you see in Figure 11.8.
4. Click the Custom radio button.
5. From the Style pull-down menu (see Figure 11.9), select what style of line you want to use as a border. I've selected a dashed line.

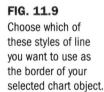

FIG. 11.9
Choose which of these styles of line you want to use as the border of your selected chart object.

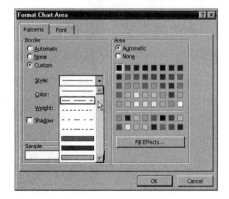

Part
IV

Ch
11

6. From the <u>C</u>olor pull-down menu (see Figure 11.10), choose what color you'd like your border to be. I've selected Sea Green.

FIG. 11.10
Choose which color you'd like to apply to your border from this palette.

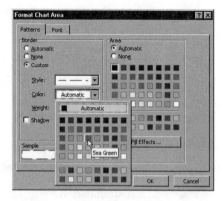

7. From the <u>W</u>eight pull-down menu (see Figure 11.11), select the thickness of the border. I've chosen the heaviest.

FIG. 11.11
Choose the thickness of the line that will be applied as a border from this menu.

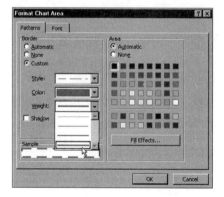

8. If you want a thin shadow effect to be added to your border, check the Sha<u>d</u>ow box. I've chosen to add it; the net result of my border-creating efforts is shown in Figure 11.12.

FIG. 11.12
Here's what the completed border looks like on a sample chart. Notice that a dashed border doesn't actually work very well with the shadow effect; this is something to be aware of when creating your own presentations.

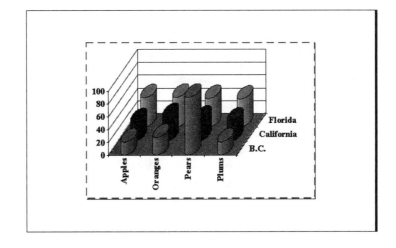

Patterns and Fills

Once you've selected a border for the chart object you're formatting, you can move on to the color in the Area area of the Patterns tab. Here again you can choose Automatic, which defaults to black, or None, which leaves the chart object you're working with empty of color, or you can choose any of the colors in the palette.

 Always be conscious of the final form your presentation will take. There's no point in using color for a black and white presentation, and no point using only shades of gray for a color computer presentation.

At the same time, even if you are preparing a computer presentation, don't go overboard with color or the patterns, gradients, and fills discussed in the subsequent sections of this chapter. The goal should always be clarity; you want these effects to enhance the presentation of your information, not obfuscate it.

It's a good idea to get a second opinion on any colors or fills you use; ask someone who hasn't seen the presentation before to tell you if your design scheme is working or if it's just confusing. If the latter, try using simpler patterns and fewer, more complementary colors. Remember, you're trying to communicate, not create optical art!

If the basic pre-selected colors don't suit your presentation, you can get fancier by clicking the Fill Effects button. This brings up the Fill Effects dialog box, which offers four tabs: Gradient, Texture, Pattern, and Picture.

Part
IV

Ch
11

Gradient   Gradient fills shade from dark to light, or one color to another, and sometimes back again, to produce a variety of pleasing effects. With the Gradient controls, you can design your own gradient fills, or choose from one of a selection of pre-designed ones.

To design a one-color gradient fill (see Figure 11.13):

1. Click the Qne Color radio button.

2. From the Color 1 pull-down menu, select the basic color you want to use in your fill.

3. Adjust the Dark/Light sliding control to your satisfaction. At the dark end the gradient will be from your chosen color to black; at the light end the gradient will be from your chosen color to white.

4. Select a Shading style from the list in the bottom left corner: Horizontal, Vertical, Diagonal Up, Diagonal Down, From Corner, or From Center.

5. Select which of the Variants you like best.

6. Click OK to apply the fill.

FIG. 11.13

Use these controls to design a one-color gradient fill for your selected chart object.

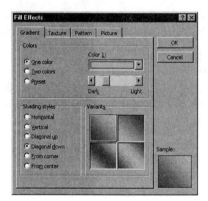

To design a two-color gradient fill (see Figure 11.14):

1. Click the Two Colors radio button.

2. From the Color 1 pull-down menu, select the first color you want to use in your fill.

3. From the Color 2 pull-down menu, select the second color you want to use in your fill.

4. Select a Shading style.

5. Select which of the Variants you prefer.

6. Click OK.

FIG. 11.14
Use these controls to design a two-color gradient fill for your selected chart object.

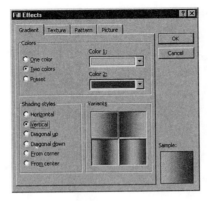

To design a preset gradient fill (see Figure 11.15):

1. Click the Preset radio button.

2. From the Preset Colors pull-down menu, select the background you want to use.

3. If you want, apply a different shading style.

4. Select which of the Variants you prefer.

5. Click OK.

FIG. 11.15
PowerPoint comes with a variety of preset gradient fills for you to choose from.

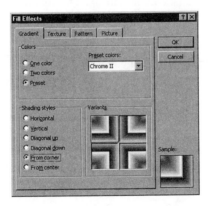

Texture   If you want something even more exotic than, say, the Rainbow preset gradient fill (it's gaudy, but eye-catching), click the Texture tab and move on to the property sheet in Figure 11.16. From here you can choose realistic-looking backgrounds of everything from Newsprint to Granite to Denim to Oak. Just click one of the choices in the Texture menu and click OK.

FIG. 11.16

Textures add creative flair to any presentation.

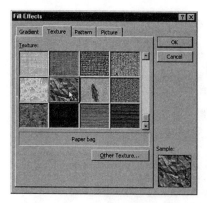

Textures such as these are used extensively as the background to World Wide Web pages, which makes the Internet an inexhaustible source of additional textures. You may also have favorite textures of your own stored on your hard drive.

To access additional textures, click Other Texture. This brings up the standard browsing dialog box. From here you can go in search of textures on your own computer, on a network or online. You can use Windows Bitmap (BMP or DIB) or Windows Metafile (WMF or EMF) files as textures, or any other graphic format for which you have an import filter installed in your computer. The most common formats for textures on World Wide Web pages are JPEG (JPG) and GIF (GIF).

Textures are very small images; if you try to choose an image that's too large to be a texture, Microsoft Graph refuses to import it. If you want to use a larger image as a background, choose the Picture tab instead. (See the section "Picture" later in this chapter.)

 To make the best use of textures, try to find one that suits the topic of your presentation. If you're in the business of selling cemetery memorial stones, for instance, a dignified Granite background to your chart of sales figures would be perfect. A newspaper might chart its circulation figures on Newsprint. And because there are literally thousands of textures available on the Internet as the backgrounds of World Wide Web pages, you can always find one that will match your presentation's topic.

Pattern   More fill effects are available under the Pattern tab, which opens the property sheet in Figure 11.17. Choose your Foreground and Background colors from the pull-down menus at the bottom, then make your choice from the Pattern menu above.

FIG. 11.17
From brickwork to weaves, you'll find presentation-enhancing fill patterns here.

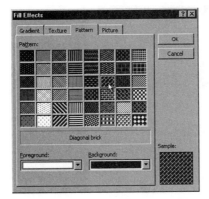

Picture   Finally, by accessing the Picture tab (see Figure 11.18), you can use any picture file from your own computer, a network, or the Internet as a background fill, provided you have an import filter to handle the specific picture format. The Office CD comes complete with a wide variety of drawings and photographs in its ClipArt file folder. To use a picture file as a fill:

1. Click the Select Picture button and open the image you want to use as a fill. It appears in the Picture preview area.

2. Choose the way you want the picture to fill the selected chart object by clicking one of the radio buttons in the Format area:

   - *Stretch*. Stretches the picture to completely fill the element.

   - *Stack*. Keeps the picture the same size, filling the selected element with as many copies of the picture as will fit.

   - *Stack and Scale To*. Resizes the picture so it can stack in however many copies of it you enter in the Units/Picture box.

CAUTION
Pictures take up a lot more memory than ordinary fills, and may slow down screen drawing time of your slide, especially if there are a lot of repetitions of the picture in the fill.

3. In the Apply To area, select which parts of the selected chart object you want to apply the picture to as a fill (see Figure 11.19). The default is all three: Sides, Front, and End. If you remove the check from any of the boxes, that part of the element is filled with the last-applied color formatting. Note that this option is only available for chart objects that have Sides, Fronts, and Ends, such as rectangular, 3-D data series in column charts.

4. Click OK.

Part
IV

Ch
11

FIG. 11.18
Any picture can be used as a fill, including photographs, such as this one of a bicycle racer that's included in the ClipArt on the Microsoft Office CD.

FIG. 11.19
Here's what a chart looks like with the photograph of the bicycle racer used to fill the entire chart area.

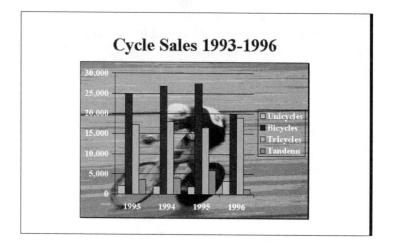

Labels and Axes

If your viewers are going to understand your chart, they have to be able to interpret the data on it. It's easy to create a beautiful chart that conveys no information at all except for the fact that you really have a knack for picking fill patterns.

To ensure your chart makes sense, see that it's well-labeled and the values assigned to the various data series can be easily deciphered. That's where formatting axes and adding labels becomes important.

Formatting Axes

To format an axis, select it using the Chart Objects pull-down chart, then click the Format button. This opens the Format Axis dialog box, which has five tabs: Patterns, Scale, Font, Number, and Alignment (see Figure 11.20).

FIG. 11.20

The Format Axis dialog box has five tabs: the first, Patterns, has the same name as, but different features from, the one discussed earlier.

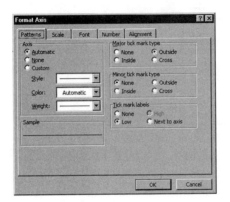

Patterns This Patterns dialog box (refer to Figure 11.20) is different from the Patterns dialog box we looked at in the last section. Instead of a Border area it offers an Axis area; however, the choices are the same: you can choose an automatic line (thin and black), no line, or a line of any color you choose, in one of several styles, in one of four weights.

On the right side of the box, where the usual Patterns dialog box offers colors, you'll find instead three areas: Major Tick Mark Type, Minor Tick Mark Type, and Tick Mark Labels.

Even if you can't always see it, most charts are built on grids. Tick marks are a way of showing where the grid marks are without drawing all of them in, for easier interpretation of the data being presented (see Figure 11.21).

Major tick marks indicate the most important gridlines; in a bar graph, for instance, they appear as separators between the categories, while in a line graph, they mark the location of each data point. Minor tick marks appear halfway between the major tick marks.

Both kinds of tick marks offer the same choices:

- *Outside.* Tick marks point outward from the axis at right angles.
- *Inside.* Tick marks point inward from the axis at right angles.
- *Cross.* Tick marks point both inward and outward at right angles (as in Figure 11.21).
- *None.* No tick marks.

Part
IV

Ch

11

FIG. 11.21

All the tick marks have been activated on this bar chart, and changed to crosses.

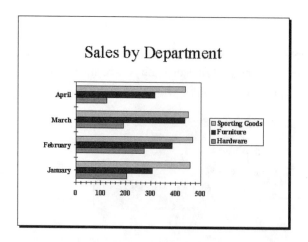

Below the Tick mark type areas is the Tick Mark Labels area. This determines the location of any labels that apply to the selected axis. High places them along the top of the chart, Low on the bottom, and Next to Axis determines their location by where you've located the axis.

Scale   This tab (see Figure 11.22) changes the way the category axis is labeled, among other things. The following discussion refers to the tab as it appears if you're formatting the category axis; if you're formatting the values axis, you see the Scale tab described in the section on gridlines later in the chapter.

FIG. 11.22

You see the Scale property sheet with the most common 2-D charts. On a 3-D chart, you don't have as many options.

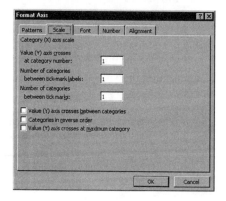

If you're working with a 2-D chart (even one with 3-D visual effects), there are three blanks to be filled in. I demonstrate some of the effects using the same chart that appears in Figure 11.21:

■ *Value (Y) Axis Crosses At Category Number.* Determines at which category the values axis will intersect the Category (X) axis. Usually that's at the first category—

the bottom-left corner of the chart—but by changing this number you can have the values axis split the category axis right down the middle or appear at the far right, if you want to.

In Figure 11.23, I've set the value at 3, which makes the value axis cross the category axis just before the third bar. Because there are four categories, this has the effect of running the values axis directly down the middle of the chart. This doesn't work well with the value axis labels; if I decided to keep this arrangement, I'd have to make further adjustments.

FIG. 11.23
The value (Y) axis has been repositioned to split the chart down the middle. This makes it easier to immediately see the values of the data series in the middle of the chart.

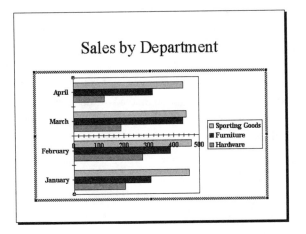

- *Number of Categories Between Tick-Mark Labels.* Determines how many categories are labeled. If this number is 1, every category is labeled; if it's 2, every second category is labeled, if it's 3, every third, and so on. For this chart, I'll leave it set at one, because I want every category labeled.

- *Number of Categories Between Tick Marks.* Determines how many categories will appear between the tick marks. I'll set it at two; the resulting chart looks just like the one in Figure 11.23, but without the tick marks directly opposite the names of the months (as in Figure 11.24).

In the Scale property sheet for a 3-D chart, only the last two choices appear.

Below these three choices (again, for a 2-D chart) are three check boxes:

- *Value (Y) Axis Crosses Between Categories.* If this check box is marked, data points are plotted between tick marks; if it's not checked, data points are plotted right at the tick-mark positions. I'll leave this blank, because I don't want my value axis running down the middle of a data series bar, which is what will happen if I check this box.

FIG. 11.24
In standard bar charts, the rightmost category in the datasheet appears at the top. You can choose to reverse that, as in this chart.

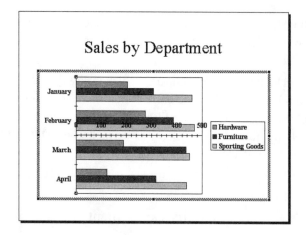

■ *Categories in Reverse Order.* Displays the last category in the leftmost position and the first category in the rightmost, instead of the usual other way around. Notice that up to now, April has appeared at the top of the chart and January at the bottom. I'll check this box to reverse that. The chart now appears as it does in Figure 11.24.

■ *Values (Y) Axis Crosses At Maximum Category.* Moves the values axis, and its labels, to the edge of the chart closest to the chart object that represents the data from the furthest right column in the datasheet. If I selected this now, it would move the values axis back to the bottom of the chart, next to the April data.

Of these, only the Categories in Reverse Order check box always appears if you're working with a 3-D chart; some 3-D charts change the Value (Y) Axis Crosses Between Categories to Value (Z) Axis Crosses Between Categories, which has essentially the same effect.

Number   This tab (see Figure 11.25) lets you determine how the values in your datasheet, and therefore along the selected axis, will be displayed.

FIG. 11.25
How would you like your labels displayed? You have got plenty of choices in the Number tab.

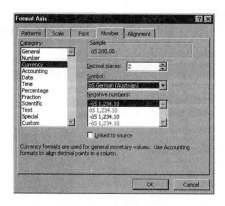

First, select the type of data the cell entry represents from the Category menu, then select the specific type of display you want. The options will vary depending on the Category you choose.

If you mark the Linked To Source check box, then whenever you change the format of the cells in the datasheet, the labels on the axis will change to match them.

Note that each time you select a different category of number, the link is broken and must be re-established by checking this box again.

Gridlines

As noted before, your chart is laid out on electronic graph paper, even if you can't see the crisscrossing lines. If you *do* want to see the crisscrossing lines, to make your data absolutely clear, all you have to do is turn on the gridlines.

There are major and minor gridlines, just as there are major and minor tick marks (not surprisingly, because they mark the same points). To toggle the major gridlines on and off, click the Category Axis and/or Value Axis Gridlines buttons on the Chart toolbar.

To turn on the minor gridlines, or turn on the third set of gridlines in a graph that makes use of three axes, such as the 3-D Surface graph, select Chart, Chart Options, and click the Gridlines tab to bring up the property sheet in Figure 11.26.

Part
IV

Ch
11

FIG. 11.26
Turn on and off the gridlines you want by checking them off on this handy list.

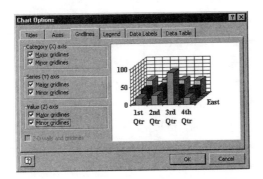

Check the boxes along the left of the property sheet to choose the gridlines you want to activate.

Check the 2-D walls and gridlines check box if you want to turn off the 3-D visual effects in 2-D charts that use them. The data series will still keep their 3-D appearance—bars, pyramids, or whatever—against a flat background.

Gridlines, like any other chart object, can be formatted. Just select them from the Chart Objects pull-down menu, then click the familiar Format button.

Again, you see the Patterns property sheet, where you can choose the style, color, and weight of the gridlines. The other option is the Scale property sheet, where you get the same options as when formatting axes.

If you're formatting the Values or Series gridlines, however, you get different options than if you're formatting the Category gridlines (see Figure 11.27).

FIG. 11.27
Here's where you can set just how far apart gridlines—and tick marks—should be, among other things.

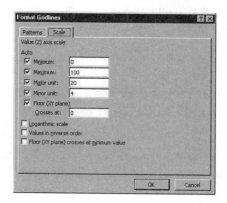

You can choose to leave everything on automatic, or you can adjust the gridlines to suit your needs. You can choose:

- *Minimum.* Sets the lowest amount indicated in your values labels.
- *Maximum.* Sets the highest allowable value.
- *Major Unit.* Determines how far apart the major gridlines or tick marks will be.
- *Minor Unit.* Determines how far apart the minor gridlines or tick marks will be.
- *Floor (XY Plane) Crosses At.* Sets the level at which the Category axis intersects the Values or Series axis (whichever you're formatting).
- *Logarithmic Scale.* In a logarithmic scale, instead of the gridlines advancing, say, from 10 to 20, they advance exponentially from 10 (10^1) to 100 (10^2) to 1000 (10^3) and so on.
- *Values in Reverse Order.* Puts the highest values at the bottom and the lowest at the top.
- *Floor (XY Plane) Crosses At Minimum Value.* Sets the intersection of the Category axis at the lowest point of the Values (or Series) axis.

Setting Up Data Labels

Sometimes when you read a chart two values are so close together that you can't tell them apart. If that's a problem, you need data labels.

To set up data labels, choose Chart, Chart Options to bring up the Chart Options dialog box again. Select the Data Labels tab (if it's present; not all charts support Data Labels). In the ensuing property sheet (see Figure 11.28), you're presented with several options:

- *None*. Displays no data labels. This choice appears by default.

- *Show Value*. Labels each data point with the precise value it represents, the original number from the datasheet.

- *Show Percent*. In pie charts and stacked charts, shows the percentage each data series is of the whole.

- *Show Label*. Labels each data point with the category it belongs to.

- *Show Label And Percent*. Labels the sections of a pie or stacked chart with both their category names and percentage values.

FIG. 11.28
Reduce ambiguity with data labels, installed using these controls.

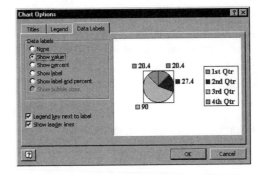

Part
IV

Ch
11

- *Show Bubble Sizes*. Labels the bubbles in a bubble chart with the value of the third data series that determines their sizes.

- *Legend Key Next To Label*. Puts a small colored square next to each label to tie it to the legend.

Formatting the Legend

Formatting the legend is very straightforward. As with everything else, you start by selecting it from the Chart Objects pull-down menu and then clicking Format.

The resulting dialog box contains the familiar Patterns and Fonts tabs, plus a third one, Placement, which offers Bottom, Corner (which places it in the upper-right corner), Top, Right, and Left. These choices are also available on the Legend tab of the Chart Options dialog box (accessed by choosing Chart, Chart Options), along with a check box that allows you turn the Legend on and off.

 TIP You can also move the legend around, along with some other chart elements, simply by clicking it inside the selected chart and dragging it from place to place.

Formatting Data Series

At the heart of the chart are the data series themselves, those colorful bars/pie slices/ bubbles, and more that you hope will both clearly convey information and capture your viewers' interest.

To format a data series, select it from the Chart Objects pull-down menu and click the Format button. In the resulting dialog box, you're given different options depending on which kind of chart you're working with. These include variations in the shape of data markers; plus options to add error markers (which indicate the margin of error in a data point) and drop lines (which tie data points in a line or area chart to a particular value), change the gap between categories in bar graphs, rotate the pie in pie graphs, and make it all one color or multicolored and more.

No matter what type of chart you're preparing, take the time to look at the options available for data series formatting; it's one more way you can hone your chart for better communication.

 TIP For added impact, use your ability to edit individual data series to create your own custom charts. You can't mix all charts this way, but you can mix, for example, bar charts and line charts (see Figure 11.29).

To do so, select a data series from the Chart Objects pull-down menu, then choose Chart, Chart Type. The Chart Type you select will apply only to the selected data series. If you try to apply a Chart Type that can't be mixed with the other data series, you get a warning message and will have to either change all data series to the new type or let the selected data series remain as it is.

FIG. 11.29
By formatting different data series as different types of charts, you can create unique, eye-catching designs.

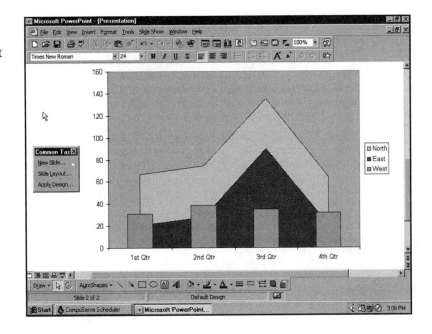

Trendlines

A *trendline* is a graphic representation of a trend in the data contained in your chart. If, for example, sales figures are doubling every month, a trendline would slope sharply upward from the end of the current data to indicate expected sales figures in coming months if that monthly doubling continues.

To add a trendline, first choose Chart. If the chart you're working with supports it, next choose Add Trendline. This brings up the dialog box in Figure 11.30.

There are several types of trendlines to choose from; click ? and then select the various types of trendlines to see the equations they're based on. You can also choose which data series the trendline should be calculated from.

The Options tab offers additional ways to modify your trendline, including labeling it and setting the number of periods you want it to forecast, either backward or forward.

Part
IV

Ch
11

FIG. 11.30
Some charts support
the inclusion of a
Trendline, which is
controlled from here.

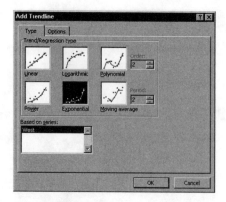

Modifying a Chart

Once you have your chart created and formatted, you may still want to relocate it or resize it. You can do both with ease; you can also adjust 3-D affects by rotating the chart through virtual space.

Resizing a Chart

Resizing a chart in PowerPoint is exactly the same as resizing anything else in Windows: grab a handle and pull. You don't even have to double-click the chart, like you do whenever you want to change formatting; a single click brings up a frame and handles. Adjust the frame as you want and the chart changes size and proportions to suit you.

TROUBLESHOOTING

I made my chart smaller, but the fonts stayed the same size and are now much too large. Is there any way to avoid this? Yes; refer to the earlier section "Formatting Fonts," and make sure that after you select Chart Area and open the Font tab, that the Scaling check box is activated. This ensures that your font automatically adjusts itself to the size of your chart.

Rotating Charts

You can't rotate a chart the way you can rotate objects created directly in PowerPoint, because the chart was actually created in Microsoft Graph. However, there is a unique kind of rotating you can apply to charts, provided they're 3-D or use 3-D visual effects.

Choose Chart, 3-D View. This brings up the dialog box in Figure 11.31. You can now rotate your chart in three dimensions, vertically using the arrows in the upper-left corner and horizontally using the buttons directly under the sample; or you can enter the Elevation and Rotation in degrees in the lower-left corner.

The Auto Scaling check box keeps things in proportion, or you can deselect it and adjust the height as a percentage of the base automatically.

FIG. 11.31
Rotate your chart through three dimensions in this small dialog box.

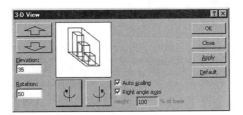

 T I P There's another way to rotate graphs in three dimensions: choose Corners from the Chart Objects pull-down menu. This creates handles at the corners of the chart. Grab these handles with your cursor to see a wireframe representation of the 3-D chart, just as you do in the 3-D View dialog box. Drag the handles around to adjust the 3-D viewing angle. This is actually simpler and makes it easier to fine-tune the chart than using the 3-D View dialog box controls.

Part
IV

Ch
11

If you're working with a true 3-D graph, as opposed to one that just uses 3-D effects, you can deselect Right Angle Axes to get the slightly different dialog box in Figure 11.32. Now you have two more buttons that allow you to add a sense of perspective to your chart, so that your columns can appear to be rising from or to a great height, or vanishing into the distance.

FIG. 11.32
Add perspective to a 3-D chart with this dialog box.

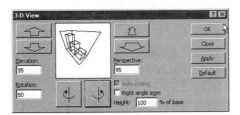

CAUTION
It bears repeating yet again: your primary goal is communication. A graph with extreme perspective applied can sometimes look wonderful but fail at its primary goal because of the distortion used to create effect. Make sure you don't lose the message in the medium.

Moving Charts on a Page

To move a chart on a slide, simply click it, hold the button down, and drag it wherever you like. To move the chart to another slide, cut and paste it.

Adding Objects to a Chart

One of the buttons active in the Chart toolbar is the Drawing button, which activates the Drawing toolbar at the bottom of the PowerPoint workspace. You can use some of the Drawing tools inside the Chart Area while it's selected. These Drawing objects become part of the chart: you can't move them out of the Chart Area, and they'll automatically resize and move with the rest of the chart.

 Instead of adding just an ordinary title to your chart, why not use the Drawing tools to add a WordArt title? Its 3-D, shadowing, and other effects aren't available with ordinary text, and can add extra impact to your chart's appearance.

Saving Your Custom Chart

You've labored long and hard to create the perfect chart for your presentation. In fact, it's such a perfect chart you'll want to use it, with variations, again and again.

In that case, add it to the list of Custom chart types that PowerPoint has on file. With your customized chart selected, choose Chart, Chart Type, and click the Custom Types tab. Click User-Defined in the Select From area, and click Add below that. Enter a name and description in the Add Custom Chart Type dialog box that opens, click OK, and your chart will be saved for future use. ●

CHAPTER 12

Working with Tables

by Edward C. Willett

Although in casual conversation we tend to use the terms *chart* and *table* more or less interchangeably, PowerPoint uses them in very specific ways. To PowerPoint, a chart (dealt with in the preceding two chapters) is a graphical display of data, while a table displays data as words or numbers. ■

Create a table

Create a Word table within PowerPoint and edit it to fit your needs.

Import a table

Import a table you may already have created in Word, and link to it so your presentation is always current.

Format a table

Change text, lines, borders, shading, and more. Do it yourself, or select one of many pre-formatted tables.

Creating a Table

Not all data is best presented as a chart. Maybe you need to cross-reference various possibilities and display the possible outcomes, or maybe you really need actual figures to appear instead of just graphical representations of them. In that case, a table may serve your purposes best. PowerPoint allows you to use the powerful Table function that's part of Microsoft Word to create a table right in PowerPoint.

Choose the Table Size

 To create a table in PowerPoint, click the Insert Microsoft Word Table button in the toolbar. This brings up the pop-up window in Figure 12.1. As you move your cursor across the blank squares (you don't have to click and hold), they turn dark. This is how you select how many cells you want to initially appear in your table.

FIG. 12.1
This small grid lets you preset the size of your table from 1 × 1 to 5 × 5.

Once you've decided how many rows and columns you want, click once, and your table appears (see Figure 12.2).

FIG. 12.2
Your table consists of a grid of columns and rows. Each box where the columns and rows intersect is called a *cell*.

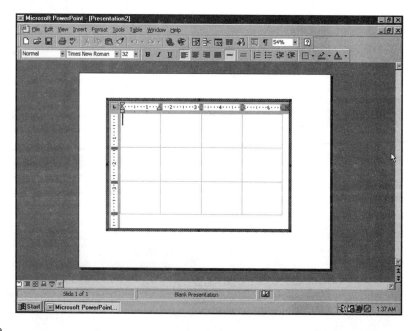

N O T E If you choose an AutoLayout slide that includes a table rather than using the Insert
Microsoft Word Table button, you won't see the grid. Instead, you see a small dialog
box that enables you to enter the number of rows and columns you want in your table. This is your
best choice if you need more than the five rows or columns shown in Figure 12.1. ■

Entering and Editing Text

To enter text into the table, click the cell where you want the text to appear. A flashing
cursor appears. Type your text, and edit it as you would any other text.

 T I P If you haven't changed the table's formatting defaults and you type more text than fits in the cell,
the cell automatically increases in height.

You can move from cell to cell using the mouse, the Tab key, or the cursor control
keys. Once you've filled in all the cells, your table will look something like the one in
Figure 12.3.

FIG. 12.3
Entering text into the
cells of your table is
as easy as pointing
and clicking.

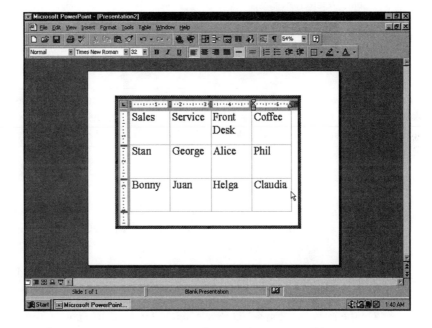

Part
IV

Ch
12

N O T E The table does not accurately show you what you see on the slide once you've finished
editing it. Not only do the rulers along the edges disappear, but the text you enter into
the table may be larger than it appears on the finished slide. You may find you have to move from
Table Formatting view to the regular Slide Layout view and back again several times to get the
effect you want. ■

Selecting Columns and Rows

To select a column or row, either click, hold, and drag your cursor across it from left to right as far as it will go, or choose Table, Select Row, or Table, Select Column.

To select multiple columns and rows or a range of cells, point at the upper-left corner of the range you want to select. Click, hold, and drag the cursor to the lower-right corner of the range you want to select.

Adding Columns and Rows

 You're not limited to the number of rows and columns you initially select for your table. If you're using the Tab key to move from cell to cell, you'll find that a new row is added automatically if you tab forward from the cell in the bottom-right corner. To add a row in between existing rows, simply place your cursor where you want the new row to be inserted, and click the Insert Row button.

Deleting a row is a little bit harder. To delete a row, you must first select it, then choose Table, Delete Rows.

To delete *or* insert a column, you must first select the column. This changes the Insert Row button on the toolbar to an Insert Column button and the Delete Rows choice under Table to Delete Columns.

 T I P An alternate way to delete a row or column is to place your cursor in a cell in the row or column you want to delete and choose Table, Delete Cells, then click Delete Entire Row or Delete Entire Column in the Delete Cells dialog box.

Resizing Columns and Rows

To change the height of columns or the width of rows, move your cursor to any of the gridlines. The cursor changes to a two-pointed arrow. Click, hold, and drag left or right to expand or shrink the column.

Another way to resize columns and rows is to change the height and width of cells. Choose Table, Cell Height and Width. This brings up the dialog box in Figure 12.4.

On the right, you can select a base height for the cell in points from the At menu; on the left is a small pull-down Height menu with three choices:

- ■ If you choose Auto, the table automatically adjusts the row height to match the height of the largest cell.

- If you choose At Least and enter a point size, the row height will be at least that height, and may be larger if it's required to fit in all the text.

- If you choose Exactly and enter a point size, the row height doesn't exceed that height, no matter how much text is entered in a cell—so if you enter too much text, some of it may not appear.

FIG. 12.4

Row height and some formatting of cells can be specified from this dialog box.

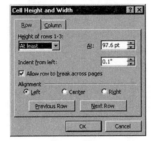

To change column width, click the Column tab, which brings up the dialog box in Figure 12.5. Here you can select the Width of the columns manually, or choose AutoFit, which automatically adjusts the width of the selected column or columns as necessary to fit in the text. You can also increase the space between your columns.

Both of these choices affect the amount of whitespace in your table. *Whitespace* is a layout term which refers to the empty space between design elements such as text and graphics. A slide with too little whitespace looks crowded and forbidding; it repels the viewer rather than drawing him or her in. Lots of whitespace, on the other hand, creates a feeling of spaciousness and simplicity, makes each layout element stand out more, and enhances readability.

Part
IV

Ch
12

FIG. 12.5

This dialog box provides an easy way to adjust the width of columns and add more whitespace to your table design by increasing the space between columns.

TROUBLESHOOTING

Some of my table cells have more text in them than others; now the size of the cells is all over the place. How can I make all the cells on my table the same size without fixing each one by hand? To make your cells all the same size again without hiding any text in the process, select the rows or columns whose width or height you want to equalize, then choose Table, Distribute Rows Evenly or Table, Distribute Columns Evenly.

Adjusting Spacing

If, to loosen up your design, you want to add whitespace between columns, call up the dialog box in Figure 12.5 again by choosing Table, Cell Height and Width, and enter the amount of whitespace you want to place between columns in the Space Between Columns box.

To format row spacing, select the rows you want to work with, then choose Format, Paragraph. In the Indents and spacing tab, add Spacing Before and After to adjust the row height for the selected rows. You can also create space by adding blank rows to your table, and adjusting their height by choosing Table, Cell Height and Width and using the dialog box in Figure 12.4.

There's also no one-step method for moving a row or column within the table, but it can be done. Just right-click the column or row you want to move, choose Edit, Cut (or press Ctrl+X), move the cursor to where you want the column or row to move to, and choose Edit, Paste (or press Ctrl+V).

If drag and drop text editing is active, you can also simply highlight the text, drag it to the point where you want to paste it, and release the mouse button. PowerPoint automatically pastes it into position.

Importing a Table

If you have already created a table in Word that you want to insert into your PowerPoint presentation, you can do so by choosing Insert, Object. This brings up the dialog box in Figure 12.6. Click Create From File and, when prompted, enter the name of the Word table you want to import. (If you don't know the name, PowerPoint allows you to browse your computer to find the file.) You can also choose Link To File; that means that whenever you change the table in Word, those changes will be reflected in PowerPoint. This is a useful way to ensure that your PowerPoint presentation always contains the latest information.

FIG. 12.6
The Insert Object dialog box allows you to place a table you've already created in Word—among many other types of files—directly into PowerPoint.

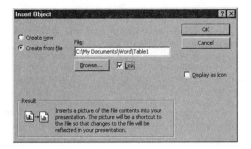

TROUBLESHOOTING

Why can't I import data from Excel into my PowerPoint table? Although it looks something like a spreadsheet, the table in PowerPoint is not. In fact, it's not really even a PowerPoint object; it's an embedded object created by Microsoft Word. Because Word doesn't allow you to directly import Excel data into a table, you can't do it in PowerPoint, either. However, you can insert an Excel spreadsheet directly, just as you've inserted a Word table, using the Insert Object dialog box in Figure 12.6.

Formatting a Table

Once you've entered text into the table, it's time to turn your attention to the visual impact of the table itself. PowerPoint makes available a number of tools to help you format lines, borders, backgrounds, and the text itself.

Formatting Text

You have more than one way to format text in a table because the table isn't really part of PowerPoint; it's really a Word document, and as a result, when you insert a table, you get several new formatting options to work with.

TROUBLESHOOTING

While I was using the Format, Font commands on my table, I noticed a tab marked Animation. I applied an Animation to my text, and it showed up while I was editing my table; but when I closed my table and returned to Slide view, the animation had quit. What's going on? This is an example of an available command that's of limited use in the context of PowerPoint. Remember that the table you're adding to your presentation is not actually produced by

continues

continued

PowerPoint; it's produced by Word. Although the Animation effects are supported in Word, they're not supported when the table is placed in PowerPoint. If you want animated text in your PowerPoint presentation, create it using PowerPoint tools as a separate object, not as part of your table.

Setting Tabs

You can set tabs by choosing Format, Tabs, or you can use the more direct approach and do it directly on the screen. Notice the rulers on the top and left sides of your table. These are just like the rulers in many word-processing systems. You can use them to adjust the margins of your table cells and add tabs.

Take a close look at these rulers. Above whichever cell your cursor is located in, the ruler has three controls: two little sliding triangles at the left, one pointing up (Hanging Indent) and one pointing down (First Line Indent), and another sliding triangle, pointing up, at the right (Right Indent) (see Figure 12.7).

The Hanging Indent and Right Indent controls set the left and right margins of the cell; the First Line Indent control sets the indent. By moving this to the left of the Hanging Indent control, you can create—what else?—a hanging indent, where the first line starts to the left of the rest of the text.

FIG. 12.7
Set margins and indents inside your cells just as you would inside a word processor, using the controls on the ruler.

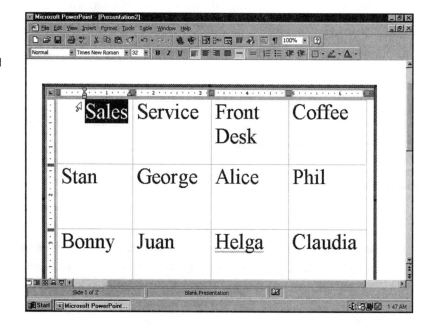

Borders and Shading

Sometimes it can be hard for your viewers to tell where information in your table's rows and columns falls, especially if it's a large, complex table. Adding borders and shading to rows, columns, or individual cells can help. Also, adding a border around the entire table gives it more visual unity and therefore more impact.

To quickly place simple borders around your table or some or all of its cells, click the arrow next to the Outside Border button to bring up another small menu of choices.

If you need more options, choose F<u>o</u>rmat, <u>B</u>orders and Shading to open the Borders and Shading dialog box in Figure 12.8.

FIG. 12.8

Specify what kind of borders you want in your table from this detailed dialog box.

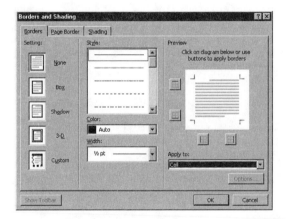

This dialog box is divided into three sections: Setting, St<u>y</u>le, and Preview.

In the Setting section, you can choose from five different types of borders:

- *<u>N</u>one*. No borders at all, the default.
- *Bo<u>x</u>*. Places a border only around the outside of the table.
- *<u>A</u>ll*. Places borders around every cell.
- *Gri<u>d</u>*. Applies special formatting that makes the selection look like it has a picture frame around it.
- *C<u>u</u>stom*. The automatic selection once you start designing your own borders with the other tools in this dialog box.

In the St<u>y</u>le area, you can choose from a variety of different lines; choose a <u>C</u>olor for your line, and apply a preset <u>W</u>idth, from 1/4 point to 6 points.

Part
IV

Ch
12

Finally, in the Preview area, you can decide exactly where the border should be applied, and how. You can apply it to the whole table, to selected cells only, or just to the selected text (so you can draw a box around a single word or phrase). You can click directly on the Preview diagram or use the buttons bordering it to decide where in the cell or table the borders should be applied.

The next tab, Page Border, is another of those that applies more to regular Word documents than to a table placed in PowerPoint; however, the third tab in the Borders and Shading dialog box, Shading, provides several options for filling cells (see Figure 12.9).

In addition to several shades of gray and color available in the Fill palette, you can create other effects by applying a shade of another color over the fill color. In the Pattern section at the bottom of the dialog box, select the Style (or shade) you want—expressed in percentages of the full color—and choose the Color below that.

As in the Borders tab, you can choose to apply this shading to just the text in the selected cells, to the cell itself, or to the whole table, by using the Apply To drop-down list menu.

FIG. 12.9
These controls that come with the table from Word provide a few more fill options than the toolbar Highlight button does.

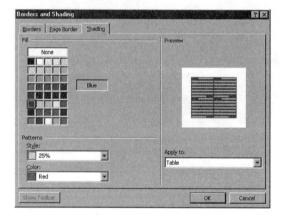

The Tables and Borders Toolbox

There's another way to achieve some of the effects I've been discussing: choose Table, Draw Table to open the Tables and Borders Toolbox in Figure 12.10. While it doesn't have all of the effects you can achieve using some of the methods mentioned previously, it does have the advantage of bringing them all together in one place. If you're formatting on-the-fly, then the Tables and Borders Toolbox is the way to go.

Let's start by looking at the text-related tools, which are mainly along the bottom (see Table 12.1).

FIG. 12.10

The Tables and Borders Toolbox puts a number of useful tools at your fingertips for quick formatting.

Table 12.1   Tables and Borders Toolbox Tools

Icon	Name	Description
	Merge Cells Split Cells	These two tools adjust cell size. Merge Cells erases the gridlines between any two or more highlighted cells in the same row or column. Split Cells splits them into the number of rows or columns you indicate in the Split Cells dialog box which opens when you click this button. (These functions are also available by choosing Table, Merge Cells or Table, Split Cells, respectively.)
	Align Top Center Vertically Align Bottom	These three buttons determine whether the text in the selected cells appears at the top of the cell, in the middle, or on the bottom.
	Distribute Rows Evenly Distribute Columns Evenly	These buttons have the same effect as the identical commands discussed earlier in the chapter.
	AutoFormat	See the discussion later in the chapter.
	Change Text Direction	Click this to rotate the text 90 degrees to the right; click it again to rotate it back 180 degrees to 90 degrees to the left of the original position; click it again to bring the text back to horizontal.
	Shading Color	Click this to change the background color of a cell or cells. Just place the cursor inside the cell you want to change, or highlight a range of cells, then click the down arrow beside the Shade Objects button. This opens a small pull-down menu from which you

continues

Table 12.1   Continued

Icon	Name	Description
		can select a background color. The color is applied to the selected cells. Notice that the Shade Objects button "remembers" which color you last used, so you can apply it to other cells by just clicking them and then choosing the Shade Objects button once.
	Outside Border	This button, which also appears on the Formatting toolbar, allows you to choose from among several standard border placements, including bordering all cells, placing a border only around the outside of the table, and placing a border along just one side of the table; it matches the button on the toolbar. Click the arrow beside it to see all the options.
	Draw Table Eraser	If the border placement you want does not appear in the Outside Border button menu, click the Draw Table tool. To draw a border along one side of a cell, place the pencil on the gridline of the side of the cell you want to border and move it along the gridline up or down (or right or left, if you're working horizontally). A line immediately appears alongside of the cell, drawn over the top of the gridline. Keep moving the pencil along the gridline from cell to cell and the border will extend cell by cell. The Erase tool works the same way, except, of course, it removes borders.
	Line Style Line Weight Border Color	To determine the appearance of the border, click Line Style, Line Weight, and Border Color. The Line Style menu gives you a variety of solid, dashed, and double lines to choose from; the Line Weight menu lets you choose how broad the line will be, measured in points; and the Border

Icon	Name	Description
		Color menu allows you to select the color you want the border to be from a basic color menu.

 TIP You can use Split Cells to quickly reconfigure your entire table to a different number of rows and columns, say from a 4 × 5 to a 6 × 6. Select all the cells in your table, then click Split Cells. In the Split Cells dialog box, enter the new number of rows and columns you want, then check the Merge Cells Before Split box. Now click OK. This will first combine all the cells in your table, then split them into the new number of rows and columns you've entered.

 TIP Unfortunately, you don't have PowerPoint's full range of patterns and fill effects available for your use when you're creating a table, because it's a Word object. However, you can still have a gradient fill, pattern, background, or picture as part of your table.

To do so, make sure that all of the cells contain no shade—click None in the Shade Objects palette in the Table and Borders Toolbox. This renders them transparent. Now use Draw to create a box the same size as the Table and fill it with the gradient, pattern, background, or picture you want highlighting your Table. Make sure it's "behind" the table. There you have it—no one will ever know you can't add those effects to a table in PowerPoint.

Other Table Commands

A few other commands accessed by choosing Table should be mentioned:

- *Headings.* Tells PowerPoint that the top row of your table should be considered a row of labels. If you select this, you won't notice any difference in your table unless you apply a formatting command that treats headings differently from regular cells, such as Sort.

- *Sort.* Sorts columns by text, number, or date, in ascending or descending order, depending on your entries in its dialog box. It also asks you if the list you are sorting has a header row or not.

- *Formula.* Turns your table into a miniature spreadsheet; you can enter a formula and use logical arguments to sum rows and columns. However, for presentation purposes, it's much more likely you do this sort of work in a spreadsheet and simply paste the results into PowerPoint, so you'll probably find this has limited usefulness.

- *Split Table.* Turns your Table into two tables, one above the other.

- *Hide Gridlines.* Does exactly what it says—making it harder to see where individual cells are, but easier to see what your table will look like when it's finished.

Part
IV

Ch
12

Using AutoFormat

 If you'd rather let the computer look after the process of formatting your table, there's another button on the Tables and Borders toolbar, you'll want to click Table AutoFormat.

This brings up the dialog box in Figure 12.11. Here you can select from a large number of preformatted table styles from the menu on the left. If you like elements of some, but not the whole table, you can also choose which formatting elements you want to keep by selecting the check boxes at the bottom.

You can choose to apply Borders, Shading, Font, or Color. You can also choose AutoFit, which automatically adjusts the size of the table to fit the amount of text in the cells. Below that, you can choose which parts of the table to apply the special formatting to: the heading row, the first column, the last row, or the last column.

FIG. 12.11

Let the computer do the work! Choose one of the AutoFormat styles you like and apply it to the table you've created.

CHAPTER 13

Creating an Organization Chart

by Dave Johnson

Perhaps the most widely used of business graphics, organization charts allow leaders and managers to convey their vision of control, communication, and operation to those who interact with an organization. Given the rate at which typical organizations restructure, any charting tool must be fast and flexible to keep you on top of the current lineup.

Microsoft Organization Chart is just that—a fast and flexible tool found inside PowerPoint 97 which makes it easy to add organization charts to any PowerPoint presentation. By using Microsoft Organization Chart, you can create charts that describe simple or quite complex personnel trees with multiple supervisors, subordinates, co-workers, and assistants. A large assortment of styles and display options means that your final product can look just as visually exciting as other components of your PowerPoint 97 presentation. ■

Building an organizational chart

Look here to get the most out of the organization chart builder in PowerPoint.

Editing an organization chart

Here's where you learn how to tweak your chart's appearance for maximum impact.

Adding a background in PowerPoint

Once you've completed the chart, add a colorful background to grab your audience's attention.

Building an Organization Chart

An Org Chart can be added to any kind of PowerPoint presentation. When you choose to start a new organization chart, PowerPoint launches an OLE-compatible application called Microsoft Organization Chart which allows you to create and modify your graphic. While this chart program is running, you may return to and work with PowerPoint; however, the chart itself is grayed-out and inaccessible.

▶ **See** "Linking Data with OLE," **p. 218**

N O T E Depending on the options you selected when installing PowerPoint, Microsoft Organization Chart may not be installed. If not, run setup again and install this component before proceeding. ▨

N O T E You cannot edit the text or structure of an organization chart directly from any of PowerPoint's various slide views. You must launch Microsoft Organization Chart to make these changes. ▨

There are two principal ways to create a new organization chart. If you are adding a new slide, follow these steps:

1. If the New Slide dialog box is not already on-screen, choose New Slide from the Common Task box on the left side of the screen.
2. Select the AutoLayout titled Organization Chart (see Figure 13.1). Click OK.
3. A new blank slide appears with the icon for an organization chart. Double-click this icon to start Microsoft Organization Chart.

On the other hand, you may need to add an organization chart to an existing slide. In this case, follow these steps:

1. Go to the slide to which you want to add an organization chart.
2. Choose Insert, Picture, Organization Chart. Organization Chart starts automatically.

Optimizing the View

Before you begin entering text in the chart boxes, you may want to change the magnification of the display. Ensure you are working in Organization Chart and choose View. Select the display option that best suits your needs: 50% of Actual is often a good starting place.

FIG. 13.1

The easiest way to start a new chart is via the AutoLayout slide templates available from the New Slide command.

Click here for AutoLayout templates

Double-click Organization Chart slide

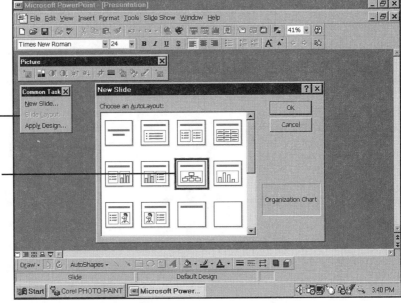

N O T E If you often switch views, it is convenient to use the function keys to change magnification:

Size to Window	F9
50% of Actual	F10
Actual Size	F11
200% of Actual	F12

The toolbar's Zoom button is a fast way to switch between the full page view (this is called Size to Window in the View Menu) to preview your chart and back to Actual Size for detail work. To use this button, select it from the toolbar and click the work area. Remember these hints for using the Zoom tool:

- Each time Zoom is selected, it cycles between Size to Window and Actual Size.
- When in Size To Window mode, selecting the Zoom tool turns the pointer into a magnifying glass. The display changes to Actual Size and Center on whatever part of the work area you click with the pointer.
- When viewing Actual Size, selecting the Zoom tool turns the pointer into a miniature Org Chart. It doesn't matter where you click with this pointer in the work area; the display changes to Full Page view.

Part

IV

Ch

13

■ When in any other mode, the Zoom tool first changes the view to Actual Size. The next time it is used, the display changes to Size To Window.

 TIP The current magnification level is always displayed in the lower-left corner of the Chart window.

If you prefer to work in a specific magnification (such as 50%) all the time, you can teach Organization Chart to always begin in that mode when launching new charts. To do this, choose Edit, Options. Make sure the box is checked for Remember the Current Magnification for New Charts. Click OK.

Entering Names, Titles, and Notes

Once you've created a chart, you initially have a template with several default chart boxes arranged in tree fashion below a single supervisor. Almost every aspect of this chart is customizable, including the style of the tree itself. For the time being, though, you learn how to enter the text data in the boxes. To enter data in a box, follow these steps:

1. Single-click the desired box. The selected box turns black.
2. Begin typing the name of the individual.
3. When you are finished with the individual's name, press the Enter key to move to the person's title (see Figure 13.2).
4. Continue pressing Enter to add up to two additional lines of comments. These lines may be left blank.
5. When you're ready to fill in another box, simply click it as per step 1. The data you entered in the current box is retained.

After you enter data in the appropriate boxes, it may be necessary to modify or change that information at a later time. To edit the text in a chart box, follow these steps:

1. Single-click the desired box. The selected box turns black.
2. Single-click again. The box expands to its "actual size," showing the contents of the various fields.
3. Double-click the field you want to change and type over the old text. Use the Enter key to move among the fields in this box.
4. When you're finished, click outside of the box to retain the changes.

 TIP When moving among fields in a chart box, you can use the Enter key, Tab key, or up and down arrow keys, depending on your preference.

FIG. 13.2
When you've finished entering data, the box fits itself to the text. Leave unused fields, like Comments, blank.

Current Box

Current Magnification

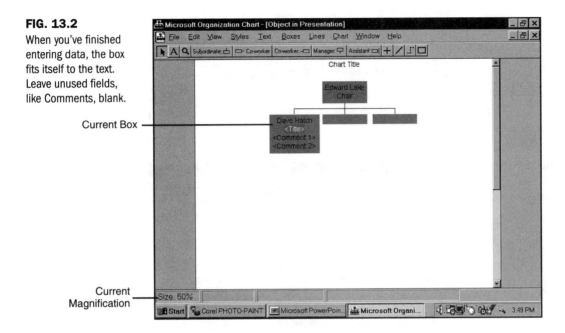

Adding Positions

The default Org Chart template consists of just one manager and three subordinates. PowerPoint lets you add various managers, subordinates, co-workers, and assistants to your organization chart to fully describe your organization. When adding boxes to a chart, you must attach them to boxes already in the project—these original boxes are called *parents*, even though occasionally the new box (if it is a manager) will end up positioned higher in the chart. Adding the personnel is actually very simple. The options are shown in Figure 13.3 and described in Table 13.1.

Part
IV

Ch
13

Table 13.1	Position Icons	
Icon	**Name**	**Function**
Subordinate:	Subordinate	This places a box one level lower than its parent.
:Co-worker	Co-worker	This places a box to the left of its parent.
Co-worker:	Co-worker	This places a box to the right of its parent.

continues

Table 13.1	Continued	
Icon	Name	Function
Manager: ⊔	Manager	This places a box one level higher than its parent.
Assistant: ☐	Assistant	This places a box below the parent, but not in the same plane as subordinates.

FIG. 13.3
Boxes—like Robert Niles—can play the role of subordinate, co-worker, and manager simulta-neously.

Assistant
Manager
Subordinate

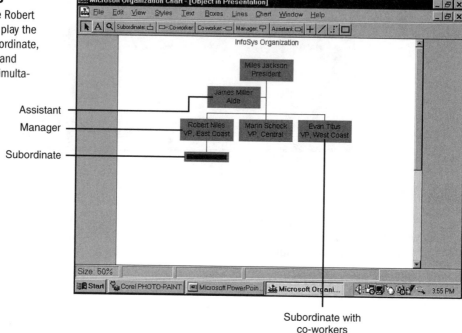

Subordinate with
co-workers

How do you actually add these objects to a chart? Try this:

1. Click the type of box (subordinate or co-worker) you want to add from the toolbar.

2. Click the box in your chart to which you want to associate a new box—this is called a *parent*. You find that the parent now has a subordinate attached.

Adding Subordinates   Enhance the default organization chart by adding subordinates. Start with a new chart by choosing Insert, Picture. Choose Organization Chart, then follow these steps:

Subordinate: ⊔

1. Click the Subordinate icon. The pointer changes shape to remind you which tool you've selected.

2. Click one of the three subordinates at the lowest level of the chart. A new subordinate appears under this box.

3. Click the Subordinate button again to add another subordinate.

4. Click the newest subordinate box you just added during the preceding step 2. Notice that there is now a string of subordinates in the chart.

What would happen if you hadn't clicked the newest box, but instead had selected the parent to that box? Try this:

1. Click the Subordinate tool one more time.

2. Click the parent box you selected in step 2. Notice that this box now has two subordinates (see Figure 13.4).

FIG. 13.4
Robert Niles has two subordinates (the Subordinate tool was used twice on his box), while Jim Thorne has a subordinate of his own.

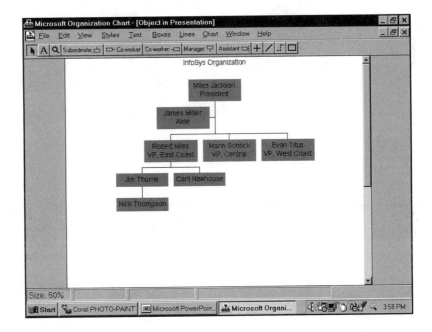

> **TIP** The tools for adding boxes aren't persistent; you must re-select the Subordinate tool for each and every subordinate you add to a chart.
>
> To add several boxes at once to the same parent, however, you can click the tool the desired number of times and then click the parent box. To add four subordinates, for instance, click the Subordinate icon four times and then select the parent box in the chart.

Part
IV

Ch
13

Adding Co-Workers   Co-workers can be added in just the same way as subordinates, and, in fact, this can ultimately have the same effect on a chart:

1. Select the Co-worker icon. The pointer changes shape to that of a co-worker. Note that there are two Co-worker tools representing left-hanging and right-hanging objects. Select which way you want the co-worker to appear on-screen.

2. Find the row of two subordinates created in step 6 from Adding Subordinates previously. Click either of these boxes (see Figure 13.5).

FIG. 13.5
Either the right-hanging co-worker or the Subordinate tool can be used to add this new box.

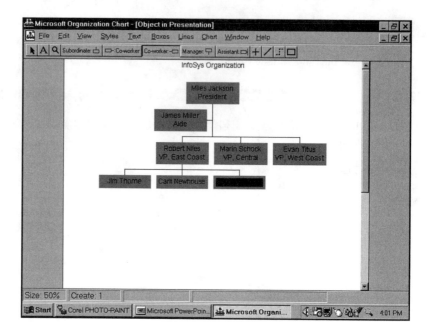

> **T I P**
> If you click a tool to add a box and then decide you don't want to add that box, press the Esc key to cancel the operation.

Adding Managers and Assistants   Unlike the other boxes discussed earlier, managers are added above the parent box. Just like in the real world, a subordinate in PowerPoint can have any number of managers or assistants. Add these boxes to your chart exactly as you would Co-workers and Subordinates (see Figure 13.6).

FIG. 13.6
The Manager boxes are used to demote the president and to drop Evan Titus to a subordinate level as well.

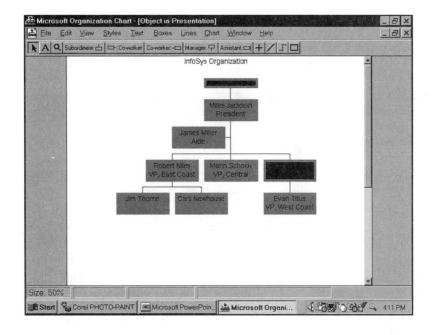

Saving Your Work

Typically, you will want to exit Microsoft Organization Chart and save your work to a PowerPoint slide. Here is how to embed your chart in a PowerPoint presentation:

1. Choose File, Exit and Return to the Presentation.

2. A dialog box asks, Do you want to update object in Presentation before proceeding?. Click Yes. Microsoft Organization Chart closes and returns you to PowerPoint.

There may be times when you want to return to PowerPoint to complete other parts of a presentation, but leave Microsoft Organization Chart open for later editing. It is a good idea to save your work before you do so. Choose File, Update Presentation. The chart is now updated in PowerPoint. Microsoft Organization Chart remains open. You can now switch to PowerPoint and resume working.

Lastly, there are situations in which it may be desirable to create organization charts that aren't embedded in PowerPoint. Microsoft Organization Chart makes it possible to save a chart to the hard disk as a stand-alone file. To use this feature, do the following:

1. Choose File, Save Copy As.

2. Name and save the file in the Save As dialog box that opens.

Part
IV

Ch
13

3. When you want to load this chart back into the program, open Microsoft Organization Chart and choose File, Open.

4. Select the file you saved and click Open (see Figure 13.7).

FIG. 13.7
You can create a library of organization charts and load them into PowerPoint on demand.

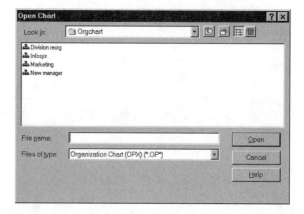

 TIP You may leave several organization charts open at once and switch among them using the Windows menu. In this way you can easily copy parts of one chart into another.

 TIP If you use several versions of the same presentation, only with different organization charts, save the charts to your hard disk and simply substitute them in the same slide show as needed.

Configuring Options for Maximum Effectiveness

You can set preferences in Microsoft Organization Chart so that it always begins just the way you need it. An Options dialog box is found under the Edit menu (see Figure 13.8). This offers the following choices:

- Use Standard 4-Box Template for New Charts. This manager plus three subordinates scheme is the default used throughout this chapter.

- Use Standard 1-Box Template for New Charts. If your chart needs are radically different from the default and you have to delete the three subordinates right away anyway, you might select this option, which opens with nothing more than a single manager.

- Remember Current Topmost Box, Use As 1-Box Template for New Charts. If your charts always begin with the same manager atop the slide, this option remembers the fields you've entered in this box for all subsequent charts.

FIG. 13.8
The options dialog
box streamlines the
process of starting
a new chart.

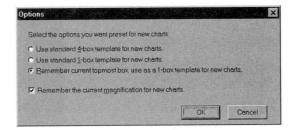

Editing an Organization Chart

Microsoft Organization Chart provides some powerful tools for editing your chart and customizing its appearance, but unfortunately, many of these are not at all obvious. Some of the things you can do to a chart include:

- Editing boxes inside the chart, including promoting and demoting members.
- Formatting text.
- Formatting the appearance of the boxes.
- Adding drawing objects.
- Changing the style of the chart.

Managing Layers

In order to edit your chart effectively, it is important to know how to select those parts of the organization which you want to modify. There are several ways to do this:

- *Shift select*. Works best for modifying boxes on the chart that aren't related to each other in an otherwise useful way. For instance, you could use Shift select to choose boxes that appear to be placed randomly on the screen and can't be grouped any other way. To Shift select boxes, simply hold down the Shift key as you click the appropriate boxes. They turn black to indicate they're selected.

- *Drag select*. Best used in situations where the desired boxes are in close proximity to each other and you can capture them all simply by expanding a rectangle around them with the mouse. Hold down the left mouse button as you drag the mouse on the screen (see Figure 13.9). All the objects completely inside the rectangle turn red, indicating they are selected.

Part
IV
Ch
13

T I P To deselect a group of boxes, simply click anywhere else on the screen.

The Edit menu also has two commands which can make selecting numerous boxes easier. Choose Edit, Select, and the following options cascade (see Table 13.2).

Table 13.2   Edit Select Menu Options

Menu Item	Function
All	Selects every object in the chart.
All Assistants	Selects every Assistant-type box.
All Co-Managers	Selects all boxes which serve as co-managers.
All Managers	Selects all boxes which have subordinates.
All Non-Managers	Selects all boxes which do not have subordinates (see Figure 13.10).
Group	Selects all the boxes which are related, such as all the subordinates to a given manager or all the co-managers supervising a set of subordinates.
Branch	Selects all the boxes in a given branch from the selected box down.
Lowest Level	Selects all the boxes in the lowest level of the chart.
Connecting lines	Selects all the lines in a chart.
Background Objects	Selects all the drawing objects added to the chart.

FIG. 13.9

Dragging the mouse draws a box around chart objects which are selected when the mouse button is released.

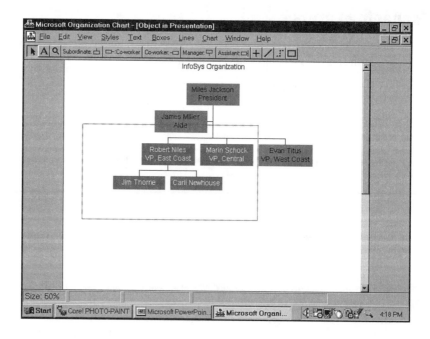

FIG. 13.10

The selected boxes are a result of choosing Edit, Select, All Non-Managers.

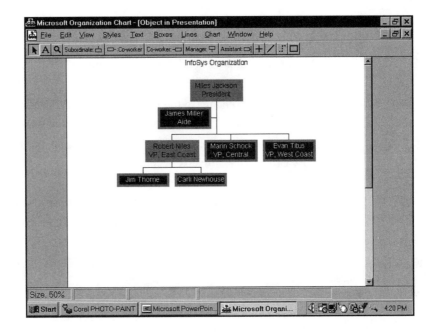

The second Edit menu command makes it easy to select a specific level or a group of levels. Choose Edit, Select Levels, and a dialog box appears in which you can specify a range of levels to select. Level 1 is always the highest manager or co-manager in the chart.

TIP Assistant boxes are considered to be part of the level which includes subordinates to the assistant's manager.

Deleting and Moving Boxes

Your organization isn't static, and the time will come when you need to modify the personnel in the chart. To delete a box, simply:

1. Click the box you want eliminated.
2. Press the Delete key.

Sometimes, personnel don't leave an organization but are re-assigned. In order to move an individual from their current location in an organization to another, do the following:

1. Make sure the box you want to move is not currently selected. If the box is already selected and you click it again, you won't be able to move it, but instead it will be in Text Edit mode. If necessary, click outside the box to deselect it.
2. Click the box you want to move and continue holding down the left mouse button.

Part
IV

Ch
13

3. Drag the box with the mouse. You see that the pointer changes to a four-direction arrow, and the box's outline moves with the mouse.

4. Move the box over another nearby box (see Figure 13.11). Three options are available:

   - If you move the pointer to the right edge of a box, a right arrow appears. If you release the mouse, the box becomes a co-worker to the right of this box.

   - If you move the pointer to the left edge of a box, a left arrow appears. If you release the mouse, the box becomes a co-worker to the left of this box.

   - If you move the pointer to the bottom edge of a box, a Subordinate icon appears. If you release the mouse, the box becomes a subordinate to this box.

5. Release the mouse in the desired position. The box moves to a new location.

FIG. 13.11

When a box is dragged over another, the new parent turns red. Depending on where it is dropped, the box becomes a co-worker or subordinate.

Selected box in old position

Outline of selected box in new position

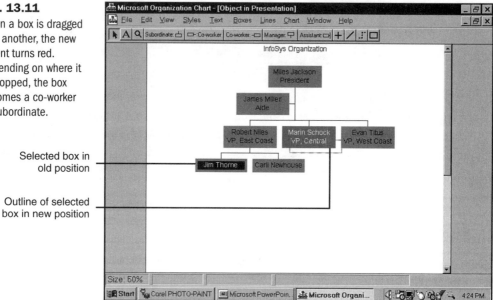

Not all positions are available at all times. If a box is already subordinate to the position to which you are attempting to drag it, for instance, the subordinate icon does not appear.

TROUBLESHOOTING

I'm having trouble making the program do what I want when moving boxes around the chart.
What's wrong? There are a few things you just can't do when dragging and dropping boxes:

- You cannot select more than one box and drag them together. All box movements must be done individually.

- You cannot drag a box in such a way that it becomes subordinate to one of is own subordinates.

- While you can drag and drop assistants to other positions in a chart, you can't turn a box into an assistant via drag and drop.

- You cannot turn a box into a manager by moving it to the top edge of a box.

Promoting and Demoting Boxes

You can use the technique described above specifically to promote and demote personnel in an organization chart. To promote a box up one level, do the following:

1. Click the previously unselected box you want to move and continue holding down the left mouse button.

2. Drag the box with the mouse until it is over its own manager (or the manager in another level).

3. Release the mouse. You may want to move the box again to position it in a more specific location (see Figure 13.12).

FIG. 13.12

Jim Thorne, dragged to the right edge of Robert Niles, has been promoted one level.

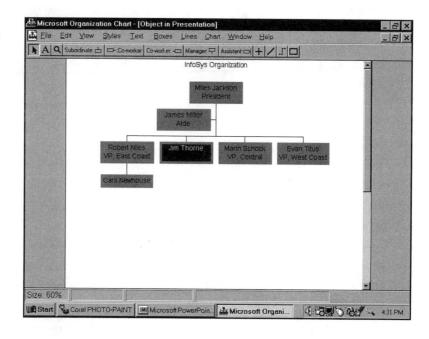

Part

IV

Ch

13

If you want to demote a manager, you cannot simply drag it to its own subordinate to move it down a level. Instead, do this:

1. Click the previously unselected manager you want to move and continue holding down the left mouse button.

2. Drag the box with the mouse until it is over another manager at the same level.

3. Release the mouse. You may want to move the box again to position it in a more specific location.

TIP When moving managers, all of the subordinates associated with that box move to the new location as well.

Editing Chart Styles

When you first begin Microsoft Organization chart, the program starts by displaying your chart in a default style. It is possible to modify the entire chart—or any part of it—via any of several styles to emphasize the specific structure of your organization.

This is one of the most powerful tools in Microsoft Organization Chart and bears some investigation. You can use the eight chart styles to change the way the organization is depicted. Some of these styles are largely cosmetic, affecting only their visual presentation, while others fundamentally change reporting structures within the depicted group. These styles are found in the Style menu (see Figure 13.13). Of these eight styles, six can be used to affect subordinates, while the remaining two options modify managers and assistants.

FIG. 13.13
Use one of six style options to organize subordinates below a manager.

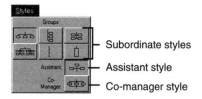

Modifying Subordinates   One of the most effective uses of styles is to control the readability of complex Org Charts. A large organization, for instance, may contain dozens of positions which take on the characteristics of an eye chart if not manipulated and displayed with care. Take a look at several ways to display subordinates. Start a new organization chart and follow these steps:

1. Label each of the four boxes in an identifiable way so you can see the effect of these styles on their position in the chart.

2. Select the lowest level by choosing Edit, Select, Lowest Level.

3. Select the Style menu. As you can see in Figure 13.13, the selected style is recessed. Click the top middle button. Note that the subordinates change from a "wide" tree in Figure 13.14 to a "vertical" tree in Figure 13.15.

FIG. 13.14
Organization Chart uses a wide subordinate "tree" as a default.

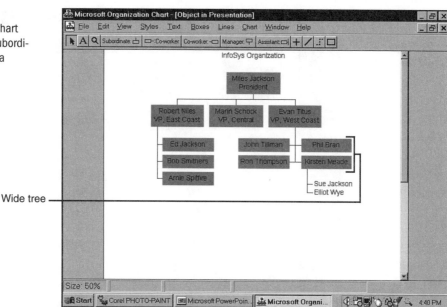

Wide tree

FIG. 13.15
This is a more efficient use of space for multiple subordinates.

Vertical tree

Part
IV

Ch

13

4. Return to the original configuration by selecting the top leftmost button.

5. Now add three new subordinates to the leftmost subordinate. Do this by clicking the subordinate button three times in the toolbar and then clicking the leftmost subordinate. Label them (see Figure 13.16).

FIG. 13.16

More than one subordinate style can be used in the same chart.

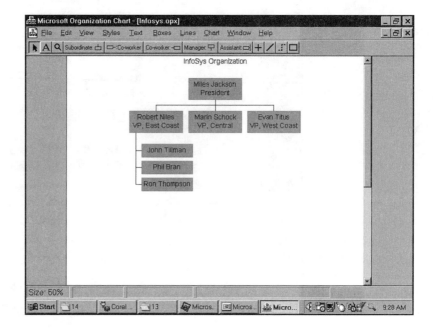

6. Note that the default for a third level subordinate is the style you just experimented with. Three subordinates can be a bit unwieldy, though, so select these (drag select them with the mouse) and change the style.

7. Now select the Style menu and choose the top-right button. Note that the lines of responsibility haven't changed, but this creates a more efficient use of space within the chart (see Figure 13.17).

Modifying Managers   Not all of the changes offered by chart styles are merely cosmetic, however. The Co-manager style changes the chain-of-command within an organization. To see how it works, continue with the previous chart:

1. Select the three subordinates in the middle level (Niles, Schock, and Titus) using the drag select method.

2. Select Style and choose the Co-Manager button. As shown in Figure 13.18, note that these three individual subordinates have now been given joint management over any subordinates below.

FIG. 13.17
Charts look best when a variety of styles are used to display the organization.

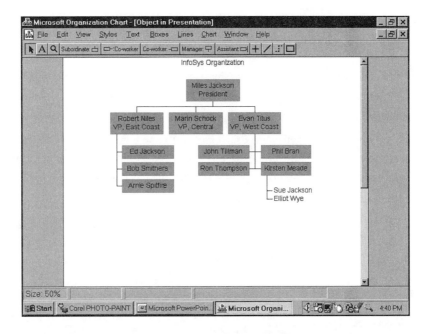

FIG. 13.18
Co-managers can be used to show joint management of personnel and departments.

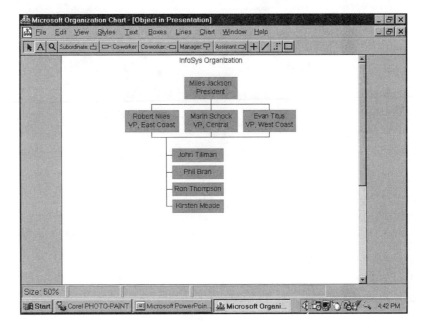

Part

IV

Ch

13

Chart styles are a powerful tool for organizing a chart. It is rare that an entire chart will need or look good with the same style. Organize individual levels and groups in the most appropriate style for maximum understandability.

Formatting Text

Microsoft Organization Chart gives you some flexibility with respect to how you display text. You have the ability to left-, right-, and center-justify text, or modify its font type, size, and color. To modify any of these attributes, do the following:

1. Select the text you want to modify.

2. From the Text menu, select the tool you want to use. Left, Right, and Center take effect immediately. Font and Color display dialog boxes for changing those attributes (see Figure 13.19).

FIG. 13.19
Both the font and text color can be modified from the Text menu.

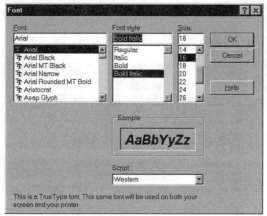
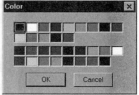

 You can modify all the text in a chart by choosing Edit, Select, All (Ctrl+A) before you choose a Text Edit tool. Alternatively, you can effect just selected boxes, or even just selected text in a particular box. You can change the font, size and color of text on a character-by-character basis by selecting just those characters you want to change.

Formatting Boxes

You can use a variety of commands to modify the appearance of boxes and lines in a chart. The tools available in the Boxes menu are:

- Color
- Shadow
- Border Style
- Border Color
- Border Line Style

You can change the attributes of a box or group of boxes very quickly for a distinctive and readable chart:

1. Open a new Org Chart and select the three co-workers in the lowest level by holding down the Shift key and clicking in each of them with the left mouse button.

2. Choose Boxes, Color.

3. Pick a shade of blue and click OK. The boxes remain selected, but you should see they have changed color. They change to the indicated color when deselected.

4. Choose Boxes, Shadow. A cascading menu of shadow options appear, illuminating the box from various angles (see Figure 13.20). Select the option below None. This makes the boxes appear as if a light source is above and to the right.

FIG. 13.20
Shadows add a sense of virtual lighting to a slide and can give a chart a professional appearance.

5. Select the Manager box, causing the subordinates to be deselected.

6. Choose Box, Border Style (see Figure 13.21). Select from the cascading menu of choices the thick frame in the lower-right corner.

7. Choose Box, Border Color and select a shade of blue from the dialog box.

8. Choose Box, Border Line Style and select the long dashes (see Figure 13.22).

FIG. 13.21
Though less useful than shadows, borders can frame important boxes and give them visual impact.

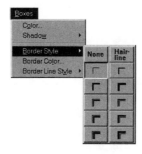

Part
IV

Ch
13

FIG. 13.22
Remember that boxes inherit the style of their parents.

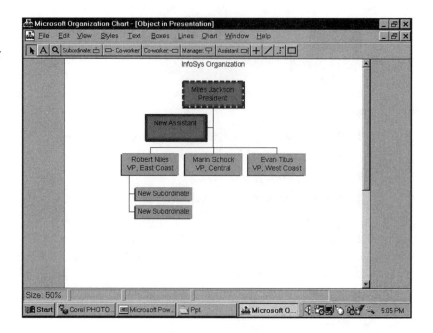

 TIP Like any graphic design elements, you should choose box styles carefully and sparingly. Stay consistent at least within groups and levels, if not the entire chart, and minimize the number of different effects you employ in a single chart.

Adding Drawing Objects

There are a small number of drawing objects you can add to organization charts which can be an important part of the overall product. They're located on the toolbar, and include the following, as shown in Table 13.3.

Table 13.3   Drawing Objects

Icon	Name	Function
A	Enter Text	You can add text outside of boxes using this tool.
+	Horizontal/ Vertical Line	This allows you to create perfectly perpendicular lines anywhere on the chart.
/	Diagonal Line	This is a freeform line that can appear at any angle on the chart.
.:	Auxiliary Line	This tool connects unrelated boxes together.

Icon	Name	Function
	Rectangle	This tool draws boxes that do not interact with the organization of the chart. You can use the Box menu to change their color, shadow, and border.

Editing Text   The Text tool allows you to enter text anywhere on the Org Chart, outside of personnel boxes. This text can be modified using any of the commands in the Text menu discussed earlier in this chapter. Place some text on the Org Chart by clicking the Text tool, then clicking the screen. Type some text. To edit it, experiment with the following:

■ Click the text. Sizing handles appear around text indicating it has been selected (see Figure 13.23).

■ You may reposition the text on-screen by clicking inside the invisible frame in which the text is stored and dragging with the mouse to a new position, or you can resize the frame by clicking a handle and dragging to make the frame larger or smaller.

■ If you resize the frame, you can use the Left, Right, and Center commands from the Text menu to position text within the frame.

■ Once the frame is selected, you can change the font, size, and color of all the text in the frame.

■ To change just a part of the text in a frame, double-click the text. Select the desired text and then modify it using the Text menu.

FIG. 13.23
When sizing handles are visible, style changes affect all the text in the frame. Double-click the text to change just part of it.

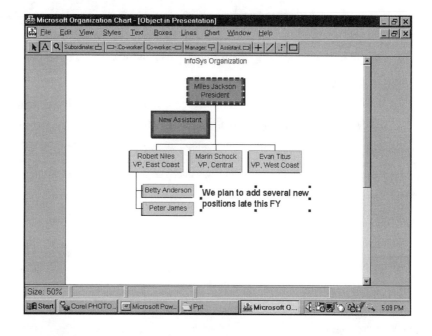

Part

IV

Ch

13

Adding Auxiliary Lines   While the other drawing tools are fairly straightforward, the auxiliary line bears a bit of explanation. Ideal for showing dual and indirect relationships between individuals in an organization chart, the auxiliary line can connect otherwise unrelated boxes together (see Figure 13.24). The line forms the necessary right angles and avoid passing through other obstacles to connect two boxes together, wherever they may be located.

FIG. 13.24

The auxiliary line can show a relationship between two otherwise unrelated co-workers.

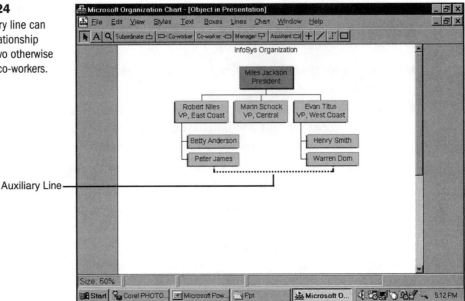

To use an auxiliary line, open a new organization chart and try this:

1. Click the Auxiliary Line icon in the toolbar.

2. Click and hold the left mouse button on the lower left subordinate.

3. Drag the mouse to the lower right subordinate. Release the mouse anywhere over the box. An auxiliary line snaps into place between the two boxes.

 TIP   The auxiliary line locks itself to its boxes wherever you begin and end with the mouse.

To change the position of an auxiliary line:

1. Carefully position the mouse over the long horizontal part of the line. Click and hold the mouse button; the pointer changes shape to two parallel lines to show it is aligned.

2. You have just grabbed the line. Drag it farther away from the boxes. Release the mouse.

You can move the vertical segments of the line in the same way.

 TIP You can use the line color, thickness, and style commands from the Line menu to make the auxiliary line stand out from other objects in the chart.

Adding a Background in PowerPoint

Once the organization chart is embedded in PowerPoint, some special tools are available for customizing the appearance of the slide. In particular, you can add background colors, patterns, and even bitmapped pictures behind the chart. To modify the slide's background, save your chart and return to PowerPoint. Then do this:

1. Single-click the chart to select it.

 2. In the Picture toolbar, click the icon labeled Format Object (see Figure 13.25).

3. The Colors and Lines tab should be on top. In the Fill section, click the Color drop-down menu (see Figure 13.26).

4. Select a color. Click OK.

FIG. 13.25
Add graphics to organization charts using the Picture toolbar.

Picture toolbar —

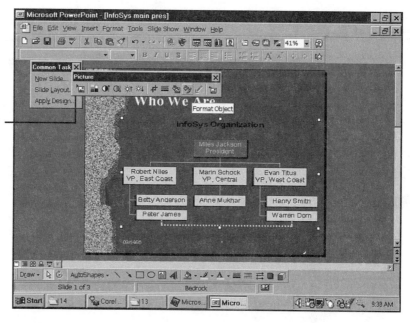

Part
IV

Ch
13

FIG. 13.26

The Format Object dialog box provides powerful controls over the chart's background appearance.

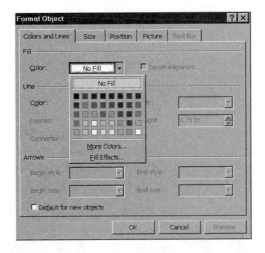

> **TIP** The transparent modifier next to the Color menu is an elegant tool for seeing through the background color to objects behind.

   5. Click the Format Object tool again and return to the Color drop-down menu.

   6. This time choose Fill Effects from the bottom of the menu; the Fill Effects dialog box appears (see Figure 13.27). The options here include:

   - *Gradient.* Gradients are configurable variations from one color to another.

   - *Texture.* This option provides a choice of a number of pre-set textures like sand, marble, and granite.

   - *Pattern.* Choose from a number of simple two-color patterns.

   - *Picture.* Load a graphic behind your organization chart.

   7. Proceed with loading a graphic. Click the Picture tab and click the Select Picture button.

   8. Choose a picture from the hard disk and click OK. A preview appears.

> **TIP** You can select an image from another drive, such as the CD-ROM, by clicking the Look In drop-down menu and choosing the appropriate drive.

   9. Click OK again. You should see a sample of the picture in the color box.

   10. Click OK. The picture should appear behind the organization chart (see Figure 13.28).

FIG. 13.27
Textures can provide a subtle, professional backdrop to your chart.

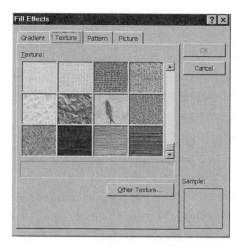

FIG. 13.28
The right picture can succinctly convey a company's image or vision.

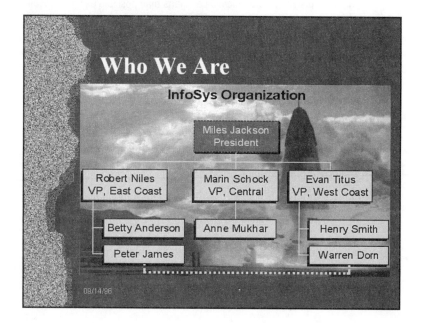

Part
IV

Ch
13

TROUBLESHOOTING

My selected picture doesn't appear behind the chart. Why? You may have set a background color in Microsoft Organization Chart, which overrides color controls in PowerPoint. Double-click the chart to return to Edit mode and check the Background menu. Set the color to the default, which is indicated by a raised square.

Org Plus for Windows

Microsoft Organization Chart is based on a more comprehensive charting program by Banner Blue Software, called Org Plus for Windows. If your charting needs are more complex than those available in PowerPoint, you might want to investigate this program, which provides the same look and feel as Microsoft Organization Chart. It offers a more robust feature set including:

- Twenty-nine Chart styles, including eight assistant styles
- Enhanced display features, such as the ability to "collapse" parts of the chart for readability
- The ability to embed pictures in chart boxes
- More box and line styles, such as different box shapes, arrowheads for lines, and more comprehensive shadow controls
- Math functions for displaying salaries and other numerical amounts
- The ability to create much larger charts than possible using Microsoft Organization Chart

Org Plus integrates into PowerPoint seamlessly—it replaces Microsoft Organization Chart.

If you want to learn more about Org Plus, you can contact Banner Blue at:

Broderbund
Banner Blue Division
PO Box 7865
Fremont, CA 94537
(510) 794-9152

Making Your Presentation

Basic Principles of Good Presentations

by Dave Johnson

A frequently-quoted magazine survey once showed that public speaking is the number one fear among Americans, even more so than wild dogs and heights.

The skills necessary to present oneself professionally while delivering a public presentation aren't magic, though, and are easily mastered. This chapter discusses the essential elements of making a presentation from designing the slide show to making the pitch. ■

Preparation and timing

This chapter shows you what you need to know about the auditorium and your audience before you even get there.

Presenting your ideas

The way you interact with the audience is half the battle. Look here for tips on how to build a rapport with your listeners.

Design issues

Effective slides aren't just text on a screen; they conform to simple rules of graphic design.

Presentation as a sales tool

Make that sale. Look here for advice on packing the most persuasiveness into a PowerPoint presentation.

Preparation and Timing

Just as with the proverbial iceberg that lies mostly under water, most of the work that goes into a presentation happens invisibly before anyone ever enters a conference room to see it unfold. You have to create the graphics in PowerPoint, of course, but also create the speech that accompanies it. For many people, that is a daunting task, but with preparation, planning, and practice, it becomes a simple and repeatable process.

Know Your Audience

Once you plan the topic, one of the first criteria you should consider is the composition of the audience. The presentation should be aimed at both the knowledge level and objectives of the intended audience. This is why standardized presentations can rarely be delivered to diverse audiences without at least some modification on each occasion.

Understand the knowledge level of the audience before you begin. Obviously, a presentation on a new product to a group of engineers will be different than the same presentation to a broad collection of consumers at a trade show. Engineers, for instance, will want to know about features, interfaces, and specifications. Consumers and sales representatives will no doubt be more concerned about benefits and capabilities, compatibility, and price. While the PowerPoint slides themselves may be the same in both situations, you will certainly have to tailor the content of your speech. You can easily save multiple versions of the same PowerPoint file, for instance, and insert unique Notes Pages in each.

It is also important to appreciate the objective of the audience. The three presentation models are:

Presentation Model	Common Examples
Persuasion	Sales Pitch, Course of Action (COA) Recommendation, Product Evangelism
Informational	Project Status, Financial or Marketing Plan
Training	Monthly or Application Training, New Employee Introductory Training

 TIP You can use the AutoContent Wizard to choose from a variety of boilerplate presentations. These include variations on all of the major presentation models.

Almost any kind of presentation fits into one of the models listed in Figure 14.1. Remember that your audience is there for a specific reason; some are paying for the opportunity to listen to you, and in other cases you will be speaking to subordinates, supervisors, or potential clients. Whatever the situation, be sure you understand why they are present. If you are speaking about a corporate strategy, for instance, such a presentation is unlikely to be informational only—make sure you close with a specific recommendation.

FIG. 14.1
The AutoContent Wizard lets you choose from many kinds of presentations, though they're all variations on the three major models.

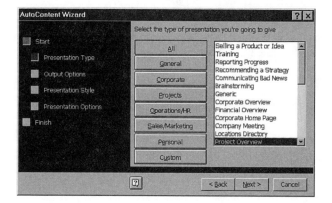

TROUBLESHOOTING

I don't know my audience. What can I do to focus my presentation to their needs? Often, the audience's needs are obvious, but that isn't always the case. You can do a bit of research early in the preparation process to better understand your audience. Try this:

- The venue often reveals the audience's needs and knowledge level. Find out if you will be speaking at a trade show or an engineering conference, for instance.

- Talk one-on-one with a representative of the audience as early in the preparation process as possible. Ideally, this is a division manager or event organizer who can speak to the group's needs.

Checking Your Equipment

Professional speakers know the importance of checking the room and its equipment prior to the presentation. This is known as *pre-flighting your equipment*, and it's as important to you as it is to the pilot who reviews his aircraft prior to flight. You should ensure that your presentation is ready to go at the proper time without any last-minute glitches. Here is a checklist to review before the scheduled start time:

Part
V

Ch

14

 TIP Plan to arrive two hours early—you need that much time to pre-flight the equipment and dry-run your presentation.

■ Spell check your entire presentation before you present it and after you've made all changes. It's easy to press a key and end up with some gibberish in the middle of your presentation.

■ Know in advance how to operate all the hardware you might need to make your presentation. Certain types of wireless control devices and multimedia equipment racks are difficult to master—practice with them before the presentation begins.

 Coordinate with the multimedia equipment technician early—an hour before the presentation, if possible—to be sure everyone understands how the equipment works and when transitions will occur between display hardware.

■ If you are using a computer, ensure that the software you need is already on the system. In particular, be sure that the correct version of PowerPoint is installed or you have the appropriate version of PowerPoint viewer.

CAUTION

You cannot view a PowerPoint 97 file on an older version of the program.

■ Make sure the environment is right for any hardware you're bringing with you. Some computer video systems, for instance, are virtually impossible to read in ordinary lighting conditions. Make sure the room can be made dark enough.

■ Display all of your slides once before attendees arrive. If you are using a 35mm projector, this will identify mis-ordered or upside down slides. On the computer, it will flag slides which display very slowly or improperly because of limited system capabilities.

■ Walk around the room as you display the slides and make sure text is readable from the back and sides of the room.

■ Ensure anything else you may need is available. Consider markers for the flip chart, chalk for the board, a VCR, and so on.

Have a Backup Plan   A well-planned presentation includes a margin for error: not everything always goes according to plan. These are more checklist items you can use to build some flexibility into your presentation:

■ If you are using a slide projector or overhead projector, know where spare bulbs are (or have someone available who does).

■ If you aren't bringing your own hardware, verify that your presentation performs adequately on the available system. If the display system is a 386 laptop connected to a projection system, for instance, you may want to use a backup slide show that forgoes extensive graphics, which will take too long to load.

■ No matter how you are delivering your presentation—whether on computer or 35mm slide—bring the presentation on overhead transparency as a means of last resort.

■ Bring 10 or 20 percent more depletable resources—such as audience handouts—than you expect to need.

 TIP Make your own pre-flight checklist and keep it with your presentation tools. Use it every time you deliver a presentation and update it frequently with "lessons learned."

TROUBLESHOOTING

What happens if something goes awry during my presentation? Stay in control and keep your head. It's important that you look like the expert throughout the presentation. Many problems can be solved by having an assistant to fix problems and run errands behind the scenes. Keep these tips in mind:

● If you have hardware or software problems, never claim that you don't understand how it works, or you're not familiar with "the new version." You're being paid to know those things—directly or indirectly—and to say otherwise undermines your credibility. Apologize and attempt to correct the problem if it is imminently correctable. If it isn't, move on as best you can.

● Never forget that you're not using your time; you're using your audience's time. Fix problems that can be solved immediately and make the best of problems that aren't immediately solvable.

● If you run out of materials such as handouts, a hotel concierge can be invaluable for getting additional copies made.

Of course, inspecting the room ahead of time gives you an opportunity to reposition the projection system (this, of course, isn't always possible), scope out where you'll speak from, and ensure your presentation is visible throughout the room.

Tailoring Your Presentation to Place and Time

The same presentation won't work in every situation. Just as the audience's knowledge and objectives vary widely, so does the environment in which you will be working. The major presentation delivery systems at your disposal are found in Table 14.1.

Part
V

Ch

14

Table 14.1   Presentation Delivery Systems

System	Maximum Audience Size
Computers	
Direct-view monitors	15
Projection monitors	50
Large screen projections	200
Overhead projectors	200
Slide projectors	200

Computers   Rather than printing slides into other formats, you can obviously use a computer as your delivery system. You can use a direct view display system—such as from a large screen television—or use a projection system for large (10 foot or larger) displays.

The logistics of such solutions are at once simpler and more complex, for different reasons. A computer is the ideal delivery system for PowerPoint. Some advantages include:

- Direct access to the PowerPoint file allows last-minute changes.
- Playback from PowerPoint provides access to advanced features like animation, slide transitions, and on-screen annotations during the presentation.

On the other hand, you must find a display system capable of supporting the desired number of viewers. Direct display systems—including televisions up to 80 inches—can provide an adequate display for no more than about 50 people. Beyond that, and you must step up to a front projection system which projects the display onto a slide projector-style screen. In order to use any of these solutions, you'll need an encoder. These are devices which convert your computer's VGA signal into NTSC, understandable by a video device.

N O T E   Some multimedia notebook computers now come with VGA-to-NTSC encoders built in, simplifying the process of taking a PowerPoint presentation on the road. Simply plug one of these computers into a VCR, video projector, or television and start your show. ■

Overhead Projectors   Overheads have the singular advantage of being fast, simple, and inexpensive to create. They have a number of disadvantages, though. In order to work well for groups larger than 100, the room's lights typically need to be completely dimmed. In addition, the projection becomes skewed as the projector head is angled sharply to accommodate larger screen sizes.

Many laser and inkjet printers have the ability to print directly to overhead transparency acetate, making it easy to create color slides rapidly.

Slide Projectors   You can print PowerPoint presentations to 35mm slides via a service bureau like Genigraphics (included in PowerPoint 97) or to a film recorder if you have one in your office. The advantage of slides is crisp color with very high saturation—you can use a wide range of tones in your slides and make very visually effective presentations. The most useful audience size for 35mm slides is between 50 and 200.

35mm is a very high resolution medium and can, if desired, seamlessly integrate ordinary 35mm slides—such as analog photography—into a set of PowerPoint slides. On the downside, the remote control is often tethered to the projector, so your ability to walk through the audience is limited while you control the pacing of the slides.

 It's a good idea to bring a back-up copy of your presentation on overhead transparencies in case of an unrecoverable hardware failure with the intended delivery system.

Presenting Your Ideas

The success of your presentation is made up of equal parts of the PowerPoint slides and your ability to address them.

Body Language

One of the reasons many people look uncomfortable or unprofessional in front of a group is that they don't understand the best way to use their own body. A relaxed speaker puts the audience at ease and makes it that much easier for them to digest the message. You should learn to think about how you use your eyes, legs, and hands when speaking and referencing your PowerPoint slides. Your body language can have a powerful effect on the audience's perception of the presentation.

Most inexperienced speakers tend to hide their hands by clasping them either in front or behind their body. While there are some reasonable Freudian interpretations for why people do this, neither position contributes to a good presentation. Instead, use your hands to convey normal body motions, as if you were in ordinary conversation. Point, wave, and gesture; natural hand motion is one of the single most powerful tools at your disposal for making you look like a pro.

Using Props   Also consider props. Pointers, both wooden sticks and laser beams, can help draw the audience's attention to specific parts of a given graphic.

Part
V

Ch
14

Props are easily abused, however, and that's why you should limit their use. Because the human eye is drawn to motion, pointers can easily distract an audience from the presentation. Remember that a six-inch hand motion translates into a wild thrust at the tip of a four-foot stick.

TIP Discipline yourself to return your prop to the podium or table when it isn't in use. Your hands will then be free to generate more natural body language.

An alternative to using a physical prop to point to the slide is the pen tool resident in PowerPoint. By using the pen, you can annotate the screen as you speak. To use the pen, enter a presentation by choosing Slide Show, View Show and do the following:

1. Move the mouse and a control panel appears in the lower-left corner of the screen.

2. Click the Control Panel. From the menu, choose Pen (see Figure 14.2). You can now annotate the screen in real-time as you speak.

FIG. 14.2
The Pen tool enables you to draw on the screen with the mouse pointer while delivering a presentation.

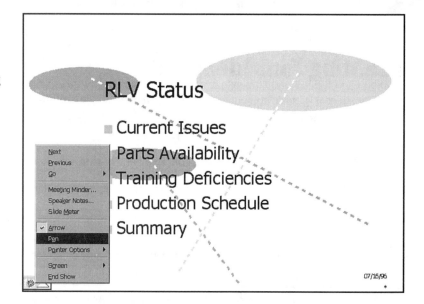

TIP When you choose a pen color, select a very high contrast color so it is visible from the back of the room.

3. To change the pen color, click the Control Panel again and choose Pointer Options, Pen Color, and select the desired color.

4. To disable the pen and continue with the presentation, choose Pointer Options, Hide Now.

 TIP You can reach the Control Panel menu at any time by right-clicking anywhere on the screen.

Moving Around the Room   One of the most powerful ways to create rapport with the audience is to move about the room. Walk around as much as is convenient, considering things like the size and layout of the room, the location of the slide or video display, and how you're controlling the presentation. New or self-conscious speakers tend to root themselves in one location—typically behind a podium.

The podium, however, is an obstacle between the speaker and audience, and it inhibits the audience from relating to the speaker and his ideas. Instead, you might want to place your notes on the podium, make your initial remarks from there, and then move away. You can always return to the podium to check your notes or get a pointer, but removing that psychological barrier helps you bond with the group.

Preparing to Speak

There are three forms of prepared narration:

- Verbatim
- Memorized
- Extemporaneous

With rare exception, speakers of all skill levels should have notes available during a speech, but reading directly and exclusively from cards—the verbatim method—has two major pitfalls:

- Reading verbatim from notes or slides carries an implicit lack of sincerity. Reading verbatim, in fact, alienates you from the audience, who can feel patronized by speakers that reiterate exactly what they can already see in handouts or on slides.
- If you're reading from notes, you're not making eye contact with the audience, which is important to building rapport with them.

Another method is rote memorization. Some speakers study their notes until they can repeat the speech, word for word, without ever looking down.

CAUTION

Rote memorization is fraught with hazard. First, this method demonstrates a lack of emotional investment in the presentation. Of course, the other danger lies in the house of cards you've built by memorizing the speech. If you forget a key phrase, the entire presentation falls apart. Even if the rote speaker has note cards with him, the lost momentum from a miscue shakes the speaker's confidence, resulting in a poor performance.

The ideal compromise is an extemporaneous speech. Great speakers always speak extemporaneously; they've practiced the presentation enough that a brief glance at the note cards is enough fuel for several minutes of speaking (see Figure 14.3). Extemporaneous speeches are notable because they have sincerity, spontaneity, and energy you'll never see from rote memorization *or* card reading. The speaker can improvise, use analogies that pop into his head on-the-fly, and never worry about it hampering his tempo or location in the speech.

FIG. 14.3
A skeletal outline of your presentation should be all you need to enter in Note Pages.

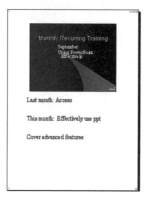

N O T E Extemporaneous speaking must be practiced. Begin by creating a complete narration of the presentation in PowerPoint's Notes Pages. Rehearse by reading the notes word for word. The second time, try to work from an outline that features just your main points. Repeat the exercise a third time the same way. Remember that it isn't important to say it exactly the same way every time. Let the freedom of working from an outline allow you to improvise the details much like a guitarist might improvise parts of a solo while keeping the overall theme, texture, and chord changes the same.

After you've made a few presentations within an extemporaneous framework, you can practice new ones without bothering to write down all the gory details for the first run-through; work from an outline all the time. ▪

TIP Experiment to find your optimum number of rehearsals. You'll want to strike a balance between memorization—which will make you seem too rigid—and unfamiliarity, which will make you appear uncomfortable with the material.

There's one last critical point to make about the way to deliver your speech. Many people are under the vague impression that when speaking in public, the speech has to flow non-stop, like a verbal conveyor belt. That drives many novices to try the verbatim or memorization approach. It also creates the nemesis of every public speaker: the verbal pause.

Verbal pauses are any phrases or word fragments you utter when preparing to say something meaningful. The most common verbal pauses are "umm" and "okay." To avoid verbal pauses, it takes a conscious effort during rehearsals to close your mouth while between thoughts. While the several seconds it takes to regroup your thoughts may seem like an eternity to you on the speaker's platform, the audience isn't likely to even notice.

N O T E More than almost any other aspect of public speaking, eliminating verbal pauses is something you absolutely must practice before you get on stage. Verbal pauses are very tricky habits to break and it takes an enormous effort of will to overcome the temptation to speak non-words. The payoff is that there is no other single enhancement which will so dramatically improve your presentation professionalism. ▪

Solicit Feedback

Many speakers are uncomfortable with speaking in front of a group. One reason for this is they tend to picture speaking as a solitary task.

That's simply not the case. The audience wants to hear your message; you simply have to channel your insecurity about being in front of a room of strangers or colleagues in a less threatening direction.

The best way to reduce anxiety is through direct eye contact. Instead of looking over the audience's heads, or "past" them to the back of the room, speak directly to individuals in the audience. The goal is to make your presentation a personal experience for the audience.

N O T E You can build rapport with an audience by focusing directly on an individual and speaking to him or her for a short time; then move to another random person in the room and continue your presentation. Try to make this natural and fluid. If the presentation is principally for a supervisor's benefit, ensure that you spend a significant amount of your time looking directly at that person. ▪

Part
V

Ch
14

Use Handouts Effectively

Handouts are an easy way to let the audience follow along with your presentation. There are several principal reasons for using handouts:

▶ **See** "Using Handouts Effectively," **p. 112**

- The audience may take notes and relate them directly to your slides.

- Handouts help audience members who may have an obstructed view of the PowerPoint display to see the slides.

- If time is limited, handouts can provide detailed information which you can't explicitly cover in your presentation.

One disadvantage to handouts is that they provide a potential distraction to the audience; audience members may be inclined to read ahead rather than listen to you. The advantages generally outweigh this pitfall, however.

Design Issues

Good slides do more than simply communicate visually the message you are trying to convey during a presentation. Good slides also adhere to some basic elements of graphic design as well. Principal among these concepts is that a slide show should be fairly minimalist in appearance. This is a hard balance to strike because PowerPoint has brought so many new visual tools and capabilities, but presentations should, in general, stick to the basics and include as little "eye candy" as possible. While there's a place for all of the capabilities of PowerPoint—like the animation tools—they should certainly not appear on every slide.

Stick to Main Ideas

An uncluttered design is very important to a slide's readability and comprehensibility. Most slides should feature text that supports the main ideas you want to convey—a slide should be a guide map to your presentation, not a detailed report that reiterates all of the things you're going to say. Use these broad guidelines when creating slides:

- Each slide should discuss just one major concept.
- Limit each slide to no more than three to five bullets that support the main idea.
- Each bullet should be just a single line of text if possible.

Even on a simple four-bullet slide such as the one in Figure 14.4, your audience's attention can easily wander from the bullet that you are currently discussing to one which you haven't begun to talk about yet. A good way to keep the audience's attention riveted on the current topic is to only introduce text on a slide as it is needed. You can reveal each bullet as needed using the Custom Animation tool. Try this:

FIG. 14.4
Don't crowd your slide with text—three to five bullets of text is ideal.

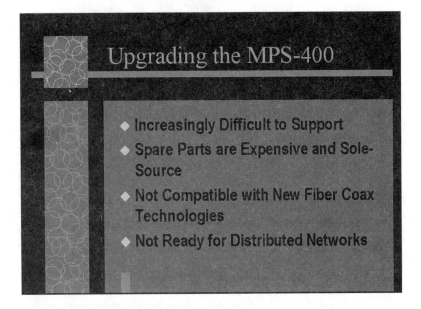

1. Create a slide with several bullets of text.
2. Choose Slide Show, Custom Animation. The Custom Animation dialog box appears.
3. In the Animation Order box in the top-left corner, click Text. This is the body of the slide which you are about to animate.
4. Click the Timing tab at the bottom of the dialog box. Select Animate and On Mouse Click (see Figure 14.5).
5. Click the Effects tab. In the Entry Animation and Sound area, select Appear and No Sound. For Introduce Text, select All at Once.
6. Click OK to close the dialog box.

This procedure creates bulleted text that appears one line at a time as you click the mouse. You can experiment with different animation styles.

FIG. 14.5
You can animate just the text bullets so they appear upon mouse clicks as you need them.

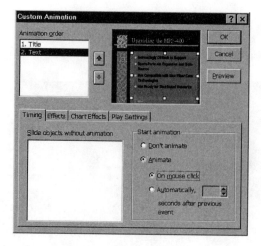

Stay Concise

A PowerPoint slide show should never overpower the overall presentation. In other words, the text, graphics, and charts on the screen—regardless of delivery system—should serve as a broad outline of what the speaker is talking about, and provide visual reinforcement when appropriate.

With that said, you should strive to minimize the number of words on any slide and also reduce the total slides in the show as much as possible. A good rule of thumb is to plan about three to five text slides per major concept in a presentation. Of course, have the flexibility to add or reduce the slides in a presentation depending on the depth of the information, but it is generally advisable to err on the low side.

Too much text is always a concern when building a presentation. Too many words can overpower the viewer, forcing the audience to spend time reading and digesting blocks of text when they should be listening to the speaker. Instead of text, try to depict the same information using charts or graphs. Typically, a business graphic such as an organizational chart, wiring diagram, pie chart, or bar graph can pack a larger quantity of information on a chart more intelligibly than attempting to do the same thing with text.

▶ **See** "Creating a Chart," **p. 203**

If you have information that lends itself to depiction as a graphic, you can insert one in this way:

1. Choose Insert, Chart.
2. A datasheet appears with sample data. Change the data to reflect the information you want to depict (see Figure 14.6).

3. Right-click one of the bars in the bar chart and select Chart Type.

4. Choose the desired Chart Type and Chart Sub-Type.

5. Click OK to close the dialog box. Click outside the graphic to close the datasheet.

FIG. 14.6
A business graphic delivers numerical information more efficiently than text on a slide.

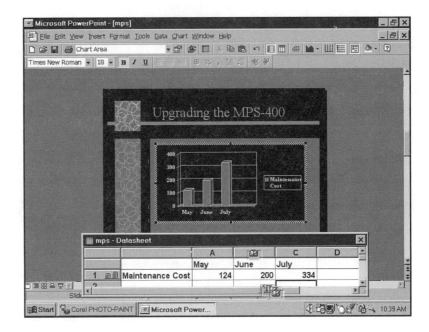

Readability of Text

The finest presentation will be of no value to the audience if it can't be read. One of the goals of an equipment pre-flight, in fact, is to ensure the display is visible and intelligible throughout the room—depending on the PowerPoint delivery system, you may need to adjust the display in different environments.

Although rules of thumb abound for configuring the text on a computer screen or video system, the fact remains that there is no substitute for viewing the presentation in the actual room ahead of time. Nonetheless, here are some general guidelines professional speakers use when creating presentations:

- Use *sans serif fonts*. These are headline-style fonts that don't have finish lines at the top or bottom of the text.

   As you can see from Figure 14.7, sans serif fonts are typically used for headlines because they are simpler and can be read more quickly. Sans serif is desirable throughout presentation slides for the same reason.

Part
V

Ch
14

- Very narrow fonts (one or two pixels) often look good on an SVGA monitor but will not be legible on a projection system. Because of the way NTSC video works, single-pixel fonts will be lost between scanlines. For the same reason, don't use very thin lines in graphics.

FIG. 14.7
Serif fonts are more attractive, but they are very difficult to read. Stick to sans serif or headline-style fonts, even in body text.

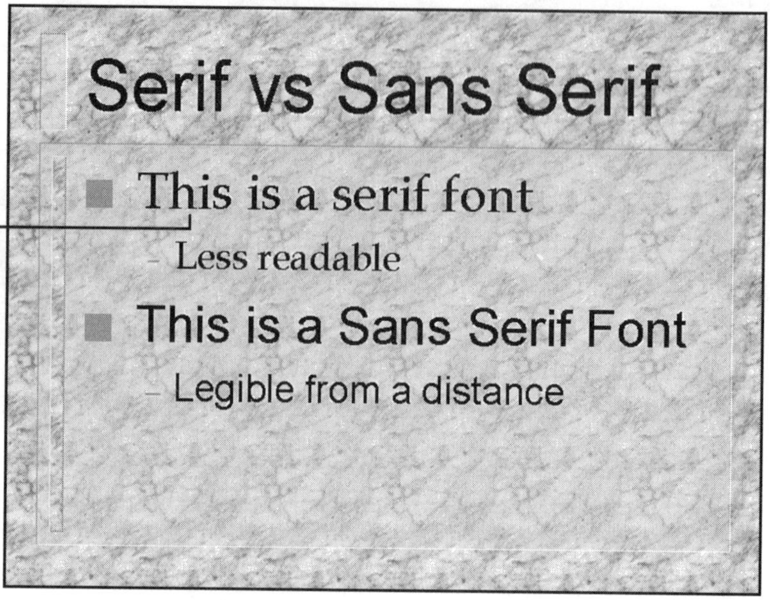

Serifs tend to connect letters visually

Serif vs Sans Serif

- This is a serif font
  - Less readable

- This is a Sans Serif Font
  - Legible from a distance

TIP When choosing a display system, you should generally ensure the text will be about an inch high for every 10 feet of distance between the display and audience. Always try to accommodate the farthest viewer.

- Keep fonts large enough to be visible from the back of the room. The smallest fonts which are generally legible on a video projection system are about 22 points. Headlines should be at least 40 or 45 points, and body text should be sized at least 32 points. If you find the need to shrink text to make it fit, move several points to another slide at a logical break point. It's better to have a series of slides on one point than have an illegible slide.

TIP You can choose Tools, Expand Slide to automatically make each bullet on a slide become the title on its own slide.

Consistency from Slide to Slide

A common problem faced by inexperienced desktop publishers is the tendency to pack documents full of incompatible fonts, layouts, and styles. The result is a garish, unprofessional, and hard-to-read product. Unfortunately, PowerPoint productions can fall prey to the same problems, particularly considering all the new features in PowerPoint 97. For that reason, PowerPoint templates are particularly valuable because they ensure a high degree of consistency between slides in a presentation. As you create slide shows, keep these style suggestions in mind:

■ Use the same background style on all the slides in a presentation. If you do switch color schemes or background graphics, do it when transitioning between major points to highlight the change in topic. To change the style of an entire presentation, choose Apply Design from the Common Tasks dialog box and select a design as seen in Figure 14.8. Click Apply.

FIG. 14.8
A basic element of graphic design suggests that the same style be used through the presentation.

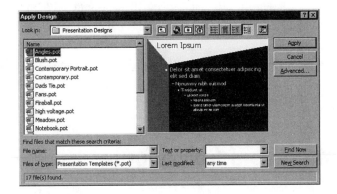

 TIP You can change the text style for every slide at once by choosing View, Master, Slide Master and making changes there.

■ Use the same fonts, sizes, and attributes throughout a slide show.
■ While the wide variety of transitions is tempting, use the same transition between each slide.

 TIP To set a global slide transition choose Slide Show, Slide Transition and choose an Effect. Then click Apply To All.

Part
V
Ch
14

Using Color Effectively

Color can dramatically improve the effectiveness of a presentation. To work well, however, you should design your slides for readability, color coordination, and the intended delivery system. Keep these guidelines in mind:

- Not all presentations need to be in color. Color is best avoided when it may distract the audience from your message; a preliminary project status meeting, for instance, should probably rely on black and white overheads. The final presentation, on the other hand, should be in color.

- If the slide show is being printed to 35mm slides or overheads, ensure the colors are acceptable in the final form. Printed products use subtractive color technology while computer displays are additive. Because of this difference, printed colors don't always resemble their on-screen counterparts.

- Keep the final presentation delivery system in mind when choosing colors. On video displays, bright reds over-saturate the display and tend to bleed. Test color schemes on a television before finalizing the project, and reduce the saturation of colors if necessary.

- Keep the contrast between backgrounds and text high; when using a dark background, for instance, make text yellow for visibility. Similar tones, like gray and light blue, blend together.

Presentation as a Sales Tool

A very common class of presentation is the Persuasion Model. By using this presentation, you are essentially trying to sell something, be it a product, idea, or strategy to someone. There are a few guidelines to consider when creating such a slide show.

Selling Ideas, Products, or Services

As a salesperson, you are trying to convince potential clients why they should purchase your product. Alternatively, you might be a product manager attempting to persuade management to choose a particular course of action with your project.

In any case, one of the most common methods of making your case is via a strategy known as *Stratification of Options*. Essentially, this method requires you to describe the options to your client in a way that it appears you are objectively describing the options available. However, you should demonstrate advantages and disadvantages of these various options, stratifying them in a manner such that your favored option is clearly the best choice. Figure 14.9 shows this stratification of options for a proposed training system.

FIG. 14.9
Stratify the options by discussing the pros and cons of each. Save the recommended option for last.

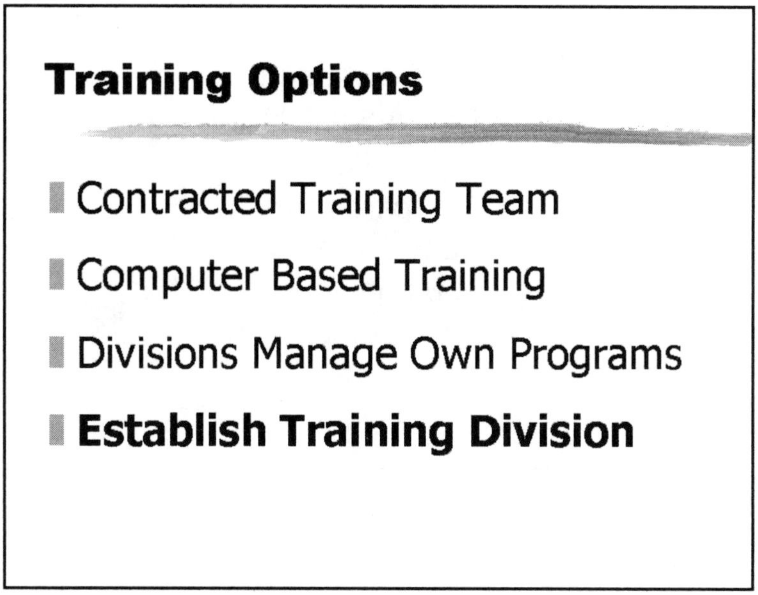

Training Options

▌ Contracted Training Team

▌ Computer Based Training

▌ Divisions Manage Own Programs

▌ **Establish Training Division**

The linchpin in any sales slide show is the discussion of your own product, idea, or strategy. This should constitute the majority of the presentation and contain these elements:

■ How does the product meet the needs of the client? You may want to preface this section with a slide—or series of slides—that reiterate what those needs actually are.

■ How is this solution cost effective? A graphical comparison of the cost benefits can work very well. You can insert a graphic which supports your argument on the same screen as the text, as shown in Figure 14.10. Demonstrate how this solution is more cost effective than either the competition or the status quo, as appropriate.

■ Why should the client choose your company? Often a sale goes beyond just the product purchase—it is important to emphasize the qualities of your company, such as product support, reputation, and reliability.

 T I P The PowerPoint template for Selling Ideas or Products captures all the essential elements needed to make a persuasive presentation.

Part
V

Ch
14

FIG. 14.10
The PowerPoint templates include placeholders for graphics in logical locations for many kinds of presentations.

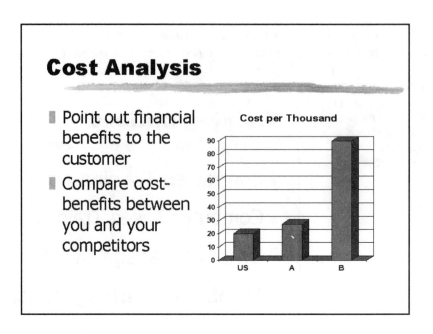

Stressing Benefits versus Features

Don't forget that in general, customers don't buy features; they buy capability and benefits. All too often, presentations get bogged down in the engineer's perspective of a product and they forget to tell the client what those features actually do for them. Compare Figure 14.11 with Figure 14.12. Always review a presentation from the client's perspective, and ensure you are telling them what they need to know, not what the engineering department would like to discuss.

Go for the Close

A compelling presentation needs a compelling finish. There are several important elements to any presentation conclusion:

■ *Summary*. Review the major elements of your presentation. Don't simply say, "We discussed the benefits of our product." Instead, drive home those capabilities one more time. The goal of the closure is to ensure the audience fully understands what you said and remembers it as well. Repetition will help the audience take your message back and make an informed decision.

■ *Recommendation*. If you are trying to persuade your supervisor to make a specific decision, be sure she knows that. All too often, persuasion presentations end anticlimactically, and the supervisor gets the impression it was an informational brief. If a decision needs to be made, ask her to make it.

■ *The sale*. If you are selling a product or service, end the presentation by asking the client to buy. When asked why they didn't buy a product after listening to a sales presentation, one of the most common responses from prospective clients is that they were never asked.

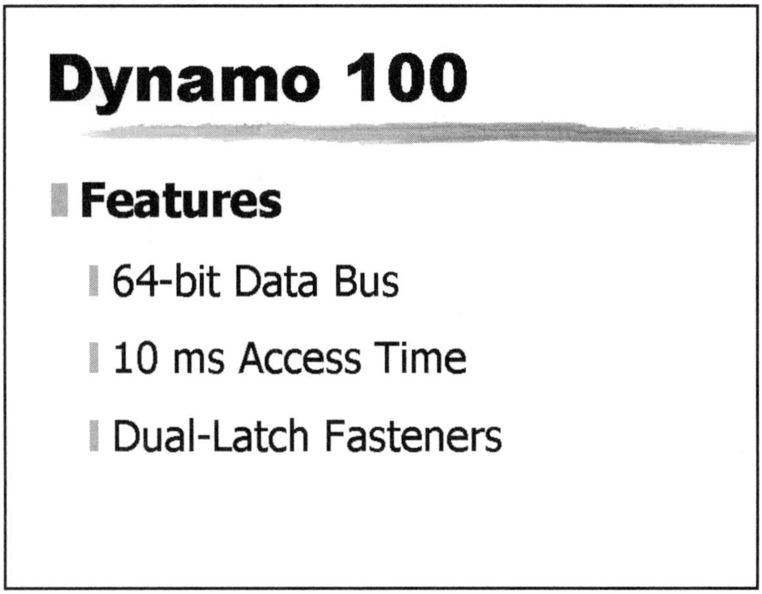

FIG. 14.11
A slide based on engineering features gives the client no basis for understanding why he would want the product.

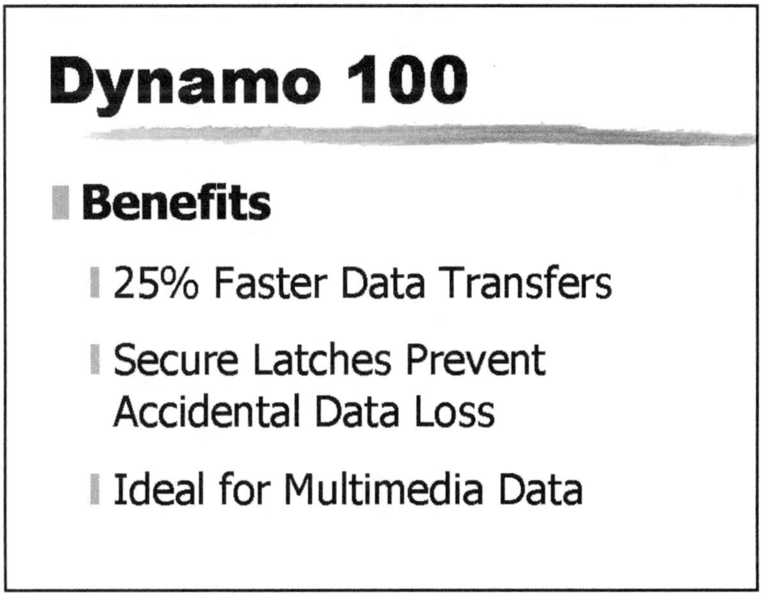

Dynamo 100

▌Features

▌ 64-bit Data Bus

▌ 10 ms Access Time

▌ Dual-Latch Fasteners

FIG. 14.12
The same slide— modified to show benefits to the user— stands a better chance of persuading a potential client.

Dynamo 100

▌Benefits

▌ 25% Faster Data Transfers

▌ Secure Latches Prevent Accidental Data Loss

▌ Ideal for Multimedia Data

Part
V

Ch
14

CHAPTER 15

Preparing Your Presentation

by Laura Monsen

From previous chapters, you've learned how to create a presentation, format text, add clip art, and even create pie charts and tables. Soon you will want to deliver your presentation and print handouts for your audience. It's time to organize the presentation so that it flows well, preview it to see what it will look like, and make final adjustments to your presentation. ■

See an overview of your entire presentation

Use Slide Sorter view to rearrange and revise the order of your slides.

Preview your presentation

See how your presentation will look when you run the slide show with an overhead projector or when it is printed.

Enhance your slide show

Learn to add visual effects to your slides. This chapter explains the best ways to use transitions, time, animation, and sound effects with your slides and charts.

Add a narrative to your slide show

You can record a narration to accompany your slides.

Organizing Your Presentation in Slide Sorter View

Slide Sorter view is ideal for getting an overall glimpse of your presentation. To switch to Slide Sorter view, click the view icon on the bottom scroll bar or choose View, Slide Sorter. When you switch to this view, miniatures of your slides appear in the order you created them. In order to enlarge the miniatures, you have to zoom in to 75 or 100 percent using the Zoom control on the Standard toolbar. While the images are larger after zooming in, however, you will see fewer of them on-screen. To see more slide miniatures on screen, reduce the zoom to 50 or 33 percent. See Figures 15.1 and 15.2 for an illustration of enlarged and reduced images.

FIG. 15.1
From Slide Sorter view, images shown at 100 percent zoom are readable.

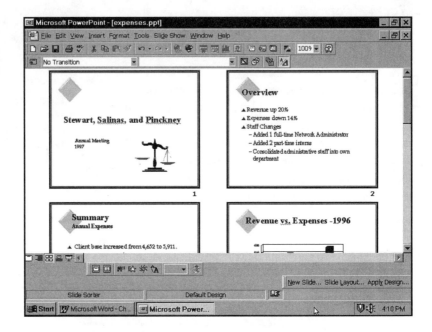

From Slide Sorter view, you can reorganize your presentation by moving, copying, or deleting slides.

FIG. 15.2

When zoomed to 33 percent, an overview of your presentation can be seen.

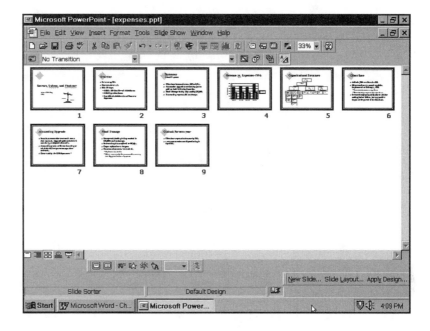

Moving Slides Around

After you've created your presentation, you may decide the slides should be in a different order. There are several techniques for moving slides around, but the simplest is by using your mouse to *drag and drop*—that is, to drag a slide from its current position and drop it into a new position. PowerPoint automatically makes room for the moved slide and renumbers all slides to reflect the new order.

To rearrange the order of your slides, follow these steps:

1. Switch to Slide Sorter view, if necessary.

2. Select the slide you want to move. A thick dark border appears around the slide. To select multiple slides, hold down your Shift key and click each additional slide.

   In other Windows products, the Shift+click method is used only to select multiple adjacent items, several paragraphs in a word processor, or a series of cells in a spreadsheet. The Ctrl+click method is used to select objects that are not next to one another, or non-contiguous items. In PowerPoint, the Shift+click method is used to select slides, whether they are adjacent or not.

NOTE If you need to select a lot of slides, use the Zoom control box and zoom out to 50 or 33 percent to see more of your slides. ▓

3. Place your mouse pointer in the middle of the slide, then click and drag. As you drag, a vertical line appears in between the miniature images. This insertion indicator shows where the slide will be placed when you release your mouse. Attached to your mouse is a small gray rectangle, as shown in Figure 15.3, displayed a reminder that you are moving slides.

FIG. 15.3
The column chart (slide 4) is being moved after the organizational chart (slide 5).

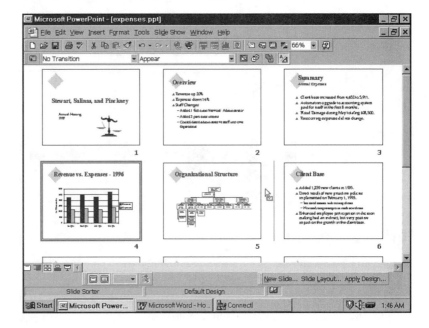

4. Drag your mouse until the vertical line is positioned where you want to move your slide. It is the vertical line, not your mouse pointer, PowerPoint uses to reposition the slide. Release your mouse button, and the slide moves to the new location.

If you prefer, you can use the standard Edit, Cut (Ctrl+X) and Edit, Paste (Ctrl+V) commands to move slides. These commands can be accessed from the Edit menu or the shortcut menu via your secondary mouse button. Once you have selected the slide to move, choose Cut.

Suppose you want to move this slide between slides 5 and 6 in your presentation. You need to click between slides 5 and 6 to indicate the destination. A vertical line appears between the slides. Choose Paste to complete the move.

Duplicating Slides

Periodically you may want to copy a slide. Perhaps you have a title slide you've created and you intend to use a similar slide at the beginning of each of the major sections of your presentation. Instead of re-creating the slide, simply copy it!

 In professional business presentations I create, I always put a copy of my first slide at the end of the presentation. That way, my audience doesn't have to keep looking at the last chart or list of bullets I discussed (or worse, the PowerPoint screen) as I wrap up the presentation, and I know I've reached the end of my slide show! I use the copy of my first slide to help the audience and me refocus our attention on the overall message of the presentation and to sum up the discussion.

There are several techniques for copying slides, but again the simplest is by using your mouse to drag and drop a copy of the existing slide to a new location.

To copy slides, follow these steps:

1. Switch to Slide Sorter view, if necessary.

2. Select the slide you want to copy. If you need to select a lot of slides, use the Zoom control box and zoom out to 50 or 33 percent to see more slides.

3. Place your mouse pointer in the middle of the slide you want to copy. While holding down the Ctrl key, click the slide and drag. As you drag, a vertical line appears in between the miniature images. This is an insertion indicator to show where the slide will be placed when you release your mouse. Attached to your mouse is a small gray rectangle; this rectangle, however, features a plus sign, indicating you are performing a copy, as shown in Figure 15.4.

4. Drag your mouse until the vertical line is positioned where you want to copy your slide. Release your mouse button, and a copy of the slide appears in the new location.

If you prefer, you can use the standard Edit, Copy (Ctrl+C) and Edit, Paste (Ctrl+V) commands to copy slides. These commands can be accessed from the Edit menu or the shortcut menu via your secondary mouse button. Once you have selected the slide to copy, choose Copy.

Suppose you want to place a copy of this slide between slides 5 and 6 in your presentation. You need to click between slides 5 and 6 to indicate the destination of the copy. A vertical line appears between the slides. Choose Paste to complete the copy.

FIG. 15.4

The column chart (slide 4) is being copied after the organizational chart (slide 5).

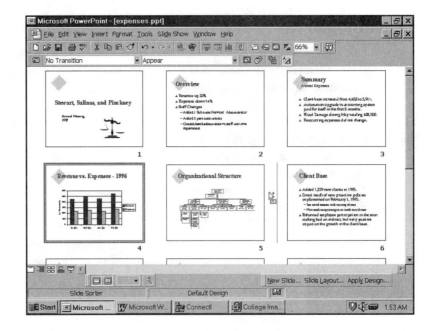

 T I P   You can also choose Edit, Duplicate Slide. This command places the duplicate to the right of the original side. You then need to move the copy to the appropriate location.

Deleting Slides

After creating your slide show, you may find some of your slides are no longer necessary or relevant to the topic you're discussing. To delete a slide:

1. Switch to Slide Sorter view, if necessary.

2. Select the slide you want to delete.

3. Press the Delete key or choose Edit, Delete Slide. You can also use the Cut icon on the Standard toolbar, but this actually places the slide on the Clipboard.

CAUTION

The Clipboard only holds one item. If you use Cut to remove a slide, anything you previously had on the Clipboard is replaced by the slide.

Also, a slide is a very large graphic item. Keeping large graphics on the Clipboard takes up valuable RAM and is not recommended.

T I P You can delete the unnecessary slides or move them to another presentation. Moving instead of deleting would be a good choice especially if you think you might use the slides in another presentation. The next section outlines the specific steps.

Copying Slides Between Presentations

One of PowerPoint's best time-saving features is the ability to copy slides between presentations. You might want to consolidate slides from several presentations into one presentation or break apart a very large presentation into smaller, more succinct ones. This technique is also useful if you create monthly or quarterly presentations; you can save yourself a lot of time by reusing slides you've already created.

Typically, you don't want to lose the original work and merely copy the slides you want to use into another presentation. The advantage of using this method instead of opening up the original presentation and using the Save As command to save a copy of the presentation under a new name is that you won't risk making modifications and accidentally save the file under the former name.

To copy slides from one presentation to another, follow these steps:

1. Open only the files you want to work with. It is important you close any unnecessary files, otherwise these presentations will appear on the screen and make it difficult to see the slides from the files you are trying to work with.

2. Choose Window, Arrange All. Your open files are arranged side-by-side in separate windows.

   Only one presentation window at a time can be active. You can tell which one is active by looking at the window title bar; the active window has a colored title bar. When you use the Arrange All command, PowerPoint places the current window on the left side of the screen and makes it the active window (see Figure 15.5).

3. To make another window active, simply click anywhere in the window, and its title bar should change colors. In Figure 15.6, the window on the right side of the screen is now the active window.

4. Each window has its own title bar, view buttons, and scroll bars. Switch to Slide Sorter view in each window. This enables you to see and select the slides in the source presentation you want to copy and the exact location you want to copy the slides to in the destination presentation.

5. From the source presentation, select the slide or slides you want to copy. A thick dark border appears around each of the slides.

`69%` ▼

FIG. 15.5

The title bar in the profex.ppt presentation is colored, indicating it is the active window.

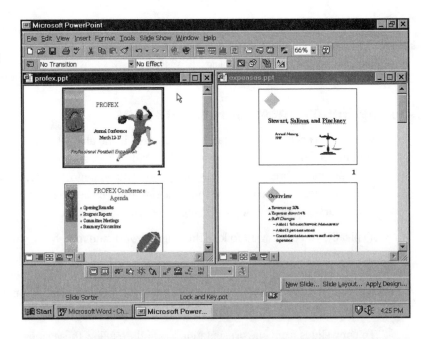

FIG. 15.6

The title bar in the expenses.ppt presentation is colored, indicating it is now the active window.

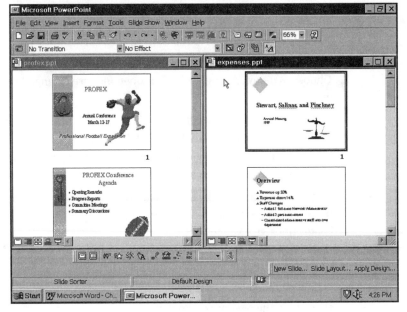

6. Place your mouse pointer in the middle of the selected slide. While holding down the Ctrl key, click and drag the selected slide into the destination presentation. A vertical line appears, indicating the slide's new position. Attached to your mouse is a small gray rectangle with a plus sign, indicating you are performing a copy, as shown in Figure 15.7.

FIG. 15.7

Slides 2, 3, and 4 have been selected in the expenses.ppt presentation and are being copied between slides 3 and 4 in the profex.ppt presentation.

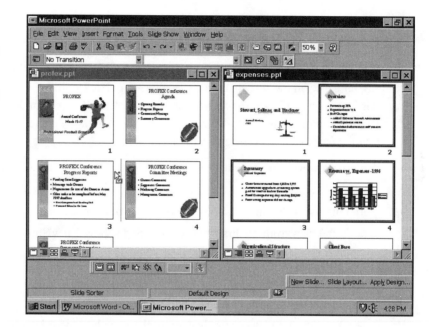

7. Drag your mouse until the vertical line is positioned where you want to copy the slides. Release the mouse button, and a copy of the slides appears in the destination presentation.

▶ **See** "Using and Editing Color Palettes," **p. 482**

The copied slides assume the template attributes of the destination presentation. Templates come with eight default colors. These colors are used for the slide background, title, text, shadows, and fill colors for your charts. If you have changed the color of the title of a slide in your source presentation to one of these eight colors, when you copy the slide it takes on the comparable color in the destination presentation. This does not always produce the look you want when you copy the slide. If you have used a custom color, the color remains unchanged when you copy the slide. In either case, look closely at the slides you have copied to ensure you have the appearance you want.

You can also use the standard Edit, Copy (Ctrl+C) and Edit, Paste (Ctrl+V) commands to copy slides. Once you have selected the slide, choose Copy. If you want to place the copy between slides 5 and 6 in your presentation, you need to click between slides 5 and 6. This indicates the destination of the copy. A vertical line appears between the slides. Choose Paste to complete the copy.

Previewing Your Presentation

WYSIWYG (What You See Is What You Get). Seeing your presentation slides, without anything else on the screen, to make certain your slides look the way you want them to—this is why you will want to preview your presentation. PowerPoint does not have a Print Preview command as do most Windows products. Instead, it combines previewing for printing purposes with previewing for a slide show.

You can preview your presentation from any view in PowerPoint, as follows:

- To preview from the current slide, click the Slide Show button, next to the four view buttons located in the lower-left corner of your screen.
- To preview from the first slide, choose Slide Show, View Show.

You can move around your presentation in several ways:

- To advance to the next slide, click your primary mouse button. The Page Down key or right arrow key can also be used to see the next slide.
- To return to the previous slide, press the Page Up key or left arrow key.

  In PowerPoint 7, you could use secondary mouse button to see the previous slide. PowerPoint 97 uses this button to provide a shortcut menu with a number of useful slide show options.

  ▶ **See** "Running Your Presentation," **p. 367**

- To get out of Preview mode, press Esc.

Now that you know the basics of previewing a presentation, you could be satisfied with merely running your slide show as it looks right now—with each slide coming up the same as the previous slide. But why be satisfied with a bland presentation that might as well be done with an old-fashioned slide projector? There is much more you can do to enhance your presentations! Read on.

Transitions and Timing

It's time to add the final touches to your slide show. One powerful method of enhancing a presentation is to add a transition style to your slides. A *transition style* is the way in which the next slide in your presentation appears on the screen. If you use the Fade Through Black transition, for example, the current slide fades to a black screen, then the next slide fades in. Applying a transition style gives your presentation a more polished look and makes it more interesting to your audience.

Another frequently used enhancement is timing your slides. Time can be attached to a slide, or just to a component of the slide. You are not bound by the time you add to a slide. The slide show can be paused if you need to discuss a topic in more detail.

As your slides transition you can have a sound play. There are 16 different sound bites in PowerPoint, including the sound a camera makes when a picture is taken, or the sound a car makes when you have to slam on the brakes.

Although you can use any of the views to apply transitions and time, Slide Sorter view provides several advantages over other views. Slide Sorter view allows you to select multiple slides at a time. The Slide Sorter toolbar has a number of tools to expedite enhancing your presentation, and beneath the miniature images of the slides appear symbols to indicate which features you have added. Some of these symbols are interactive.

▶ **See** "Moving from View to View," **p. 26**

One exciting feature is the ability to add time and animation effects to a specific component of a slide, like a series of bullets or a chart. You might decide to add timing effects to a list of bullets, so that as you finish discussing one bullet, the next bullet appears. One of the greatest changes to this version of PowerPoint is the ability to add time or transition effects to the parts of a chart. This wonderful feature helps to focus the audience's attention on the specific item you're explaining. See the section "Using Builds Effectively" later in this chapter for specific steps on animating your text and charts.

Selecting a Transition Style

There are 45 different slide transition styles in PowerPoint 97. You can apply a transition style to one slide, a group of selected slides, or every slide in your entire presentation. Generally, I have found it is best to use the same transition throughout a presentation, especially if it is a formal or business presentation. In very long slide shows, I sometimes use one transition style for all the slides dealing with the first major topic, then as a method of signaling a shift to another major topic (and keep the audience's attention), I apply a different transition style to the slides covering the next major topic.

T I P It is distracting to have a different transition style for each slide in your presentation. Your audience will tend to notice the cool transitions and miss the information you're presenting!

To select a transition, follow these steps:

1. Switch to Slide Sorter view.

2. Select the slide or slides you want to apply the transition to.

   If you plan on applying the same transition to all your slides, it is not necessary to select all the slides first. However, if you want to apply a transition to one or several slides, you must select the slides you want to work with. To select multiple slides, hold down the Shift key and click each slide additional slide. A dark border appears around each of the selected slides. Figure 15.8 shows the first three slides selected.

FIG. 15.8

Slides 1, 2, and 3 are selected.

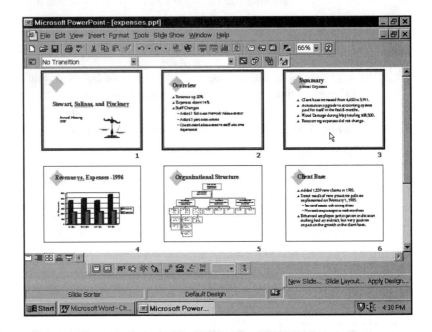

 3. Click the Slide Transition tool on the Slide View toolbar or choose Slide Show, Slide Transition. The Slide Transition dialog box appears, as shown in Figure 15.9.

 T I P You can also use the shortcut menu to access the Slide Transition command.

Allow me to introduce to you Petey. (I call him that because he reminds me of that wonderfully odd looking dog from the "Little Rascals.") Petey is here to illustrate how the transition will look.

FIG. 15.9

The Slide Transition dialog box is used to add transition and sound effects, and add timing to your slides.

4. Select the desired transition effect from the drop-down list box in the Effect section of the dialog box, just underneath Petey (see Figure 15.10). Every time you choose a transition, Petey switches places with another image, the Big Gray Key. Choose another transition, and Petey reappears. Petey and the Big Grey Key illustrate how the transition you've selected will look on your slides. The transitions are listed in alphabetical order.

FIG. 15.10

The Fade Through Black transition is selected. The Big Gray Key replaces Petey.

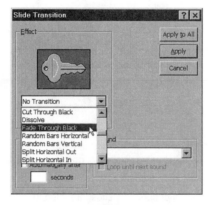

The default effect is No Transition; the next slide in the presentation just appears on the screen. By using the drop-down list box, you can choose from 45 different effects. Take a few minutes to explore the different transitions that are available. As you work more and more with transitions, you'll find yourself going back to a few that you really like and work well with the type of presentations you create. My personal favorites are Fade Through Black and Box Out.

5. Select the desired speed for the transition.

Initially, the speed of the effect will be set to transition Fast, which may be too fast while you're exploring the various transitions. Click the Slow radio button to get a better feel for exactly how the transition will come up. Once you have determined the transition you want to use, the speed selected becomes important. The speed you choose will impact how quickly the transition takes place in the slide show. You can set all your slides to be one speed or vary the speed. The choice is yours!

6. Click the Apply button to add the transition and speed to only the selected slides. Click the Apply To All button add the transition to every slide in your presentation.

If you're in Slide Sorter view, an interactive slide transition symbol appears beneath the miniature images of the slides in the lower-left corner. If you click the symbol, the slide actually previews the transition, showing you the previous slide and the transition effect to the active slide. You don't have to run the slide show to see the effects!

 From the Slide Sorter toolbar, the Slide Transition Effect drop-down list box indicates the name of the transition applied to the slide. Once you become familiar with the transitions, you can set or change the effect using this tool. However, the speed can only be changed through the Slide Transition dialog box.

Setting the Timing

By setting an amount of time for each slide to be on screen, you can run the slide show without using the mouse or keyboard to advance to the next slide. But you're not limited by these timings. If you reach a point in the presentation that you (or the audience) need to discuss a topic at greater length, you can easily pause the slide show and resume whenever you and the audience are ready.

As with transitions, you can use any of the views to apply timing, but Slide Sorter view provides several advantages over other views. Slide Sorter view allows you to select multiple slides at a time, and the miniature slide images display the time added to each slide.

T I P The first slide in most slide shows is a title or summary slide, designed to introduce the topic being presented. Generally, the first slide will appear on-screen when the audience enters the room. To avoid having to pause the first slide, simply don't put any time on it. When you're ready to begin the presentation, advance to the next slide, and the show will run with the timing you have set.

The same holds true for the last slide in a presentation. You don't want the audience distracted by the PowerPoint program while you're wrapping up your final comments. Because the last slide is usually a summary of the presentation or a copy of the title slide, don't assign any time to the last slide, either. The audience should walk out of the room with your last slide up on the screen.

Adding the Time   By default, a slide show is set up to advance manually, so that you can control the slides by using the mouse or keyboard. Setting a timed presentation is a two-step process. The first step is adding the desired time; the second is telling PowerPoint to advance the show using the timings.

Part
V

Ch
15

To assign time to a slide, follow these steps:

1. Switch to Slide Sorter view.

2. Select the slide or slides you want to have the same timing.

   To select a group of slides, hold down the Shift key and click each additional slide. A dark border appears around each of the selected slides.

   If the same amount of time is being applied to all your slides, it is not necessary to select all the slides first.

3. Click the Slide Transition tool on the Slide Sorter toolbar or choose Slide Show, Slide Transition. The Slide Transition dialog box appears.

T I P   Access the Slide Transition command on the shortcut menu via your secondary mouse button.

Time is added to a slide by using the Advance portion of the Slide Transition dialog box. The default setting is On Mouse Click. Leave this box checked if you want the option of using your mouse to advance the slides.

CAUTION

If you do not keep the On Mouse Click option checked, you will not be able to use your mouse to advance the slides. This is a change from previous versions of PowerPoint. In older versions, the Advance options were radio buttons; only one option could be selected. Automatically After *n* Seconds would add time to your slides *and* allow you to use your mouse. With this version, you should check both boxes for the greatest flexibility in working with slide shows.

4. Select the Automatically After *n* Seconds check box and enter the number of seconds you want the slide to be up on the screen (see Figure 15.11).

5. Click the Apply button to add the timing to only the selected slides. Click the Apply To All button to add the timing to every slide in your presentation.

If you're in Slide Sorter view, the time appears underneath the bottom-left corner of the miniature images.

FIG. 15.11
In the Advance section of the dialog box, 15 seconds is set as the time for the selected slides.

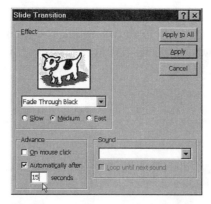

Activating the Timing   The second step in running a slide show with timings is to use the Set Up Show command to let PowerPoint know you want to run the show with the timings.

If you are using PowerPoint 7.0 instead of PowerPoint 97, choose View, Slide Show to set up this option.

To set up the show using the timings, follow these steps:

1. Position your mouse pointer over the slide. By using your secondary mouse button, access the shortcut menu and choose Set Up Show. You can also choose Slide Show, Set Up Show.

2. At the bottom of the dialog box, click Use Timings, If Present (see Figure 15.12).

3. Click the OK button.

FIG. 15.12
Slide Shows can be run Manually (by clicking the mouse click or pressing Enter) or automatically using the timings in the Slide Transition dialog box.

You can set the slide show up to either use the timings or advance manually. Sometimes you may want to run the slide show, but prefer to advance to the next slide using your mouse or keyboard. In other situations, you may want use the timings you've assigned to your presentation. The S̲et Up Show command provides you with the flexibility to switch back and forth between manual and automatic advance based on your needs.

Part

V

Ch

15

> **T I P** If you need to pause the presentation, simply press the S key. This stops the presentation. To resume, press the S key again.

Adding Transition Sounds

As you learned in Chapter 9, "Adding Animation and Sound," there are a number of ways you can use sound in your PowerPoint presentations. One way to incorporate sound in your presentation is to make it part of your slide show. The sound is played when you make the transition from one slide to another.

There are 16 different sound bites in PowerPoint 97. Sounds of clapping hands, glass breaking, the "cha-ching" of an old-fashioned cash register, and even a ricochet can be heard in your presentation. The same sound can even repeat over and over again until the next sound effect is played.

 You can apply transition sounds from any view. The advantage to using Slide Sorter view is its use of the interactive slide transition symbols. Earlier in this chapter, you learned that this symbol can be used to preview the slide transition. It is also used to hear the transition sounds you've applied. The Slide Transition symbol appears underneath the miniature images of the slides in the lower-left corner. If you click the symbol, you can preview both slide and sound transition effects. You don't have to run the slide show to see or hear the effects.

To add sound effects as the slide transitions, follow these steps:

1. Switch to Slide Sorter view.
2. Select the slide or slides you apply the same sound to.

   To select a group of slides, hold down the Shift key and click each additional slide. A dark border appears around each of the selected slides.

 3. Click the Slide Transition tool on the Slide View toolbar or choose Sli̲de Show, Slide T̲ransition. The Slide Transition dialog box appears.

   Sound effects are added to a slide by using the So̲und portion of the Slide Transition dialog box. The default setting is No Sound.

4. Open the Sound drop-down list and choose the desired sound effect (see Figure 15.13).

FIG. 15.13
The Clapping sound has been selected. This sound plays when the slide transitions.

5. If you want the sound to play over and over again, check Loop Until Next Sound.

CAUTION

The sound keeps playing without stopping not only for as long as this slide is on the screen, but until there is another sound played. This could be a sound attached to text, other objects on the same slide, or 10 slides into your presentation! If you only apply one transition sound at the beginning of your presentation, it continues to be played over and over throughout your entire presentation.

 Clapping is better than Applause for a continuous sound. Applause has a gap in the sound bite.

6. Choose Apply to add the sound to only the selected slides. Select the Apply To All button to add the sound to every slide in your presentation.

In addition to the 16 built-in sounds, you can also apply other sounds to your slides. To see a list of the sounds used by Office 97, scroll to the bottom of the Sound drop-down list box and choose Other Sounds. The Add Sound dialog box appears. The sound files listed here include the 16 sounds used for transitions, as well as other sounds Office 97 plays when you cancel, delete, or undo.

 To find all the sounds used by the various programs you have on your computer, perform an Advanced Find from the Add Sound dialog box. Search your entire hard drive and all subfolders to locate files with a WAV extension.

The sound files have a WAV extension. You can use the built-in sounds, sounds you've recorded, or even music on a CD. Refer to Chapter 9 for more information on using sound in PowerPoint.

Using Builds Effectively

A *build* is a special effect where objects appear on the slide, one after another. This powerful feature gives you greater control during a slide show. Your audience's attention is focused on the item your discussing. In previous versions of PowerPoint, you could only build slides with bulletized text. A list of bullets would be displayed, one at a time, to "build" the slide.

One of the most important enhancements made to PowerPoint 97 is the ability to build charts. Imagine, if you will, a column chart which compares Revenue and Expenses for each quarter of this year. The X axis displays the four quarters. A series of blue columns represents revenue, and red columns (naturally) show expenses. As you begin the discussion, your slide comes up with the title, the frame for the graph, and the legend. When you click your mouse, the revenue and expense columns for Quarter 1 appear (and only Quarter 1). After a brief discussion of the figures, another mouse click displays the second Quarter columns. You begin to compare Quarter 1 and Quarter 2. Clicking with your mouse when you want to display Quarter 3 and 4. Alternatively, you can display all of the revenue columns at one time, then add in the expense columns.

Don't like column charts? No problem! You can also build a pie chart, one piece at a time until the entire pie is "built." In fact, you can use a build with any of the chart types in PowerPoint. In addition to being able to build a series or category, even individual data points on a chart can be "built."

▶ **See** "Creating a Chart," **p. 201**

As you may know, when you create a graph in PowerPoint, a separate program called Microsoft Graph is launched. This program is used by all Microsoft programs, like Excel and Access, that have graphing capabilities. Because all these programs use Microsoft Graph to create charts, the ability to "build" graphs is available in those programs, too!

In PowerPoint 7, Microsoft began to refer to the build feature as *animation* to encompass the different types of effects available (such as time or sound). PowerPoint 97 continues to use the phrase *animation*. *Build* and *animation* are used interchangeably in this chapter.

Working with Text Preset Animation

There are two ways you can build text animation in your slide show. PowerPoint has built-in or preset animation effects designed to help you quickly enhance your presentation. You can also customize the animation effects. In this section, I focus on the text preset animation capabilities. Later sections discuss different methods of customizing text or chart animation.

You can work with preset animation in either Slide Sorter or Slide view. Using Slide Sorter view provides a wider variety of transition animation options and allows you to add enhancements to multiple slides at one time.

There are two methods of applying a transition effect:

- Use the Text Preset Animation drop-down list box on the Slide Sorter toolbar. Select from the 46 transition effects listed. The same transition effect is applied to all the bulletized text (unless you use the Random Effects animation).

- Choose Slide Show, Preset Animation to find 12 text animation effects. Some apply only a transition effect, while others combine transition and sound. See Table 15.1 for a breakdown of these effects.

Table 15.1   Text and Preset Animation Effects (from the Slide Show Menu)

Preset Animation Name	Transition Effect	Sound Effect
Drive-In	Fly From Right	Screeching Brakes
Flying	Fly From Left	Whoosh
Camera	Box Out	Camera
Flash Once	Flash once, Medium	No sound
Laser Text	Fly From Top-Right	Laser
Typewriter	Wipe Down	Typewriter
Reverse	Wipe Right	No sound
Drop In	Fly From Top	No sound
Wipe Right	Wipe Right	No sound
Dissolve	Dissolve	No sound
Split Vertical Out	Split Vertical Out	Laser
Appear	Appear	No sound

N O T E   Preset text animation can be applied to a slide in Slide view. You must first select the
bulletized text and use the Slide Show menu. The 12 transition effects listed in Table
15.1 are the only transitions available with preset animation. ▪

Customizing Text Animation

Unlike preset animation, you must be in Slide view to customize text animation. As with
the slides themselves, there are a number of animation effects you can implement in conjunction with a build. Here is a list of the effects with a brief description:

- *Apply timing to an animated build.* You can set a specific time interval between
  bullets. For example, you might have 10 seconds between the appearance of each
  bullet. If more time is needed, you can pause the presentation and resume whenever
  you're ready.

- *Select the level of the build.* When performing a build, PowerPoint can display groups
  of bullets together or show each level separately. You can even have the text appear
  one word or character at a time!

- *Use a transition effect when displaying text.* As with slide transitions, you can apply a
  transition effect to text on your slide. Your Title can Fly From Left, and each bullet
  can Crawl From Top or Peek From Bottom. There are 46 different transition effects.

- *Play a sound bite as each item builds on the slide.* A variety of sounds can be played
  when your bullets appear on the screen. Sixteen sound effects are available,
  including two types of clapping, a drum roll, and a ricochet.

- *Recolor or hide the previously animated text.* To focus your audience's attention on
  the item you're discussing, have PowerPoint change the color or hide the previously
  viewed text.

> **CAUTION**
>
> Preset Animation should be turned off before using custom animation. Choose Slide Show, Preset
> Animation, and select Off.

T I P It is distracting when each and every slide in your presentation uses animation. Your audience will
tend to notice the animation and miss the information you're presenting.

To manipulate the animation features, you must be in Slide view. From Slide view, select
the Custom Animation tool from the Animation Effects toolbar or choose Slide Show,
Custom Animation. The Custom Animation dialog box appears (see Figure 15.14).

FIG. 15.14

You can animate text and charts from the Custom Animation dialog box.

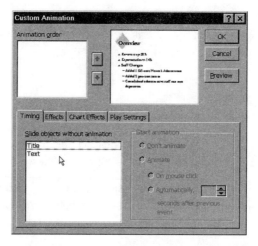

At the top of the dialog box is an area labeled Animation Order and a miniature of your current slide. Unless you have animated other objects, the Animation Order box is empty. Below, there are four tabs: Timing, Effects, Chart Effects, and Play Settings. Timing is the default tab.

Timing a Build   If you are working with a typical bullet slide and are looking at the Timing tab, the words Title and Text appear in the Slide Objects Without Animation box. The options on the right side of the tab under Start Animation are not activated and appear grayed out.

The time you add will depend on how you intend to animate the bullets. If you plan on showing the text all at once, your time interval should be set long enough for you to discuss the entire list. However, if you plan on building the bullets, the time you set here is the interval between the display of each of the components.

To add time to a list of bullets, follow these steps:

1. Select Text from the Slide Objects Without Animation box (see Figure 15.15).

   The miniature of your slide in the upper-right corner of the dialog box indicates that a portion of your text is selected. The Start Animation area of the dialog box becomes activated. By default, the Don't Animate button is selected.

2. Select Animate.

   Several things happen when you choose Animate. The animation is set to occur only on a mouse click (or if you press your Enter key). The word Text has moved and becomes the first item in the Animation Order section of the dialog box.

FIG. 15.15
When you select an object to animate, the object name is highlighted and selection handles appear around the object in the preview area.

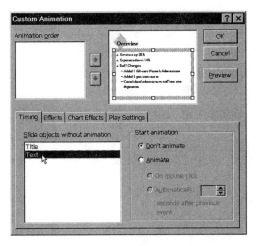

3. Choose Automatically *n* Seconds After Previous Event, and type in the number of seconds you want to pause between the display of each bullet.

4. Choose Preview. The miniature of your slide illustrates the timing effects.

5. Choose OK to save the animation timing.

If you find in the course of delivering your presentation you need additional time to discuss a topic, you can pause the presentation.

TROUBLESHOOTING

I've set up builds on my bullet slides and used the On Mouse Click setting (from the Custom Animation dialog box) instead of building the bullets automatically with time. When I run the slide show, my mouse doesn't work. I have to use my Enter key or the shortcut menu to activate the build. In the Slide Transitions dialog box, you do not have the On Mouse Click option checked. You'll find the Slide Transitions option under the Slide Show menu. You should always keep this option marked. It not only controls slide transitions, but, as you've discovered, slide build as well.

Selecting the Level   PowerPoint considers each bullet level a different "paragraph." There are five levels. Suppose you have a list of bullets, like the ones in Figure 15.16, and you set the slide to build on the first paragraph level. Team Sports and all the bullets indented underneath it would appear. Then, after a preset time or a mouse click, Individual Sports and all its sub-bullets appears. If you set the slide to build on the second paragraph level, Team Sports appears by itself, then Football and its sub-bullets display, followed by Softball and its sub-bullets, and so on.

FIG. 15.16
There are three levels of text in this bullet slide.

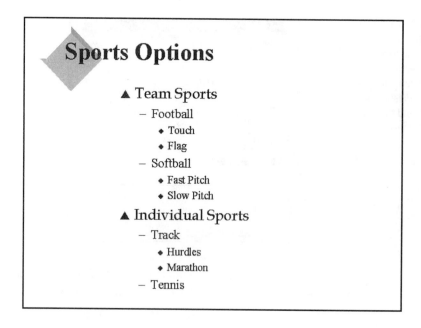

To select the level of the build, follow these steps:

1. From Slide view, select the Custom Animation tool from the Animation Effects toolbar or choose Slide Show, Custom Animation. The Custom Animation dialog box appears.

2. Click the Effects tab (see Figure 15.17).

3. Select the Grouped By *n* Level Paragraphs box, and choose the desired level.

FIG. 15.17
From the Effects tab, you can select whether you want the text to appear all at once or by each level. Choose the desired transition or sound effect, and what should happen after the effect is over.

To further enhance the build, several options can be used for introducing the text. On the right side of the Effects tab in the Custom Animation dialog box is an area labeled Introduce Text (see Figure 15.18). By default, text is displayed all at one time. However, you can choose to build the text word by word, or even letter by letter.

FIG. 15.18

The text appears grouped by the second bullet levels. Team Sports appears, followed by the Football and its sub-bullets, then Softball and its sub-bullets.

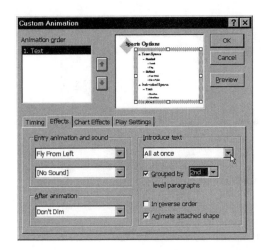

As a unique alternative to a traditional build, you have the option of building bullets from the bottom up. One great use for the In Reverse Order option is when you have a ranking or a hierarchical order of some kind, such as the Top Ten Sales Reps or Top Ten Reasons to Buy Your Product. To foster excitement and anticipation in the audience, you can present the 10th item first and work your way up the list to the first or highest ranking.

Applying a Build Transition Effect   As with slide transitions, you can apply a transition effect to a build. Each bullet or chart item can Fly From Left or Peek From Bottom. You can choose from 45 different transition styles. Once applied, the same transition is used to build all the bullets on the slide. The only exception is the Random Effects transition which, of course, selects transitions at random to build your text.

If yours is a business presentations, it is best to use the same transition on most of your builds, then using a different transition to emphasize a particular slide further.

To select a transition, follow these steps:

1. From Slide view, select the Custom Animation tool from the Animation Effects toolbar or choose Slide Show, Custom Animation. The Custom Animation dialog box appears.

2. In the Timing tab, select the item you want to enhance.

3. Click the Effects tab. From the Entry Animation and Sound section, use the Effects drop-down box to choose the transition style. The default effect is Fly From Left. By using the drop-down list box, you can choose from 45 different effects (see Figure 15.19).

FIG. 15.19
The Box Out effect has been selected from the drop-down list box.

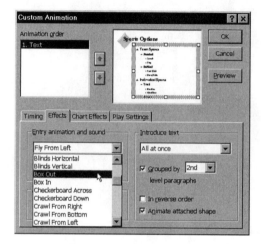

4. Choose Preview. The miniature of your slide shows how the transition will work.

5. Choose OK to apply the transition effect.

 In Slide Sorter view, the Text Preset Animation drop-down list box indicates the name of the effect applied to the text. If you have applied one animation effect to your title and another to your bullets, the Text Preset Animation indicates the effect on the bullets. You can use this tool to change the effect.

Selecting the Animation Order   Most slides have several objects on them: the title, bulleted text, shapes you've drawn, and clip art objects you've added. The order in which these objects appear on the screen is the order in which you animated the items. If you want a shape or clip art to appear before the bullets, you need to adjust the order of the animation effects.

To select or change the order on your slide, follow these steps:

1. From Slide view, select the Custom Animation tool from the Animation Effects toolbar or choose Slide Show, Custom Animation. The Custom Animation dialog box appears (see Figure 15.20).

FIG. 15.20
In this list, the bulleted text is animated first, followed by the Title, then the clip art Object. The Title has been selected in order to move it before the Text.

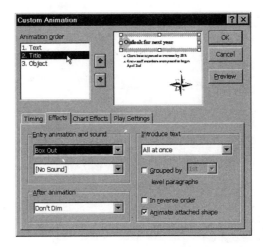

2. In the upper-left corner of the dialog box is a list of the animated items. Select the item you want to reorder. To move the item up in the list, click the up arrow until you have the order you want. To move an down in the list, click the down arrow.

3. Choose OK to save the new order.

Sound   A variety of sounds can be played when your bullets appear on the screen. An explosion, a music chime, and even the sound of a slide projector is among the 16 sound bites in PowerPoint. When applied to animated text or an object, it can liven up your slide show.

To add sound effects to the text in your slide, follow these steps:

1. From Slide view, select the Custom Animation tool from the Animation Effects toolbar or choose Slide Show, Custom Animation. The Custom Animation dialog box appears.

2. In the Timing tab, select the item you want to enhance.

3. Click the Effects tab. The default effect is No Sound. From the Sound Animation drop-down list box, make your selection (see Figure 15.21).

4. Choose Preview. As the miniature of your slide shows the animation effects, you will hear the sound play.

5. Choose OK to save the sound effect.

T I P   Sound is best used with slide titles, drawn objects, and clip art. The same sound repeating over and over again each time a bullet appears might prove annoying to your audience. Instead of a repeating sound, consider playing music for the entire slide or presentation.

FIG. 15.21
The Whoosh sound
has been selected to
play.

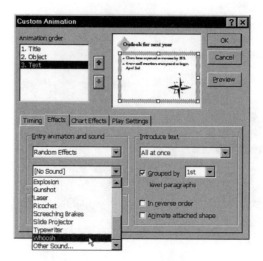

The sound files have a WAV extension. You can use the built-in sounds, sounds you've recorded, or even music on a CD. Refer to Chapter 9 for more information on using sound in PowerPoint.

▶ **See** "Adding Animation and Sound," **p. 187**

After the Effect   Once the animation effect is complete, PowerPoint can change the color or hide the previously viewed text. This technique helps your audience to focus their attention on the item you're discussing.

To dim or hide the previous animation, follow these steps:

1. From Slide view, select the Custom Animation tool from the Animation Effects toolbar or choose Slide Show, Custom Animation. The Custom Animation dialog box appears.

2. In the Timing tab, select the item you want to work with (see Figure 15.22).

3. Click the Effects tab. The default setting is Don't Dim. Click the After Animation drop-down list box and make a selection.

   The text color can be changed so it appears lighter (or dimmer) than the current color. You can hide the text, either just after the animation or with a mouse click.

4. Choose Preview. As the miniature of your slide shows the animation effects, you will hear the sound play.

5. Choose OK to save the sound effect.

FIG. 15.22
The Text object has been selected. After the animation, the text color changed to red.

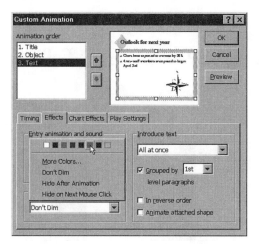

TROUBLESHOOTING

I've set up builds on my bullet slides and used the Hide On Next Mouse Click setting (from the After Animation option in the Custom Animation dialog box). When I run the slide show, my mouse doesn't work. I have to use my Enter key or the shortcut menu to activate the build. Choose Slide Show, Slide Transitions. In the Slide Transitions dialog box, you do not have the On Mouse Click option checked. You should always keep this option marked. Though part of the Slide Transition settings, this setting impacts animation as well.

Customizing Chart Animation

One of the more exciting animation capabilities in PowerPoint is the ability to animate charts. Similar to building your text slides, animation can build a pie chart one piece at a time, or a bar chart by the group of bars or individual bars.

Suppose you have a slide like the one shown in Figure 15.23. You could animate your chart by displaying just the Revenue columns for all four quarters, then adding the columns for Expenses (see Figures 15.24 and 15.25). Series are the items in the legend of a chart.

Alternatively, PowerPoint can show both Revenue and Expenses for Quarter 1, adding the other quarters one at a time (see Figures 15.26 and 15.27). Categories are the items along the x-axis of the chart.

And, if you're really ambitious, PowerPoint can display each and every column separately!

FIG. 15.23
Revenue and
Expenses for each
quarter in 1996.

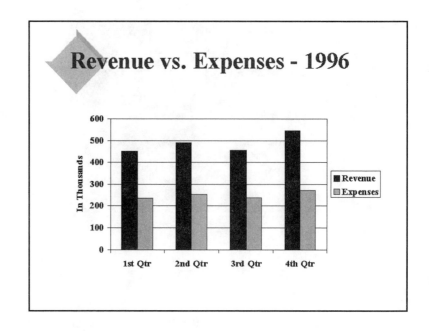

FIG. 15.24
The slide is animated
by series, first dis-
playing only the
Revenue information.

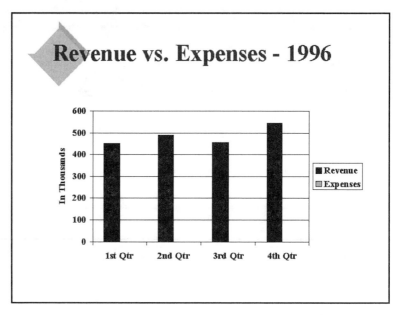

FIG. 15.25
The animation continues by displaying the next series, the Expenses information.

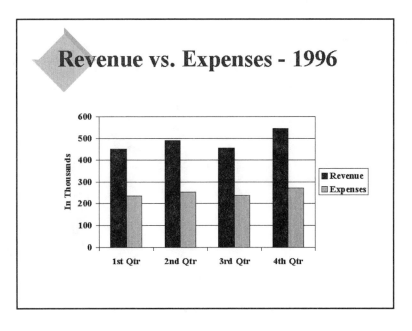

FIG. 15.26
The slide is animated by category, first displaying only the first quarter information.

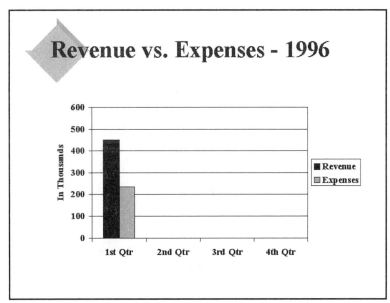

FIG. 15.27
The animation con-
tinues by displaying
each category, one
after another.

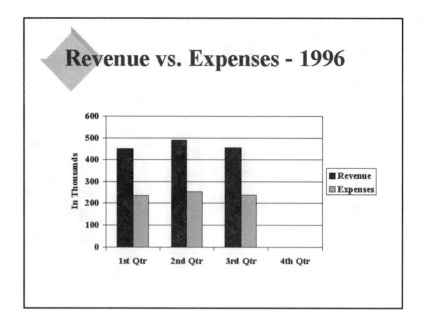

You must be in Slide view to customize chart animation. As with the slides themselves, there are a number of animation effects you can implement in conjunction with building a chart:

- *Apply timing to an animated build.* You can set a specific time interval between displaying pieces of a pie or bars on a chart. For example, you might have ten seconds between the appearance of each item. If more time is needed, you can pause the presentation and resume whenever you're ready.

- *Select the level of the build.* When building a chart, you can have PowerPoint display a series of bars together or add each individual bar one at a time.

- *Use a transition effect when displaying charts.* As with slide transitions, you can apply a transition effect to the elements in your chart. Your chart can come in Box Out or Wipe Up. There are 46 different transition effects.

- *Play a sound bite as each item builds on the slide.* A variety of sounds can be played when your chart components appear. Sixteen sound effects are available, including sound made by a camera click, gunshot, and typewriter.

Unless you are providing a very detailed presentation, you will probably not animate each and every chart in your slide show. On some slides you might build the slide title separately from the chart, and show the entire chart all at once. On other slides you may need to discuss each series or category of the chart as it appears on the screen. Planning ahead on what you'd like to emphasize in your presentation is important.

To work with the chart animation features, you must be in Slide view. Select the Custom Animation tool from the Animation Effects toolbar or choose Slide Show, Custom Animation. The Custom Animation dialog box appears (see Figure 15.28).

FIG. 15.28
From the Custom Animation dialog box, you can choose which objects to animate and how you want them to appear.

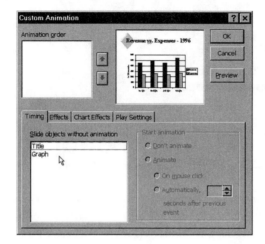

At the top of the dialog box is an area labeled Animation Order and a miniature of your current slide. Unless you have animated other objects, the Animation Order box is empty. Below, there are four tabs: Timing, Effects, Chart Effects, and Play Settings. Timing is the default tab.

Timed Animation   If you are working with a typical chart slide and are looking at the Timing tab, the words Title and Graph appear in the Slide Objects Without Animation box. The options on the right side of the tab under Start Animation are not activated and appear grayed out.

To add time to a chart, follow these steps:

1. Select Graph from the Slide Objects Without Animation box, as shown in Figure 15.29.

   The miniature of your slide in the upper-right corner of the dialog box indicates that the graph is selected. The Start Animation area of the dialog box becomes activated. By default the Don't Animate button is selected.

2. Select Animate.

   Several things happen when you choose Animate. The animation is set to occur only on a mouse click (or if you press the Enter key). The word Graph has moved and become the first item in the Animation Order section of the dialog box.

3. Choose Automatically, *n* Seconds After Previous Event, and type in the number of seconds you want to pause between the display of component of the graph.

FIG. 15.29
The Graph has been selected. When you select an object to animate, the object name is highlighted and selection handles appear around the object in the preview area.

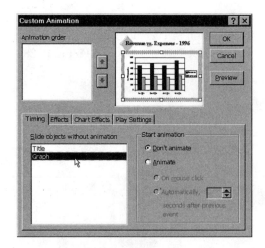

N O T E   The time you add depends on how you intend to animate the chart. If you plan on showing the chart all at once, your time interval should be set long enough for you to discuss the entire chart, for instance 180 seconds (2 minutes). However, if you plan on building the chart, the time you set here is the interval between the display of each of the components. Two minutes is a long time to wait for each piece of pie to appear! ■

   4. Choose Preview. The miniature of your slide illustrates the timing effects.

   5. Choose OK to save the animation timing.

If you find in the course of delivering your presentation you need additional time to discuss a topic, you can pause the presentation. See the section "Previewing Your Presentation" earlier in this chapter for basic information on running your slide show. Chapter 16, "Running Your Presentation," provides more detailed information on slide show keyboard shortcuts and pausing a presentation.

Introducing Chart Elements   One of the things you need to decide is how you want to build your chart. Table 15.2 lists and describes the choices.

Table 15.2   Animating Chart Elements

Introducing Chart Elements	Description
All At Once	The default setting. In effect, this shows the entire chart at one time. No building of the chart takes place.
By Series	The items represented in the legend are the "series" in the chart. Figure 15.30 shows a Revenue series and an Expenses series.

Introducing Chart Elements	Description
By Category	The groups along the X-axis are the "categories" in the chart. In Figure 15.30, each quarter is a category.
By Element in Series	Each component in a series is displayed one at a time. The revenue column in quarter 1 of Figure 15.30 appears first, followed by the revenue column for quarter 2. When all of the revenue columns have appeared, the first expense column comes up on the screen.
By Element in Category	Each component in a category is displayed one at a time. The revenue column in quarter 1 appears, followed by the expense column for quarter 1. The columns for the remaining quarters appear in the same order, first revenue then expenses.

FIG. 15.30

A typical column chart. Expenses and Revenue are the series. The four quarters are the categories.

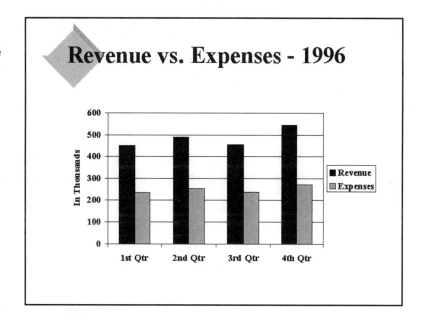

To build your chart elements, follow these steps:

1. From Slide view, select the Custom Animation tool from the Animation Effects toolbar or choose Slide Show, Custom Animation. The Custom Animation dialog box appears.

2. Select Graph from the Timing tab.

   In order to "build" the chart elements, you must turn on the Animate option on the Timing tab of the Custom Animation dialog box.

3. Click the Chart Effects tab. From the Introduce Chart Elements drop-down list box, select a level of introduction. The default effect is All At Once (see Figure 15.31).

FIG. 15.31
The graph is animated by Series.

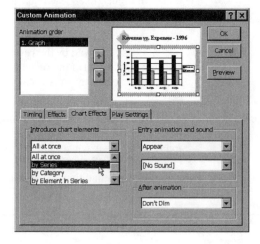

4. Choose Preview. The miniature of your slide illustrates how the build will work.

5. Choose OK to apply the build effect.

TROUBLESHOOTING

I've attached a time to build my chart components. As soon as the last part of my chart is displayed, the next slide appears before I've had a chance to finish talking about the chart. The time you've attached to your slide transition is not long enough. To lengthen the time on the slide, choose Slide Show, Slide Transition.

Applying a Transition Effect   In order to add a transition to a chart, you need to have turned on the animate option on the Timings tab in the Custom Animation dialog box.

You can apply a transition effect to build a chart, just as you can build a list of bullets. Chart elements Wipe Up or Appear on the screen. You can choose from 45 different transition effects, though depending on the type of chart you have, some transitions will not be available.

In the previous section, you learned about the level you want to use to introduce your chart elements. If you selected All At Once from the Introduce Text option, the transition you choose is applied as the chart appears on the screen. If you selected one of the options which introduces the elements by series or category, the transition you select here is applied to each element that is built.

N O T E The Random Effects transition does not work the same way with chart elements as it
does with text. If the Random Effects option is selected, the first time you run the slide
show, PowerPoint selects a transition, and all elements of the chart appear using that one
transition. The next time you run your slide show, a different transition is selected, and all the
elements of the chart appear using the new transition. ▨

If yours is a business presentation, it is best to use the same transition on the majority
of your charts, then apply a different transition as a way to emphasize a particular slide
further.

To select a chart transition, follow these steps:

1. From Slide view, select the Custom Animation tool from the Animation Effects
toolbar or choose Sli̲de Show, Custo̲m Animation. The Custom Animation dialog box
appears.

2. The Chart Effects tab should appear, if you have animated the chart. If you have not
animated the chart, then select Graph in the S̲lide Objects Without Animation from
the Timing tab.

3. On the Chart Effects tab, choose the transition style from the Effects drop-down list
box in the E̲ntry Animation and Sound area. The default effect is No Effect (see
Figure 15.32).

FIG. 15.32
Strips Up-Right is the
selected animation
effect. Each column
appears from the
bottom-left to the
upper-right corner.

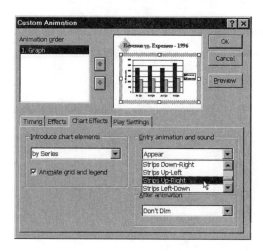

4. Choose P̲review. The slide miniature in the dialog box shows how the transition will
work.

5. Choose OK to apply the chart transition effect.

Although not specifically noted in the dialog box, when your chart animates, first the frame, axis, and legend for the chart will appear, followed by the other elements.

T I P   No Effect ▼   On the Slide Sorter toolbar, the Text Preset Animation drop-down list box indicates the name of the effect applied to the chart. If you have applied one animation effect to your title and another to chart, the Text Preset Animation indicates the effect on the chart. You can use this tool to change the effect.

Selecting the Animation Order   Most slides have several objects on them: the title, graph, shapes you've drawn, and clip art objects you've added. The order in which these objects appear on the screen is the order in which you animated the items. If you want a shape or clip art to appear before the chart, you need to adjust the order of the animation effects.

To select or change the animation order on your slide, follow these steps:

1. In the upper-left corner of the Custom Animation dialog box is a list of the animated items. Select the item you want to reorder. To move the item up in the list, click the up arrow until you have the order you want (see Figure 15.33). To move the item down in the list, click the down arrow.

FIG. 15.33
In this list, the Graph is animated first, followed by the Title. The Title has been selected in order to move it before the Graph.

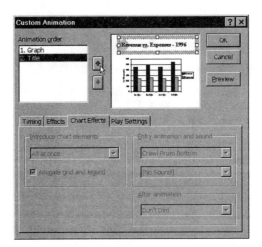

2. Choose OK to save the new order.

Sound   A variety of sounds can be played when your bullets appear on the screen. An explosion, a music chime, and even the sound of a slide projector is among the 16 sound bites in PowerPoint. When applied to animated text or an object, it can liven up your slide show. Now, having said that, I would *not* recommend using sound when building your chart for the following reasons.

The sound you apply when your chart is animated is heard when each element appears. For example, suppose you have animated a column chart, decided to introduce the elements by series, and have applied the Applause sound to your animation. The first elements to animate are the frame, axis, and legend (they appear all at once), and you hear Applause when they come up. When the first series appears, you hear Applause. Each time a series appears, you hear Applause. How often do you hear this Applause in the chart illustrated in Figure 15.34? Three times—once for the frame and other elements, once for the Revenue columns, and once for the Expense columns.

Now, if you have elected to introduce the chart elements by each element in a series, how often do you hear the Applause sound? Nine times! This can be really irritating to your audience.

Also, you cannot apply a sound to a particular element (like a great revenue number in the third quarter). If you could apply a sound to an individual element, it would have a great deal more impact on the audience.

FIG. 15.34

A typical column chart. Use sound with animation sparingly, if at all.

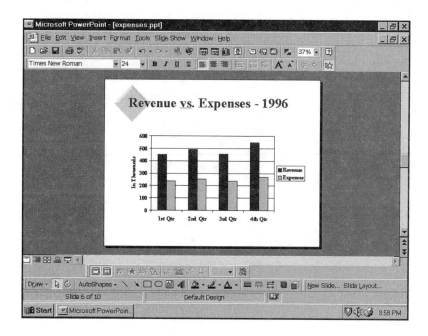

To add sound effects to the elements of your chart, use these steps:

1. From Slide view, select the Custom Animation tool from the Animation Effects toolbar or choose Slide Show, Custom Animation. The Custom Animation dialog box appears.

2. In the Timing tab, select the item you want to enhance.

3. Click the Chart Effects tab. The default effect is No Sound. From the Sound Animation drop-down list box, make your selection (see Figure 15.35).

4. Choose Preview. As the miniature of your slide shows the animation effects, you will hear the sound play.

5. Choose OK to save the sound effect.

 T I P Sound is best used with slide titles, drawn objects, and clip art. The same sound repeating over and over again each time a bullet appears might prove annoying to your audience. Instead of a repeating sound, consider playing music for the entire slide or presentation.

FIG. 15.35
The Chime sound plays twice—once when the Revenue columns first appear, then again when the Expenses columns appear.

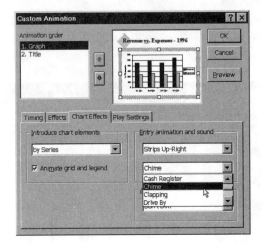

You can use the built-in sounds, sounds you've recorded, or even music on a CD. Refer to Chapters 9 and 23 for more information on using sound in PowerPoint.

▶ **See** "Using Action Buttons," **p. 189**

After the Animation Effect   Once the animation effect is complete, PowerPoint can change the color or hide the previously viewed text. This technique helps your audience to focus their attention on the item you're discussing.

To dim or hide the previous animation, follow these steps:

1. From Slide view, select the Custom Animation tool from the Animation Effects toolbar or choose Slide Show, Custom Animation. The Custom Animation dialog box appears.

2. In the Timing tab, select the item you want to work with (see Figure 15.36).

FIG. 15.36

After the animation, the text changes color. The color is selected from the PowerPoint color palette using the More Colors option.

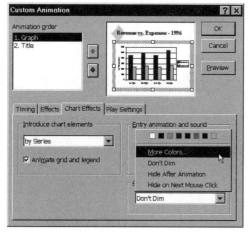

3. Click the Effects tab. The default setting is Don't Dim. Click the After Animation drop-down list box and make a selection.

   The text color can be changed, so it appears lighter (or dimmer) than the current color. You can hide the text, either just after the animation or with a mouse click.

4. Choose Preview. As the miniature of your slide shows the animation effects, you will hear the sound play.

5. Choose OK to save the sound effect.

Play Settings   The items on this tab are primarily used with video and sound. However, if you are in a situation where you want to be able to edit a graph or chart, as you are running a slide show, you can activate that option using Play Settings. To use this feature, you have selected the graph or object before you go into the Custom Animation dialog box. Depending on the object you are working with, you may have two or three choices.

To invoke the Play Setting options, use these steps:

1. Switch to Slide view, if necessary.

2. Select the chart. The options for Play Settings only appear when you have selected the graph or object before you go into dialog box.

3. Select the Custom Animation tool from the Animation Effects toolbar or choose Slide Show, Custom Animation. The Custom Animation dialog box appears.

4. In the Play Settings tab, click the Object Action drop-down list (see Figure 15.37), and make a selection. The default setting is Don't Play.

FIG. 15.37

The Edit option from the Play Settings tab. Being able to edit a graph during internal meetings or rehearsals is particularly useful.

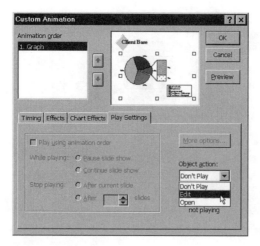

The Edit option appears in the drop-down list box only if you have activated animation on the Timing tab. This option allows you to edit the graph or chart while you are running the slide show.

Let's say you have a pie chart on the third slide in your presentation. You've animated the pie chart to build one piece at a time. You run the slide show and on the third slide, and your pie begins to build, like the one in Figure 15.38. Once the animation has built the pie chart, while you are still running the slide show, the system opens up Microsoft Graph (the program that launches when you create or edit a graph), giving you the opportunity to edit the chart (see Figure 15.39). This capability is particularly useful for internal meetings or rehearsals, where you have not finalized the presentation and need the input of others. Once you have received the input, you will want to change the play setting back to Don't Play. The Open option applies to video and sound clips.

▶ **See** "Assigning Action Settings to Other Objects," **p. 194**

Once you have completed your changes, the Microsoft Graph program closes and your slide show continues.

5. Choose OK to save the setting. The slide show continues.

FIG. 15.38
The slide as it appears when running the show.

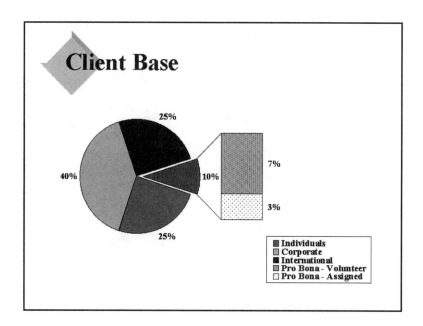

A Word About Organization Charts   Organization charts can be animated with timing, transitions, and sound. Unlike data, bar, and pie charts, organizational charts cannot be "built." Rather, PowerPoint treats organization charts as objects, like clip art, rather than data charts, and are animated differently. You can activate play settings for an organizational chart as described in the previous section.

▶ **See** "Creating an Organization Chart," **p. 269**

To animate an organization chart, follow these steps:

1. In the Timing tab of the Custom Animation dialog box, select the item you want to enhance. Choose Animate from the Start Animation options. The animation can be set to begin on a mouse click or automatically after a set time. The whole chart animates all at once.

2. From the Effects tab, choose the transition and sound effect from the Entry Animation and Sound drop-down list boxes.

3. From the Play Settings tab, choose Edit from the Object Action drop-down list box if you want to edit the chart while you are running the slide show.

4. Choose Preview. The miniature of your slide shows how the options you've selected will work.

5. Choose OK to activate the settings.

FIG. 15.39
The Microsoft Graph program opens, enabling you to edit the chart. The slide show is still active in the background.

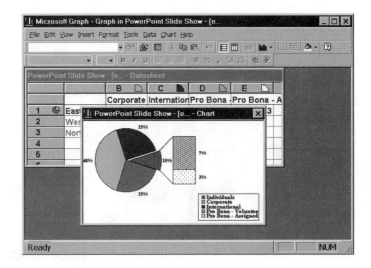

Adding Narration

Recording a narration to accompany your slide show is a great way to deliver a presentation if you can't be there in person. Perhaps you want to show your presentation to perspective clients, but can't afford the time (or money) to deliver it personally. Or to raise your company's visibility at a trade show, you can run the narrated presentation continuously while talking to perspective clients.

To add voice narration to your slide show, follow these steps

1. Choose Slide Show, Record Narration. The Record Narration dialog box appears. The amount of free disk space and the number of minutes you can record is shown (see Figure 15.40).

FIG. 15.40
The system displays the quality, amount of free disk space, and maximum recording time available in the Record Narration dialog box.

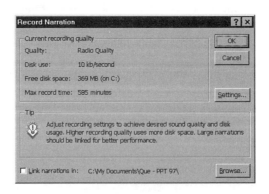

2. Adjust the recording options by clicking the <u>S</u>ettings button. The Sound Selection dialog box appears.

3. To insert the narration on your slides as an embedded object and to begin recording, choose OK. To insert the narration as a linked object, select the <u>L</u>ink Narrations In check box, located in the lower-left corner of the dialog box. Then choose OK to begin recording.

4. Advance through the slide show as you normally would, narrating as you go.

5. At the end of the slide show, a confirmation message appears (see Figure 15.41). Choose <u>Y</u>es to save the slide timings along with the narration. Choose <u>N</u>o to save only the narration. An icon appears in the lower-right corner of each slide that has narration.

FIG. 15.41

If you have changed the timings as you have been recording, you have the option of saving the revised timings.

When you run the slide show, the narration will automatically play with the show. If you want to run the slide show without narration, choose Sli<u>d</u>e Show, <u>S</u>et Up Show. Click the Show Without <u>N</u>arrations check box.

While you're recording, the other sounds inserted in your slide show will not be heard. You can't record and play sounds simultaneously.

▶ **See** "Adding a Narration Track to Your Presentation, **p. 556**

CHAPTER 16

Running Your Presentation

by Dave Johnson

Now that you've got a slide presentation put together, PowerPoint offers a slew of tools and techniques to help you run your show exactly the way you want. Not only can you automatically generate notes and action items during the slide show, but you can play the slides in any order on-the-fly. You can even bundle your PowerPoint presentations together with Viewer so that you can take the show on the road. ■

Taking notes during a presentation

Learn how to make the most of real-time annotations while you deliver a presentation.

Playing your presentation

PowerPoint presentations can be automated—here's how to run a hands-off show.

Taking your show on the road

Road shows are stressful enough without worrying about PowerPoint trouble. Look here to keep your blood pressure down.

Taking Notes During a Presentation

PowerPoint solves the problem of tracking action items, comments, and corrections throughout the actual presentation. Instead of jotting notes on a pad of paper or the Notes Pages, you can now enter the data directly into the presentation as it occurs.

Annotating Slides as You Go

You can use the pen tool to annotate slides as they are displayed. The pen provides a simple way to make course marks on the screen to draw attention to specific objects on the screen. The results will look only as good as you are skilled at drawing with the mouse, and, in fact, often resemble the graphics used on television to diagram football plays.

You can use the pen tool at any time during a presentation. To draw, do the following:

1. Move the mouse while displaying a slide. The Control Panel appears in the bottom-left corner of the screen.

2. Click the Control Panel. A pop-up menu appears.

3. Choose P<u>e</u>n (see Figure 16.1).

FIG. 16.1
The presentation menu provides access to a simple drawing tool.

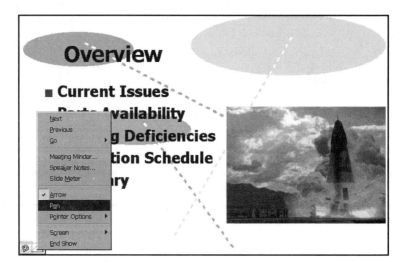

4. Draw on the screen by dragging the mouse while holding the left mouse button down (see Figure 16.2).

FIG. 16.2
It's not sophisticated, but the pen can draw attention to specific parts of a slide.

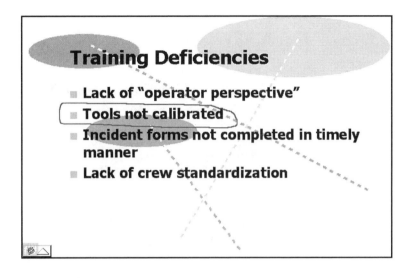

Part

V

Ch

16

CAUTION

Annotations are not saved. If you return to a slide that was previously marked-up, the annotations will be gone.

 T I P You can right-click the slide show to produce the pop-up menu anywhere on the screen without using the Control Panel.

You may find that the default pen color doesn't provide enough contrast to be visible against the slide background. If this is the case, you can change the pen's color as follows:

1. Click the Control Panel again.
2. Choose Pointer Options, Pen Color.
3. Select a color from the menu as shown in Figure 16.3.

 T I P For best results—and to avoid wasting time during your actual presentation—you should select a pen that contrasts with the background color before the presentation begins.

 T I P To permanently set the pen color for a presentation, choose Slide Show, Set Up Show and set the Pen Color at the bottom of the dialog box.

FIG. 16.3
You can change the
pen color for the
duration of the slide
show from the
presentation menu.

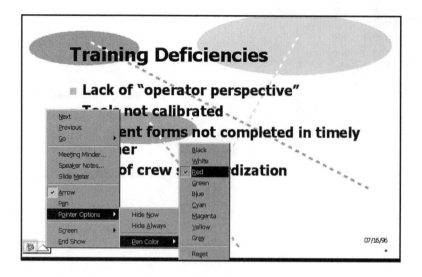

If you change the pen color from the control panel during a slide show, you can return to the default pen simply by choosing Pointer Options, Pen Color, Reset.

When you are ready to move to the next slide, you can't advance via a mouse click if the pen is active. There are several ways to disable the pen, described in Table 16.1.

Table 16.1 Hiding the Pen Tool

Action	Effect
Press the spacebar	Pen changes back into a pointer and the presentation advances to the next slide.
From the Control Panel, choose Pointer Options, Hide Now	Pen changes back into a pointer and the Control Panel is hidden from view until the mouse moves again. The slide doesn't advance until you click the mouse button (see Figure 16.4).
From the Control Panel, choose Pointer Options, Hide Always	Pen changes into an invisible pointer, and the Control Panel is hidden for the duration of the slide show. The slide doesn't advance until you click the mouse button.

 T I P If you choose to always hide the Control Panel, you can still access the pop-up menu via the right mouse button.

FIG. 16.4
By using the Pointer Options and choosing Hide Always, you can disable the pointer and prevent the Control Panel from becoming visible when the mouse moves.

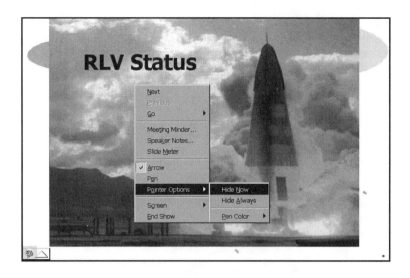

The pen is not a true drawing tool; PowerPoint doesn't allow you to use straight lines, shapes, or any unique tools for creating images on the slide. If you truly need to draw an image in the middle of the slide show, you have two options:

- Switch to a specialized Windows drawing program
- If you anticipate needing such a capability when you create the presentation, link the paint program to the appropriate slide in this way:

▶ **See** "Adding Action Buttons," **p. 189**

1. In Slide view, choose a slide that you want to be able to call a paint program from.

2. On the Drawing toolbar, click the AutoShapes button. A pop-up menu of options appears; choose Action Buttons.

3. Click a button. To keep the button inconspicuous, choose the first button that looks like an empty rectangle (see Figure 16.5).

4. Place a square in a corner of the slide by dragging the crosshair while holding down the mouse button.

5. When you release the mouse, a Properties dialog box appears. If the presentation has not already been saved, a dialog box prompts you to save your work before proceeding. Click Run Program, then Browse.

6. Select the program you want to run (see Figure 16.6). For instance, you could enter **C:\Windows\Pbrush.exe** to run the Paint program from this slide. Click OK.

FIG. 16.5
Action buttons come in many shapes and act as "hot spots" when clicked during a presentation.

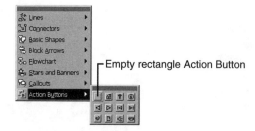

— Empty rectangle Action Button

FIG. 16.6
Action buttons can launch programs from a PowerPoint slide, such as this paint program.

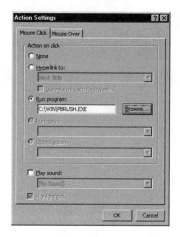

When you run this slide show, you can click the action button in this slide and have access to a more sophisticated paint program (or any other application, such as a calculator).

Using the Meeting Minder to Annotate Slides

While the pen allows you to draw crude figures on slides, another tool—Meeting Minder—is designed to store notes, comments, and action items that you may encounter during the presentation. Meeting Minder puts you in control of this information as well. Using Meeting Minder, you can:

■ Create an end slide which summarizes action items.

■ Export notes to a professionally formatted Microsoft Word file.

■ Schedule actions via Microsoft Outlook.

To use the Meeting Minder while running a presentation, follow these steps:

1. Move the mouse while displaying a slide. The Control Panel appears in the bottom-left corner of the screen.

2. Click the Control Panel. A pop-up menu appears.

3. Choose Meeting Minder.

 T I P If you're using PowerPoint's View on Two Screens feature, Meeting Minder only appears on the speaker's monitor and the audience cannot see it, you can leave the dialog box on the screen as long as needed.

When the Meeting Minder dialog box appears, you see two tabs: Meeting Minutes and Action Items. The Meeting Minutes tab provides a free-form text box where you can enter any notes on the presentation as they occur. The Action Items tab is a bit more structured, as it requires you to enter specific data. To create a list of action items:

1. With the Meeting Minder open, click the Action Items tab (see Figure 16.7).

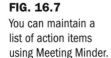 **FIG. 16.7**
You can maintain a list of action items using Meeting Minder.

2. Enter a task in the Description box.

 T I P Only the Description is required. It's optional to assign a task to an individual.

3. Enter a name in the Assigned To box.

4. Change the Due Date if necessary.

5. Click the Add button to enter the Action Item to Meeting Minder's database.

6. When you have added all of the action items desired, click OK to close the dialog box.

Meeting Minder remembers all the action items throughout a presentation. If you need to add more items later in the presentation, you can open and close the Meeting Minder at your convenience and add new ones to the existing list. When you reach the end of your presentation, PowerPoint adds a new slide that lists all of the action items created with Meeting Minder (see Figure 16.8).

CAUTION

Only action items that are saved by closing the Meeting Minder dialog box with the OK button are added to the Action Item slide at the close of the presentation. If you leave the Meeting Minder open, action items won't be created on the last slide.

FIG. 16.8
Action items are automatically added to a new slide at the end of the presentation for review by your group.

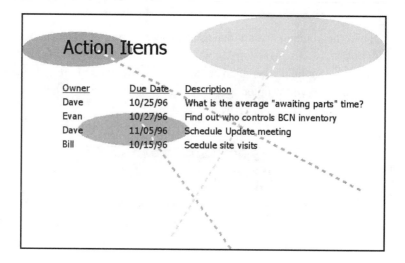

Using Meeting Minder with Outlook and Word

Meeting Minder provides connectivity between PowerPoint and two other applications: Microsoft Outlook and Word. By using Meeting Minder, you can directly schedule appointments by clicking the Schedule button at the bottom of the dialog box. This launches an Outlook appointment dialog box such as the one in Figure 16.9, which you may complete in the ordinary way. This is useful for annotating future meetings that occur as a result of the presentation. You can also create Action Item reports in Word with a single button in Meeting Minder.

Alternatively, you can send Meeting Minder's action items to Outlook as to-do tasks:

1. With the Meeting Minder open, click the Export button at the bottom of the dialog box.

2. A new dialog box appears, presenting two options. Select only the top one: Post Action Items to Microsoft Outlook (see Figure 16.10).

3. Click Export Now to send the data to the desired application.

4. Switch to Outlook. You'll find that the action items have been entered in the task list.

FIG. 16.9
Outlook can be launched from within a slide show via Meeting Minder to schedule events that arise as a result of the presentation.

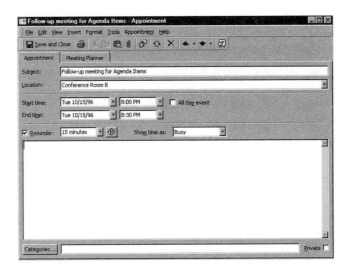

CAUTION
Export Meeting Minder data only after you have completed adding items to its database. If you choose Export Now and later add new items, you need to export again, which creates duplicate reports.

FIG. 16.10
Outlook's to-do's can automatically track action items created with Meeting Minder, but you must remember to export them first.

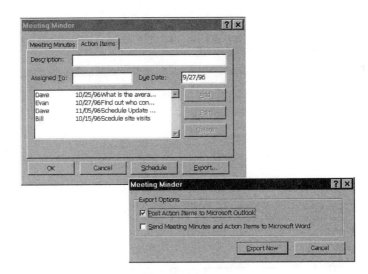

N O T E The format for Meeting Minder action items in Outlook is:

Johnson: Update specifications

where the action item is preceded by the individual assigned the task. ■

In addition to exporting action items to Outlook, you can also use the Export dialog box to create a report in Microsoft Word. This file lists all the items created during the presentation. When this option—Send Meeting Minutes and Action Items to Microsoft Word—is selected, Word automatically starts and creates a formatted report.

CAUTION

If you send the minutes and action items to Word, be sure to save your Word file before shutting down. Meeting Minder does not name or save this file for you.

Playing the Presentation

You don't always want to run just a single slide show or play the slides in the same order they were built. PowerPoint anticipates those needs and gives you some tools for doing it your own way.

Navigating Through a Presentation

PowerPoint offers several different ways of navigating through your presentation. While the left mouse button provides a linear path through the slide show, there are times when you will want to navigate differently.

 You can use the spacebar rather than the mouse to advance slides in a presentation.

During a slide show, move the mouse while displaying a slide. The Control Panel appears in the bottom-left corner of the screen. The menu has three primary navigation controls, described in Table 16.2.

Table 16.2   PowerPoint's Slide Navigation Controls

Menu Item	Effect
Next	Advances to the next slide; same as clicking the mouse.
Previous	Backs up one slide.

Menu Item	Effect
Go	The most powerful navigation control. A submenu lets you move within the slide show rapidly to specific slides.

Finding Slides with the Slide Navigator and By Title   Among the options in the Go menu is the Slide Navigator. To use it, follow these steps:

1. Move the mouse while displaying a slide. The Control Panel appears in the bottom-left corner of the screen.

2. Click the Control Panel. A pop-up menu appears.

3. Choose Go, Slide Navigator.

4. A dialog box appears with a list of all the slides in the presentation (see Figure 16.11). Choose the one you want to switch to and click Go To.

TIP   The Slide Navigator only appears on the speaker's monitor, so you can use it without obscuring the audience's view of the current slide.

FIG. 16.11

The Slide Navigator provides a means of switching to another slide in the presentation.

TIP   If you lose track of where you are, the Slide Navigator displays the last slide viewed at the bottom of the dialog box.

Another, often easier way to reach a certain slide is by choosing Go, By Title. This menu selection drops a list of all the slides in the show by their title text (see Figure 16.12). Choose the slide, and you are taken immediately to it.

Part

V

Ch

16

FIG. 16.12
Choosing Go, By Title takes you to specific slides without opening the Navigator dialog box.

N O T E   If you have "hidden" a slide, you can switch to it by choosing Slide Navigator or By Title. ■

Using a Custom Show   Yet another way to navigate through a slide show in a non-linear fashion is via a *custom show*. By using this feature, you can create any number of alternative slide arrangements and switch to any sequence on demand, without ever rearranging the true order of the slides in the slide sorter. Create a custom show in this way:

1. While in any view other than Slide Show, choose Slide Show, Custom Shows.
2. Click New. A dialog box opens. This is where you will arrange the slides in a unique order for later playback.
3. Rename the show in the Slide Show Name box.
4. Select the first slide title for the new show, and then click the Add button to copy it to the window on the right. If you make a mistake, select the appropriate slide and Remove it (see Figure 16.13).

FIG. 16.13
Create any number of unique presentations from the same set of slides using Custom Shows.

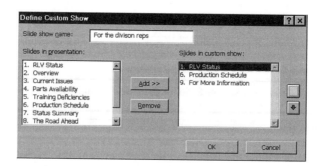

 T I P   You can select a range of slides at once by clicking the first slide, holding the Shift key, and clicking the last slide in the range.

5. Rearrange slides in the new show by clicking the desired slide and using the up and down arrows at the right edge of the window.

6. Click OK when you are finished building a custom show. Click the Close button to close the dialog box.

When you want to show this custom presentation, simply use the Control Panel menu and choose Go, Custom Show. The names of each custom show are listed in this submenu.

N O T E   Often, professional speakers create a series of "backup slides" which are only used if needed. By convention, these backups are appended to the end of the slide show. You can choose Go, By Title, or Custom Show to rapidly switch to these slides if the need arises. ■

Running a Show in a Loop

There are occasions, such as at trade shows and in kiosk displays, when it is appropriate to run a presentation in an ever-repeating loop. This way, the presentation repeats continuously without any human intervention. This is very easy to accomplish:

1. While in any view other than Slide Show, choose Slide Show, Set Up Show.

2. A dialog box opens that allows you to set numerous options for the playback of the slide show. Select Loop Continuously Until 'Esc' (see Figure 16.14).

3. If the presentation will run autonomously, be sure Using Timings, If Present is checked.

4. Click OK to close the dialog box.

FIG. 16.14
Kiosks and trade shows rely on continuously looping slide shows, and now PowerPoint can do it with a single step.

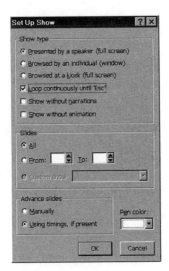

N O T E Because the Esc key ends a looping slide show, be sure the keyboard is hidden or out of reach of the audience, or the show could accidentally be terminated. ▦

Using a Play List

Often it is desirable to run multiple presentations back-to-back. This is easy to do, though it can't be accomplished from inside PowerPoint. Instead, you need to create a text file that PowerPoint Viewer interprets when it is run:

N O T E Play lists are useful in situations such as training classes, where various lessons are taught one after the other. Play lists prevent the instructor from having to return to Windows simply to load the next lesson. ▦

1. Open a text editor, such as WordPad.
2. Type the name of the first PowerPoint presentation you want to run. Press Enter and type the second file. Repeat until you've entered every file, each on its own line (see Figure 16.15).
3. Save this file as a plain text document in the folder that contains all of these PowerPoint files using the extension LST.

FIG. 16.15
Don't include the path name in the play list; all the files must be stored in the same directory as the list.

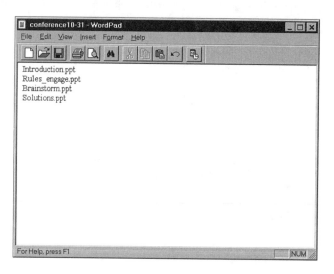

N O T E All of the files you intend to play must be stored in the same folder. ▦

4. When you want to run these files together in a presentation, start PowerPoint Viewer.

5. In the file requester, select the LST file you created in steps 2 and 3.

N O T E PowerPoint Viewer is a small program that can play PowerPoint presentations on computers that don't have a full version of PowerPoint installed. It is part of the Microsoft PowerPoint package, but you may need to install it if you did not perform a complete installation when you first got PowerPoint 97. ■

Part

V

Ch

16

Taking Your Show on the Road

Road shows are an ugly fact of life; pack up the presentation and board a late flight to Cincinnati. PowerPoint is a great tool for traveling because of the many ways a slide show can be delivered—by overhead, 35mm projector, or computer. If you're planning to display it via computer, you have the capability to modify the show right up until the last moment, and there's no risk of accidentally scrambling a batch of slides.

Using a computer to display PowerPoint slides while away from the home office used to be a hassle, but now it is fairly simple. Even if the available computer doesn't have PowerPoint 97, you can simply bring PowerPoint Viewer with you or use the Pack and Go Wizard.

Using the Pack and Go Wizard

The Pack and Go Wizard can copy your PowerPoint presentation and all the associated files to a floppy, Zip drive, or any other kind of portable media. Simply "unpack" the presentation when you arrive, and you're ready to start your presentation. To pack up a presentation:

1. Choose File, Pack and Go.

2. The Pack and Go Wizard appears. Click Next.

3. Select the presentation you want to pack (see Figure 16.16). The current presentation is the default—if you want to pack a different presentation, or multiple presentations, click Other Presentations. Click Browse to choose files from the file requester. When you're finished choosing, click Next.

FIG. 16.16
You may pack the
current presentation or
any number of files
from disk into a single
Pack and Go package.

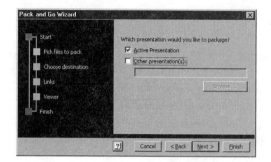

 TIP   Pack and Go creates a Play List automatically. This is useful if you are packing multiple presentations. The Play List is organized in the same order as the files appear in the wizard's file list.

   4. Choose a destination for the packed file, such as a floppy, Zip drive, or the hard disk.

   5. Choose whether to include linked files and TrueType fonts (see Figure 16.17):

      • If you include linked files, you can edit the source data in the original applica-
        tion. If you don't include linked files, the data will still be visible in PowerPoint,
        but it can't be changed.

      • If the destination computer doesn't have the same TrueType fonts you used to
        create your presentation, you should select the option. If in doubt, include the
        fonts.

FIG. 16.17
While these options
make the packed file
larger, it's probably
worth the effort in
case you need the
extra power they
provide.

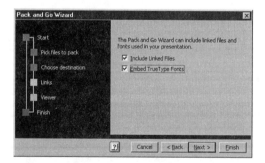

   6. Choose whether to include the PowerPoint Viewer. If you aren't sure if the destina-
      tion computer has PowerPoint 97, include it. Click Next.

CAUTION
PowerPoint 97 and its Viewer can only run on Windows 95 or Windows NT.

---

   7. Click Finish. The wizard copies the required files to the destination drive.

Once you reach your destination and you're ready to install your presentation, insert or install the media on which your packed slide show resides and follow these steps:

1. Open the folder in which you packed the presentation. Double-click the icon called Pngsetup (see Figure 16.18).

2. A dialog box appears asking for the destination directory. Specify where you would like the presentation to be saved on the new computer.

3. Click OK. The presentation is now ready to run.

Part

V

Ch

16

FIG. 16.18
Double-click the Pngsetup icon to expand the presentation and associated files—such as PowerPoint Viewer.

Managing Hardware Issues

On the road, Murphy's Law often intervenes and make the simplest tasks seem insurmountable. To reduce the stress of delivering presentations on the road, keep the following tips in mind:

▶ **See** "Checking Your Equipment," **p. 301**

- Not all video encoders use the same interface. Be prepared to use a variety of connectors, like BNC and RCA jacks.

- You can use an IR cordless mouse to control your presentation, but range is usually limited. Try a corded mouse with a long (25-foot) extension or a specially designed pointing device like the AirMouse.

- Restart Windows immediately before beginning a presentation to reduce the risk of sluggish performance or crashes during the show.

- Always have a backup plan. Bring traditional overhead slides with you in case the computer or display system fails.

- Arrange access to a spare projector, bulbs, and any other hardware that can fail at just the wrong moment.

CHAPTER 17

Selecting and Generating Output

by Steve Rindsberg

You've labored long and hard on your presentation. You've formatted and tweaked it to perfection. Now you've come to the place where the rubber meets the road. Or more aptly, where the pixels meet the paper.

It's time to print.

PowerPoint gives you plenty of options to meet nearly any printing need you can think of. Some choices are obvious, some aren't. In this chapter, you learn about all of them.

It's always a good idea to give your presentation a quick final check before you press the Print button, so before you look at the details of PowerPoint's print features, you can learn how to review your presentation efficiently and make certain that your printouts look exactly the way you want them to. ■

Previewing your presentations

Save time and materials by previewing your presentation in black and white before printing it. PowerPoint not only shows you how your presentation will print but lets you correct problems...*before* you click the Print button.

A guided tour of the Print dialog box

Printing slides, handouts, and notes pages involves more than just pressing the Print button. Learn about all of PowerPoint's Print dialog box options.

35mm slides

Creating Slides is easy with PowerPoint. Learn about getting 35mm slides and other unusual output from your PowerPoint presentations, and how to work with the service bureaus that provide these output services.

Troubleshoot printing problems

Find out how to troubleshoot and solve printing problems.

Previewing Your Presentation

Nobody likes to waste time waiting for printouts; it's even less fun when you find that they're wrong and have to be re-done. It only makes sense to use the tools PowerPoint puts at your disposal to make sure that your presentation prints the way you want it to the first time.

It's always a good idea to use PowerPoint's spelling checker (choose Tools, Spelling or press F7 to see the Spelling dialog box shown in Figure 17.1), but don't assume that it will catch every spelling error for you. It won't. Inn fact, if ewe we're to run this sentence threw you're spelling checker, it wouldn't complain a beet.

The spelling checker simply compares the words in your presentation against a list of correctly spelled words it knows. "Ewe" and "You" are both correctly spelled, and until spelling checkers get smart enough to understand the context in which each is properly used, they won't flag either one as misspelled.

TIP Use the Spelling Checker as your first line of defense against errors, but try to find somebody else to proof your presentation for you. Sure, it's embarrassing when they catch silly mistakes you've been staring at and not seeing for days, but it beats making the same mistakes in front of an audience.

FIG. 17.1
The Spelling Checker is a handy tool, but don't count on it to catch all your mistakes.

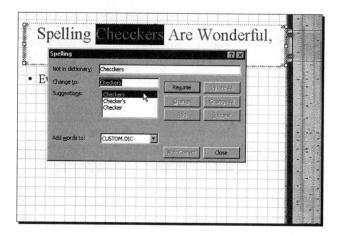

Once the presentation has been carefully proofed, you'll want to make certain it looks its best on the printout.

Black and White Preview

One of the most frequent complaints about earlier versions of PowerPoint is the lack of control it allows you over presentations printed in black and white. The Print dialog box offers several options for changing the appearance of printouts, but there are always times when the option that fixes one printing problem causes other slides to print badly.

The truth of the matter is that PowerPoint 95 gives very precise control over the way each item in a presentation is printed in Black and White (B&W). Unfortunately, it's a feature that few people learn how to use.

What you're about to learn is one of the best-kept secrets of PowerPoint 95. Let's hope that PowerPoint 97 users get more familiar with it, because it's tremendously useful. You can have near total control over your printouts when you learn how to use PowerPoint's Black and White view and Black and White mode features.

Part

V

Ch

17

Black and White view enables you to display your presentation on screen in the same shades of black, white, and gray that PowerPoint will print to your black and white printer. Black and White mode lets you alter those shades to suit your own needs. You can change the way PowerPoint treats individual objects, groups of objects, a whole slide, or even the entire presentation. There's also a handy Slide Miniature feature that lets you view a black and white mini-preview of your slide while you work on it in full color.

PowerPoint includes three toolbar buttons to make the Black and White features easier to use. Make sure that you have the icons shown in Figure 17.2 on one of your toolbars.

If you can't find one or more of them, don't worry. You can easily install them yourself.

To install the icons on one of PowerPoint's toolbars:

1. Choose Tools, Customize. This displays the Customize dialog box (see Figure 17.3).

2. In the Customize dialog box, choose the Commands tab.

3. Click View in the Categories panel on the left, then scroll down the list in the Commands panel until you see Black and White view.

4. Drag the Black and White View icon to any convenient toolbar. You can put it wherever it's handiest for you.

5. Drag the Black and White Mode icon to a toolbar also. It is the second entry below Black and White view. It's most convenient to use if you drop it next to the Black and White View icon.

6. Drag the Slide Miniature icon, beneath Black and White, to the same toolbar as the other two icons.

7. Choose Close to close the Customize dialog box.

Black and white icons

FIG. 17.2

If you don't have these icons on your toolbar, it's simple to add them.

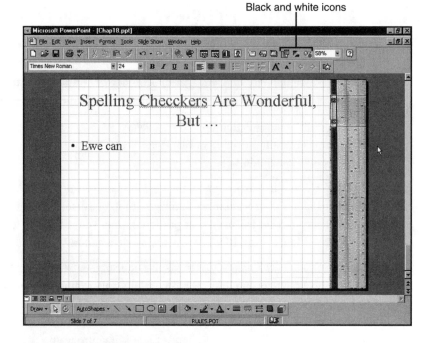

FIG. 17.3

Add icons to your toolbars; choose Tools, Customize and select the Commands tab.

PowerPoint makes it easy to keep an eye on how your presentation will print in black and white, even as you work on it in full color. Click the Slide Miniature button to get a mini view of how PowerPoint will print your presentation on a black and white printer (see Figure 17.4). You can right-click the slide miniature to choose Color or Black and White views. The title bar of the miniature changes to remind you which mode is active.

FIG. 17.4
PowerPoint's Slide Miniature gives you an on-screen preview of your black and white printouts.

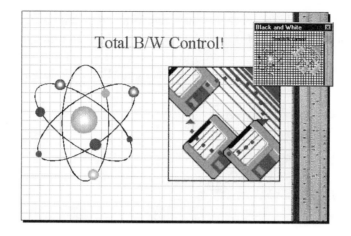

You can also preview your animation settings without having to run a slide show. Click the slide miniature to see your animation play without pauses for slide changes.

TROUBLESHOOTING

I don't see your animations when I click the slide miniature. Right-click it and make sure there's a check mark next to Animation Preview.

 Sometimes the slide miniature doesn't show you enough detail. This is when you should choose View, Black and White, or press the Black and White View button to see your presentation in full-screen black and white.

OK, so maybe black and white is not so impressive, especially if you've just forked over big bucks for that nice new color monitor. Understand, though, that PowerPoint is now showing you the exact shades of black and white that it will print to your black and white printer. This helps you determine if you will be able to see all the text, graphics, and other information on your slides clearly when you print them.

I promised you control over your black and white printing, though, not just accurate previews of what it will look like. Now that you know what PowerPoint plans to do when you press the Print button, let's look at the other button that we've ignored so far, Black and White mode.

 The Black and White Mode button is disabled unless your presentation is in Black and White view first, so if you haven't done so already, click the Black and White View button.

With nothing selected, click the Black and White Mode button to see a list of options that control how you want the entire slide to print in black and white. If you select individual objects or groups of objects first, you can change the way they print without affecting the rest of the slide. Figure 17.5 shows the Black and White Mode button in action.

FIG. 17.5

Control your presentation's appearance slide by slide or object by object with the Black and White Mode button.

The effect each option has on your slide depends on the sort of graphics you've placed on it; here's what you can expect:

If You Choose:	The Slide or Object:
Automatic	Prints however PowerPoint would ordinarily print it.
Grayscale	Prints in shades of gray.
Light Grayscale	Prints in very light shades of gray.
Inverse Grayscale	Prints in reversed gray (dark values print light and vice versa).
Gray with White Fill	Prints with a gray outline and white fill.
Black with Grayscale Fill	Prints with a black outline and grayscale fill.
Black with White Fill	Prints with a black outline and white fill.
Black	Prints in black.
White	Prints in white.
Don't Show	Will not appear on the printout (not available unless an object or objects are selected).

You can set options for the entire slide, then pick objects and fine-tune them one by one or in groups until your slide looks perfect in Black and White view. Just as with the options in the Print dialog box, there'll be times when a particular option fixes some problems but causes others on the same slide. When that happens, pick the option that produces the best black and white rendition for the overall slide, then select any problem objects on your slide and pick another Black and White Mode option for them. Once everything on the slide looks just right, you can print perfect black and white printouts.

You can just as easily change your entire presentation by working with the Slide Master rather than changing Black and White Mode settings slide by slide:

1. Choose View, Master, Slide Master and adjust the black and white settings for the Master.

2. To work with individual objects on the Master, you have to ungroup them. Right-click the master then choose Grouping, Ungroup.

3. Select the individual objects you want to work with. You may have to ungroup several times, as some of PowerPoint's masters are made up of groups of groups.

Don't forget to modify the Title Master as well, if the presentation includes one. PowerPoint treats the Title and Slide Masters as two separate items. Choose View, Master, Title Master to change the way your title slides print in black and white.

One important thing to note (and it's very good news indeed): the Black and White Mode settings have no effect whatsoever on PowerPoint's color output. This means that you can create a presentation to be used as a screen show or 35mm color slides and still tweak your black and white printouts to perfection. PowerPoint veterans will instantly fall in love with this feature. In previous versions of PowerPoint, you might have had to maintain two completely different presentations, one in color, the other in black and white, just to get decent printouts without ruining the colors in the "real" presentation.

PowerPoint's Black and White printing features are the best in the presentation graphics market. They allow you the control necessary to make presentations that are as appealing on paper as they are on-screen.

Now that you know how to fine tune the way PowerPoint prints your presentation, let's take a look at printing itself.

Part V

Ch 17

A Guided Tour of PowerPoint's Print Dialog Box

The Print dialog box isn't especially complex, but the functions of some of the options are not immediately obvious. While things you do in PowerPoint can be undone quickly with just a keystroke or click of the mouse, printing once started can't be undone.

Well-designed Windows dialog boxes group complex sets of options into related areas; that's what PowerPoint's designers did with the Print dialog box. Let's look at it area by area and learn what all the controls do. Choose File, Print (or press Ctrl+P) to see the Print dialog box shown in Figure 17.6.

FIG. 17.6
PowerPoint's Print dialog box is similar to other application Print dialog boxes.

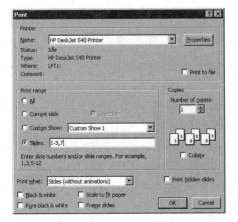

N O T E   *Slides* can mean several different things depending upon the context. To avoid confusion, I use this definition throughout the chapter. A slide is the basic unit of a PowerPoint presentation. If you choose View, Slides, a single slide is what you see. In Slide Sorter view, you see all of the slides in your presentation.

When I refer specifically to 35mm slides, I use the term *35MM slides* to make it clear that I'm not talking about a PowerPoint slide. ▨

Printer Area

The Printer area is where you choose the printer you want to use and set printer-specific options:

- *Name.* Contains the names of all the printers installed on your system (including your Fax, if you have a fax modem on your computer). Click the down arrow at the right of the list box to see the complete list, then click the name of the printer you want to use.

- *Status, Type, Where, and Comment.* Give you information about the current printer. They tell you whether it's currently printing another document, what kind of printer it is, what printer port it's attached to, and so forth.

- *Properties.* Changes your printer settings from its defaults temporarily. Changes you make from within PowerPoint are only effective until you quit PowerPoint. Once you quit, printer properties revert to their default settings. Because of this, you can set the printer up specifically for your PowerPoint session. You don't have to remember to set it back to its normal settings for use with other programs.

■ *Print to File*. Causes PowerPoint to send print data to a disk file rather than directly to your printer. This allows you to "print" to any printer even if it isn't connected to your printer directly. Some service bureaus may ask you to use this feature to create PostScript or other "print" files.

Print Range Area

This is where you specify which slides of the presentation to print:

■ *All*. Prints your entire presentation, beginning to end.

■ *Current Slide*. Prints only the slide you're currently viewing in Slide view.

■ *Selection*. Ordinarily grayed out, but if you have one or more slides selected in Slide Sorter view, Selection is available. Choose it and PowerPoint prints only the currently selected slides.

■ *Custom Show*. If you've created custom shows, they are listed here. Choose one, and PowerPoint prints only the slides that are part of the custom show.

■ *Slides*. Enter specific slide numbers or ranges of slides into the text box to the right. Here are some examples of what you can enter and the result you get:

You Enter	PowerPoint Prints
1,2,3	Slides 1, 2, and 3
2-7	Slides 2–7 inclusive
1,3,5-9,12	Slides 1, 3, 5 through 9 inclusive, and 12
12-4	Slides 12 through 4 (for example, slides 4–12 in reverse order)
1,20,15-12	Slides 1, 20, 15, 14, 13 ,12 in exactly that order

Copies Area

The Copies area sets the number of copies of the selected slides that are printed, and how they are printed:

■ *Number of Copies*. Sets the number of copies PowerPoint will make of each page you print.

■ *Collate*. Controls the order in which PowerPoint sends pages to the printer when you've elected to make more than one copy per page.

Miscellaneous Options

A few options in the Print dialog box aren't grouped. These options fine-tune the way PowerPoint prints and the way it's printed:

- *Print What.* PowerPoint can print Slides, Handouts in several formats, Notes Pages, or the Outline (see Figure 17.7). This is where you tell it which you'd like to print. Here's what the various Print What options do:

If You Choose	PowerPoint Prints
Slides or Slides (Without Animations)	One page per slide, full page size.
Slides (With Animations)	One page per slide, full page size. Each step in an animation prints on a new page.
Handouts (2 Slides Per Page)	Two slides per page, each approximately half-page size.
Handouts (3 Slides Per Page)	Three slides per page, small, with lines for annotations.
Handouts (6 Slides Per Page)	Six slides per page, small.
Notes Pages	One page per slide formatted according to your Notes master (choose View, Masters, Notes Master to see and edit the master).
Outline View	The text in your presentation's outline.

FIG. 17.7
Slides, handouts, notes, or outline? Choose what you want here.

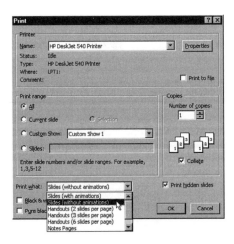

- *Black and White*. Tells PowerPoint to send only black and white data to your printer. This may speed up your printouts on some printers.

- *Pure Black and White*. Causes PowerPoint to convert everything to pure black or white on the printout. Eliminates all shades of gray, removes fills from most objects, and converts all text to black. Produces graphics that are very simple for your printer to handle, so you get your printouts very quickly.

- *Print Hidden Slides*. Lets you choose whether or not to print hidden slides. This option is not available unless you have hidden slides in your presentation.

- *Scale to Fit Paper*. PowerPoint reduces the printout to fit the imageable area of your printer. This prevents your printouts from getting cut off at the printer's unprintable margins.

- *Frame Slides*. Tells PowerPoint to put a thin black rectangle around your slides when it prints. Useful to delineate the edges of your slides, especially when printing Pure Black and White.

Whether multiple copies and collated print jobs print quickly or not depends on your printer. Some printers build the image for an entire page in memory then transfer it to paper all at once, as many times as needed for the number of copies you want.

All PostScript laser printers work this way. Many non-PostScript laser printers have a feature called *Page Protect*. If Page Protect is turned on, they can print multiple copies very quickly, too.

Inkjet and dot matrix printers don't have enough memory to store a full page of graphics, so your computer must send the print data a line or two at a time. For each copy of a page, it has to send the whole page over again, so printing the entire presentation twice or printing two copies of each page takes about the same amount of time.

 TIP
If you're not sure which sort of printer you have, it pays to do a quick test before you set PowerPoint to printing multiple copies of any large presentations. Pick a moderately complex page, set Number of Copies to **2** and print it. If the printer thinks a while then prints out two pages in rapid succession, it's storing the whole page in memory. If it thinks, prints a page, thinks some more, then prints the second page, it doesn't have enough memory to store a full page, so multiple copies will be slower.

When you choose Collate, PowerPoint prints all of the slides you've asked for then starts over and does it again. And again. Once for each copy you've requested.

When it's finished, you have however many copies you asked for, each pre-sorted into presentation order. In a word, your output has been collated for you.

As convenient as that may sound, there's a good reason not to choose Collate when time is short. Because PowerPoint prints the entire job start to finish once for each collated copy, even a PostScript laser printer will have to process each and every copy of each page. That always takes extra time. It's usually faster to print uncollated then manually collate your printouts. If you have the extra time, it's convenient to let PowerPoint collate for you.

TROUBLESHOOTING

I often have to reprint entire presentations because I've lost track of which slides I revised since the last print session. Hiding slides is a handy trick to know about. Before you make revisions, switch to Slide Sorter view, select all of your slides (Edit, Select All; or press Ctrl+A). Hide them all by choosing Slide Show, Hide Slide or click the Hide Slide button. As you revise each slide, unhide it. From any view, choose Slide Show, Hide Slide again to unhide the slide.

When you're ready to print, choose All in the Print Range area of the Print dialog box, make sure that Print Hidden Slides is not checked, and print. Only the newly revised slides will print.

> **N O T E**   PowerPoint can't control the colors in some types of inserted graphics. If it can't control the colors, the Black and White printing options won't have any effect.

If you run into this situation, select the graphic and try to ungroup it. When PowerPoint ungroups a graphic, it converts it to PowerPoint objects. Once it does that, it can control the colors, so your Print dialog box's black and white options settings work as expected.

If the graphic is a bitmap, PowerPoint can't ungroup it. To change the way it prints in black and white, select it and use the Black and White Mode options we described earlier. ■

PowerPoint's Ideal Print Settings

PowerPoint has a few built-in notions about what constitutes "ideal" print settings. You may have different ideas. In earlier versions of PowerPoint, you had to change all of the settings in the Print dialog box every time you printed. With PowerPoint 97, you get to take charge. Choose Tools, Options then click the Print tab to choose the default Print dialog box settings you want. The settings, shown in Figure 17.8, are saved with each PowerPoint file, so you can have different defaults for different files if you like.

If you prefer, choose Use the Most Recently Used print settings to have PowerPoint store the most recent print settings with the file and use them the next time you print.

In this same dialog box, you can turn Background Printing off and on. With it on, you regain the use of your computer quickly after starting a print job, but your presentation won't print as fast.

Your computer will respond a bit more slowly while a background print job is running, because it has to divide its time between keeping you and the printer happy. You get faster printouts with Background Printing turned off, but you have to wait longer to use your computer for something else.

Print TrueType fonts as graphics can cure printing problems with some printers that have trouble printing TrueType fonts. With this option on, PowerPoint sends TrueType text as graphics (that is, bitmaps) rather than as fonted text. This is easier for some printers to handle. Turn this option on if your printer won't print large TrueType text or if it sometimes drops text altogether. This option won't be available if your printer doesn't support printing TrueType text as graphics.

Print Inserted Objects At Printer Resolution tells PowerPoint to pre-scale bitmap graphics to the printer's resolution before sending them to the printer.

If you have a PostScript printer, you should normally disable this setting. The printer will do as good a job of scaling the bitmaps as PowerPoint. Pre-scaling bitmaps results in more data being sent to the printer, so printouts will take longer. However, if you have a large bitmap that you've reduced considerably on the slide, pre-scaling it can actually reduce the amount of data going to the printer. In this case, you get faster printouts (and less likelihood of printer errors) if you turn this setting on.

With non-PostScript printers, PowerPoint can probably scale bitmap graphics faster (and better) than the printer, so leave this setting on all the time.

FIG. 17.8
Control Print dialog box default settings, background printing, and TrueType and graphics options by choosing Tools, Options, Print tab.

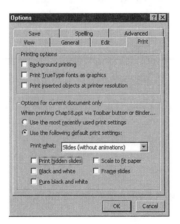

Part
V

Ch
17

Working with a Service Bureau

There are always going to be times when you need to do something that you can't afford to buy the hardware to do. That is when you use a service bureau. A service bureau buys all of the expensive equipment to make color transparencies, color copies, photo-realistic prints, or 35mm slides. They then take your file and convert it to good-looking output in whatever medium that you need.

The most common reason to use a service bureau today is to do 35mm slides for a presentation. This is as simple as two steps:

1. Before starting on a presentation, choose File, Page Setup. From the Slides Sized For list, pick 35mm Slides (see Figure 17.9).

2. Create and save your presentation, then send it to a service bureau for output to 35mm slides.

FIG. 17.9

Nearly everything you need to know to make 35mm slides with PowerPoint: File, Page Setup, 35mm Slides.

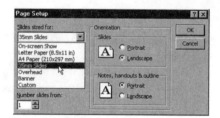

Choosing a Service Bureau

If you go shopping for a service bureau, you'll find them in all sizes, from small local shops to big national firms. Any good service bureau, small or large, can have finished 35mm slides ready for you in 24 hours or less.

If you have the U.S. version of PowerPoint, it came with a printer driver and modem software that hooks you up to one of the largest service bureaus in the country, Genigraphics.

For a more personal touch, check your local Yellow Pages under Slides & Filmstrips; look for service bureaus advertising 35mm slide output. Any moderately large city should have several to choose from.

ON THE WEB

You can also point your Web browser at one of the search sites like Yahoo and do a search for **35mm**:

http://www.yahoo.com

Are They Competent?

How can you determine whether a service bureau is competent before you hand over your presentation for production? Ask a few well-chosen questions, and you'll be able to learn a lot about a service bureau you're thinking of doing business with. Here are some things you'll want to find out about:

- What kind of equipment they use. Brands like Agfa-Matrix, Management Graphics or LaserGraphics are all professional-grade film recorders that produce high quality results.

- What's their standard resolution setting? Look for a bureau that uses 4K (they might call it *4000-line*) or higher. If they produce 35mm slides at lower resolution than that, you might not be happy with the results.

- Will they send you a few sample slides or, better yet, produce samples from your presentation? If so, take them up on it. Examine the results carefully with a good 8-power magnifying glass. You can find decent ones for less than $10 at most camera shops. Give special attention to text and fine lines, which should be crisp and sharp. You can also project the slides if you prefer. A good magnifying glass will be sharper than the average projector lens; it will give you a more accurate look at how sharp the slides really are.

- What kind of files do they want you to send them? Most service bureaus accept your PowerPoint files, but some may ask you to install a special printer driver and send them PostScript files instead. Many accept either, and may offer a discount for PostScript files.

- Do they have PowerPoint 97 and do they use it for their own work? If they're hesitant about accepting your PowerPoint files, it probably means that they don't. They won't be much help if you need advice about using it and they certainly won't be able to make any last-minute corrections for you. When you discover that you've spelled the chairman of the board's name wrong and the slides are already at the service bureau for the presentation tomorrow morning, you will want a service bureau that is familiar with PowerPoint 97 and can make those last-minute fixes for you.

- Do they use the same computer system as you? If you're PC and they're strictly Mac, plan on trouble sooner or later. It's all but inevitable. For the same reason, if they ask you to save your PowerPoint 97 files in PowerPoint 95 or 4 format, or worse, if they ask you to give them an EPS file, you'd better shop around some more. The better service bureaus have both Macs and PCs and keep several versions of PowerPoint on their computers. They'll try their best level to open your files on the same computer and software version you use to avoid the font and version differences that otherwise result.

- What other services do they offer? You might be shopping for 35mm slide output now, but what if you need a few color overheads next month? If they seem to know what they're doing, why not give them a shot at that work also?

Part
V

Ch
17

- What about training, design, and scanning services, or technical consultation?

- Do they have a 24-hour BBS or Internet connection you can use to send them your files? You just never know when the next panic deadline might strike, so it's nice to know you can modem your files to the service bureau in the middle of the night from halfway around the world.

- And of course, don't forget to ask the all-important question: "How much?" If all the other answers to your questions are right on target, it doesn't make sense to quibble over small differences in price, but be sure they're quoting you prices for the service and turnaround times you need. Sometimes those low, low prices you see in the advertisements are only applicable when you place a large order and don't need it done quickly.

Now that You've Chosen a Service Bureau...

How do you make sure you get what you want when you send them your presentations for output?

Tell the service bureau what you need (and when you need it), and then listen carefully to their instructions. It's easier to learn how to avoid problems than it is to fix them later. They are generally quite forthcoming with advice. Assuming they know PowerPoint well, they'll be able to tell you how to:

- Set PowerPoint up for the kind of output you want. It will save time if you do the setup before you start work on your presentation.

- Install and use any special printer drivers they require you to use.

- Avoid any of PowerPoint's features that don't work well on their film recorders. For instance, patterned fills don't print correctly on any film recorder; EPS graphics print beautifully, but only if your service bureau uses PostScript to run their recorders.

- Choose fonts. Which fonts do you plan to use, and what can be done about the ones they don't have. In general, it's easiest to stick with the fonts that came with PowerPoint, and they should be able to give you a list of these. It shouldn't be a problem if you want to use other fonts, but make sure you check with the service bureau to find out how they want you to handle it.

> **CAUTION**
>
> Just because a font shows up in PowerPoint's font list doesn't mean that it came with PowerPoint. Any font installed in Windows, no matter where it came from, is available to all Windows programs.

T I P To check which fonts you've used in your presentation, choose F<u>o</u>rmat, <u>R</u>eplace Fonts to use the Replace Fonts dialog box shown in Figure 17.10. The Re<u>p</u>lace list shows you the fonts you've used and the <u>W</u>ith list lets you replace a font you've used with any other font on your system.

You can also choose <u>F</u>ile, Proper<u>t</u>ies, Contents tab to see what fonts your presentation uses (but do not replace them with others).

FIG. 17.10

Choose Format, Replace Fonts to see what fonts your presentation uses.

Part

V

Ch

17

Think of the service bureau as your partner in producing successful presentations. You each have a role to play and clear communication is crucial. Expect them to bring technical expertise and fanatical devotion to meeting deadlines to the partnership. In return, they'll expect you to follow their instructions thoroughly and to provide ample details about your deadlines, billing information, and so on.

They're only asking because they want to ensure your satisfaction. They want to see you again. After all, there are plenty of other service bureaus out there who'd be delighted to have your business.

Dealing with Printing Problems

By and large, printing from PowerPoint is trouble-free, but there's always the occasional exception to the rule. If you run into printing problems, here are a few troubleshooting suggestions.

Printed Colors Don't Match what's On-Screen

To some extent, this will always be the case. The computer's video screen and your printer use very different methods of displaying images. Some mismatch between the two is nearly inevitable.

Some printer drivers include color matching features that help the printer match your screen colors more closely. Check to see if your printer has this type of feature and enable it.

If predictable output is more important than exact screen/printer color matching, create a test file, including rectangles of the colors you plan to use plus more rectangles of similar color. Print this file on the same printer and media you'll use for your final output. Make your color selections from the printed sample rather than basing them on what you see on-screen. That way you'll know precisely what you'll get on the final printouts.

PowerPoint (Or the Computer) Crashes When Printing

If PowerPoint or your computer crash or lock up when you print a particular presentation, check for corrupt graphics files. The quickest way to do this is to make a copy of your presentation, delete the first half of the slides from it, then print. If it works, you know that the problem is on one of the slides in the other half of the presentation. Make another copy of the original, delete the second half, then delete half the remaining slides and print again. Repeat the process until you've narrowed it down to the slide that won't print. Delete and re-create or re-insert any graphics on that slide and try printing again.

Try printing to a different printer or install a printer driver for a similar printer and use that instead. Some programs and printer drivers just don't seem to be able to get along. If using a different driver prevents problems, contact your printer manufacturer to see if they have an updated driver for your printer.

Try printing with Windows in Safe Mode. Re-start your computer and press F8 when you see `Starting Windows 95`. Choose Safe Mode from the resulting menu. If you can now print the presentation without problems, there may be a problem with your video driver. Contact the video board manufacturer for an updated driver.

Presentations Print Slowly

Turn off background printing in PowerPoint. Choose Tools, Options then click the Print tab to reach the dialog box that controls background printing. With it off, it will take longer to create the print job and return control of the computer to you, but your print job may finish more quickly.

Check your printer driver settings, especially the Spool settings. If there are several available options for how graphics are handled, try switching settings.

If you just need faster proof prints, click Pure Black and White in the Print dialog box.

Text or Graphics are Missing from Printouts

Check the Spool settings for your printer driver. The usual possibilities are EMF or Raster. Try a different setting.

If your printer driver offers a choice between Raster graphics and HP/GL2 graphics, choose Raster.

Changing the thickness of lines can help prevent their dropping out in some cases.

Printouts Just Don't Look Right

Contact the printer manufacturer for an updated driver. Some printer drivers simply don't support all of PowerPoint's features.

If your printer offers several emulation modes, try changing to a different mode. If PostScript is one of the available options, try that first. ●

Part

V

Ch

17

Working with Drawings, Clip Art, Sounds, and Animation

CHAPTER 18

Publishing to the Internet

by Michael O'Mara

PowerPoint has always provided multiple choices for presenting the materials you create with the program. You might create 35mm slides, overhead transparencies, or printed handouts; or you might create a screen show. Your choice of presentation medium depends on the audience you're trying to reach and the facilities that are available for your presentation.

An emerging new presentation medium—the World Wide Web—is rapidly becoming the standard way to view information on the Internet (and on corporate intranets as well). PowerPoint, like all the Office 97 programs, has built-in Web support that integrates Web browsing facilities into the program and allows you to create hyperlinks in your presentations. Moreover, PowerPoint allows you to use the Web as a presentation medium by saving your presentation in the proper format to be viewed by anyone with a standard Web browser. As a result, it has never been easier to share your presentation with the World (Wide Web).

The advantage of publishing your presentation via the Web is the broad distribution your presentation can

Two steps to Internet publishing

Publishing a PowerPoint presentation on the Internet is a two-step process. First, you save your presentation in the proper format, then you make the saved presentation available on the Internet.

Creating presentations to be published on the Internet

PowerPoint includes several templates to make it easier to create presentations that are destined to be published on the Internet.

Installing the Web Authoring tools

You'll need to install two wizards in order to take advantage of PowerPoint's Internet publishing capabilities.

Posting your presentation on the Web

In order for your presentation to be available on the Web, you must copy the presentation files to a Web server. You can copy the files manually, or, in some cases, the Web Publishing Wizard can help automate the process.

Viewing Web-based presentations

Learn what to expect when you view a presentation with a Web browser.

receive on the Internet. Your audience can be anyone with an Internet connection and a Web browser. They don't need to have PowerPoint (or even the PowerPoint Viewer) installed; and they can view your presentation at their convenience. Of course, there are some disadvantages, too. When you publish a presentation on the Internet, you lose a measure of control over that presentation. Also, although a Web browser makes a suitable viewer for standard slides, some of the features and effects you can pack into a PowerPoint screen show presentation won't survive the translation to the Web. ■

An Overview of the Publishing Process

When you publish a PowerPoint presentation to the Internet, you go through two distinct steps. The first step is to transform your PowerPoint presentation from its native PowerPoint file format into a format suitable for viewing with a Web browser. The Save As HTML Wizard automates much of the process. After you accomplish that task, you must copy the Web presentation files to a Web server where other Internet users can access them. Another wizard—the Web Publishing Wizard—can make this part of the Internet publishing process easier for some users. However, if you have access to basic Internet utilities such as an FTP program, copying the files manually is fairly simple.

N O T E Everything in this chapter that applies to publishing PowerPoint presentations to the Internet, applies equally to publishing to corporate intranets—the rapidly developing class of local area networks (LANs) that use the same standards as the Internet. As long as intranet users can use a standard Web browser to access and view documents on the network, they will be able to view your PowerPoint presentation as well. The only difference is scope. On an intranet, the World Wide Web is only company-wide. ▓

Save As HTML

The Save As HTML Wizard is the key to preparing your PowerPoint presentation for publication on the Internet. It's the Save As HTML Wizard that translates your PowerPoint presentation file into a set of Web pages that can be viewed with a Web browser.

The wizard's name might suggest that it simply converts the PowerPoint presentation file to the HTML file format that is the standard of the World Wide Web. However, converting a PowerPoint presentation for use on the Web is a more complicated undertaking than a simple file conversion. The Save As HTML Wizard must transform a single PowerPoint presentation file into not one, but a series of Web-compatible files—and only a few of those files are actually in the HTML format. You have the option of saving your presentation as a set of individual graphics pages—one for each slide—or as an animation file that is similar to a screen show.

What is HTML?

HTML stands for *HyperText Markup Language*—the standard language of the World Wide Web. Basically, it's a set of codes that can be embedded in a plain text file to tell a Web browser program how to display the text with different type sizes, fonts, colors, and so on. But HTML goes beyond simple text formatting. It also includes provisions for displaying graphics on a Web page and for the hypertext links that are the hallmark of the World Wide Web. It's these features that the Save As HTML Wizard uses to create a Web-based version of your PowerPoint presentation.

The HTML file format is continually evolving to support new features to give Web authors more control over the appearance of the Web pages they create. Fortunately, you don't need to be concerned with the details of HTML in order to translate your PowerPoint presentation into a Web-based presentation. The Save As HTML Wizard can take care of the details for you. All you need to remember is to choose Save As HTML Wizard when you need to prepare your presentation for publication on the Internet.

Saving Slides as Individual Pages   The standard conversion creates a separate graphic file (you can choose GIF or JPEG format) for each slide in your presentation, plus separate files for buttons and other navigation aides that will appear on the Web pages. In addition to the graphics files, the wizard creates one or more HTML files for each page to serve as containers for the graphics and to present a text-only version of the page for those users whose systems can't handle the graphics. Finally, the wizard creates a plain text-based HTML page that serves as an index or introduction to the Web presentation.

N O T E   GIF and JPEG are both popular file formats for storing graphics in a compressed form for speedy transmission on the Web. GIF is the older, more universally supported format. JPEG offers more flexibility by allowing you to adjust the amount of compression that is used. Less compression produces higher quality graphics, while more compression creates smaller files. Both formats are supported by most Web browsers in use today. ■

When the Save As HTML Wizard completes its work, a typical PowerPoint presentation that started out as a single presentation file becomes a collection of dozens, perhaps hundreds, of smaller files. To keep this potentially massive collection of files manageable, the wizard creates a new folder to hold them all. (You learn how to specify the location of the folder, along with other options, later in this chapter.)

The resulting Web presentation contains an introduction page and a separate page for each slide in your PowerPoint presentation. In addition to the slide graphic, the wizard adds navigation buttons to each page that allow the viewer to do things such as select the next or previous slide, return to the home page, or display a text-only version of the page. The Save As HTML Wizard also offers the option of using *frames*—dividing the Web page into separate panels—to organize the presentation and aid in navigation. See the section "Viewing a Presentation on the Web" later in this chapter for examples of presentations with and without frames.

> **CAUTION**
>
> Consider your options carefully before you elect to lay out your Web presentation using frames. Frames are a relatively new development, and older Web browser software may not display your pages properly. Also, reserving on-screen space for frames devoted to navigation aids effectively reduces the space available to display the graphic representation of your slides.

Saving a Presentation as Animation In addition to saving each slide as a separate Web page, the Save As HTML Wizard offers the option of saving your presentation as an animation file. Unlike saving your presentation as a set of graphics which the users can view one-slide-at-a-time, saving it as an animation file preserves the slide transitions and text animations of your original PowerPoint presentation. The result is similar to showing your presentation as a screen show, except that it appears within the Web browser window.

When you choose to save your presentation as an animation file, the Save As HTML Wizard doesn't create as many files. Instead of separate graphic files for each slide, one animation file exists for the entire presentation. There are still several files involved to create the presentation index, navigation buttons, frames, and so on; but the file inventory is much smaller than when you save the presentation as individual slides. While this seems to simplify things somewhat, it can also be a problem—the animation file can be quite large and therefore time-consuming to transfer over slower Internet connections. That may not be a problem on a corporate intranet where all the potential users have direct network connections. But users who access the Internet via dial-up connections over slower modems may not want to invest the time it takes to download your whole presentation before they can view it. The individual graphics files of the other Save As HTML options may actually total more data that must be transferred, but the wait for the first slide to appear is shorter with the graphics files than it is with the animation file—especially with a large presentation.

Perhaps a more important consideration if you're planning to save your presentation as an animation file is that the animation file will not display in a standard Web browser—it requires special playback software. The Microsoft PowerPoint Animation Player for ActiveX is an add-on for recent versions of Microsoft Internet Explorer and Netscape

Navigator. It's available free of charge from Microsoft's Web site, and the Save As HTML Wizard adds a button to the index page for your presentation that will download the software automatically. Even though the PowerPoint Animation Player is free and easy to obtain; it's an extra step users have to go through before they can view your presentation (unless, of course, they've already installed the software). The PowerPoint Animation Player takes several minutes to download and requires about 2.5M of hard disk space; in addition, some users may be reluctant to download any software from the Internet due to fears of viruses.

ON THE WEB

You can download Microsoft PowerPoint Animation Player for ActiveX from the Microsoft Web site: **http://www.microsoft.com/powerpoint/internet/player/installing.htm**. This page provides installation instructions, and links you to the downloadable file.

Copy Files to the Internet Server

The Save As HTML Wizard creates a set of files—graphics files, HTML files, and perhaps an animation file—from your PowerPoint presentation that can be viewed by a Web browser. However, those files don't do much good as long as they reside only on your hard disk. To publish your presentation on the Internet, you must copy the Web presentation files to a *Web server*—a computer that is connected to the Internet and is set up to allow other Internet users to access the information by referencing the address of the Web site (such as www.domain.com).

In order to transfer the presentation files from your hard disk to the Web server, you need to know something about the Web server and how to access it. You may need to consult with the system administrator to get the required information and arrange to post your files on the Web server. Normally, you need all of the following:

- Web site address
- Name of the Web server
- Directory where the files need to be stored on the Web server
- User ID and password for access to the server
- Access permission for the target directory so you can write files to that location

You also need to know what technique to use to copy the presentation files from your hard drive to the Web server. If you are working on a LAN, you may be able to use standard file-copying commands. However, to transfer files to another Internet location, you'll usually need to use FTP (File Transfer Protocol). If you need to use FTP to transfer files, you can employ any of the popular FTP utilities (such as WS_FTP) to do the job.

Part
VI

Ch
18

To make the task of transferring files to a Web server easier, Microsoft provides the Web Publishing Wizard. It can automate the file transfer process after you enter the necessary information about the destination Web server. In fact, the wizard is preconfigured to upload files to a few of the more popular Internet service provider's Web servers with minimal information from you. (See the sections "Installing the Web Publishing Wizard" and "Publishing Your Presentation with the Wizard" later in this chapter for more information.)

Installing Web Authoring Support

The typical PowerPoint installation doesn't include either of the wizards that facilitate publishing your presentations on the Internet. The Save As HTML and the Web Publishing wizards are both available on the Office 97 CD-ROM, but they weren't installed with the rest of your software unless you (or whoever installed your software for you) specifically elected to install those options. So, before you can publish your presentations on the Internet, you'll probably need to install the wizards.

Installing the Save As HTML Wizard

To determine whether the Save As HTML Wizard is installed, open PowerPoint and pull down the File menu. If the Save As HTML command is available, you're in good shape— the Save As HTML Wizard is already installed and ready to use. If the command is grayed out, you'll need to install the wizard.

To install the Save As HTML Wizard, follow these steps:

1. Insert the PowerPoint 97 or Office 97 CD-ROM in the drive and start the Setup program.

2. When the Setup program displays a dialog box giving you the option to change your current installation, choose the Add/Remove button.

3. In the Maintenance dialog box, click the Web Page Authoring (HTML) option to make sure it's checked, as shown in Figure 18.1; then choose the Continue button.

4. The Setup program displays a series of messages as it copies files and updates your system to install the Save As HTML Wizard. When the final message appears to confirm the successful installation, choose the OK button to close the Setup program. The Save As HTML command should be available on the File menu the next time you run PowerPoint.

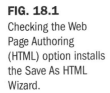

FIG. 18.1
Checking the Web Page Authoring (HTML) option installs the Save As HTML Wizard.

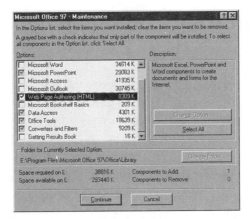

N O T E If you have other Office 97 programs installed, this procedure adds Web Page Authoring capability to all those programs, not just PowerPoint. ▇

Installing the Web Publishing Wizard

Unlike the Save As HTML Wizard, installing the Web Publishing Wizard is optional. Using the wizard to transfer presentation files from your hard disk to the Internet server is merely a convenience. You can do the same thing with a simple FTP program, so the wizard isn't required.

You don't need to use the Setup program to install the Web Publishing Wizard. The wizard isn't really part of the PowerPoint program or Office 97 suite. It's a separate utility that Microsoft distributes with several of its programs. (The Web Publishing Wizard is also available for download from Microsoft's Web site.) You'll find the Web Publishing Wizard in the ValuPack folder on the Office 97 CD-ROM. It's in the Webpost subfolder and the filename is WEBPOST.EXE. To install the wizard, just double-click the file icon in an Explorer window. The installation is automatic.

The Web Publishing Wizard is installed as a Windows accessory—it's not an integral part of Office or any of the Office suite of programs. After it's installed, you'll find the Web Publishing Wizard on the Windows 95 Start menu. However, it's not listed with the Office 97 programs; instead, you'll find it by choosing Programs, Accessories, Internet Tools.

Creating Presentations Destined for the Internet

It isn't really necessary to create a PowerPoint presentation specifically for publication on the Internet. You can use the Save As HTML Wizard to convert any PowerPoint presentation to a Web-based presentation that you can then publish to the Internet. You don't need to do anything special as long as you avoid obvious problem areas (such as type sizes that are too small to read on-screen). Keep your presentation simple—no hyperlinks to documents and files that won't be available on the Internet. Generally, if a presentation looks good as a screen show, it also works when viewed in a Web browser.

On the other hand, PowerPoint includes some options specifically tailored to creating a presentation that will end up on the Internet. Using these options can make your job a bit easier.

Starting a Presentation with the AutoContent Wizard

PowerPoint's AutoContent Wizard offers a few presentation formats specifically targeted for use on the Internet. You can choose the Internet as an Output option for the rest of the presentation formats. Choosing the Internet as the Output option in the wizard usually adds navigation buttons to each slide (it varies with the presentation template you choose), and prompts you for information (such as a copyright notice and an e-mail address) to add to each slide that is appropriate for a presentation that will be published on the Internet.

N O T E   A *navigation button* on a slide is simply an Action Button with a hyperlink to another slide in the presentation—typically the next slide. ▨

To use the AutoContent Wizard to create a presentation destined for the Internet, follow these steps:

1. Launch the AutoContent Wizard. You can do this by choosing the AutoContent option from the PowerPoint dialog box that appears when you start PowerPoint. Alternatively, you can launch the wizard by choosing File, New, clicking the Presentations tab in the New Presentation dialog box that appears, and then double-clicking the icon for the AutoContent Wizard.

2. From the AutoContent Wizard dialog box that appears, choose the Next button to proceed past the Start page.

3. On the Presentation Type page (see Figure 18.2), select the type of presentation you want to create. The Information Kiosk presentation (under the Operations/HR button) and the Personal Home Page (under the Personal button) are both intended primarily for use on the Internet. However, any of the other presentation types can be tailored to Internet publication as well. After you make your selection, choose the Next button to advance to the Output Options page of the wizard.

FIG. 18.2

Some of the presentation types listed in the AutoContent Wizard are specifically designed for publication on the Internet.

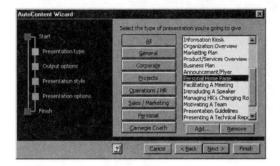

N O T E As its name implies, the Personal Home Page presentation type is a template for a personal home page on the World Wide Web. However, the Personal Home Page presentation doesn't produce a stellar-quality Web site. It's serviceable, and a bit more interesting than the simple text-based home pages many people use as their personal home page. But it's probably more useful as a simple demo than as a viable tool for creating your home page. ■

4. On the Output Options page, select the Internet, Kiosk option. This causes the AutoContent Wizard to skip the usual questions about the various output options on the Presentation Style page (since you've already specified the Internet as the output, the other output options don't apply) and go directly to the Presentation Options page when you choose the Next button.

5. Instead of the usual prompts for information to go on a title slide, the Presentation Style page (shown in Figure 18.3) prompts for information that is more apropos for a publication on the Internet. You can instruct the wizard to place a copyright notice, the current date, or an e-mail address on each slide of your presentation. Simply check the box beside each item you want to include on each slide and type in the appropriate text. When your selections are complete, choose the Next button to proceed to the final page of the wizard.

6. On the final page of the AutoContent Wizard, you can choose the Back button to step back through the previous pages and review your selections, or choose the

Finish button to create the presentation. After a short wait, your new presentation appears in the PowerPoint window ready for you to begin replacing the placeholder text with your copy. Figure 18.4 shows a typical slide created by the AutoContent Wizard using the Internet output settings. Notice the navigation buttons at the bottom of the slide, and the copyright notice and e-mail address the wizard added.

FIG. 18.3
The AutoContent Wizard prompts you for information that is typically displayed on each page of a Web presentation.

FIG. 18.4
The AutoContent Wizard adds the copyright notice and e-mail address to each slide automatically.

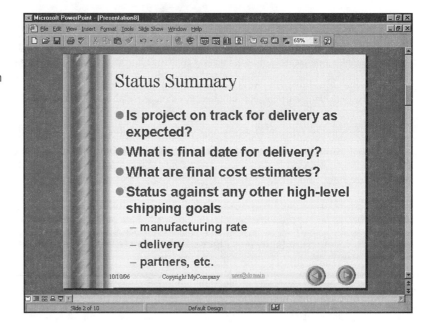

Creating a New Presentation with a Template

Of course, you don't have to start your presentation with the AutoContent Wizard. You can build a presentation from scratch or start a new presentation based on one of the many presentation templates supplied with PowerPoint. Most of the templates come in both standard and online versions as shown in Figure 18.5. Have fun exploring the many options and variations that are open to you.

FIG. 18.5
Most presentation templates come in Standard and Online versions.

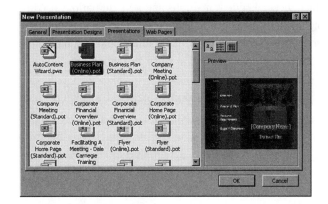

If you create a presentation based on the online version of a template, the result is very similar to starting a presentation using the Internet Output options of the AutoContent Wizard. Most templates include navigation buttons on each slide to allow the user to page through the presentation. The only element missing from most templates is the copyright notice and e-mail address you can elect to add to each slide when you use the AutoContent Wizard.

N O T E Because the Save As HTML Wizard adds navigation buttons to each page of a standard Web presentation, the navigation buttons that are part of many online templates may be redundant. You might want to use the standard version of your favorite template to avoid having two sets of navigation buttons in your Web presentation. ▪

What Happens to Special Features and Effects?

PowerPoint has many powerful presentation features you can use to add interest to your presentation when you present it as a screen show. There are slide transitions, text animations, action buttons, hyperlinks, sounds, and video clips. When you create a Web-based version of your presentation and view it with a Web browser, it seems very similar to a screen show. You might expect to see all the same special effects in the Web-based presentation that you see in a screen show. However, although some of the effects survive the translation to the Web, others don't—and there's a significant difference between saving a presentation as an animation file and saving it as an individual graphics file.

The following list tells you what happens to your screen show effects when you save a presentation for publication on the Internet:

- *Slide transitions and text animations.* When you save your presentation as individual graphics files, all slide transitions and text animations are lost. The Web browser simply loads the next graphic when you choose to view the next page of the presentation. On the other hand, slide transitions and text animations are fully supported when you save the presentation as an animation file. In fact, this is the primary reason for using an animation file.

- *Action buttons and hyperlinks.* When the Save As HTML Wizard encounters a slide with an action button or hyperlink, it creates an image map—a graphic with clickable hot spots—of the slide and attempts to link the hot spots to the same hyperlinks as the corresponding action buttons and hyperlinks in your presentation. Action buttons and hyperlinks are supported in a similar fashion in presentations saved as animation files. When you view the slide in the Web browser, the pointer changes from an arrow to a hand when you point to a clickable button or link. You can click the hotspot to follow the associated hyperlink, provided the target of the hyperlink is available to the browser on the Internet. Links to other pages of the presentation and to other Web sites and Internet resources should work. However, links to documents, presentations, and files stored on your hard disk usually fail because the files won't be accessible from the Internet.

> **CAUTION**
>
> Remember, the targets of hyperlinks must be available on the network in order for the links to work for the viewer of your presentation. Links to other pages of the presentation and to other Web sites should work, but links to files stored on your hard disk fail.

- *Multimedia objects.* Sounds and video clips in your presentation can present special challenges when you translate your presentation to the Web. Generally, sounds and video clips are supported when you save your presentation as an animation file. However, when you save your presentation as a set of graphic pages, The Save As HTML Wizard may not recognize multimedia objects and convert them to hotspots on an image map as it does action buttons. You could get around that problem by creating an action button and linking it to a multimedia file. However, the user must have the appropriate playback software installed in order for the multimedia object to play properly—and you can't necessarily count on that.

Saving Your Presentation as Web Pages

After your presentation is complete, the process of transforming it into a set of files that can be viewed with a Web browser is relatively simple. The Save As HTML Wizard does most of the work after you answer a few questions to specify file formats and layout of the Web pages.

To save your presentation as a set of Web pages, follow these steps:

1. Choose File, Save As HTML to launch the Save As HTML Wizard.

2. When the Start page appears in the Save As HTML dialog box, choose the Next button to get started.

3. On the Layout Selection page (shown in Figure 18.6), click the New Layout option, or if you've previously saved HTML layout settings, you can click the Load Existing Layout option and select the name you assigned to the layout settings from the list box to load those settings as the default values for the options in the rest of the wizard. (If you choose New Layout, the options throughout the wizard default to the values you selected the last time you used the wizard.) Regardless of your choice, you can change any of the options as you go through the wizard. Choose the Next button to proceed to the next page of the wizard.

Part
VI

Ch

18

FIG. 18.6
You can choose from previously saved layout settings, or start from scratch with new selections.

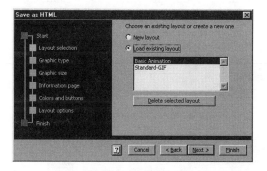

4. The next page of the wizard (shown in Figure 18.7) lets you choose whether to use frames to display your presentation pages in the Web browser. Choose Standard or Browser Frames, according to your preference. The standard option places your slide and a set of navigation buttons on each Web page. The Browser Frames option uses the frames feature of newer Web browsers to create separate on-screen boxes for the slide, navigation buttons, and list of the slides in the presentation. After you make your selection, then choose the Next button to proceed to the wizard's Graphic Type page.

FIG. 18.7
Choose whether you want to use frames to display your slides on the Web page or simply place the slides directly on the Web page.

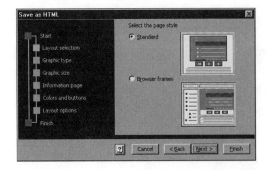

5. The Graphic Type page (shown in Figure 18.8) is where you specify the file format the wizard should use for your presentation pages. You can choose to create individual graphic files for each slide using either the GIF or JPEG file formats.

    If you choose the JPEG format, you can also specify the degree of compression by selecting a value from the Compression value drop-down list box. A 100% setting renders the slides as high-quality graphics with minimal compression. In contrast, a 50% setting creates much smaller graphic files from each slide at the expense of image quality. Your third choice is to save the entire presentation as a PowerPoint Animation File.

    After you make your selection, choose the Next button to move to the Graphic Size page of the wizard.

FIG. 18.8
GIF, JPEG, or animation file—it's your choice.

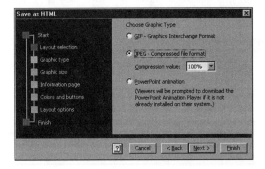

6. On the Graphic Size page (see Figure 18.9), you specify how much screen space your presentation pages should occupy. You determine the image size by combining a screen resolution with a Width of graphics selection that specifies how much of the selected screen size the image should fill. For example, choosing 800 × 600 resolution and 1/2 width of the screen would instruct the wizard to make the image files 400 pixels wide. Choose the Next button to proceed.

FIG. 18.9

The goal is to make your slides easy to read without requiring the viewer to scroll around too much to see the whole image.

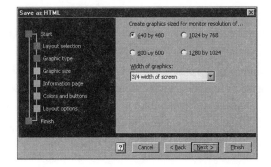

 Try to select an image size that is large enough to make the text in your presentation readable, yet small enough to allow the entire slide to be displayed within the Web browser window. If the slide is too big, it becomes awkward to scroll each page of a presentation in order to see all of the image. An added bonus of creating smaller graphics is that the resulting smaller files will load faster, thus reducing the time it takes for each page to appear on-screen.

7. The next page of the wizard is labeled Information Page (see Figure 18.10). This is where you enter some of the information you want to appear on the opening index page of your presentation Web site. (This information, and the index page on which it appears, is separate from the similar information the AutoContent Wizard adds to each slide.) There are text boxes for your Email Address, Your Home Page, and Other Information. In addition, there are two check box options that, if checked, instruct the wizard to add buttons to the page to allow the user to download a copy of your original presentation file or to download the Internet Explorer software. Choose the Next button to move on to the Colors and Buttons page of the wizard.

FIG. 18.10

This is where you supply some of the information the wizard will place on the index page for your presentation.

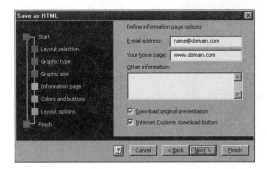

8. On the first Colors and Buttons page of the Save As HTML Wizard (see Figure 18.11), you can elect to Use Browser Colors from the user's browser or define

Custom Colors. (These color choices affect the index page and the buttons and background page on which your presentation slides appear. The graphic images of your presentation pages aren't affected.) If you chose Custom Colors, you can choose the Change Background, Change Text, Change Links, and Change Visited buttons to select a different color for the corresponding part of the Web page. Check the Transparent Buttons option to create buttons that appear to be shades of the background color instead of shades of gray. After you make your selections, choose the Next button to proceed to the next page of the wizard.

FIG. 18.11
Rely on the Web browser's default colors for the Web pages the wizard creates or select your own color scheme.

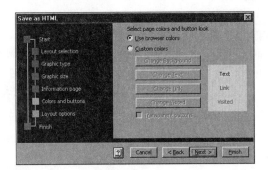

9. The second Colors and Buttons page enables you to select one of the four button styles shown in Figure 18.12 for the navigation buttons the wizard places on each Web page outside the slide image area. Make your selection, and then choose the Next button to continue through the wizard.

FIG. 18.12
Select the style of the navigation buttons the wizard adds to each Web page.

10. Next comes the Layout Options page shown in Figure 18.13. Here you can define the standard layout for the Web pages by selecting the position of the navigation buttons (above, below, left, or right) relative to the slide. There is also a check box option if you want to include on the Web page the slide notes from your presentation along with the graphic slide image. Choose the Next button after you make your selections to proceed to the next page of the wizard.

FIG. 18.13
Specify the location of the navigation buttons that the wizard adds to each Web page.

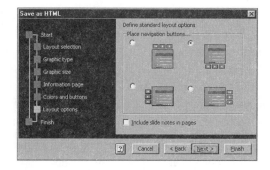

11. The next page of the wizard (shown in Figure 18.14) contains a text box where you can enter the drive and folder where you want the wizard to place the files it creates. If you prefer, you can choose the Browse button to open a Browse dialog box where you can select the folder instead of having to type it in. Choose the folder and then choose the Next button to move to the final wizard page.

FIG. 18.14
You must tell the wizard where to place the folder full of files it will create.

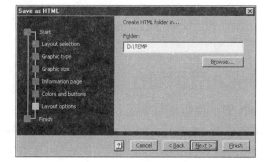

12. That brings up the final page of the Save As HTML Wizard shown in Figure 18.15. Choose the Finish button to begin the process of creating Web pages according to your specifications.

FIG. 18.15
Choose the Finish button to put the wizard to work creating files for the Web version of your presentation.

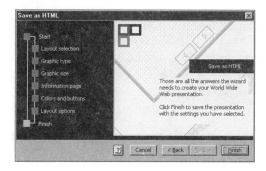

13. A small dialog box appears, giving you the option to save the HTML layout settings you've just defined. If you expect to create more Web presentations using the same settings, type a name for the settings in the text box and choose the Save button. The next time you launch the Save As HTML Wizard, the name appears in the list of options under the Load Existing Layout option on the Layout Options page. If you don't expect to use the same settings again, choose the Don't Save button.

14. The Save As HTML Wizard starts creating a set of Web pages from your presentation according to your instructions. The process takes a while to complete. How long depends on the speed of your system and the number of slides in your presentation. When the conversion is finished, the wizard displays a message to that effect. Choose OK to close the message box and return to your PowerPoint presentation.

After the Save As HTML Wizard completes its work, you will find a set of Web presentation files in a folder bearing the name of your presentation. That folder is located in the destination folder you specified in step 11. If you want to preview how your presentation will look in a Web browser, you can load into your browser the INDEX.HTM file you will find in the presentation folder and then follow the links to step through the presentation pages one-by-one or run the animation file.

Posting Your Presentation on a Server

After the Save As HTML Wizard creates a set of Web pages and graphics (or animation file) from your PowerPoint presentation, your next task is to post the presentation on a Web server where it can be accessed from the Internet. Basically, this step is nothing more than copying files from one location (your hard disk) to another (the Web server). However, you'll need to know the name of the Web server and the directory where your Web presentation is to be stored; and you'll need a user ID and password to gain access to the server. Usually, you'll need to get this information from the system administrator in charge of maintaining the Web server.

Also, in most cases, you'll need to use FTP instead of normal file copy commands to transfer files over the Internet. An FTP utility program, such as WS_FTP, will handle the task quite nicely. If you prefer a semi-automated approach, the Web Publishing Wizard can help some by prompting you for the necessary information about the Web server and handling the FTP file transfer.

N O T E The Web Publishing Wizard is most useful for uploading files to the Web server of a major online service such as America Online or CompuServe that adhere to a known naming convention for user directories. For uploading Web files to a Web site at a local Internet Service Provider, the wizard offers very little advantage over using an FTP program to transfer the files. ■

Viewing a Presentation on the Web

Once you get your presentation posted on a Web server, you (and other Internet users around the world) can access it just like any other Web site. The heavy reliance on graphics to display the presentation's slides makes a Web presentation a little different from the typical Web site that is composed primarily of text. Still, the Web presentation isn't so strange or different that it's likely to confuse the average Web user.

Viewing a Standard Presentation

When you first access a Web presentation, you see the presentation's text-based index page (see Figure 18.16). It contains basic information about the presentation and links to each of the presentation pages. Click the Click Here to Start link to view the first slide of the presentation and begin paging through the presentation in sequence.

Part
VI

Ch
18

FIG. 18.16
The index page is a plain but functional table of contents for your presentation.

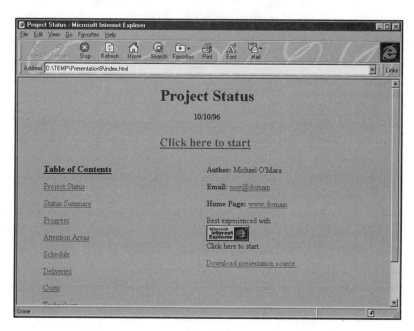

Each page of the presentation includes navigation buttons that enable the user to move from page to page through the presentation. Figure 18.17 shows a typical presentation page that uses the standard (non-frame) layout. The four arrow buttons link to the first, previous, next, and last pages of the presentation. The other buttons provide links to the index page for the presentation, to your home page, and to a text-only version of the slide for users who can't (or don't want to) view the graphics. To step through the presentation, simply choose the Next button (the single right arrow) to bring up each new page in sequence.

FIG. 18.17

A typical slide using the standard layout.

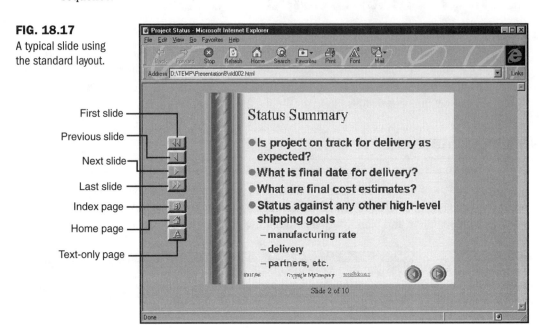

If you elect to layout your Web pages using frames, the Save As HTML Wizard creates a slightly different set of navigation tools. As Figure 18.18 shows, the large frame contains the slide graphic with the navigation buttons appearing in a frame above the graphic. Along the left side is an outline of the presentation with each slide title appearing as a hyperlink that you can click to jump directly to that slide. It looks and works a lot like the list of slides on the index page. However, this framed outline can do more. The two buttons above the outline frame enable you to expand the outline to display text from each slide or collapse it to show only slide titles.

FIG. 18.18
The Frames Layout
option adds an
outline of the
presentation to
each Web page.

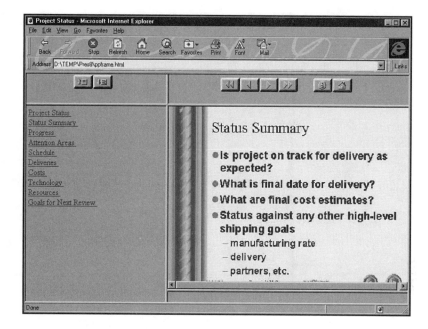

Viewing a Presentation with Animation

If you chose to save your presentation as an animation file, viewing the presentation will be a different experience. First of all, you will need to have the PowerPoint Animation Player installed in order to view the presentation. The index page for the presentation (see Figure 18.19) includes a button that enables you to automatically connect to Microsoft's Web site and automatically download and install the Animation Player software if you don't already have it installed.

Once the PowerPoint Animation Player is installed, you start the presentation the same way you begin viewing the pages of a standard, graphics presentation—simply click the Click Here to Start link. Your browser downloads the presentation file and launches the PowerPoint Animation Viewer to play back the presentation in a protected window as shown in Figure 18.20. The presentation runs like a movie, complete with slide transitions, text animations, builds, and so on.

You can click anywhere on the page to advance to the next slide, just like a PowerPoint screen show. Because the slide sequencing is part of the animation file, there are no navigation buttons for moving from slide to slide. The only navigation buttons in the animation window are to return to the index page or display the text-only version of the slides.

Part
VI

Ch
18

FIG. 18.19
Click the button to download the PowerPoint Animation Player automatically.

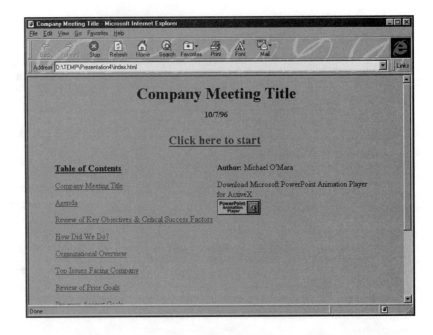

FIG. 18.20
Viewing an animation file allows the viewer to experience slide transitions, text animations, and the associated sound effects.

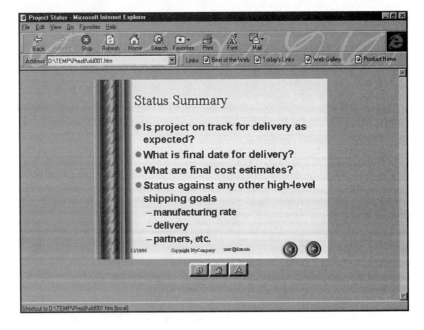

CHAPTER 19

Using Hyperlinks in Presentations

by Todd White

During the past several years, you have witnessed the Internet emerge as a rich information source, as well as an inexpensive publishing medium for companies and individuals. Today it is easier than ever to publish and access up-to-the-minute information from virtually anywhere. Keeping information fresh in a presentation is a challenge for every presenter. However, if your latest sales figures or building plans or product specifications are available over the Internet or your private intranet, using PowerPoint allows you to access this information online *during* your presentation. ■

Creating hyperlinks

Any text or object displayed on a PowerPoint slide can be created as a "clickable" hyperlink.

Using hyperlinks

It takes practice to effectively use hyperlinks during a presentation. This section explains how you can use hyperlinks while keeping your presentation smooth and professional.

Maintaining hyperlinks

While Internet hyperlinks enable you to access specific information over the Internet, make sure that your hyperlinks remain valid and current.

Internet hyperlinks in presentations

Hyperlinks can enhance the quality of your presentations by keeping your presentations fresh and up-to-date, but always check the hyperlink before giving a presentation to verify the address.

Saving presentations to HTML file format

Presentation Internet hyperlinks are maintained when saving presentations to HTML for World Wide Web publishing.

Creating Internet Hyperlinks

Any text or visual object in a PowerPoint slide can be an Internet hyperlink. Standard text, clip art, Word Art images, AutoShape images, charts, and more—anything in a slide that can be selected—can be an Internet hyperlink. PowerPoint provides a variety of images that can be used as hyperlinks. One such type of image is called Action Buttons, intended to be used as hyperlink icons in slide presentations.

Hyperlinks can be created so that during a presentation the link may be clicked or simply passed over with the mouse pointer to activate the link.

Insert Hyperlink

 Using the Insert Hyperlink button is the easiest method for engaging an Internet hyperlink. In Slide view:

1. Select the object or highlight the text that is to become the hyperlink (see Figure 19.1).

FIG. 19.1
Highlight the text that will become the Internet hyperlink.

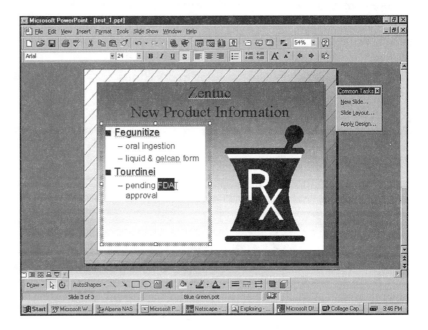

2. Click the Insert Hyperlink button; or choose Insert, Hyperlink; or press Ctrl+K.
3. Enter the Internet URL in the Link to file or URL field (see Figure 19.2).
4. Click OK.

TIP URL stands for *Uniform Resource Locator*, which is an Internet addressing standard. For example,

http://www.some.company.com/public/sales/June/weekly.html

has three distinct components—the specific protocol (http://), the Internet computer name (www.some.company.com), and the directory path to the desired document (/public/sales/June/ weekly.html). If you are ever unsure of the exact document path, just type in the first two components (**http://www.some.company.com/**) to access the home page from which you should be able to find the information you are looking for.

FIG. 19.2
Enter the
Internet URL.

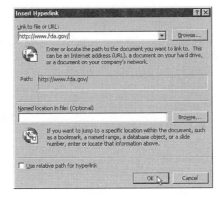

The object or text is now an Internet hyperlink that can be activated during a presentation by clicking it with the mouse pointer. Text hyperlinks appear as underline text; when your mouse pointer is placed over the hyperlink, it turns into a small hand pointing the index finger. Graphical hyperlinks are not underlined, but your mouse pointer still appears as a small pointing hand when placed over a hyperlink object.

Action Settings

 While the Insert Hyperlink command is the easiest method for engaging text and objects as Internet hyperlinks, it does not allow the ability to control *how* hyperlinks are activated during a presentation. The Action Settings command of the Slide Show menu offers a wider variety of options when engaging hyperlinks. One additional option in particular is to make the hyperlink activated by Mouse Click or by passing the Mouse Over the object or text.

 TIP For a more animated presentation, create a sound for a Mouse Over action and create an Internet hyperlink for a Mouse Click on the same object or text. When you move the mouse to the object or text during a presentation, the sound activates, and then the Internet URL is activated when the object or text is clicked.

Part
VI

Ch
19

To apply an action setting to your hyperlink:

1. Select the object or highlight the text (see Figure 19.3).

FIG. 19.3
Select the object that
is to become the
Internet hyperlink.

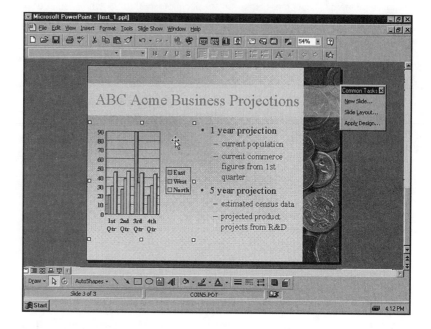

2. Select Slide Show, Action Settings.
3. Select either the Mouse Click tab or the Mouse Over tab, depending on whether you want the Internet hyperlink to be a Mouse Click or Mouse Over hyperlink.
4. Select Hyperlink to open the drop-down menu.
5. Select URL from the list (see Figure 19.4).

FIG. 19.4
Select URL from the
Hyperlink To drop-
down menu.

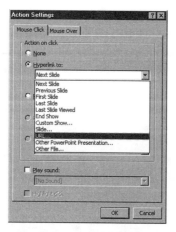

6. Enter the Internet URL to be opened through the hyperlink (see Figure 19.5).

FIG. 19.5
Enter the Internet
or intranet URL
and click OK.

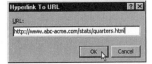

7. Click OK in the Hyperlink To URL dialog box.

8. Click OK in the Action Settings dialog box.

The selected object or text is now an Internet hyperlink.

 T I P If your presentation is equipped with a variety of hyperlinks, including URL hyperlinks, links to Excel spreadsheets, and links to other presentations or slides, it may become difficult to remember where each hyperlink will take you and your audience. Employing certain conventions when engaging your hyperlinks can assist you during a presentation. For example, you might use a specific action button for one type of hyperlink and another action button for another type of hyperlink.

You might also consider "sound coding" your links by engaging a Mouse Over sound to activate each type of hyperlink. For example, one sound for an Internet hyperlink, another sound for an Excel spreadsheet.

Action Buttons

 Action buttons are a set of icons available in PowerPoint for creating hyperlinks. Generally, action buttons are intended for linking to other slides and presentations. However, action buttons can also be used in presentations for setting up Internet hyperlinks. Perhaps the most logical action button to be used as an Internet hyperlink is the Information action button.

To add an action button to your presentation as an Internet hyperlink:

1. In Slide view, choose Slide Show, Action Buttons.

2. Select the desired Action Button from the palette (see Figure 19.6). Your mouse pointer turns into a large plus (+) sign.

3. Move your mouse to the location on the slide that you want to place the action button, and click your primary mouse button. The Action Settings dialog box opens.

4. Select Hyperlink To.

5. Choose URL (see Figure 19.7).

FIG. 19.6

The Action Button palette allows you to choose from a variety of standard icons.

FIG. 19.7

Select URL from the Hyperlink To drop-down menu to engage the selected action button as an Internet hyperlink.

6. Enter the Internet URL to which you want to link (see Figure 19.8).

FIG. 19.8

Enter the Internet URL to engage the action button as an Internet hyperlink.

7. Click OK in the Hyperlink To URL dialog box.

8. Click OK in the Action Settings dialog box.

The action button is now an Internet hyperlink that can be activated during a presentation by clicking it with the mouse pointer.

Linking to the Internet During a Presentation

Giving a professional presentation is one of the primary goals for any presenter. Linking to the Internet through URL hyperlinks challenges that goal by introducing several new variables. Perhaps the best way to prepare for a flawless presentation is through practice, practice, practice. Never is this more true than when using Internet hyperlinks.

Hyperlinks present choices for you during a presentation. Hyperlinks should be thought of as supporting evidence to your presentation; and you may find that certain evidence just isn't necessary when presenting. If it isn't necessary to utilize a certain hyperlink during a presentation, then don't. Think of yourself as an army that comes prepared for the worst. If you need to access an Excel spreadsheet, you can; if you need to access your corporate WWW server, you can. These options are available, but if they are not necessary to clinch the sale or pass the budget or teach the class, then don't clutter your presentation by accessing "outside" information.

Practicing your presentation helps you become familiar with the variety of available "resources." You should know exactly where each hyperlink takes you during a presentation. Surprise for the audience can be good; surprises for the presenter can be tragic. Know where your links take you and your audience, and know how to quickly and smoothly return everyone to the presentation.

Activating Hyperlinks to the Internet

Upon arriving at a slide in your presentation that has an Internet hyperlink, be sure you are prepared to talk to your audience while you wait for the Web browser to open and acquire the requested information through the defined URL. If the computer being used for the presentation is a powerful system, and it is connected to the Internet through a high-speed network connection, it may only take seconds to access the desired Internet information. However, on a slower, less powerful system, connected over a dial-up modem connection, you may need to plan on talking to your audience for up to a minute or more while you wait for the requested Internet information.

Part VI
Ch 19

> **CAUTION**
>
> Be aware that if an Internet Explorer window is currently open when you activate an Internet hyperlink, another Internet Explorer opens, but not as the active application. The PowerPoint slide show remains the active presentation. Use Alt+Tab to navigate to the needed Internet Explorer window.

To activate an Internet hyperlink during a presentation:

1. Move your mouse to the hyperlink object or text.

   Your mouse pointer turns into a hand with a pointing finger when you are pointing to the hyperlink (see Figure 19.9).

Pointing hand

2. If the hyperlink is created as a Mouse Over hyperlink, it can be activated by simply pointing to it; if the hyperlink is created as a Mouse Click hyperlink, you need to click the object or text to activate the hyperlink.

Upon activating an Internet hyperlink, the Web browser opens and acquires the information requested through the defined URL.

Data may actually arrive to your computer in "pieces." You may first see a background, then the text of the HTML document, then any images in the document will display one by one. Over a fast Internet connection, on a powerful computer system, this entire process may complete in a single second. You should have some idea of how long each Internet hyperlink will take before beginning the presentation. And be aware of the steps that must be accomplished in order to acquire information over the Internet.

Creating Internet hyperlinks with URLs that do not use domain names (for example, **www.company.com**) but rather IP addresses (for example, **190.208.78.101**) eliminates the need for a DNS request. This can shorten the time needed to acquire information over the Internet.

Returning to Your Presentation

Every time an Internet hyperlink is activated during a presentation, the Microsoft Internet Explorer opens a new window. If your presentation is rich with Internet hyperlinks, you will want to be aware of how many Internet Explorer windows are open at any single time. Many Internet Explorer windows open during a presentation can tax your computer system resources and cause the system to perform slower. After activating an Internet hyperlink and displaying the necessary Internet information, it is recommended that you close Internet Explorer to return to your presentation.

If you want, you may use the Windows Alt+Tab feature to navigate back to the PowerPoint slide show, leaving the Internet Explorer window open for reference. Alt+Tab can be employed throughout the presentation to navigate smoothly through all open applications. This allows you to refer back to "outside" data as needed for your audience. It is highly suggested that the number of open applications be kept to a minimum for simplicity and to maintain efficient system performance.

Editing Hyperlinks

Part
VI

Ch
19

Information on the Internet changes and moves. It is critical that you check and edit your Internet hyperlinks regularly for presentations that are given on a regular basis. Make sure that what you expect to display on a screen in front of your audience when you activate an Internet hyperlink is in fact what displays.

In some instances, you may link to information on the Internet that simply goes away and cannot be found. While you may not want to remove the hyperlink object or text on a certain slide, you certainly need to disengage the hyperlink so that you don't find yourself attempting to use it during a presentation.

In other cases you may just need to slightly modify the URL hyperlinks in your presentation. Changing Internet hyperlinks is similar to the process that originally created the hyperlink. Refer to the section "Creating Internet Hyperlinks" for detailed instructions on how to create/edit Internet hyperlinks.

Checking Current Internet Hyperlinks

Check your Internet hyperlinks before each presentation. The best method for checking your Internet hyperlinks is by running through your presentation and checking each hyperlink.

Perhaps a quicker method for checking your Internet hyperlinks is to maintain a folder of Internet favorites in your Internet Explorer that contains all of the URLs used in a given presentation. On a regular basis, as time allows, you can open your Microsoft Internet Explorer and check each URL in your Favorites folder.

Removing Dead Links

When you find an Internet hyperlink that is no longer valid, resulting in an `Object not found` error from the WWW server, this is called a *dead link*. It is critical that dead links either be changed to a new URL or altogether removed.

To disengage an Internet hyperlink:

1. In Slide view, select the object or highlight the text that is currently an Internet hyperlink.

2. Click the Insert Hyperlink button on the Standard toolbar; choose Insert, Hyperlink; or press Ctrl+K.

3. Select None in the Action Settings dialog box.

The object or text is now disengaged as an Internet hyperlink. You should note that text will no longer be underlined as it was as an Internet hyperlink. If the text or object was only necessary as a hyperlink, you may consider removing it from your slide after disengaging the link.

 TIP Internet hyperlinks can be disengaged by simply removing the object or text to which they are tied. Select the object or text and press Delete.

Changing Internet Hyperlinks

Changing the URL for any Internet hyperlink is similar to the process of engaging an Internet hyperlink. In the event that you find the needed information has moved to a new URL:

1. In Slide view, select the object or highlight the text that is currently an Internet hyperlink.
2. Click the Insert Hyperlink button on the Standard toolbar; or choose Insert, Hyperlink; or press Ctrl+K.
3. Change the URL in the Link to File or URL field to the new URL.
4. Click OK.

Considering Internet Hyperlink Issues

PowerPoint allows you to present information in a clear, concise, and professional manner. Internet hyperlinks can introduce a variable to a presentation that may make a presentation more dazzling and professional than ever before, or make for a presenter's nightmare.

This section highlights some of the nightmares that you should be aware of before adding and relying on Internet hyperlinks in your presentation. It also provides some tips for recovering from nightmares if they occur.

Internet Hyperlinks Slow Down Presentations

Several things must occur every time you click an Internet hyperlink during a presentation:

1. Click the hyperlink object or text in a slide during a presentation (see Figure 19.10).
2. The Microsoft Internet Explorer opens.

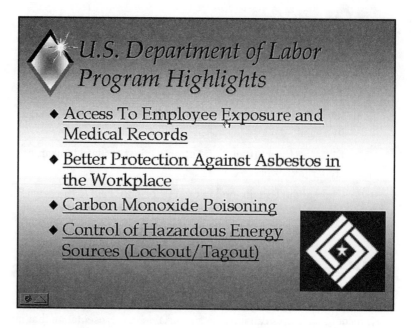

3. The URL is sent to the Internet Explorer and the request for information is sent across the Internet.

4. The requested information is transferred across the Internet to your computer.

5. The Internet information is received and formatted for viewing in the Internet Explorer (see Figure 19.11).

This entire sequence can take as little as a few seconds, during which you can continue speaking to transition your audience to this departure from your slide presentation. This entire sequence can also take up to a minute or more, which you may not anticipate. Several variables determine how fast this sequence occurs:

■ Speed of your computer

■ Speed of your Internet connection—modem or network interface connection

■ Current Internet network traffic

■ Current traffic on the Internet host from which information is being requested

■ File size being transferred across the Internet

Fortunately, you can plan for some of these expected bottlenecks so that they do not interrupt the flow of your presentation.

After considering the issues associated with live Internet access during a presentation, you elect to present data locally. Many of the other chapters in this book provide a wide range of alternatives, for presenting information during a presentation.

FIG. 19.11
The Internet Explorer displays the information requested by an Internet hyperlink activated during a PowerPoint presentation.

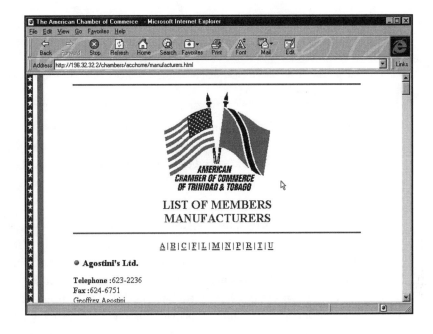

Your Computer   Know your computer and how quickly it can exit your PowerPoint slide presentation and start the Microsoft Internet Explorer. The Internet Explorer must start *every* time you click an Internet hyperlink during a presentation.

 If you have multiple Internet hyperlinks in a presentation, close the Internet Explorer each time you return to your presentation. Otherwise, each time you click a hyperlink, another Internet Explorer starts each time, slowing your system down further.

Part
VI

Ch
19

Your Internet Connection   What speed is your Internet connection? Are you connected via a T3, T1, ISDN, 56K, 28.8Kbps modem connection, and so on? Know how quickly Internet information generally travels across the network connection on which you are presenting.

CAUTION
Be sure to also consider the type of network connection for the Internet server from which you are requesting information. You may have the fastest connection in the world, but if the server computer delivering the information has a slower network connection, the bottleneck will occur on the delivery side, and the information will still load slowly.

If you will be traveling and presenting on a network with which you are unfamiliar, check with the network administrator before you arrive to acquire the general information of their Internet connection. Find out what type of connection they have and perhaps even get some ping or tracert information in critical presentation situations.

 TIP   Ping and tracert are network utilities that allow you to monitor network path and performance between two network computers.

If you will be presenting over a modem Internet connection, be sure to test that connection first. A wide variety of variables contribute to the performance speed of a modem Internet connection. If you are used to surfing the Internet over a T1 or T3 connection, a 28.8Kbps or slower modem connection can be an unpleasant surprise during a presentation.

If you are unable to travel to the area where you are presenting—which is the case for most people—you should dial long distance to the modem pool in that area for testing. Acquire ahead of time the phone number for the modem pool. By using the presentation computer, dial up to that area modem pool and test the performance of that Internet connection. It is not uncommon for Internet modem pools to be overloaded with modems, thus not allowing for maximum performance of the line connecting it to the Internet. Again, consider using tools like ping and tracert to test the network performance.

If you do plan a presentation using Internet hyperlinks over a modem Internet connection, you should strongly consider incorporating the needed information into your presentation through other methods. A modem Internet connection may simply be too slow for the caliber of presentation you are intending on conducting.

Current Internet Network Traffic   Be aware of the dramatic fluctuation in Internet network traffic over the course of a day. Information that loaded in seconds from an Internet site in the morning, may not be accessible in the afternoon due to increased Internet traffic. If possible, be aware of the various networks between you and the needed information, and become familiar with traffic on those networks.

Tools such as ping and tracert can assist you in discovering the general network path and performance between you and the information you will link to during a presentation. These tools are available in your Windows directory. Refer to your network documentation or network administrator for assistance in using these tools and understanding the output.

Current Traffic on Internet Host Server   Be aware that if you will be linking to an extremely popular Internet site during the middle of the day, you may have to "wait in line" for the information you are requesting. For example, think of the millions of people connecting to the Netscape WWW servers on a daily basis. If you want to present information to your audience that resides on the Netscape WWW server, you will find that it can take more time to acquire information during peak Internet usage than it does during non-peak times.

T I P Be sure to test any Internet network performance several times a day or specifically around the time of day that you will be presenting. Internet network traffic can fluctuate dramatically throughout the day.

File Size Being Transferred   Consider the file size or the amount of information you might request through an Internet URL. For example, if you are linking to a URL that opens with a large graphic, you may have to wait several seconds for the image to load.

In the most rural of areas over a slow 14,400 bps modem, even small files might be too large. Over a T3 connection, almost anything will transfer immediately, unless there is a bottleneck before your incoming T3 connection.

Internet Information Moves or is Unavailable

Perhaps one of the most critical issues to consider when relying on Internet information during a presentation is the possibility of a URL becoming invalid because the information on the Internet server moved (see Figure 19.12) or the Internet server is currently down (see Figure 19.13). You need to check your Internet hyperlinks frequently and always have a backup for when Internet information is simply unavailable.

FIG. 19.12
Information on the Internet sometimes moves making URLs invalid.

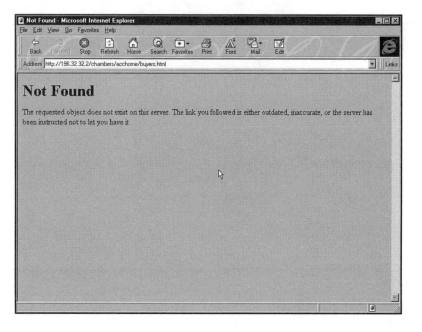

Part
VI

Ch
19

FIG. 19.13
Internet servers can be
unavailable due to
technical difficulties
that are out of your
control.

Copying Internet Information versus Linking

Based on the issues discussed thus far in this section, you need to decide if you are going to use a hyperlink to information available on the Internet, or if you are going to copy that information manually and add it to your presentation.

Linking to Internet information can be added flash that impresses your audience, not to mention ensuring that you have the most current information in your presentation. If, however, after studying the issues of linking to Internet information, you decide that you shouldn't do it or you find that you will be presenting in a place where you simply can't connect to the Internet, consider linking to data or information stored locally on your system.

If it is critical to maintain the Internet "flavor" to your presentation, consider saving the needed HTML file(s) locally to your system and linking to local URLs (see Figure 19.14) for display in the Microsoft Internet Explorer.

FIG. 19.14
Linking to local HTML
documents is a useful
alternative to Internet
hyperlinks.

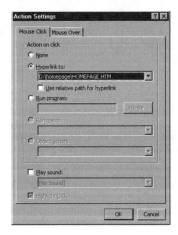

Understanding what Internet Assistant Does with Internet Hyperlinks

Chapter 18, "Publishing to the Internet," details publishing your PowerPoint presentations to the Internet and using the PowerPoint Internet Assistant to simplify the process. I would like to quickly explain how the Internet Assistant handles existing Internet hyperlinks in your presentation when converting to HTML.

When you save your PowerPoint presentation to an HTML format using the Internet Assistant, several hypertext links are created to assist the Internet user in navigating through the presentation via the WWW. Hypertext links are created between each slide, but presentation Internet hyperlinks are also maintained and turned into active hypertext links on the HTML pages.

It is a rather natural transition from a PowerPoint presentation format to HTML documents linked together via hypertext links. The links that were once activated during a presentation as Internet hyperlinks, simply become hypertext links in the HTML document of the same slide. This allows the Internet user navigating through the presentation via the WWW the same options to the same information as you had conducting the presentation through PowerPoint. ●

Part
VI

Ch
19

CHAPTER 20

Using PowerPoint on an Intranet

by Todd White

Networks greatly increase the utility of computers. Before networks, computer users were severely limited to the programs and information loaded on the hard-drives of their computers. Networks changed this limited world of computing by allowing users to link to other computers to gain access to a broader range of programs and information. Over time, networks even gave way to an efficient method of communication which came to be known as e-mail.

Today, you know better than anyone what a crucial role your company intranet or the Internet plays in your day-to-day, corporate life. The "paperless office" is becoming more of a reality each day that you begin by reading your e-mail, sending and receiving online faxes, and conducting electronic PowerPoint presentations for the monthly sales meeting. Through your company intranet, PowerPoint 97 brings new and better capabilities for conducting and participating in presentation conferences over a computer network and using your e-mail to collaborate with others on presentations. Read on to learn how... ∎

Collaborating on presentations with others on your intranet

PowerPoint now makes it easier than ever to distribute presentations to a defined group for review and collaboration. Via e-mail, you can now quickly and easily pass along an entire presentation to an individual or a group of recipients. Presentations can even be routed through a defined group or posted to a public Microsoft Exchange folder for public access.

Conducting or receiving presentations over a network

Presentation Conferences provide new opportunities for distance-training, corporate meetings, and long-distance information sharing. Enjoying the multimedia benefits of a PowerPoint presentation no longer requires presenter and audience to be in the same location; just connected via a computer network.

How to link to existing PowerPoint presentations on your intranet

Know of a presentation available on the company intranet that will explain your second bullet point on your seventh slide? Why not link to it? Learn how to use the resources already created and made available on your company intranet, and learn how to link to another presentation over a network.

Distributing Presentations to Others on a Network

PowerPoint offers three simple methods for sharing your presentations with others on your intranet. To list them, you may:

- E-mail your presentations to an individual or group.
- E-mail your presentation to a routing slip that will distribute the presentation from recipient to recipient.
- Post your presentation to a Microsoft Exchange public folder for your associates to access at their convenience.

E-mailing a Presentation

If there is no need to route a presentation through a group of recipients one by one, you may simply e-mail a presentation to an individual or group.

One important note to keep in mind is that when sending a PowerPoint presentation through e-mail, you are sending a normal e-mail message with an attached file. Therefore, whatever capabilities in e-mail that you have grown accustomed to are still available when sending a presentation via e-mail. The largest difference is that you will initiate the "sending" from PowerPoint.

N O T E   Certain e-mail gateways may not allow e-mail file attachments. Contact your e-mail administrator to find out if you can send a specific recipient on another network a PowerPoint presentation attachment. ▦

To e-mail a presentation:

1. Open the presentation.
2. Choose File, Send To, Mail Recipient.

N O T E   If the option is Next Routing Recipient, the presentation has an attached routing slip. You may select this option and choose the Send Copy of Presentation Without Using the Routing Slip option; this will allow you to send the presentation to a group or individual without using the attached routing slip. See the section "Routing a Presentation" later in this chapter for more information regarding routing slips. ▦

3. Enter the recipient(s) of the presentation in the To field. Take note that the PowerPoint presentation file is displayed as an attachment to this e-mail message (see Figure. 20.1).

FIG. 20.1

Enter a recipient's e-mail account name or Internet address to send the person a copy of the presentation.

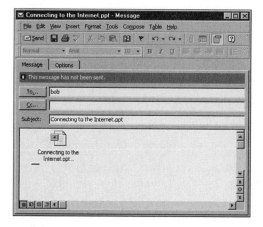

4. Continue composing the e-mail message. Feel free to add any text to the message for the recipient(s).

5. Send the message by Choosing File, Send. The small Send envelope icon at the far left of the Standard toolbar may be used to send as well (see Figure. 20.2).

FIG. 20.2

Use the Send icon in the upper-left corner to quickly send your presentation.

Send

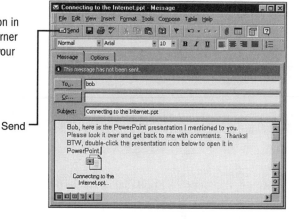

The presentation is sent to the recipient(s) of the e-mail message as an attached file. If your recipients are using Microsoft Outlook or Exchange to receive the message, they can simply double-click the attachment icon to open the presentation in PowerPoint.

Routing a Presentation

Routing presentations is an easy, efficient, paperless method for distributing presentations to a select group for review or direct modification. Routing presentations makes collaboration enjoyable and simplifies sharing presentations with others in your department. If

Part

IV

Ch

20

collaborating with a group on a single presentation, each recipient can make the necessary additions, deletions, and general changes before sending the presentation along to the next recipient on the routing slip.

Creating a Routing Slip   When preparing to route a presentation, consider a few options:

- Decide whether you want to route a copy of the presentation through the group individually or all at once.

- Track the progress of a routed presentation; by default this option is turned off.

- Return the presentation to you when it has completed its route; this feature is turned on by default.

All of these options are available to you when you create the routing slip. To create a routing slip:

1. Choose <u>F</u>ile, Sen<u>d</u> To, <u>R</u>outing Recipient; the Add Routing Slip dialog box appears (see Figure. 20.3).

FIG. 20.3

Create and define your routing slips in this dialog box.

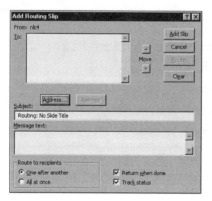

2. Click the A<u>d</u>dress button; the Address Book dialog box appears (see Figure. 20.4). By default, the Postoffice Address List is initially displayed; you may switch to another address book by opening the Show Names from the menu located in the uppermost right corner of the Address Book dialog box.

3. Either manually type the name of the first recipient or select a name from the list of addresses.

4. Click the T<u>o</u> button to add the selected name to the box on the right.

5. Enter or select another person to be added to the list of recipients. Continue this procedure until you have added each person to whom you want to route this presentation.

FIG. 20.4

Select the recipients to be included on the routing slip.

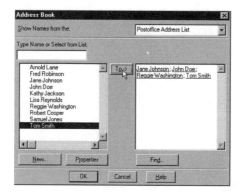

N O T E You may select individual and group aliases for your routing slip. Be aware that if you select a group alias, the entire group will receive the presentation at once when the presentation is routed to that group alias. ▨

6. Click OK to return to the Add Routing Slip dialog box.

7. Modify the order of the routing by using the up and down Move buttons. Select a recipient's name, and click the up Move button to move the user closer to the top of the routing list. Likewise, select a recipient's name and click the down Move button to move the user closer to the bottom of the routing list.

8. To remove a person from the routing slip, click the person's name on the To list and click the Remove button.

9. When a presentation is routed using e-mail, be sure to enter an appropriate subject in the Subject field. By default, PowerPoint provides a subject based on the Title of the presentation, "Properties." You may modify the presentation Title by choosing File, Properties, and the Summary tab.

10. Enter any text that you want to be sent to each recipient when he/she receives the routed presentation (see Figure. 20.5).

N O T E There is no need to explain to each recipient that the received presentation is being routed and must be passed along to the next recipient. PowerPoint automatically adds the following text to every routed presentation:

```
The Presentation below has a routing slip. When you are done
reviewing this Presentation, choose Send from the Microsoft
PowerPoint 8.0 File menu to route it to the next recipient. ▨
```

Part

IV

Ch

20

FIG. 20.5

Enter the text to be included in the e-mail message sent to the routing slip recipients.

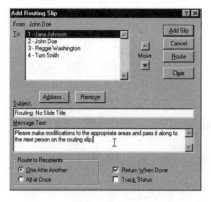

11. In the Route to Recipients section of the Add Routing Slip, select whether you want your presentation distributed to the whole routing list at once or one after another. By default, <u>O</u>ne After Another is selected. To change this so that the whole list receives the presentation at once, click the A<u>l</u>l at Once radio button.

12. By default, the Return <u>W</u>hen Done option is selected. This feature ensures that you will be the final recipient after the presentation has been distributed to everyone on the routing slip. If this is not desired, click the box next to this option to remove the check mark.

13. If you would like to track the status of the routing process to perhaps ensure that it doesn't get "stuck" somewhere in an individual's e-mail, turn on the Trac<u>k</u> Status option.

14. Select <u>R</u>oute to begin the routing process immediately. Click <u>A</u>dd Slip to postpone routing the presentation to a later time. You might postpone routing for various reasons, including a person on the routing slip currently being out of the office for vacation or any other extended period of time. When you are ready to begin routing, choose <u>F</u>ile, Sen<u>d</u> To, <u>N</u>ext Routing Recipient.

Upon clicking either <u>R</u>oute or <u>A</u>dd Slip, the Add Routing Slip dialog box closes and returns you to your original spot in PowerPoint. If you selected <u>A</u>dd Slip, you may open the presentation at any time and follow the procedure detailed in the next section.

Sending a Routed Presentation   Once you have received a routed presentation or added a routing slip to a presentation without starting the routing, you may pass the presentation along to the next recipient on the routing slip at any time.

You may make any changes necessary to a presentation before routing it to the next recipient on the routing slip. When you are ready to send the presentation to the next recipient, follow these steps:

1. Choose File, Send To, Next Routing Recipient; the Send dialog box appears (see Figure. 20.6).

FIG. 20.6

You have two Send options once you add a routing slip.

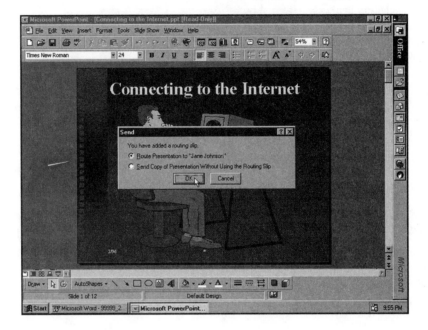

2. You have the option of either routing the presentation to the next recipient on the routing slip or sending a copy of the presentation to someone without using the routing slip (refer to the section "E-Mailing a Presentation" if you choose to send without the routing slip). By default, the next recipient on the routing slip is selected. Click OK to pass the presentation along.

Immediately upon clicking OK in the Send dialog box, the presentation is sent to the next recipient on the routing slip. You may exit from PowerPoint, which will eliminate the temporary copy of the presentation from your system.

Receiving and Opening a Routed Presentation   If the message that you receive is a routed message, you may find that the originator of the routing slip did not include any specialized instructions or text in the message. The originator has the option to include such text, but if he/she elected not to, a generic instruction to continue routing the presentation appears by default (see Figure 20.7).

Using Microsoft Outlook or Microsoft Exchange to receive the presentation e-mail message, simply double-click the presentation icon displayed in the message to open the presentation in PowerPoint.

Part
IV

Ch
20

FIG. 20.7
Double-click the
presentation icon to
open the attached
Connecting to the
Internet.ppt presenta-
tion in PowerPoint.

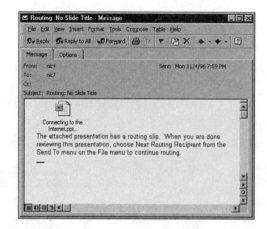

Once opened, you may elect to either simply view the presentation or modify it as needed. When finished, save any changes made using the Save command, and either send it along to the next routing slip recipient (see the section "Sending a Routed Presentation" earlier in the chapter) or save the presentation to your system using the Save As command. You may also elect to use any of the other features described in this chapter.

Posting a Presentation to a Microsoft Exchange Folder

If you would like to make your presentations available to others on your intranet without e-mailing a copy to everybody or all appropriate parties, then you should post your presentations to a Microsoft Exchange public folder. This will allow others who have access to the public folder to open the presentation anytime they want. They may even take copies of any presentation posted to the public folder for their own use, or to review or modify.

N O T E To post presentations to a Microsoft Exchange public folder, your network must be attached to a system running the Microsoft Exchange Server. ▪

To post a presentation to a Microsoft Exchange public folder:

1. Open the presentation in PowerPoint.

2. Choose File, Send To, Exchange Folder.

3. In the Send To Exchange Folder dialog box, double-click the Microsoft Mail Shared Folders to open the public folders (see Figure. 20.8).

4. Select the folder that you want to save the presentation to.

5. Click OK.

FIG. 20.8

Open the Shared
Folders to place the
presentation in a
publicly accessible
folder over your
intranet.

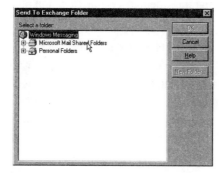

By using Microsoft Outlook, users can open the folder to which you posted the presentation in order to view or copy it.

Holding Presentation Conferences

Whether your audience is across the room or across the continent, a computer network allows you to conduct your flawless electronic presentation just the same. What's the magic? PowerPoint's Presentation Conferencing feature and your corporate intranet.

In short, Presentation Conferencing enables you to transmit a PowerPoint presentation to any computer on a network, in real-time as though you were sitting at each receiving computer conducting the presentation.

Coupled with any telephone conferencing system and the on-screen PowerPoint pen available to both presenter and audience, Presentation Conferencing truly is the next best thing to being there. In fact, you may still employ Presentation Conferencing even when in the same room as your audience. If you are unable to display a clear image of your presentation for an audience that is sitting in front of you, you may elect to use Presentation Conferencing to send clear, easy to read slides straight to their computer screens. A classroom or training session is perhaps the best application of this idea.

Part

IV

Ch

20

Preparing for a Presentation Conference

Presentation Conferencing is so cool, there isn't any other way to describe it. In fact, it's such an outstanding feature, that most people assume they don't have what it takes to use it. In most cases those people are wrong.

So what is needed to conduct a Presentation Conference? A Presentation Conference is conducted over an intranet. Therefore, the instructor's computer must be connected to a network and be able to run PowerPoint. Likewise, each receiving computer must be on the same network and also running PowerPoint. The single largest challenge in preparing a Presentation Conference is collecting the names of each computer that will participate in the conference.

N O T E Whether your audience is connecting to your presentation conference via your local area network or the Internet, each audience member will be given his/her computer name during the process of running the Presentation Conference Wizard. ▓

On every computer network, each attached computer is identified by a unique name. For example, a computer network set up by an administrator with a liking for trees might name each computer on the network after a different tree. If your network administrator likes trees, you might be sitting at a computer right now named **redwood**. To conduct a Presentation Conference, you must know the network names of each computer that will be receiving your presentation.

Each audience member can acquire the name of his/her computer by doing the following:

1. Open the Windows 95 Start menu, point to Settings and choose Control Panel.
2. Locate and double-click the Network icon to open the Network dialog box.
3. Click the Identification tab located at the top of the Network dialog box. The computer's unique identity is listed in the Computer name field.

While you are collecting the names of each participating computer, make sure that each of those computers is running PowerPoint 97 as well.

N O T E If you will be conducting your presentation to computers connected to the Internet, you may be using longer computer names—often referred to as *domain names*—or you may perhaps specify the audience of computers by IP (Internet protocol) numbers. In any case, you may need to contact your network administrator or the network administrator of your audience for the specific computer network names before you begin your Presentation Conference. ▓

Conducting a Presentation Conference

Everything you learned from "Part V: Making Your Presentation" should also be employed when you are conducting a Presentation Conference. If you are unsure about basic PowerPoint presentation principles, be sure to consult Chapters 14, 15, and 16 before going any further. If you are already familiar with the "principles of conducting good presentations" material and just want to know how to start the Presentation Conferencing feature to conduct an online presentation, then read on.

After you have acquired the names of each computer that will be participating in your virtual conference, open your presentation in PowerPoint and make sure that you are coordinated in time with all members of your audience; be sure to account for time zone changes when coordinating with others over long distances. Conference telephone calls are the easiest method to insure that everyone is in sync.

Before beginning, make sure that all audience members are logged on and have PowerPoint running. With your presentation open and your audience members' computers ready to receive your presentation, do the following:

1. Choose Tools, Presentation Conference, to start the Presentation Conference Wizard (see Figure 20.9).

FIG. 20.9
The opening dialog box to the Presentation Conference Wizard.

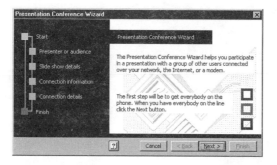

2. As the instructions indicate, before continuing be sure that all audience members are connected to the network. Once you are sure that your audience is on the network, Internet, or modem, click Next to continue.

3. As the presenter, you want to make sure that the Presenter radio button is selected; if it is not and you find that Audience is selected, click the Presenter radio button (see Figure. 20.10).

4. After selecting Presenter, click Next to continue.

Part
IV

Ch
20

FIG. 20.10
Select Presenter to command the presentation from your computer.

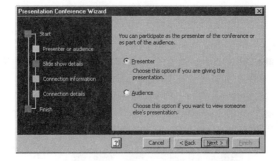

5. PowerPoint reviews before continuing what you will be presenting based on the Set Up Show command of the Slide Show menu (refer to Chapter 15, "Preparing Your Presentation" for more detail regarding the Set Up Show command). If slide show setup is incorrect, click Cancel and modify the Show. If the Show is correct, click Next to continue (see Figure 20.11).

FIG. 20.11
Check your slide show setup before continuing.

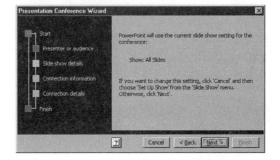

6. If you are connecting to your audience over the Internet, make sure at this time that your Internet connection is established. If you are connecting via your corporate intranet or once the Internet connection has been established, click Next to continue (see Figure 20.12).

FIG. 20.12
Establish your network connection before continuing.

7. As instructed, enter the names of the audience computers participating in your Presentation Conference. Enter the first computer in the Computer Name field and click Add. Enter the next computer name in the Computer Name field and click Add. Continue this process until each audience member's computer is added to the list (see Figure 20.13). PowerPoint verifies the presence of each computer as you Add computer names to your audience list. If a specified computer cannot be found on the network, PowerPoint indicates this and asks you to Check name and try again.

N O T E If teleconferencing with your audience during this process, you may ask them at this time for each computer name. As each audience member runs the Presentation Conference Wizard, each member will be given his/her computer name. ▨

FIG. 20.13

Enter each audience member's computer name or Internet address to establish the connection.

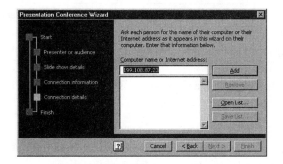

 T I P If you will be conducting Presentation Conferences with the same audience on a regular basis, consider using the Save List button to save the audience list for later use. If you have already saved an audience list from a previous Presentation Conference, use the Open List button to open the list, saving you the time of re-entering each computer name.

8. After completing the list of audience computer names, click Next to continue.

9. The final dialog box of the Presentation Conference Wizard reminds you that Each member of the Audience must select Finish before you do. This is important to keep in mind; be sure to check that each audience member has chosen Finish.

10. Upon ensuring that your audience is prepared to receive your presentation, click Finish to begin the presentation.

CAUTION

Be sure to wait for your audience to click Finish before you. When you, the presenter, select Finish, the connections are made at that time. If an audience member has not yet chosen Finish, that person is unable to join the conference.

If all audience members are not ready for the presentation, you receive an error box indicating that PowerPoint `Couldn't make a connection`. Press OK to return to the wizard and check the highlighted name for accuracy.

If the highlighted name turns out to be correct and correctly entered, you may have a networking issue to be resolved by your network administrator or even perhaps your Internet service provider.

It may take a small amount of time for your computer to connect and initialize each audience member computer. During this process you will see a dialog box with the following message:

```
Please wait for the connections to be made and the file to be sent to the
audience. This may take a moment.
```

 TIP To avoid a long unexpected delay while the network connections and file transfers initialize the Presentation Conference, be sure to test this process prior to an important online meeting. Large multimedia presentations will take longer to initialize over long distance networks.

Once the connection and initialization is complete, conduct your presentation just as you would any other—flawlessly!

When the presentation begins, you will have several tools available to you called Stage Manager tools. *Stage Manager tools* help you to review notes and take new notes during the presentation, control the navigation of the presentation for each audience member, and monitor your timing. Each of these tools are available by clicking your right mouse button.

Only you will see the Stage Manager tools on your screen. Your audience members only see the presentation as you control it, and any on-screen notes your or any other audience member draws using the Pen; the Pen is controlled by the movement of the mouse.

Participating in a Presentation Conference

To be an audience member in a Presentation Conference, you need to have:

- A computer connected to the same network as the presenter.
- A copy of PowerPoint 97 running on Windows 95.
- A unique network computer name to give to the presenter.

It is not necessary to acquire your computer name ahead of time, except for advanced preparation; the Presentation Conference Wizard presents your computer name to you before the final connection is made. You can give the presenter your computer name at that time.

To participate in a Presentation Conference as an audience member, you must have PowerPoint running and at least have a blank presentation open to gain access to the Presentation Conference feature. The Presentation Conference feature is available on the Tools menu which is not available if all presentations are closed in PowerPoint.

To join a Presentation Conference:

1. Choose Tools, Presentation Conference to start the Presentation Conference wizard. The opening dialog box simply introduces the Presentation Conference Wizard, explaining that the wizard helps you participate in a presentation with a group of other users over your network, the Internet, or a modem (refer to Figure 20.9). Click Next to continue.

2. By default the Presenter radio button is chosen. To be an audience member in this Presentation Conference, select the Audience radio button and click Next to continue (see Figure 20.14).

FIG. 20.14
Select Audience to participate in the Presentation Conference as an audience member.

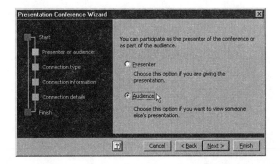

3. Choose the type of connection you are employing to connect to the presenter (see Figure 20.15). If you are connecting via your local area network or corporate intranet, select the Local Area Network (LAN) or Corporate Network. If you are connecting via the Internet, select the Dial-in to Internet radio button. After making your selection, click Next to continue.

Part
IV

Ch
20

FIG. 20.15
Select the type of connection you are using to connect into the Presentation Conference.

4. If you selected a LAN connection, you are now presented with the network name of your computer, which you should pass along to the presenter if he/she does not already have it (see Figure 20.16).

FIG. 20.16

For a LAN connection, your computer name is presented to you so that you may pass it along to the presenter setting up the conference connection.

If you selected a dial-in Internet connection, you are asked to get connected at this time to your Internet service provider. Click Next once connected (see Figure 20.17).

FIG. 20.17

Connect to your Internet service provider before continuing.

After connecting to your Internet service provider and clicking Next, PowerPoint queries your dial-up connection for the assigned IP address to your computer. The number displayed next to Your IP Address is: is your unique Internet address while connected (see Figure 20.18). Supply this IP number to the presenter so that he/she can complete the Presentation Conference setup. Click Next to continue.

5. Make sure that you click Finish before the presenter. All audience members must click Finish before the presenter in order to prepare the computer for receiving the presentation (see Figure 20.19).

FIG. 20.18
Your uniquely as-
signed IP address is
displayed. Give this
number to the
presenter.

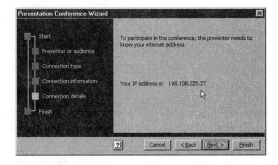

FIG. 20.19
Click the Finish button
before the presenter
and wait for all
connections to be
established.

The Connecting to the Conference message box appears immediately after you click Finish at the final Presentation Conference Wizard dialog box. The message box reads:

```
Please wait for the network connection to be made with the presenter.
```

This message box remains until all audience members and the presenter have completed
the Presentation Conference Wizard. Once all participating parties have completed the
Presentation Conference Wizard, the presentation appears on your screen.

The presenter conducts the presentation and manages the slide navigation. You are unable to control the movement of the slides or the builds used in each slide. You may, however, use your screen pen to annotate slides for the both the presenter and the rest of the
audience to see.

Linking Among Presentations on an Intranet

PowerPoint hyperlinking allows you the flexibility of linking to specific slides within your
presentation, linking to Internet sites, linking to Word or Excel documents, or even linking to other presentations.

You may know that your colleague recently created a PowerPoint presentation with the latest quarterly market share statistics. Without copying any of your colleague's slides, you can create hyperlinks in your presentation that you can click during your presentation to display the appropriate slides regarding the "decline over last year's fourth quarter earnings."

To link to a presentation on your intranet, you must make sure that the PowerPoint presentation is stored in a public folder to which you have access. For example, if the file you are linking to is stored on the computer named **Pine**, make sure that you either have read-only or full access to the Pine disk drives or to the folder in which the file is stored. Once you know the name of the computer, and the folder and file name of the presentation, linking to it is simple:

1. Select the object or text in the presentation to be activated as the hyperlink. This will be your "clickable" object or text.

2. Choose Slide Show, Action Settings.

3. In the Action Settings dialog box, click the Hyperlink To radio button (see Figure. 20.20).

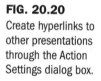

FIG. 20.20

Create hyperlinks to other presentations through the Action Settings dialog box.

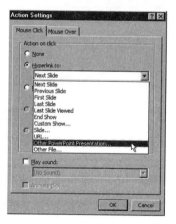

4. Open the Hyperlink To drop-down menu and select Other PowerPoint Presentation from the list of possible hyperlinks.

5. In the Hyperlink to Other PowerPoint Presentation dialog box, you may either browse your local disk drives, or navigate your Network Neighborhood for the presentation file by opening the Look In menu. To link to a presentation available through your intranet, open the Look In menu and select Network Neighborhood for a full listing of computers on your network (see Figure. 20.21).

FIG. 20.21

Your Network Neighborhood provides access to the various computer resources available over your intranet.

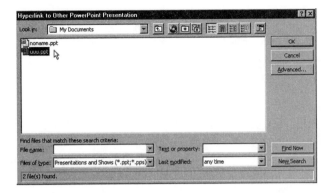

6. Either select a computer listed on your network, or select the Entire Network to browse further on your intranet. Once you have identified the computer that stores the presentation, click that computer.

7. Click Open.

8. Opening a computer on the network reveals a list of all "shared" folders; select the folder containing the presentation.

9. Click Open.

10. Locate and click the needed PowerPoint presentation. Click OK.

11. In the Hyperlink to Slide dialog box, select the slide to which you want to link (see Figure 20.22). Click OK.

12. After returning to the Action Settings dialog box, click OK.

FIG. 20.22

Select the specific slide to which you would like to link during your presentation.

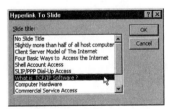

Part
IV

Ch
20

Your selected text or object is now a hyperlink specifically to the selected slide on the presentation located across your intranet. To call the slide during a presentation, simply place your mouse pointer over the hyperlink during the presentation and click once. PowerPoint immediately navigates your intranet, connects to the appropriate computer, opens the presentation, and displays the pre-defined slide on your screen for your audience. Your audience won't even know anything special occurred in the process. ●

PowerPoint Charts and Tables

CHAPTER 21

Customizing PowerPoint

by Edward C. Willett

When you first start working with PowerPoint, you may find yourself overwhelmed by all the possibilities it presents. It takes awhile to figure out what does what and how—that's why you bought this book. But after awhile, when you begin to get the hang of things, you'll start to notice that there are times when PowerPoint's standard menus and toolbars just don't quite provide exactly what you need. That's understandable; what seemed logical to the folks at Microsoft who programmed PowerPoint won't necessarily make perfect sense thousands of miles away under entirely different circumstances. Fortunately, PowerPoint provides you with plenty of ways to make it fit you, instead of the other way around. ∎

Create your own toolbars

Place the control buttons you depend on most onto your own custom toolbar so they're always there when you need them!

Change options

Change printing, text editing, and other options so the program works the same way you do.

Develop your own templates

Edit PowerPoint's existing templates or create your own so you don't have to reinvent the wheel every time you prepare a presentation.

Customize colors

Always have just the right color you need—even if you have to invent it yourself!

Creating and Modifying Toolbars

One of the best ways to customize PowerPoint is to develop your own toolbars, with your own favorite tools on them for immediate use whenever you need them. With PowerPoint, you can modify any existing toolbar and then save it for later use.

To customize toolbars, follow these steps:

1. Choose Tools, Customize.

2. The menu on the left in Figure 21.1 displays a list of all the available toolbars, with check marks indicating which ones are currently open or displayed. If a toolbar you are planning to customize is not open at the moment, place a check mark beside it and it will appear.

FIG. 21.1
PowerPoint already has an extensive list of toolbars for all of its many functions, but if this isn't enough, you can change them to suit yourself!

3. Click the Commands tab to bring up the window in Figure 21.2. The list on the left this time shows categories of commands. When you select a category, the preview box on the right shows you the icons for the various commands. Commands that don't have icons are shown simply as text. If you're not sure what a particular command does, click the Description button below the Categories list.

FIG. 21.2
PowerPoint divides its many commands into categories to make finding the one you want for your custom toolbar easier.

4. To add a command to a toolbar, simply click and drag it onto the toolbar you want to modify. To remove a command from a toolbar, drag it off the toolbar and back into the preview box with the other icons.

5. Once you have modified the toolbar to your heart's content, choose Close. The toolbar keeps its new configuration until you change it again.

If you don't like the buttons that are offered for the various commands, you can even change those, too, from the <u>C</u>ommands dialog box. Click the button you want to change on the selected toolbar, then click <u>M</u>odify Selection, or simply right-click. This will display the pop-up menu in Figure 21.3.

FIG. 21.3

By using this menu, you can replace those boring old buttons with just about anything you want.

Here, you can choose from the following:

- *Reset.* Returns the button to its default appearance and function.

- *Delete.* Removes the button from the toolbar.

- *Name.* Enter the new name you'd like to assign to the button here, and set the hotkey by typing an ampersand (**&**) in front of the letter you want it to be.

- *Copy Button Image.* The button's image. If you see a button whose image you particularly like, copy it using this command.

- *Paste Button Image.* Once you've copied a button's image, you can use this command to paste it in place of another button you've selected to modify.

- *Reset Button Image.* Returns the selected button to its default appearance.

- *Edit Button Image.* Opens the Button Editor in Figure 21.4. There are four sections to the Button Editor: Picture, Move, Color, and Preview. The Picture box shows you what's on the button now. Each little square within the box is an individual pixel. The Move buttons below the Picture allow you to move the picture up, down, and sideways within the button. To change the picture, choose a color, or Erase, and click a pixel. The pixel's current color changes to the color you've chosen, or, if you chose Erase, to the button's background color. (If you've chosen the same color as the color of the pixel you click, that erases the pixel as well.) Click, hold, and drag

Part

VII

Ch

21

the arrow to erase or color a string of pixels. You can see the effect of your changes on the button's appearance in the Preview area. Click Clear to completely erase the button's picture.

- ▮ *Change Button Image.* Brings up the selection of optional pictures in Figure 21.5; choose the one you'd like to apply to the selected button.

- ▮ *Default Style.* Returns the selected button to its default style of image only, text only, or image and text combined.

- ▮ *Text Only (Always).* Choose this, and no matter where the command shows up— whether on the toolbar or in a pull-down menu—it will be labeled only as text, without an associated image.

- ▮ *Text Only (in Menus).* Choose this, and on a toolbar, the command is represented by a button image, but if it appears in a pull-down menu, it is labeled only with text.

- ▮ *Image And Text.* Choose this, and the command is labeled with both an image and text, both on a toolbar and in a menu.

- ▮ *Begin a Group.* Places the selected button inside its own distinct area, represented on the toolbar by "engraved lines," such as those that enclose the bold, italic, and underline commands in the Formatting toolbar.

FIG. 21.4
The Button Editor lets you draw your own command button icon.

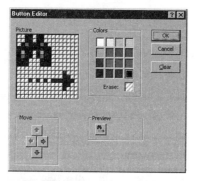

FIG. 21.5
If you'd prefer, choose one of these shapes for your new command button.

If you have several commands you use frequently that PowerPoint has split up among several toolbars, you might want to create your own personalized toolbar to group all those commands in one easy-to-access place. To do so:

1. Click the Toolbars tab.

2. Click New.

3. In the New Toolbar dialog box that appears, enter the name of your new toolbar and click OK.

4. A new toolbar with that name appears in the Toolbars menu on the left. You can now select and modify it using the methods I've just discussed, just like the pre-existing toolbars.

There are four more toolbar settings you can change by selecting the Options tab (see Figure 21.6).

Your choices on this tab are:

- *Large Icons.* Makes the icons larger and easier to see. This is especially useful if you're using a high screen resolution of 1024 × 278 or finer; because icons are made up of a fixed number of pixels and the pixels are smaller at higher screen resolutions, the icons shrink as the resolution increases.

- *Show ScreenTips on Toolbars.* Activates a small label when pointing to the mouse pointer at a command button or control. In previous versions this was called ToolTips.

- *Show Shortcut Keys in ScreenTips.* Adds shortcut keys for the labels activated by the mouse pointer.

- *Menu Animations.* Provides you with four choices in the drop-down list: if you choose Unfold, menus seem to open up from the upper-left hand corner; if you choose Slide, they seem to appear on the screen like a panel sliding down from above; if you choose Random, you get a mixture of both unfold and slide animations. If you stay with the default None, menus just seem to appear out of nowhere.

FIG. 21.6

The Options tab lets you put the finishing touches on your new, improved toolbars.

Exploring PowerPoint 97 Options

In addition to allowing you to edit toolbars, PowerPoint provides many more options you can tweak. Most of these are found by choosing Tools, Options, which brings up the Options dialog box shown in Figure 21.7.

FIG. 21.7
The Options dialog box includes many different options that you can change. It defaults to the View tab.

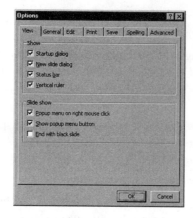

View Options

The tab the Options dialog box defaults to is the View tab. The Show area of the View tab offers you four choices:

- *Startup Dialog.* If this is selected, every time you open PowerPoint you'll see the dialog box that asks if you want to use the AutoContent Wizard, open an existing presentation, or open a blank presentation.

- *New Slide Dialog.* Select this one to make sure that each time you insert a new slide the New Slide dialog box appears, which offers you several different types of preformatted slides.

- *Status Bar.* Checking this box activates the bar at the bottom of the screen that displays information about the status of the program and the presentation you're currently working on.

- *Vertical Ruler.* If this is checked, the vertical ruler comes on every time you turn on the horizontal ruler.

In the Slide Show area at the bottom of the View tab, you have three options:

- *Popup Menu On Right Mouse Click.* Makes it possible to activate the pop-up menu while a slide show is in progress by right- clicking the mouse.

■ *Show Popup Menu Button.* Places a menu button in the lower-left corner of the screen during a slide show.

■ *End With Black Slide.* Ends every presentation by "fading to black" in the great Hollywood tradition.

General Options

The General Options tab (see Figure 21.8) contains miscellaneous options that you can customize.

FIG. 21.8

The General Options tab provides a grab-bag of customizable options that apparently just didn't fit under any of the more specific titles.

In the upper area, the redundantly named General Options area, there are four controls:

■ *Provide Feedback With Sound To Screen Elements.* In other words, this turns on or off all those little clicks, swooshes, and other sounds Office plays when certain events happen. If your computer doesn't have a sound card, you don't have to worry about this one at all.

■ *Recently Used File List.* Use the scroll box to determine how many recently opened files will be displayed under File, from zero to nine.

■ *Macro Virus Protection.* Brings up a warning message whenever a user opens a file that contains macros or customized toolbars, menus, or templates—all of which could are capable of carrying viruses. The message doesn't mean PowerPoint has detected a virus; it's just letting you know that you're treading on potentially dangerous ground.

■ *Link Sounds With File Size Greater Than.* If you include a sound file in your presentation larger than the size you enter in the box here, PowerPoint links to it instead of embedding it. This helps keep your presentation a manageable size.

Part
VII

Ch
21

In the lower area, you can change the name and initials Office has on record to identify you.

Save Options

In the Save tab (see Figure 21.9), you can customize how your computer saves your PowerPoint presentation.

FIG. 21.9

Decide how thoroughly and how often you want PowerPoint to save your precious presentation in the Save tab of the Options dialog box.

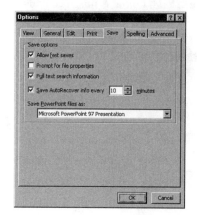

The tabs you see include the following:

- *Allow Fast Saves.* Saves only the changes in your presentation that have occurred since the last full save. Using fast saves can save time, but you'll still want to do a full save when you've finished working on your presentation; often it will take up less drive space.

- *Prompt For File Properties.* File properties are additional information about a file, including title, author, subject, and keywords, that can be saved along with the file. If this box is checked, PowerPoint prompts you for that additional information whenever you save a presentation for the first time.

- *Full Text Search Information.* If this is selected, PowerPoint stores full-text search information with your presentation—which means if you want to open it later and can't remember where you've filed it, all you'll need to remember is a keyword in any of the text in the presentation, and PowerPoint should be able to find it for you.

- *Save AutoRecover Info Every.* If you select this box, PowerPoint saves information every few minutes—how ever often you've entered in the box—that helps prevent the loss of data should your computer crash or the power go out.

CAUTION

AutoRecover is *not* an Auto Save feature. If you turn off your computer at the end of a session without saving your presentation, it won't be there when you turn the computer back on, no matter how often you've been saving AutoRecover information.

■ *Save PowerPoint Files As.* This defaults, naturally enough, to Microsoft PowerPoint 97 Presentation, but you might want to change it to, for example, Microsoft PowerPoint 4.0 Presentation if most of the computers in your company have not yet been upgraded to the new version.

Advanced Options

Exactly why Microsoft calls these "advanced" options is anyone's guess. In any event, what you get in this tab (see Figure 21.10) are two options concerning pictures and one option concerning where you save your work.

FIG. 21.10

Picture options and your default file-saving location are, for some reason, what Microsoft PowerPoint considers "advanced" options.

Under the Picture area, you can check Render 24-bit Bitmaps at Highest Quality, which ensures your pictures look great on the screen and take longer to appear, and under Export Pictures, you can decide whether you want them exported in a fashion Best for Printing or Best for On-Screen Viewing.

In the File Locations area, you can select the Default File Location to which your work will be saved.

Part

VII

Ch

21

Choosing Printing Options

It's happened to more than one person that the presentation which looked so good on the computer screen either looked lousy when printed, or didn't print at all. Some possible problems can be overcome by picking the right options in the Print tab of the Options dialog box (see Figure 21.11).

FIG. 21.11

PowerPoint provides several options you can choose from to ensure your presentation prints the way you want it to.

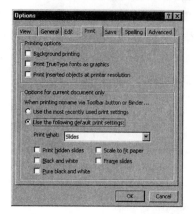

In the Printing tab there are two areas: General Printing Options, and options for the Current Document Only.

General Printing options are:

■ *Background Printing.* If this is selected, you can continue using PowerPoint even while it's busily printing presentations.

■ *Print TrueType Fonts As Graphics.* If this is available, you can choose to have your printer print TrueType fonts as graphic images rather than having the fonts downloaded to it. This could mean faster printing, although it typically also means lower quality, because many printers use special techniques to "smooth" fonts that aren't available if the fonts are printed as graphics. If this command is grayed out, then your selected printer doesn't support this option.

■ *Print Inserted Objects At Printer Resolution.* Just as it says, selecting this box causes objects inserted in your presentation to print at the printer's default resolution—which may be lower than the resolution of the objects themselves. Again, this might speed up printing while lowering quality. On the other hand, it can also ensure that the overall look of your objects will be similar, which gives your presentation a more integrated look than if different objects print at different resolutions.

Setting Options For Current Document Only allows you to fine-tune printing for each presentation. If you select Use The Most Recently Used Print Settings, then when you click the Print button, your presentation will print using whatever options or setting the last item to be printed used. If you choose Use the Following Default Print Settings, then whenever you print this document, it will use its own customized print settings.

The available choices are:

- *Print What.* You can choose to print one slide per page; handouts with two, three, or six slides per page; the Notes pages; or the Outline view of your presentation.
- *Print Hidden Slides.* Does just what it says.
- *Black and White.* Prints everything in the presentation in black and white, and colors in shades of gray—in other words, what you get from a black-and-white printer anyway.
- *Pure Black And White.* Prints even more black-and-white than it will if you select Black and White. This choice prints all text and lines in black and even adds black outlines to all the filled objects—which, no matter what color they are on your screen, will be filled with white. Only pictures are printed in shades of gray.
- *Scale To Fit Paper.* If you've designed 11 × 17-inch slides and you're printing it on 8 1/2 × 11-inch paper, you'll want this box selected. Selecting this option shrinks (or expands) slides to fit the paper they're being printed on.
- *Frame Slides.* Places a thin border around each slide.

 TIP Print your presentation in black and white, even if you have a color printer, if you want to see how it will look in photocopied handouts or simple overhead projections.

Using Text Editing Options

Two of the tabs in the Options dialog box relate to how PowerPoint deals with text: the Spelling and Edit tabs. Each provides several options that can help you make sure that PowerPoint "thinks" the way you do.

Edit Options

In the Edit tab (see Figure 21.12), there are six options you can change, beginning with four in the top area, labeled Text:

Part
VII

Ch
21

FIG. 21.12

Graphics are nice, but it's text that conveys most of your message, so you'll spend a lot of time working with it. Change these options to make that work go as smoothly as possible.

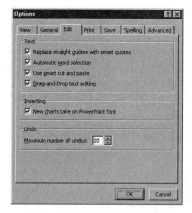

- *Replace Straight Quotes With Smart Quotes.* Smart quotes curl to embrace quotations; straight quotes just hang there. Smart quotes look better, although watch out for those occasions when the computer gets fooled and puts the quotes curling the wrong way—then they just look silly.

- *Automatic Word Selection.* If this is selected, PowerPoint automatically selects an entire word, and the space on either side of it, whenever you select part of the word.

 If your presentation requires you to change a lot of individual figures or uses a lot of names (prone to errors that require single-letter fixes), make sure automatic word selection is off. Nothing is more annoying than trying to select a single letter and having the computer insisting on selecting the entire word.

- *Use Smart Cut And Paste.* "Smart" cut and paste is smart because it knows enough to watch out for those extra spaces that are sometimes left behind when you cut text and delete them—and, better yet, knows enough to insert a space between words when you paste text in that doesn't come with its own space.

- *Drag-And-Drop Text Editing.* If this is selected, highlighted text can be copied and/or moved just by dragging it with the mouse. (You can copy it if you hold down Shift while you drag it; otherwise, it's pulled out of one place and placed in another.)

In the Inserting area, there's just one choice: New Charts Take On PowerPoint Font, which, if selected, makes any charts you insert into PowerPoint switch to 18-point Arial. If you prefer that the charts you insert use their original fonts, don't check this box.

There's also just one choice in the Undo area: Maximum Number Of Undos. Whatever number you put in the box is how many steps back you'll be able to undo your recent actions—all the way up to 150.

> **CAUTION**
>
> Don't set the maximum number of undos too high; it could slow down the program appreciably, because it has to "remember" everything you've done for so many steps. The default number of 20 is probably more than you'll ever need.

Spelling Options

Spell check is a wonderful invention for the many people who have never been entirely sure of all the exceptions to the "i-before-e-except-after-c" rule. In the Spell tab of the Options dialog box (see Figure 21.13), you can set five options that affect how spelling is checked in PowerPoint.

FIG. 21.13
You *don't* want a spelling mistake in your all-important business presentation; in this tab, you can decide how you want PowerPoint to help prevent that.

PowerPoint can check your spelling as you type, if you tell it to by checking the Spelling box. It will mark any errors—or words it doesn't recognize—by underlining them with a wavy red line (which you can right-click to get a list of suggestions of how the word should be spelled) unless you check the other box marked Hide Spelling Errors.

Besides checking your spelling as you type, PowerPoint can also be asked to check your spelling after a document is complete. If it finds a word it doesn't know, it stops and points it out to you—but it won't automatically make suggestions unless you click the Always box.

N O T E Don't worry about all those wavy red lines (assuming the words they're marking are actually correct, and just unrecognized by the spelling checker). They won't show up in your presentation or in any print-outs; they're strictly for your own information. ▪

Part
VII

Ch
21

Finally, to keep the spelling checker from stopping so frequently and asking about words that aren't in the dictionary because they're acronyms or contain numbers, check Words in UPPERCASE and Words with Numbers in the Ignore area.

Editing Templates

PowerPoint comes with many different templates which can serve as the basis of your presentation—presentations in which a great deal of the design work has already been done. As you work with PowerPoint more and more, however, you'll rely less on the pre-designed templates and more on your own experience.

If you create a presentation you think you'll be using over and over again, with modifications, then save it not only as a presentation, but also as a presentation template. Choose File, Save As, and you'll see the dialog box in Figure 21.14.

FIG. 21.14
Save your award-winning presentation as a Presentation template, and it will always be there for use again in the future.

Enter the name you want to give your presentation template in the File Name pull-down menu, and choose Presentation Templates from the Save as Type pull-down list. The file folder listed in the Save In pull-down list automatically changes to Templates, and you'll see a list of folders in the window. Select Presentations and then click the Save button. The next time you are looking for a template to use, the one you created will be listed with those provided with PowerPoint.

Using and Editing Color Palettes

No matter which tool you're using in PowerPoint, you'll frequently be given the opportunity to select a color for whatever element you're working with. You'll usually be given a small selection of colors to choose from, with a button to choose for More Colors. That, in turn, leads to the Color palette. If none of the preselected colors are right for you, then the

Color palette invites you to find the one that is by choosing from predefined colors or creating your own.

There are two types of Color palettes: the Standard one, seen in Figure 21.15, and the Custom one, seen in Figure 21.16.

FIG. 21.15
The Standard Color palette gives you many more colors to choose from than the small selection offered first when you start looking to change the color of a PowerPoint object.

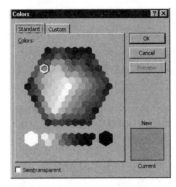

FIG. 21.16
The Custom palette offers you all the colors your computer is capable of displaying.

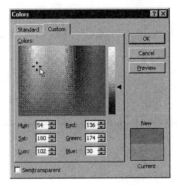

In the Standard Colors palette, you select a color or a shade of gray by moving the small white hexagonal marker around the hexagonal display of colors using the mouse or cursor controls. In the New/Current box at right, you can contrast the color you're choosing with the current color of the object.

If you check the Semitransparent box in the bottom-left corner of either palette, the color you've chosen is displayed partially transparent, which means it will allow whatever background color is beneath it to partially show through. This effect isn't displayed in the New/Current box, but you can see how it will look in your selected object by clicking Preview.

If the colors in the Standard palette aren't enough, you can click the Custom tab. Now, instead of many pre-defined colors, you can choose from any color your computer can display by moving the crosshairs around the Colors palette, using the mouse, and adjusting the light/dark slider by moving the triangle up or down it.

The other option—which is sometimes helpful if you're trying to exactly match another color—is to type in values in the Hue, Sat, and Lum or Red, Green, and Blue boxes. These are two different ways of identifying colors. Hue is the color itself; Sat (for Saturation) is the color's intensity—the higher the number, the more intense the color (for example, a high saturation would make red look blood-red, while a low saturation would make it look pale pink)—and Lum (for Luminance) is how bright or dark the color is. The Red, Green, and Blue values, meanwhile, are based on the fact that all colors of light can be created by mixing Red, Green, and Blue in various amounts.

The New color you've selected is contrasted with the Current color in a box at the right, and again, you can choose to make the color Semitransparent.

With all of the colors your computer is capable of displaying at your disposal, you're sure to find exactly the right color that your presentation needs. ●

CHAPTER 22

Automating Your Work with Macros

by Brian Reilly

The Visual Basic for Applications (VBA) language has been incorporated into PowerPoint 97. With this language, PowerPoint 97 gives you the ability to write your own macros to perform time-consuming, repetitive tasks with just the click of a button. If you're an advanced user, you can also develop new solutions either entirely in PowerPoint or by integrating the solution across PowerPoint, Excel, Word, or Access.

With macros, you can not only automate repetitive tasks, but you can also program decision-making within the program, based on additional input from whoever is using it in a given situation—for example, a salesperson making a presentation. If you've already written macros in Excel or Word, you'll find PowerPoint's macro language very exciting. And even if you've never written a piece of macro code before, PowerPoint's macros can increase your productivity in a variety of ways. Whether you're experienced at creating macros or not, this chapter helps you understand PowerPoint's macro environment, and shows you how to plan and create your own macros. ■

Write macros that automate tedious repetitive tasks

The macro recorder can record your actions and play them back for you at the touch of a key, so you don't need to be nervous about writing code. It writes the code for you as you go.

Modify code written by the macro recorder to perform decision making for you

As powerful as the macro recorder is, there are many things it just cannot or does not record.

Write advanced code that will let you perform some advanced operations with only a few lines of code

Code shortcuts can accomplish tasks by looping back through the same instructions until finished.

Visualize the Object Model

The Object Model is the hierarchy of the PowerPoint code. Every object has its place in the model and a relationship to other objects. The Object Model is the underlying structure of PowerPoint commands.

What is a Macro?

If you're new to macros, the first order of business is to understand just what a macro is. In simple terms, a *macro* is a series of commands that are all executed in sequence. For example, you might describe the series of steps associated with making a cup of instant coffee as the following:

1. Go into the kitchen.
2. Find the tea kettle.
3. Add water to the tea kettle.
4. Put the tea kettle on the burner.
5. Turn on the burner (the one with the tea kettle on it).
6. Wait until the water in the tea kettle boils.
7. Turn off the burner.
8. Add a teaspoonful of instant coffee to an empty coffee cup.
9. Pour the boiling water into the coffee cup.
10. Add milk or cream and sugar, if desired.

If you had a macro that could do this chore for you, you could perform all 10 steps with one command. The macro is the equivalent of saying to one's spouse, "Darling, please make me a cup of coffee."

The coffee example may seem simplistic, but it has all the necessary comparisons to a macro. It has objects (tea kettle, water, coffee cup, burner, instant coffee, milk, sugar). It has methods (boil, turn on/turn off the burner, add). It has properties (empty). It has sequence. It even has decision-making (if).

There are many similar tasks in PowerPoint that might be automated in this fashion. Suppose, for example, you want to be able to turn all your drawing toolbars on or off in just one step. Your steps might be:

1. Turn on the Drawing toolbar.
2. Turn on the Picture toolbar.
3. Turn on the WordArt toolbar.
4. Turn off all other toolbars.

Or you might want to print several presentations overnight while you're in bed, and you don't want to get out of bed repeatedly to issue the File, Print command for each new copy of the file. Here, the steps would be:

1. Print the first file in this directory.
2. Print each successive file in this directory.
3. When you have finished the last file in this directory, stop.

Both of these examples have several things in common. They are repetitive tasks and they both can be executed from the keyboard. But in the first example, you have to use several keystrokes, and in the second example, you have to wait for the prior command to finish executing before the next command can be given.

Such tasks can be automated with macros, which can save you a great amount of time, especially if you frequently perform these tasks. In the second case, the printing of several long presentations to a color printer may take quite a few hours. You could not, until now, issue the command to print the second presentation until the first presentation was finished printing. Now with one keystroke, you can print them all at once, literally in your sleep.

Automating Repetitive Tasks with a Macro

What tasks can be automated? Virtually anything that can be created on the keyboard can be automated with a macro. There are two caveats here:

- The macro recorder only records what is going on in PowerPoint. If you switch to Excel during the recording of a macro, the recorder does not record the process in Excel. There are ways to activate other programs like Excel, but that has to be performed with specifically written code and not through the macro recorder.

- Some things that may be recorded may not be performed often enough to warrant the time involved in creating a macro. You need to decide if the time involved to automate a simple task outweighs the amount of time that may be necessary to do it manually whenever that situation arises.

Certainly, if you find yourself doing a specific task frequently, then you should consider automating the task with a macro. When the task is very time-consuming and subject to possible keyboard error, you should definitely consider creating a macro. If it takes substantial time to execute sequential commands before you get access back to your computer—as in the printing of the series of files to a color printer—you should definitely consider automating the process with a macro, because you will be able to do something else while the computer is doing all the work.

There are two ways to build macros. You can create them by:

■ Recording steps, saving the recording, then telling PowerPoint to play them back whenever you need to

■ Actually scripting the macro's code

Using the Macro Recorder

PowerPoint's macro recorder is just like a good assistant who writes down exactly what you did and can reproduce those actions any time you tell him to. Assume you have added the text to a presentation and want to start adding graphics to the pages, but you first want to have the Drawing, Picture, and WordArt toolbars on-screen. Instead of opening each of the toolbars individually (then closing them when you're finished, then re-opening them later), you can record a macro to display the toolbars all in one step. Here's how to record this macro:

1. Choose Tools, Macro, Record New Macro.

2. The Record Macro dialog box appears, as shown in Figure 22.1. This dialog box gives you three options:

   • A chance to name the macro. Descriptive names can help, but PowerPoint also lists a default name such as Macro1 if you don't choose a name of your own. In this case, name your macro **Show_Graphics_Toolbars**.

   • A file location to store the macro. The active file is the default.

   • A text description to help you remember what you are doing in this particular macro; this is for documentation purposes only and has no effect on the macro. The default is the current user name and the current date. A good documentation practice is to type a description of what the macro does—for example, **Shows the Drawing toolbars**.

After filling in the dialog box in step 2, make sure that the toolbars you are trying to open through the macro are not already open, and choose OK to start recording the steps of the macro. Then just perform the operation that you want to record. In this case, the operation is displaying three toolbars. First, choose View, Toolbars and highlight the Drawing Toolbar option, and select it by clicking the mouse. The Drawing toolbar should appear on-screen. Remember that the macro records whatever you do. If you make a mistake, fix it, and then go on, the macro thinks that all of this was intentional and records it. So it's a good idea to rehearse the steps you plan to put in the macro, and perhaps even write them down so you don't trip up.

3. Display the Picture toolbar by choosing View, Toolbars. Then highlight the Picture option and select it by clicking the mouse.

4. Display the WordArt toolbar by choosing View, Toolbars, then highlight the WordArt option, and select it by clicking the mouse.

5. Now that you have finished recording the steps to your macro, click the Stop Recording button. (This icon appeared automatically on the screen when you clicked the OK button to start the recorder.)

FIG. 22.1

Recording macros is like recording on a VCR.

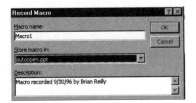

Now you are ready to test that macro. But because you have already displayed the toolbars, let's record a second macro to hide them. This new macro is handy when you no longer need the toolbars on-screen and want to hide them quickly.

Repeat the preceding steps and name the macro **Hide_Graphics Toolbars**. Note that this time, you are deselecting each of the toolbars.

You can now test the first macro, which displays the toolbars. To do this:

1. Choose Tools, Macro, Macros or press Alt+F8. The Macro dialog box appears, as shown in Figure 22.2. The dialog box contains a list of available macros.

2. Select Show_Graphics_Toolbars, then click Run. The macro runs, and the three graphics toolbars should appear on your screen.

To hide the toolbars, just repeat the preceding steps and choose the Hide_Graphics_Toolbars macro. The macro should run, and the three toolbars should disappear.

FIG. 22.2
The Macro dialog box lists all available macros.

> **N O T E** You save macros in your presentation files. This can be beneficial; if you are sharing a file with someone else, you can share macros as well. Remember, however, that some macros can actually cause trouble.

Following the creation of the Word Concept virus that was carried in an AutoOpen macro (one that opens automatically when a Word document is opened), Microsoft and its consumers became very wary of opening files from unknown sources because the files might contain macros which in turn may contain viruses. New with Office 97 is a warning box that appears prior to opening any file that contains a macro. The new warning box permits you to open the file with macros enabled or disabled, or not to open the file at all. Figure 22.3 shows the dialog box. If you prefer, you can disable this warning altogether.

While this warning may be irritating to some computer users, it's reassuring to those whose systems have been infected by a virus. If you are receiving files from any outside sources, even your co-workers on a network, it might be in your best interest to leave the warning on. However, the warning doesn't necessarily mean that a virus is present, and it does not clean a virus if one exists. It's just a device to allow you to disable macros if you want. ▪

FIG. 22.3
Office 97 alerts you when you open a file that contains a macro, because the macro may carry a virus.

The Structure of a Macro

Now that you've created and run a simple macro, it's a good time to take a look inside it to see what makes the macro work. The macro recorder translated your actions into VBA code and recorded that code. While VBA code looks somewhat like English, as with any computer code there are some very specific syntax issues that are necessary to address for the code to run without error. Let's look at the code, then explore the structure of the macro. To view the code in the Show_Graphics_Toolbars macro, take the following steps:

1. Choose Tools, Macro, Macros.
2. Select Show_Graphics_Toolbars, then choose Edit. You see a window that looks similar to Figure 22.4. For the time being, let's focus only on the macro's code:

```
Sub Show_Graphics_Toolbars()
'
' This macro displays the Drawing, Picture, and WordArt toolbars.
'
Application.CommandBars("Picture").Visible = True

Application.CommandBars("Drawing").Visible = True
Application.CommandBars("WordArt").Visible = True
Application.CommandBars("Formatting").Visible = False

End Sub
```

FIG. 22.4

The code that the macro recorder generated for the Show_Graphics_Toolbars macro.

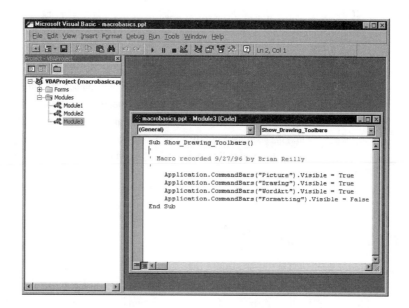

What is the Code?

The code is everything that appears between the words Sub and End sub. It includes three critical elements:

■ The first line which names the macro command. This is defined by the words Sub Command Name(). Note that the command name is restricted to just one word. The use of _ is actually a character just like any typed character and is used for making the command names easier to read.

From the code's perspective, it would also be acceptable to name the command `Sub ShowGraphicsToolbars()`. Uppercase or lowercase is also irrelevant to command names; uppercase letters are used only to make the code easier to read later. The command must always be ended by parentheses, which tell the program that this is a command name line and not part of the commands to execute.

■ The group of commands which perform the task you want the macro to accomplish. These are the lines sandwiched between the first and the last lines of the macro. In the example, the first line of code to execute is `Application.CommandBars("Picture"). Visible=True`. The Application.CommandBars tells the application (PowerPoint) to do something with the CommandBars, which is the program's name for the toolbars. `("Picture")` isolates the Drawing toolbar. `.Visible = True` tells the program to set the property of that specific toolbar to be visible as opposed to not visible. Note that in the last line of the group, the Formatting toolbar had been visible and was turned to not visible when you recorded the macro.

■ The last line, which tells the macro to stop working. This is defined by the words `End Sub()`.

N O T E There can be a fourth part of a macro that is actually not code. It serves purely to document what is happening in the macro so that you can remember what you were trying to accomplish. It is always preceded by an apostrophe because any line of code preceded by an apostrophe is ignored by the program and is for human readership only. If you have ever changed a line in a file such as your AUTOEXEC.BAT file, you may have "remarked" out a line with an apostrophe or *REM* (remark). This remark tells the code to ignore this line because it does not contain code to execute. ■

The Visual Basic Editor

Visual Basic 5.0 is the language used in Office 97 to write macros. It exists in a different environment than it did in previous versions of Visual Basic for Applications (VBA). The program that controls VBA code in PowerPoint, as well as the other Office applications, is the Visual Basic Editor (VBE).

The VBE is a separate program that works with all the programs that support VBA. The VBE exists separately from the main application such as PowerPoint. However, the code is kept in Project folders that are stored in specific presentations. In a sense, the VBE is similar to Microsoft Graph in that Graph creates and edits the datasheet and chart, but the chart and datasheet are stored inside of PowerPoint.

The *Project folder* is the container document for all elements of a specific project, whether it be one simple macro or a complex set of commands that develop an Office solution across several Office applications. See Chapter 25 for some examples of more complex solutions.

Several kinds of different elements can be contained in the Project folder:

- A number of modules where the code for various macros is stored.

- UserForms, which are custom-designed dialog boxes to get information from the user to use in the program. Actually, all modules are stored in a subfolder named Modules; UserForms are stored in a subfolder called Forms.

Figure 22.5 shows the VBE open and the module with the code to show/hide the Drawing toolbars open.

FIG. 22.5

All modules and UserForms are contained in the VBAProject folder.

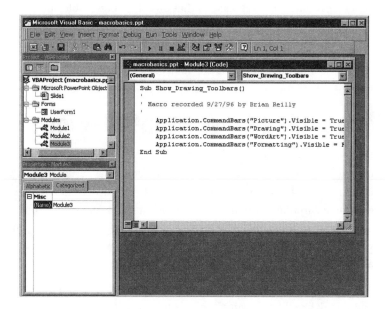

While you looked at the VBE and wrote code in the macros to show/hide Drawing toolbars, there is another way to view the Project folder and all its components. To open the VBE:

1. Open the presentation for which you want to view the Project folder, if it is not already open.

2. Choose Tools, Macros, Visual Basic Editor or press Alt+F11.

When you open the VBE, you are presented with three potential separate elements:

- The Project Explorer, which is docked to the VBE frame
- The Property window for Project Explorer
- A separate window for the editor

The *Project Explorer* is just like the Explorer program for showing folders and files in a tree format. You can click the + or - check boxes to expand or collapse any folder. The Project Explorer displays the Project files for any open file that has a Project file. Advanced users can use this excellent tool to copy macros from one project to another.

The *Property window* contains information about an object. For example, an object may be visible or not. It will have other characteristics depending on the object, such as a font will have a font name, font size, and font color. The information about a specific object is contained here, and if the property of that object is changeable, it can be changed here.

The third window is where one records or writes the specific code associated with a macro. You may know the term *method*; a method is the code that is assigned to an object that knows how to manipulate the object's data.

Understanding PowerPoint Macros

While using the macro recorder is a good way to record specific actions, there are many occasions when you will have to modify the code that is recorded. A good example of this is in the Show_Drawing_Toolbars macro—the recorder did not take into account the existing environment when recording the changes you wanted to make. You may need to go in and manually change the recorded code to do exactly what you want. And if you want to use decision-making in the code or if you want to activate another application such as Word or Excel, you will certainly have to write some of the code yourself.

The macros for showing and hiding toolbars really should reference all the toolbars, and might look like the following:

```
Sub Show_All_Toolbars()
'
' Displays all non-custom and one custom toolbars in PowerPoint 97
'
    Application.CommandBars("Standard").Visible = True
    Application.CommandBars("Formatting").Visible = True
    Application.CommandBars("Animation Effects").Visible = True
    Application.CommandBars("Common Tasks").Visible = True
    Application.CommandBars("Control Toolbox").Visible = True
    Application.CommandBars("Drawing").Visible = True
    Application.CommandBars("Picture").Visible = True
    Application.CommandBars("Reviewing").Visible = True
```

```
        Application.CommandBars("Visual Basic").Visible = True
        Application.CommandBars("Web").Visible = True
        Application.CommandBars("WordArt").Visible = True
    End Sub
```

To be able to change the code, you need to examine the structure of the VBA Project, which is the first main level of creating macros in the VBE.

Assigning Macro Code to Objects and Toolbars

Now that you have learned how to record simple macros and modify them in the VBE, you can learn about the three different ways to run a macro as shown in Table 22.1. You can use any or all of the following methods. Note the differences between executing a macro while in Slide Edit and Slide Show modes.

Table 22.1 Assigning Macros to Objects in PowerPoint

How to Run the Macro	Works in These Modes	Comments
From the menu	Edit, Outline, Notes, Slide Master, Slide Sorter.	You may have to reference the specific page with a line such as **With Activeslide**.
From a toolbar	Edit, Outline, Notes, Slide Master, Slide Sorter. Could add custom toolbar buttons to the Web toolbar that is available under certain Slide Show view options.	
From an object on the page	Only in Slide Show view.	

Let's take each of these options separately and define the steps. You've already learned how to run a macro using the menu (Tools, Macro, Macros). Let's now learn how to assign a specific macro to a toolbar button. To do this, you need to have created a specific button on either a custom toolbar or added one to an existing toolbar. To create a new toolbar button and assign a macro command to it, perform the following steps:

1. Open the presentation that contains the macro you want to add to the toolbar, if it is not already open.

2. Choose Tools, Customize.

3. Select the Toolbars tab from the dialog box and click New.

4. Name the new toolbar and click OK.

5. Click the Commands tab in the dialog box, and select Macros from the Categories window.

6. From the Commands window, drag the macro you want to use to the new toolbar.

7. Click Close.

Assigning a macro command to a toolbar button permits you to execute the code associated with that macro any time you click that toolbar button.

In the third case, attaching macro commands to page objects in Slide Show view permits you to perform a variety of tasks during a slide show. For example, you can launch a data collection session from a user during a self-running slide show at a trade show, or even collect data from a viewer of your Web page if you've chosen to use PowerPoint 97 to create your Web page. Or, you can use it to attach commands to simple navigation buttons such as the forward arrow for the next page and the backwards arrow to return to the most recent page.

To attach a macro command to any object on a page, choose Slide Show, Action Settings to tell it to launch a macro either when the object is clicked or when the mouse passes over the object. The following steps show specifically how to assign a macro to an object on the page:

1. Select the object you want to assign the macro to.

2. Choose Slide Show, Action Settings.

3. From the Action Settings dialog box that is presented, choose Mouse Click or Mouse Over to register the settings based on the action you want to set.

4. Click the Run Macro button and choose the macro to assign from the now available pull-down list.

5. Click OK to finish.

These steps enable you to assign a macro command so that you can execute macros when you need to.

TROUBLESHOOTING

Why doesn't my macro work now? Sometimes when you record or even write a macro, the code tests fine but it doesn't work later. The most frequent cause of this is that the macro does not run from the same location you originally tested from.

For example, Let's say you have a slide with a picture it in the top-left corner and the macro is programmed to select that picture and move it to a new location. If you run that macro from a page with no picture, you receive an error message. Placing the line of code `On Error Resume Next` in the macro tells the macro to skip over errors and continue to execute. But use this line of code with caution. It may cause the macro to ignore other errors that you may not want to ignore.

Writing Your Own Code

Now that you know about the macro recorder and the VBE, it is time to write some of your own code that cannot be written solely with the macro recorder. You may encounter several situations when you need to write your own code. Here are two examples:

- When you don't know how many times you need to perform an operation. For example, when printing of a series of files, you will likely have a varying number of files from day to day, and they will likely have different names from day to day. In a case like this, it would be handy to be able to tell the program to print all the files in the specific directory and to stop when it has printed them all.

- When you have to decide what action to take based on a condition that you cannot predict. For example, you might not be able to make a decision about what presentation design to apply until you know whether a financial statement shows a profit or a loss.

These are only two examples of how writing your own code can make the macros you write much more powerful than those written solely with the macro recorder. Let's take a look at these two examples and how each situation can be structured.

One of the first principles of writing code is to write short, easy-to-understand sets of commands. These commands can then be used over and over again by other macros that combine these commands together in order to execute what you are after.

As a good example of this, you should think of the task of printing all files in a given directory as two different tasks. The first task is to get a list of all the presentations in a directory. The second task is to print each of those presentations sequentially. If you create two macros, one for each task, you could then reuse the first macro, getting a list of all files in a specific directory, and reuse that again later if you wanted to show each of these files in sequence in a screen show instead of printing them. Then you would only have to write the code to show each file and let the new macro to show these files *call* the first macro to repeat the Get All Files list.

Calling a macro from another macro runs the called macro. This is an excellent technique for reusing code in many places. To place a call to a macro from another macro, just type the name of the macro to run without the Sub or ().

For Each...Next

Let's write the code to print all the files in a given directory. Because you have defined this procedure as having two steps, you can create two separate macros—one for the first step and one for the second:

1. List all the files in a specific directory.
2. Print each of those files.

To create the first macro, the one that lists the files in the correct directory, do the following:

1. Switch to the VBE by choosing Tools, Macro, Visual Basic Editor (or press Alt+F11).
2. Choose Insert, Module to get a blank module.
3. Type **Sub Print_All_Files( )** and press Enter. Notice that the program automatically adds End Sub for you.
4. Type the following lines of code:

```
Sub Choose_Files()

Set fs = Application.FileSearch
With fs

'    Substitute your target directory here
    .LookIn = "C:\My Documents"
    .FileName = "*.ppt"
    If .Execute(SortBy:=msoSortByFileName, SortOrder:=msoSortOrderAscending)
> 0 Then
        MsgBox .FoundFiles.Count & " files(0s) found."

'   Open and print each presentation found there
        For i = 1 To .FoundFiles.Count
            Presentations.Open FileName:=.FoundFiles.Item(i),
ReadOnly:=msoFalse

'   Here's where we call the other macro:
            Print_Presentation
        Next i
    Else
        MsgBox "No files found."
    End If
```

```
    End With

    End Sub
```

 TIP I added the MsgBox line to provide feedback that this is performing the correct task. It is a useful technique that you can use to give yourself feedback while you are testing the code that ensures you are indeed getting the correct value to that point. You can delete it after the code is debugged and running correctly.

The important thing to realize here is that the For Each...Next command lets you get all instances of a circumstance when you don't know how many times that circumstance might occur. When the command finds no more values, it stops looping and proceeds with the next line of code.

For the second macro—the one to print the active file—you can just turn on the macro recorder and record your actions as you print the current file using the print settings you'd like to use for your files. You should get something like this depending on the choices you make in the Print dialog box:

```
    Sub Print_Presentation()
    '
    ' Macro recorded 9/29/96 by Brian Reilly
    '
        With ActivePresentation.PrintOptions
            .RangeType = ppPrintAll
            .NumberOfCopies = 1
            .Collate = msoFalse
            .OutputType = ppPrintOutputSlides
            .PrintHiddenSlides = msoTrue
            .PrintColorType = ppPrintBlackAndWhite
            .FitToPage = msoTrue
            .FrameSlides = msoFalse
            ' Substitute the name of your printer or remove this line to use the
    default printer
            .ActivePrinter = "HP LaserJet 4L"
        End With
        ActivePresentation.PrintOut

    End Sub
```

To test the two new macros, choose Tools, Macro, Macros or press Alt+F8. Pick Choose_Files and click OK. Your two new macros will do all the work of locating, opening and printing every file in the directory you entered.

Note that there are always several ways to write the code to perform the same task. Many programmers try to write the shortest amount of code possible because the macro will run somewhat faster. Others try to spend the least amount of time writing the code and let the machine take a few more seconds to execute it. It is all a matter of personal style, and as you gain experience in writing code in VBA and especially in PowerPoint, you will undoubtedly find faster ways to do things. The most important thing is to get started and write some code that helps make you more productive.

If Then...Else

The command to judge a conditional statement is extremely powerful. It can cycle through many possibilities for you and automatically execute different commands depending on the condition that is met. The following example changes the design template based on whether a range in the Excel sheet shows a profit or loss for the current period. While this is a very simple example, you can easily adapt it to change the design template for each division if you have some divisions in the black and some in the red.

The presentation will have been created with links to the spreadsheet range. The If statement is used to define whether to apply an upbeat background for a profitable period or a downbeat background for an unprofitable period.

Again, because the decision is a choice of two potential outcomes, you should create three macros:

- One to apply the upbeat design scheme
- One to apply the downbeat design scheme
- The master macro to decide what the outcome is and then call the appropriate macro to apply the correct scheme

The two following macros are very simple; they apply either template to the active presentation. Both have been created as new templates and saved as UPBEAT.POT and DOWNBEAT.POT, respectively.

```
Sub Apply_Upbeat_Design()

    ActivePresentation.ApplyTemplate
➥FileName:="C:\Office97\Templates\Presentation Designs\Upbeat.POT"
End Sub


Sub Apply_Downbeat_Design()

    ActivePresentation.ApplyTemplate
➥FileName:="C:\Office97\Templates\Presentation Designs\Downbeat.POT"
End Sub
```

The controlling macro is a bit more complicated because it needs to open a specific spreadsheet in Excel and check the value of the range named Profit_Loss to determine if that value is greater than zero (profit) or less than or equal to zero (loss). Refer to the Excel application as an object and therefore declare the variable name you will assign to the Excel application. In this case, the variable name is declared in the first line of the module so it is available to any macro that runs within this module. Then, open the Excel application and the specific file. Check the value of the range Profit_Loss. Based on the returned value, you can choose which design to apply. The code that does this is as follows:

```
Dim appxl as Object
Sub Open_Excel_Profit_Loss_file()
Set appxl = CreateObject("Excel.Application.8")   '\sets the variable
                                                  '\name to the application
Appxl.Visible = False                             '\operates invisibly
            '\next line opens the file
Appxl.Workbooks.Open "c:\Excelfiles\Profit_Loss_file.xls"
        '/checks to see if value is profit
If appxl.Range("Profit_Loss").Value > 0 Then
        '\run the Apply_Upbeat_Design macro
Apply_Upbeat_Design
ElseIf appxl.Range("Profit_Loss").Value <= Then
Apply_Downbeat_Design
'\must end all If statements with End If
End If
        '\closes Excel and does not save since file is unchanged
Appxl.Quit
End Sub
```

This application runs entirely inside of PowerPoint. It references the outside program—Excel—opens that program with the command from PowerPoint, checks the value in the Excel file, and returns that value to PowerPoint so that the PowerPoint macro can decide what option to execute. There is no need in this case to operate a macro in Excel. Similar examples can be executed with Word and Access. You can get values from any of these programs, and copy to or from any of these programs all from within PowerPoint.

Exploring the PowerPoint Object Model

In the first macro written in this chapter, Show_Drawing_Toolbars(), there are two lines that show the hierarchy of the objects relevant to that macro:

```
Application.CommandBars("Drawing").Visible = True
    Application.CommandBars("Formatting").Visible = False
```

In these particular lines, four levels of this hierarchy are shown. This hierarchy is known as the Object Model. The *Object Model* is a visualization of how every object in PowerPoint relates or does not relate to another object. By accessing the correct object through the commands, you can manipulate it with code manually.

While the Object Model may look difficult to understand at first, it is really the easiest way to conceptualize PowerPoint code. Figure 22.6 shows the relationship between the objects in the top two levels of the model. In this example, the top level is the Application—Power-Point. The next level down is Presentations (if it is a collection of Presentations) or Presentation (if it is a single presentation you are referring to). Figure 22.7 repeats the objects in the Presentation level and shows the relationship to one type of object—Shapes, the next level down.

FIG. 22.6

This figure shows the top two levels of the Object Model for PowerPoint 97.

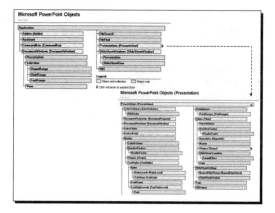

FIG. 22.7

The second and third levels of the Object Model are continued in this figure.

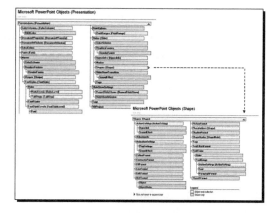

To refer to an object such as a shape and refer to its fill property, you would first have to reference the Application, then the Presentation, then the shape, then the fill property. In code it might look like the following:

```
'This opens the presentation
Presentations.Open FileName:="D:\My Documents\Model.ppt", ReadOnly:=msoFalse
'This selects the third page in the active presentation which is Model.ppt
    ActiveWindow.View.GotoSlide Index:=3
'this actually uses the presentation in the Active Window and selects the
'Rectangle #8 on that page
```

```
ActiveWindow.Selection.SlideRange.Shapes("Rectangle 8").Select
' Then it sets the properties for that shape
    With ActiveWindow.Selection.ShapeRange
'the Fill is visible for this particular shape
        .Fill.Visible = msoTrue
'the fill is a solid fill instead of a patterned or shaded fill
        .Fill.Solid
'it sets the color property in RGB colors
        .Fill.ForeColor.RGB = RGB(0, 0, 255)
'the End With means you stop referring to this particular shape.
    End With
```

You can access the Object Model while in the VBE by pressing the F2 key. When you do this, you see something similar to Figure 22.8. You can select an object in the left-hand pane of the window and see all the possible objects available to that object. To use the toolbars example, follow these steps:

1. If you are not already in the VBE, press Alt+F11.

2. Press the F2 key to bring up the Object Browser. You can use the Object Browser to find the potential relationships from any object.

3. From the choices in the scroll bar on the screen, click CommandBar.

4. If you scroll the Members of Command Bar window downward, you see the property value of Visible.

FIG. 22.8
The Object Model is available by pressing the F2 key.

TIP Whether you are an advanced code writer or a new code writer, I advise you to pick several commands you may understand—such as File, Save—and explore the Object Browser to get a better feel for it. It will be time well spent when you need to troubleshoot some errors in the code you write.

CHAPTER 23

Linking to Other Applications

by Brian Reilly

PowerPoint 97 has added a host of new linking opportunities to this version which makes it very easy for you to link information across documents, even if you don't know how to program. As in earlier releases of PowerPoint, PowerPoint 97 supports Object Linking and Embedding (OLE), and is enhanced to include the capability to link to graphics files. More importantly, PowerPoint 97 adds the capability to create HTML (Hypertext Markup Language) links to presentation objects, which enable you to quickly make non-sequential jumps to other slides, presentations, documents, and even to other Web sites from your own home page. ■

Exploit links to and from many other applications

Linking to data in other applications eliminates the need for retyping or updating changes twice.

Create links to Word and Excel

Word makes great tables and terrific outlines; Excel lets you summarize numbers easily. Using both can make you more productive.

Understanding Links

The PowerPoint links you can create are two-directional in some cases and one-directional in other cases. Figure 23.1 shows a schematic flow of a partial list of the links that are available from the perspective of a PowerPoint presentation. Each of the links is explained in more detail later in this chapter and in other chapters.

The links shown in Figure 23.1 enable you to easily accomplish a wide variety of tasks (see Table 23.1).

FIG. 23.1
Ways to use linking to other applications are now easy and diverse in PowerPoint 97.

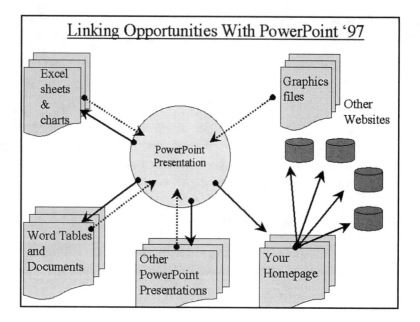

Linking Opportunities With PowerPoint '97

Table 23.1   Links and Potential Uses

Type of Link	OLE or HTML	Implications	Potential Uses
Excel Sheets and Charts	OLE HTML	Links work to and from Excel sheets and charts. You can link data in Excel sheets that will change, and it automatically updates, with no re-keying in PowerPoint.	When numbers are likely to change and affect a lot of other numbers and charts. Also use to jump to back up data or to dynamically change assumptions and instantly update all calculations during a presentation.

Type of Link	OLE or HTML	Implications	Potential Uses
Word Tables and Documents	OLE HTML	Links work to and from Word.	Let your presenters prepare their text in Word, which they may be more familiar with, and then link their text to a presentation. When they change the text in Word, it updates the presentation. Also, embed PowerPoint presentations in Word documents that you send electronically to other users.
Other PowerPoint	OLE HTML	Jump automatically to any slide in any presentation at the click of the mouse.	Jump to backup documentation when needed. Skip the jump when not needed.
Your home page	HTML	Create links from data files to a PowerPoint presentation and link that PowerPoint presentation to your home page for periodic updates.	Automate the updating of home page content.
To other Web sites	HTML	Add HTML links easily to other Web sites.	This adds value to your home page and may be synergistic with related pages and subject matter.

Part **VII**

Ch **23**

Given all the linking options and the differences between OLE and HTML links, the following sections give a rather simplistic explanation of how each type of link works so that it is easier for you to plan for and exploit their uses. You then learn some of the benefits and drawbacks of each kind of link and when you might want to use or avoid it. This is truly a case of judgment, and the use or lack of use of these two types of links have benefits and drawbacks in some situations.

Using Object Linking and Embedding

OLE, short for *Object Linking and Embedding*, might be more appropriately named Object Linking *or* Embedding. The simplest explanation for what can be done with the concept of OLE is right in the Word Help file written by Microsoft:

"You can link or embed all or part of an existing file created in an Office application or in any other application that supports linking and embedding. You can also create a new object and then link or embed it. If the file you want to use was created in an application that does not support linking and embedding, you can still copy and paste information from the file, but you may not be able to link or embed from it.

The main differences between linking and embedding are where the data is stored and how it is updated after you place it in your file.

When you *link*, information gets updated if you modify the source file. Linked data is stored in the source file; the file into which you place the data stores only the location of the source and displays a representation of the linked data.

When you *embed*, information does not change if you modify the source file. Embedded objects become part of the container file itself. Double-clicking an object after you embed it opens the object in the source application. You can then edit it in place, and the original object in the source application remains unchanged."

The time to link is when the source document will change, and these changes need to be reflected in the target—in this case, a PowerPoint presentation. The time to embed is when you want to edit the pasted document without changing the original source document. In either case, with OLE, you get to edit the document in question in the original source application.

With an embedded document, the document is entirely inside the PowerPoint presentation and moves with the presentation wherever it goes. With linked documents, the object in the PowerPoint presentation contains a pointer to the location of the source document. Moving files across drives or computers can sometimes lose the links; the pointer may not be able to find the source document because it is no longer there.

To see what happens with linking, look at an example of an Excel spreadsheet and chart where the chart is linked to a PowerPoint presentation. Figure 23.2 shows three things:

- A simple chart
- The data the chart is based on in an Excel worksheet
- The appropriate slide in PowerPoint

If your data comes from a spreadsheet (such as Excel) and is likely to change, you can save a tremendous amount of time by linking the chart or table in PowerPoint directly to the source spreadsheet.

Changing any number in Excel changes the chart in Excel, and because the chart is linked to the PowerPoint chart object (assuming the PowerPoint presentation is open), it is updated there as well. Figure 23.3 shows the change just made in Excel and reflected in the PowerPoint presentation.

FIG. 23.2
The original chart in Excel is copied and pasted into PowerPoint by choosing Edit, Paste Special, Link.

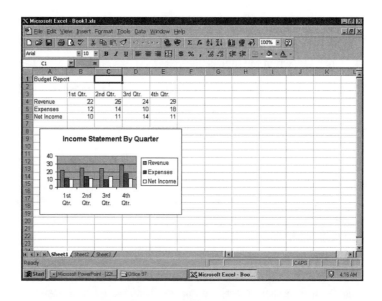

FIG. 23.3
The changes in the Excel sheet are updated in PowerPoint with no re-keying.

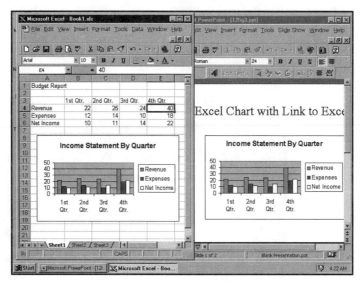

The following steps show how to copy a chart or table from Excel and use the Paste Special command in PowerPoint to create an OLE link:

1. Select the chart in Excel and choose Edit, Copy.

2. Switch to PowerPoint and select the correct page (it should not be a page that is formatted to contain a chart or table).

3. Choose Edit, Paste Special and select the Paste Link radio button. You see the choices of object types reduced automatically to the appropriate type of object.

4. Click OK when finished.

The same technique works for Excel charts, Excel ranges, Word tables, and even Word text and charts. If the two programs are *OLE compliant*—meaning they allow OLE links between them—then linking from a source document to a target document is this easy.

CAUTION

When you create an OLE link as shown in the preceding steps, you are placing a tag in the target document that shows a picture of what that object really is in the source document. Therefore, the PowerPoint presentation shows the picture of the object exactly as it appears in the source. You may want to change some of the formatting (such as colors, fonts, and font size) in the source document so that it appears correctly in the presentation. This avoids many of the undesirable results of trying to resize linked objects in PowerPoint.

Figure 23.4 shows some objects in a Word and in an Excel document and the results in PowerPoint with callouts explaining what has happened. When text objects are sized correctly in Word or Excel, they reproduce correctly in PowerPoint. If they are resized in PowerPoint, they are stretched upwards and outwards proportionately. The pasted object is no longer type in the strict sense but artwork—a picture of what was type in the source document (see Figure 23.4).

FIG. 23.4
The Word and Excel objects should be sized in the source before placing them into PowerPoint to avoid distortion problems.

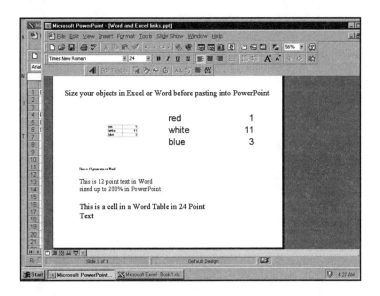

Knowing When to Link or Embed

The choice to link or to embed is a matter of personal choice with factors to consider such as file location, file size, frequency of changes, life cycle of the documents, available disk space, confidentiality, and others. Table 23.2 lists several of these considerations and the advantages and disadvantages of each approach.

Table 23.2 Advantages and Disadvantages of Using OLE		
Factor	**Linking Considerations**	**Embedding Considerations**
Location of files	If files are going to move to other locations, such as other drives, across networks, or outside computers, both files must be moved. Additionally, links are very path-specific, and unless the links were established with both files in the same directory, it can be tedious to reestablish unfound links.	Embedded files travel inside the container file and travel with the container file.
File size	File sizes are counted only once on the hard drive. That means they only occupy space on the hard drive once.	Embedding adds the entire file into the container file. In essence, this can double the file size and can fill up small hard disks quickly.
Frequency of changes	If data is likely to change near the time of presenting, links update automatically.	If someone else is doing many "what if" scenarios with a spreadsheet, you may be better off embedding and protecting your presentation from these changes.
Life cycle of documents	If a source changes periodically but is essentially the same document, just the data changes; linking eliminates re-keying.	If the source is likely to change before you want to present the old results, you are better off to embed and protect yourself from the unwanted changes.
Available disk space	Linking only counts file sizes once.	Embedding embeds a complete copy of the source file and can fill small hard disks quickly, especially if a file is embedded in more than one presentation.

So far you've learned about using either linking or embedding of documents as the only options. There is, however, a third option for those users worried about every byte of disk space.

You do not have to choose to either link or embed an object. You can generally paste only a picture of that object which consumes much less file space, but you are limited in that it is a picture and is therefore not editable and cannot be updated. But, if file size is a critical issue, as it is for many, this is an excellent option. You copy the object to the Clipboard in the normal manner and then in PowerPoint, do the following:

1. Choose Edit, Paste Special.
2. Select the Paste radio button and choose from one of the options other than the Microsoft Word/Excel document as shown in Figure 23.5.
3. Click OK when finished.

FIG. 23.5
Edit, Paste Special lets you choose how to paste an object.

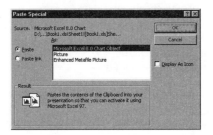

Table 23.3 describes the options for Excel and Word objects that you can paste without the overhead of an OLE object.

Table 23.3	Excel and Word Paste Special Options		
Paste Special Object Choice	**In Excel**	**In Word**	**Comments**
Picture	Yes	Yes	Un-editable in PowerPoint.
Enhanced Metafile Picture	Yes	Yes	Un-editable in PowerPoint, but can be resized without loss of quality.
Device Independent Bitmap	Yes		Un-editable in PowerPoint.
Bitmap	Yes		Un-editable in PowerPoint.
Formatted Text (RTF)	Yes	Yes	Can be ungrouped, text changed, and font colors changed.

Paste Special

Object Choice	In Excel	In Word	Comments
Unformatted Text	Yes	Yes	Displays without formatting, but can be ungrouped and text changed and font colors changed.

Exploring HTML

HTML (Hypertext Markup Language) is the language of the Internet. It provides a way to link documents of different types and different locations. Simply put, if you think of it as "Click here and then go there," that is all you need to know. It basically jumps from one location in a file to another location in the same file, or even to a location in another file. It's like a road map for the computer to follow.

If you have spent any time at all on the Internet, you are familiar with the end result of hypertext links. For example, you have probably *jumped* from one location to another, and maybe not even known it. That is a *hypertext link*.

The term *hyperlink* is relatively new to PowerPoint; the concept appeared in PowerPoint 95. However, the ease of use and the great amount of power that hyperlinks possess in PowerPoint 97 make them an invaluable tool for preparing presentations in screen show format or on the World Wide Web.

What do hyperlinks do and how do they work? Hyperlinks let your presentations operate much more like the human mind does—in non-sequential format, instead of in the traditional, linear way slide shows and most computer associations work. For example, how many times have you been in meetings when you have a nicely organized structure to your presentation and the boss asks a very valid question that doesn't fit your structure? For example, she might ask, "You say sales are down in the fourth quarter, but is it in all product lines in all regions, or is it a mixture of product lines that vary by region?" This is a valid question, but one that requires a lot of detail to explain. And you may not have wanted all that detail in your presentation.

With a hyperlink, at that point you could link to a completely different presentation or a detailed spreadsheet that quickly explains the pattern of one particular product line across most regions. And it would explain it in much greater detail than you would have originally planned for your presentation. Basically, hyperlinks let you add informative footnotes and appendices to your slide shows.

Of course, you have to create these hyperlinks when you create the slide presentation, which means you have to anticipate where these questions may arise.

For the most part, none of us should care how they do this. The important thing to know is that PowerPoint 97 handles all the hidden code for hyperlinks behind the scenes. All you have to supply is the knowledge of where to go to get the information. PowerPoint asks you to connect a hyperlink to a specific location—whether it is a particular file (such as an Excel workbook, a Word document, or another PowerPoint presentation)—and maybe a particular location (such as a range or page in a document) within that file. You also can specify another location, such as a URL location on the Web.

You have a variety of options to link with an HTML link to different locations:

- Another PowerPoint presentation
- A spreadsheet range
- A Word document
- Another program
- Another Web site

Just as Windows 95 provides many ways to accomplish the same task, there are a variety of ways you can establish hyperlinks to another presentation. You also can mix the uses without a problem. It is up to you which of the methods you prefer and what you want your presentation to look like.

Two methods enable you to create hypertext links to another presentation:

- Create your own custom object and create the link from that object.
- Find the target of the link and let PowerPoint create an object in your main presentation for you to use as an icon to jump to the other presentation.

You can create a hyperlink to another PowerPoint presentation from any object on a page:

1. Select any object on a page in PowerPoint, or add a new object.
2. Choose Slide Show, Action Settings to access the Action Settings dialog box.
3. At this point, two tabs enable you to choose whether you want the link activated by a Mouse Click or by merely passing the Mouse Over the object. Either one is appropriate.
4. Click the Hyperlink To radio button for and use the drop-down list, as shown in Figure 23.6 to select Other PowerPoint Presentation.
5. Select the presentation to link to by browsing.
6. You are presented with a choice of each slide in that presentation. Choose which slide in that presentation you want to hyperlink to.

7. Set any other options in the dialog box as appropriate for Play Sound or Highlight Click or Highlight When Mouse Over.

8. Click OK.

FIG. 23.6
You can link to other pages in your presentation or other presentations.

N O T E While it is easy to set hyperlinks in PowerPoint, PowerPoint does not automatically return you to the original presentation. If you are just branching instead of jumping and want to return to the original presentation, you have to set another hyperlink in the second presentation to return you to the original.

Additionally, these hyperlink jumps don't just jump you between different presentations. They change the way the screen views the show. And the new view is not a traditional screen show view because it introduces Web-like menus to go forward and backwards, as well as to Favorite places. ▨

The other way to establish a hyperlink in a PowerPoint presentation is to establish the link from the target rather than from the original presentation. The following steps show how to do this:

1. Select an object on the page or create a new one.

2. Choose Edit, Copy.

3. Choose Window and select the other presentation if it is open, or choose File, Open to open the other presentation.

4. Select the correct page where you want the hyperlink object to be placed.

5. Choose Edit, Paste as Hyperlink. You see a rectangle with a light copy of the title of the linked slide inside the rectangle.

In both cases of placing the hyperlink object, the text that shows on the screen can be edited. In the first situation of attaching a hyperlink to an object, you can use any object. In the second example of placing the hyperlink object from the target presentation, the format of the rectangle can be changed only as far as size, color fill, line color and text in the rectangle. In this second case, use caution when trying to hide this object by placing it behind other objects or grouping it with other objects on the page because the hypertext link will be hidden as well.

Adding Hyperlinks to Spreadsheet Ranges or Charts

You can also use a hyperlink to a spreadsheet range or a chart sheet in a specific Excel workbook. It is similar to the process used in linking to another PowerPoint presentation but with a few variations. Here's how to do this:

1. Select an object on the page or create a new one.
2. Choose Insert, Hyperlink.
3. Browse to select the file in the box that says Link to File or URL.
4. You can also type a range name and range address in the Named Location in File (Optional) box.
5. Click OK to return to Slide Edit mode in PowerPoint.

N O T E There is also an option to check a check box to let you use a relative path for a hyperlink: Use Relative Path For Hyperlink. Links of any kind are pathed. If you place all files that are related by links in the same directory before you establish any links, you can then move them to another computer, drive, or directory without losing this path-specific information.

For example, if you created all the links in the D:\linkshere\ directory on one computer and you move all the files to another computer to H:\newdir\, then all the links will maintain their integrity. If you plan on establishing hyperlinks to other files and using them on your home page, it is critical to check the Use Relative Paths box and maintain the relationship of files in directories in order for the links to remain in place. ■

Adding Hyperlinks to Another Program

Another terrific use of hyperlinks during a presentation is to launch another program. This is especially appropriate for salespeople who are demonstrating a program that is not actually a presentation program but want to use PowerPoint as the primary presentation program. You can launch any EXE program, even a DOS program if you need to. This other program is launched in its own window on top of the slide show view screen, just like you saw when linking to a specific Excel file. You can use the browser to find the EXE file to launch, or you can just type the correct path to the file, such as **d:\MyDir\custom. exe**, as shown in Figure 23.7.

FIG. 23.7
The Action Settings
dialog box is where
you can set many of
the hyperlink options.

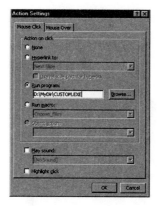

Here's how to set the hyperlink options for an object to launch another program:

1. Select an object on the page or create a new object.
2. Choose Sli_de Show, Ac_tion Settings.
3. Click the _Run Program radio button.
4. Browse to find the EXE file or just type the command line in the _Run Program box.
5. Set any other options on the Action Settings dialog page for _Play Sound or Highlight _Click.
6. Click OK.

Adding Hyperlinks to a URL Web Site

PowerPoint 97 also enables you to establish hyperlinks to another URL or Web site. Be-cause the Web can be thought of as just one very big hard drive, the hyperlink only needs to know the address for that site. The hidden code behind PowerPoint links does all the work; you just have to point to it.

When you publish your presentation to HTML format, these hyperlinks stay in place and function just like the links you can establish with higher-end Web publishing programs. These are the hyperlinks that make the Web such a robust environment. Setting the links to other URLs is just as easy as establishing links to other presentations or docu-ments on your own hard drive.

The following steps show you how to create hyperlinks in PowerPoint to other Web sites:

1. Select an object on the page or create a new object.

2. Choose Insert, Hyperlink to access the Insert Hyperlink dialog box.

3. Enter the URL to link to or choose the Link to File or URL pull-down menu if you have already linked to that site.

4. Click OK.

Linking to Your Favorite Places

There is yet another very handy linking feature to this version of PowerPoint. You might find very helpful in working on Web pages or even in presentations that want to exist in a very fluid and unpredictable environment. This type of link is directly lifted from the experience that is common to the Internet experience. That is Favorite Places. While the Internet can be sometimes compared to a wild connection of tangled fish lines, there is a feature that the browsers offer that helps keep users from getting entirely lost.

The concept of Favorite Places is not the same as the Most Recent File list common to software programs. It is an entirely customizable personal list of just that—favorite places I like to visit. It's very much like the Speed Dial feature on telephones. There is no re-typing long URL names. Just go back to your Speed Dial key and get automatically reconnected. ●

CHAPTER 24

Advanced Multimedia Presentations

by Michael Desmond

You want your presentations to make an impact, and studies show that there is no better way to do so than to include audio and video elements in your show. PC-based presentation software like PowerPoint lets you do just that, with facilities for adding video clips, audio elements, and eye-catching animation to your presentations. PowerPoint 97 provides incremental improvements in multimedia support over earlier versions, while including key features such as the Clip Gallery for keeping track of multimedia elements. ■

Exploring multimedia issues

Make sure you have the right equipment and proper software to make multimedia work.

Working with video and audio

Learn your way around Windows 95's multimedia file formats and tools.

Working with video clips in presentations

Learn how to add exciting digital video footage to your multimedia presentations.

Using PowerPoint's Animation Settings feature to trigger multimedia events

Customize your PowerPoint video clips with transitions, animation, and timing cues.

Adding a CD soundtrack to your presentation

Using a $2,000 PC to play audio CDs may sound silly, but the effect can be powerful in your presentations.

Adding a narration track to your presentation

PowerPoint's new narration feature lets you create precisely-timed voice overs for your presentations.

Exploring Multimedia Issues

By its very nature, multimedia is hard to manage. You need to be aware of issues affecting audio and video playback, while juggling diverse file formats and Windows tools. Of course, it takes skill to effectively capture, edit, and incorporate video and audio into presentations. But the payoff is significant: incorporating these elements can transform a me-too effort into a star-turning performance. This section will help you learn the basics.

The Multimedia-Ready Presentation PC

First things first: you need the right hardware for the job. After all, a poor presentation can be worse than no presentation at all, and an under-powered system will turn even the best source video and audio into bad output. Here are some guidelines to a properly-equipped system for multimedia presentations:

- *Fast Pentium CPU with 16M of RAM.* A 100MHz Pentium is a good minimum for reliable playback of video and audio, while at least 16M of RAM is needed to avoid performance-sapping hard disk memory swaps.

- *A PCI bus graphics card with 2M of memory.* At least 2M of graphics RAM is needed to deliver high-resolution displays at true color, while fast PCI bus connections allow for quick slide updates and smooth video.

- *Windows 95 DirectDraw software and hardware.* A DirectDraw-capable graphics board and drivers offload performance-intensive tasks from the CPU to boost frame rates. The combination also lets graphics hardware scale up video to full screen while maintaining acceptable visual detail.

- *A sound card with 16-bit, 44.1KHz wave audio recording and playback.* Most boards sold over the past two years can record and playback CD-quality sound—a vital feature if you want to use music in your presentations. Also consider a good pair of powered speakers with about 5 watts of amplification for small audiences.

- *A sound card with wave table MIDI hardware.* While the hardware will add to the cost of the board, the payoff is realistic-sounding playback of scores based on compact MIDI files.

- *Large and fast disk storage.* A 4X CD-ROM drive and 1.6G or larger hard disk enable the use of space-consuming video and audio files while maintaining quality playback.

If you intend to create your own video and audio, also consider these additions to your system:

- *A video capture card.* A PCI bus capture card lets you import 640 × 480 resolution video files for use in presentations.

- *Video and audio editing software.* Third-party software such as Adobe Premiere and Blue Ribbon SoundWorks Software Audio Workshop let you precisely control and enhance video and audio content.

Understanding Media Handling Under PowerPoint

PowerPoint 97 manages video and audio files either as native PowerPoint media objects or as embedded Media Player objects. Embedded media objects can be edited within your presentations using Windows 95's standard media tools, while native PowerPoint media objects feature more precise controls for playback in presentations. In both cases, you get a video clip or sound file that plays as part of your presentation.

Part

VII

Ch

24

PowerPoint gives you several ways to import media files into your presentations, many of which are accessible from the Insert menu command, as shown in Figure 24.1.

FIG. 24.1
The Insert menu item provides quick access to multimedia elements for your presentations.

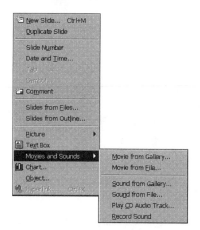

The way you import a clip determines whether a media clip is treated as a native PowerPoint object or as an embedded Media Player object. For this reason, it is important to know how the different commands will affect your control over media objects. The following shows you what kind of media object you get when using different methods of importation (see Figures 24.2 and 24.3).

FIG. 24.2

Right-click an embedded media object, such as this video clip, and you can access external Windows 95 applications like Media Player and Sound Recorder to edit and play back media files.

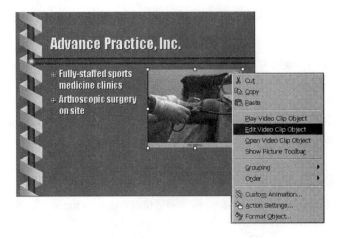

FIG. 24.3

Right-click a multimedia file inserted as a native PowerPoint media object, and you can access PowerPoint's basic editing tools.

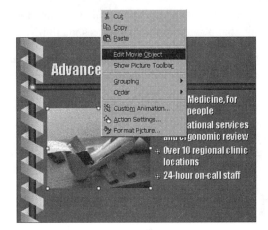

■ *Insert, Movies and Sounds menu commands.* Selected video and audio files embedded as PowerPoint-native media objects. These clips can not be edited by using Media Player.

■ *Insert, Object menu command for video files.* Selected video files embedded as Media Player objects.

■ *Insert, Object menu command for audio files.* Selected audio files embedded as Sound Recorder objects.

■ *Insert, New Slide menu command.* AutoLayout templates with media clip placeholders embed selected video and audio files as Media Player objects.

■ *Using Windows 95 copy and paste to insert video files into PowerPoint layout.* Selected video files embedded as a Media Player object.

■ *Using Windows 95 copy and paste to insert audio files into PowerPoint layout.* Selected audio files embedded as a Sound Recorder object.

N O T E You can also drag and drop media clips into your presentations. PowerPoint treats dragged file items the same way it does those copied and pasted into the layout. ■

As a general rule, PowerPoint-native media objects are easier to work into the timing of presentations, because the program provides more timing controls. However, once these clips are inserted into PowerPoint, it is difficult to edit them. You need to go to the original file, make your changes and cuts, and then reinsert into PowerPoint.

Media clips inserted as embedded Media Player objects, on the other hand, enjoy one key advantage: you can edit the media clip to suit your needs at any point during the presentation design.

Optimizing Your PC for Multimedia Presentations

Sound and video require a well-maintained environment to ensure smooth playback and good results. This section helps you get the most from your presentations by showing you how to use the tools built into Windows 95 to optimize playback.

Mastering Windows 95's Graphics Settings   Digital video requires full color and high resolutions to provide realistic playback. Fortunately, today's Pentium PCs are up to the task. Most systems now come with 2M of graphics RAM, which can support 800×600 pixel resolutions while displaying 16.7 million colors—more colors than the human eye can actually perceive.

Windows 95 or Windows NT makes it easy to change the graphics settings of your system. To change color depths and resolutions, do the following:

1. Right-click the Windows desktop and select Properties from the context menu.
2. Click the Settings tab.
3. To change the screen resolution, drag the slider bar in the Desktop Area section to the left or right (see Figure 24.4). The text below the slider bar changes to reflect the new resolution settings.
4. To change color depth, click the Color Palette drop-down list box and choose from the available settings. Note that Windows 95 prompts you to restart the system when you change color depths.

Part
VII
Ch
24

FIG. 24.4

The powerful Display Properties dialog box lets you adjust resolutions, color depths, and graphics drivers—and is only a right-click away from the Windows 95 desktop.

TROUBLESHOOTING

The video playback seems very choppy, and certain graphics settings fail to work. It could be because you have the wrong graphics drivers installed. To update the drivers for your graphics board or monitor, go to the Settings tab in the Display Properties dialog box and click the Change Display Type button. In the Change Display Type dialog box that appears, click Change to install a new driver for your graphics hardware. To set up a new display driver, click the Change button.

TIP

Often, Windows 95 uses drivers that correspond to the graphics chip on your graphics board, but not for the specific board itself. If you want access to all the features of your graphics hardware, you should load the drivers supplied by the manufacturer of your graphics board. You can often find graphics board drivers at the vendor's Web site.

CAUTION

Selecting the wrong monitor type can cause your graphics hardware to send a higher frequency signal than your display is designed to handle, possibly resulting in damage to the display.

Boosting CD-ROM Performance   The CD-ROM drive can have a major impact on system performance—and your presentation—if you use it to play back video and audio files. Therefore, you should ensure that your CD-ROM is working at peak efficiency. To get the most from your drive, do the following:

1. Open the Windows 95 Control Panel and double-click the System icon.

2. In the System Properties dialog box, click the Performance tab. If you see a message indicating that your CD-ROM drive is not using Windows 95 32-bit drivers, your drive will not provide optimal performance (see Figure 24.5). Run the Hardware Troubleshooter to try to diagnose and solve the problem. To access the Hardware Troubleshooter from the Windows 95 Help system, search for the phrase "hardware conflict troubleshooter" in the Help Index.

Part

VII

Ch

24

FIG. 24.5
Is your CD-ROM drive letting you down? It just might be the drivers.

3. Click the File System button to go to the File System Properties dialog box.

4. Click the CD-ROM tab, as shown in Figure 24.6. Make sure the Supplemental Cache Size slider bar is pushed all the way to the right. If you are using a 4X or faster CD-ROM drive, make sure the Optimize Access Pattern For drop-down list box is set to Quad-speed. Otherwise, set it to match the speed of your drive.

FIG. 24.6

Smooth out video playback by tweaking the cache settings of your CD-ROM drive.

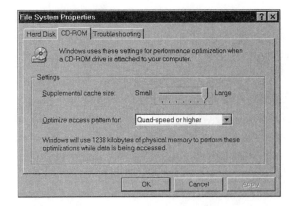

Understanding Video and Audio

Audio and video are at the heart of PC-based multimedia, and can help add excitement to presentations. However, both video and audio can be difficult to work with, because they both require knowledge of editing tools in order to create appropriate clips. Video, for example, requires significant system resources, as well as some compromises in order to maintain smooth playback. Audio, meanwhile, can grab attention at key junctures.

Understanding Video Formats and Compression

To play on a PC, digital video must be presented in a recognizable format. For Windows 95, that format is Microsoft's Video for Windows, which uses the familiar AVI file extension. The other popular format, Apple's QuickTime, is used with many multimedia CD-ROM titles. To recognize Video for Windows AVI files and QuickTime for Windows MOV files, your system must have the proper drivers and software loaded.

In both cases, the formats build video files from thousands of individual frames. An interleaved audio soundtrack is synched up with the video frames, resulting in the digital equivalent of a movie.

The problem is that all the images and audio require an immense amount of data—date which must be played back without delay to avoid unsightly dropped frames and jerky motion. A true-color, 640 × 480 video playing back at 30 frames per second would require your system to pour more than 26M of data *per second*, and that doesn't include the additional data needed for audio!

What makes digital video possible is compression. Compression/decompression schemes—called *codecs*—reduce file sizes by compressing the data stream, and by using complex algorithms to crunch down images and audio. To play back a video compressed using a certain codec, your PC must have that codec driver installed. So a Video for Windows file compressed using Intel's Indeo 4.0 codec will only play back on your system if you have the Indeo 4.0 codec installed.

T I P To see what codecs you have installed, open the Control Panel, double-click the Multimedia icon, and click the Advanced tab. Click the plus sign next to the Video Compression Codecs item in the Multimedia Devices list box, as shown in Figure 24.7.

FIG. 24.7
The Multimedia Properties dialog box in the Windows 95 Control Panel provides a useful inventory of video compression drivers and other key components.

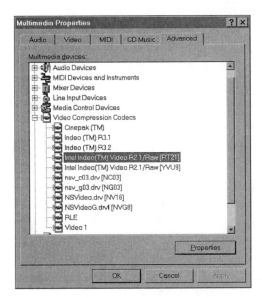

Part
VII
Ch
24

Understanding Wave Audio

Wave audio sounds are digitally recorded sounds that are played back from disk. While you can record—or *sample*—wave audio sounds using a microphone or line input source, the resulting files tend to be extremely large. In fact, one minute of high-fidelity sound can consume 10M of disk space. As a result, it is usually necessary to reduce file sizes by either limiting the fidelity of the audio, or by compressing the audio file during capture. In either case, compromises are made to the quality of the digital audio.

Today, virtually all sound boards can handle CD-quality digital sound, usually described as 16-bit, 44.1KHz audio. 44.1KHz refers to the number of times each second a sound board samples incoming sound to produce the digital equivalent of analog audio—in this particular case, 44,100 times each second. The 16-bit refers to the amount of data used to store each sample. The lower these numbers, the less realistic the digital product will sound. Most sound boards also provide stereo playback, which means that the sampling and storing is done in pairs, for the separate left and right channels.

T I P   You'll want to crank up the audio quality for multimedia presentations, because distorted or unrealistic sounds will distract from your pitch. Use at least 16-bit, 22KHz stereo audio in your playback. The files will consume disk space, but the effect will be worth it.

Wave audio is generally used for slide transitions, most sound effects, and all recorded sounds such as voice or recorded music.

Understanding MIDI Audio

Unlike wave audio files, which store millions of bits to recreate analog sounds, *MIDI files* consist of commands that tell MIDI hardware what notes and instrument sounds to play. In effect, a MIDI file is similar to the paper roll in a player piano, telling your sound board what to play. MIDI stands for *Musical Instrument Digital Interface,* and was created by the music industry to let synthesizers and other electronic musical instruments work with a standard music interface.

The biggest advantage of MIDI scores is that they are compact. Long compositions consume only a few kilobytes of disk space, as opposed to the tens of megabytes the same wave audio file might take. MIDI files are also easy to edit, allowing users to create or customize MIDI scores.

The two types of MIDI are:

- *FM synthesis.* Found on inexpensive sound cards, this scheme emulates the sounds of real instruments by mixing signals. Generally, FM synthesis can re-create instrument sounds, but yields poor results.

- *Wave table synthesis.* This method uses digitally-recorded sounds of real instruments to create realistic playback. Wave table MIDI sound boards are more expensive due to the ROM chips used to store the instrument sounds, but playback quality is much better than FM synthesis.

MIDI audio is used almost exclusively to play instrumental musical scores, such as for background music in a presentation. Some special effects sounds may also be played using MIDI sounds.

Mastering Windows 95's Media Player

To get the most from video and audio in your presentations, you need to know your way around the Windows 95 Media Player (see Figure 24.8). This built-in application provides standard tools for creating, editing, and playing back full-motion video and digital audio files. In addition, many media files are embedded in PowerPoint as Media Player objects.

This section can help you access all the controls and features of the Media Player for these embedded clips.

FIG. 24.8
The Windows 95 Media Player has a key role in handling multimedia elements within PowerPoint.

The Media Player has five top-level menu items: File, Edit, Device, Scale, and Help. The File item is used to open and close video files, while Help contains the standard help features. The other three menu items, discussed in the following sections, offer many valuable tools.

Exploring the Edit Menu   The following commands are available under the Edit menu:

■ *Copy Object.* Copies the loaded media file to Clipboard so it can be pasted to another application or document.

■ *Options.* Opens the Options dialog box, which provides key controls over the playback of video and audio inside Windows 95 applications, as shown in Figure 24.9. The available items are:

Auto Rewind. Resets the video or audio clip back to the beginning after playback. (Clips do not reset to the beginning unless this item is checked.)

Auto Repeat. Sets the video or audio clip to repeat in an endless loop until the user interrupts it with a mouse click during the presentation.

Control Bar on Playback. When selected, video and audio clips will display a control bar at the bottom of the window offering standard Play/Pause and Stop buttons. The user may click the control bar buttons during playback. Most presentations should leave this box unchecked to avoid distracting the audience.

Caption. Displays the file name of the video or audio clip in the control bar. Note that this item is only active if the Control Bar on Playback check box is enabled.

Border Around Object. Displays a window border around the video or audio object when it is played.

Play in Client Document. This item allows video and audio files to play directly within an application, without displaying the Media Player interface. This item should be selected for embedded clips inside PowerPoint presentations in order to enable seamless playback of video and audio within the PowerPoint screen.

Dither Picture to VGA Colors. This feature, which applies only to video clips, resets the color palette of video clips to a basic 16-color palette. This item should only be selected if you are limited to using 16 colors in your presentation. This item is grayed out on systems displaying more than 256 colors. Be warned that 16-color video will look very poor on playback. I recommend that you only use video if your system is able to support at least 256 colors.

FIG. 24.9

The Options dialog box controls how video and audio elements will look when playing back in your presentation.

■ *Selection.* Opens the Set Selection dialog box, which lets you select a subset of the loaded video or audio clip for playback or editing. Depending on the unit of measure being used, the values in the From:, To:, and Size:, spinner controls is displayed in seconds or frames (see Figure 24.10).

FIG. 24.10

The Set Selection dialog box gives you precise control when selecting areas of media files for editing or other operations.

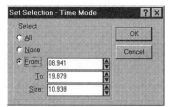

Exploring the Device Menu   The Device menu of the Media Player provides access to powerful customization features for media of all types. The following functions are accessed from the Device menu:

■ *File types.* The top section of the Device menu gives you quick access to files of media types registered with the Media Player (see Figure 24.11). Clicking one of the options works identically to choosing File, Open menu items, except that you will only see files corresponding to the file types specified. For example, selecting the 4 MIDI Sequencer item displays an Open dialog box tailored to MIDI files with MID and RMI file extensions.

FIG. 24.11
The Device menu gives you a quick shortcut to media types recognized by your system.

■ *Properties.* This command accesses tools for customizing media playback and capabilities. The available tools change depending on the media type loaded into the Media Player. Users will encounter the following Properties controls for video and audio files:

Wave audio file. The MCI Waveform Driver Setup box appears, as shown in Figure 24.12, allowing the user to change the amount of memory used to buffer audio data during playback. Move the Seconds slider bar to the right to ensure uninterrupted playback of long WAV files.

FIG. 24.12
Ensure smooth audio playback by adding memory to your Windows 95's audio buffer.

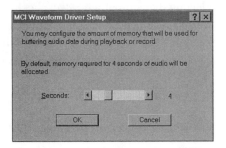

MIDI file. The MIDI Properties dialog box appears, as shown in Figure 24.13. Here you can add support for an external MIDI instrument, such as a MIDI keyboard, using the Add New Instrument button. You can also assign different MIDI instruments to different Channels by selecting the Custom Configuration radio button and clicking the Configure button.

FIG. 24.13
Sophisticated users
can add custom flair
to presentations by
installing their own
MIDI instruments onto
their systems.

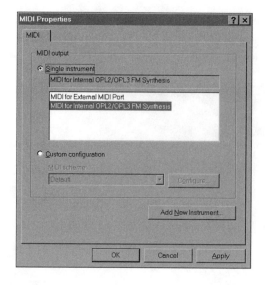

Video for Windows file. The Video Properties box appears as shown in Figure 24.14. Click the Window drop-down list box to play video clips at original size, double original size, as a maximized window, or at 1/16, 1/4, or 1/2 the original size. The Full Screen radio button knocks out the Windows 95 GUI during video playback to maximize frame rates. When the clip finishes, your presentation or another application will resume.

■ *Volume Control.* The Volume Control dialog box lets you set the volume and balance of the various audio devices installed under Windows 95 (see Figure 24.15). You can mute devices by deselecting the appropriate Select check box, or disable audio altogether by selecting the Mute All check box at the bottom left of the dialog box. Depending on the installed sound hardware and drivers, the Options menu may include an Advanced Controls item that accesses further audio features and controls.

TROUBLESHOOTING

I'm experiencing unwanted noise in my audio playback. It may be because other devices are playing in the background. Try muting devices you are not using, such as the microphone or CD devices, to eliminate signals from unused devices. You can do this by double-clicking the speaker icon in the Windows 95 taskbar to open the Volume Control dialog box. Deselect the Select check box for any device not needed for audio playback.

FIG. 24.14
The Video Properties dialog box lets you set the size of the video window when it plays back.

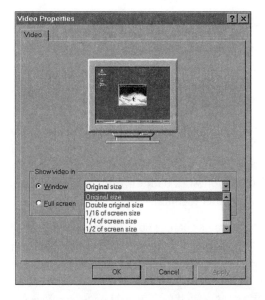

FIG. 24.15
Pump up the volume, or pump it down for that matter, with the Windows 95 Volume Control.

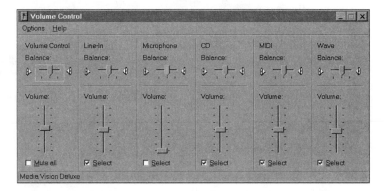

Exploring the Scale Menu   Click the Scale menu item in Media Player to toggle the unit of measure used to depict the duration of video or audio files. Three possible selections under the Scale menu are available, not all of which may be present at the same time:

- *Time*. Media Player shows the length of the loaded clip in seconds.

- *Frames*. Media Player shows the length of the loaded clip in frames. (Only applicable for video and animation files.)

- *Tracks*. Media Player shows the length of the loaded media in tracks. (Only applicable for audio CD discs.)

Introducing Video and Audio Editing Tools

Creating multimedia presentations requires the right software. While the tools built into Windows 95 are enough for basic tasks, third-party software gives you impressive control over your media. Applications such as Adobe Premiere 4.2 and Ulead VideoStudio Pro can turn your PC into a desktop studio.

Video editing software lets you capture and edit digital video that can then be imported into PowerPoint. These tools let you cut down video footage to just the portions you need in your presentations, and allow you to add compelling special effects and transitions such as fades and wipes. They let you work both with video you have captured and with video files stored on CD-ROM or other medium.

Similarly, audio editing programs enable you to work with wave audio and MIDI files. These packages give you sophisticated controls for recording audio to disk—a process called sampling—as well as for editing digital audio files. You can mix audio tracks together, add special effects, or create your own MIDI scores to use as background music in your presentations. Programs such as Blue Ribbon SoundWorks' Software Audio Workshop provide these capabilities.

Working with Video Clips in Presentations

Of all the tools at your disposal for multimedia presentations, none are as powerful and challenging as video. Full-motion video clips add compelling content to your presentations, immediately drawing the attention of the audience. Best of all, inexpensive Pentium PCs and the video-savvy Windows 95 operating system have combined to make digital video more effective and attractive than ever before.

PowerPoint 97 lets you take advantage of video, providing several ways to incorporate video clips into your presentations. In fact, you can use any of six methods:

- Insert video clips as movies from a file
- Insert video clips as movies from the Clip Gallery
- Insert video clips as objects from a file
- Insert video clips as new objects
- Insert video clips from the Slide AutoLayout
- Pasting video clips from Windows 95 Explorer

Inserting Video Clips as Movies from File

PowerPoint 97 gives you plenty of options for bringing video into your presentations, but the most straightforward method is to insert video clips as movies. You can import your movies either from a file or from the Microsoft Clip Gallery. To insert from a file, follow these steps:

1. If you are not already in Slide view, choose View, Slide.
2. Select the slide that will contain the video clip.
3. Choose Insert, Movies and Sounds.
4. From the menu that appears, click Movie from File.
5. From the Look In drop-down list, choose the drive and folder in which your video files are located. The Files of Type box at the bottom automatically shows Movie Files, as shown in Figure 24.16.

FIG. 24.16

The Insert Movie dialog box automatically filters for media files matching your description.

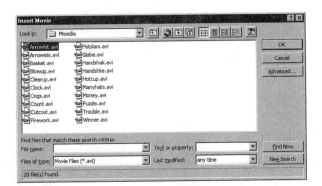

6. Double-click the file icon.

PowerPoint embeds the video clip into your slide as a native PowerPoint media object.

TIP Preview video clips from the Insert Movie dialog box by right-clicking the desired file icon and selecting Play from the context menu. The video will play in a separate window that closes when it is finished.

Part

VII

Ch

24

Inserting Video Clips as Movies from the Clip Gallery

You can also insert clips as PowerPoint videos using the Microsoft Clip Gallery. This new feature is particularly useful for multimedia presentations, because it lets you organize your graphics, sounds, animations, and videos. To insert a video clip from the Clip Gallery, follow these steps:

1. If you are not already in Slide view, choose View, Slide.
2. Select the slide that will contain the video clip.
3. Choose Insert, Movies and Sounds.
4. From the menu that appears, click Movie from Gallery.
5. Click the Videos tab in the Microsoft Clip Gallery 3.0 dialog box.
6. Use the scroll bar to view the first frames of the video files, as shown in Figure 24.17. Click an image to select the video clip.

FIG. 24.17
PowerPoint Clip Gallery's visual interface makes it easy to organize and find video clips for use in your presentations.

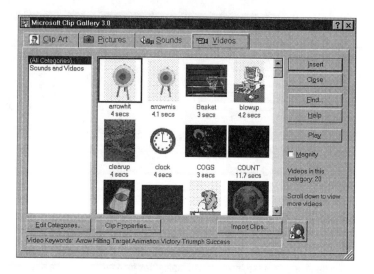

7. To get a better view of a selected video image, click the Magnify check box.
8. To insert the selected clip, Click the Insert button or double-click the selected image. PowerPoint embeds the video clip into your slide as a PowerPoint native media object.

T I P To preview a selected video clip, click the Play button. To stop playing, click the button again (it toggles to Stop Playing), as in Figure 24.18.

FIG. 24.18
Clip Gallery lets you
preview video files
before inserting them
into your presenta-
tions.

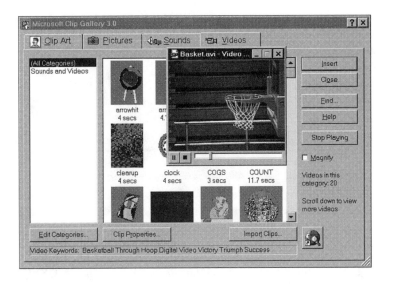

Part

VII

Ch

24

Inserting Video Clips as Objects

PowerPoint 97 also lets you insert video clips into your presentations as embedded Media
Player objects, by choosing Insert, Object. In this case, video files are accessed using the
Windows 95 Media Player, which allows you to use its controls for editing and playback.
There are two ways to embed videos as objects:

- Insert video clips as objects from a file
- Insert video clips as new objects

The main advantage of the insert object from file method is that it lets you search for all
file extensions. So if you are selecting among Video for Windows, QuickTime, and MPEG
videos, you will see the respective AVI, MOV, and MPG file extensions. To load a video
clip as an object using the Create from file method, follow these steps:

1. Choose Insert, Object. The Insert Object dialog box appears as shown in Figure
   24.19.

FIG. 24.19
The Insert Object
dialog box presents a
laundry list of file
types recognized by
Windows 95, including
multimedia file types.

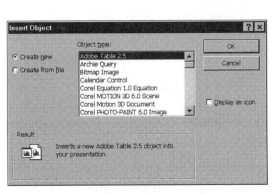

FIG. 24.20

If you choose to Create From File, you can browse freely for files of all types.

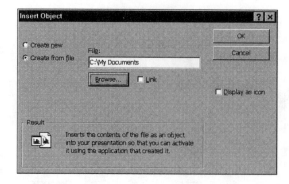

2. Click the Create from File radio button. The dialog box changes appearance to that shown in Figure 24.20.

3. Choose the Browse button. The Browse dialog box appears.

4. Select the drive, folder, and file you want, then choose OK. The Insert Object dialog box reappears, displaying the name of your selected video clip.

5. Choose OK. The video clip is inserted into your slide. When you play the slide back, the clip appears in its own separate window.

You can also load a video clip as an object using the create new method. This approach lets you first identify your media type, so that you can focus only on AVI files, for example. To load a video clip as an object using the create new method, follow these steps:

1. Choose Insert, Object. When the Insert Object dialog box appears, click the Create New radio button.

2. In the Object Type list box, select the Video Clip item and click OK. The screen now changes to show the Media Player interface.

3. Choose Insert Clip, 1 Video for Windows as shown in Figure 24.21.

FIG. 24.21

PowerPoint sports a Media Player interface when you load a video file using the Insert Clip command.

4. A standard Open dialog box now appears. Select the drive and directory containing your clips from the Look In drop-down list box and click the AVI file that you want to insert in your presentation.

The Media Player interface is still displayed.

5. To embed the video object, click anywhere on the PowerPoint slide outside the clip.

Inserting Video Clips with the Slide AutoLayout Feature

The easiest and surest way to get a video into a presentation is to use the Slide AutoLayout feature explained in earlier chapters. AutoLayouts ensure that your video clips are properly embedded into your slides and won't invoke a separate playback window when activated during a presentation.

▶ **See** "Selecting AutoLayouts," **p. xxx**(Chapter 2)

N O T E Video clips inserted using the Slide AutoLayout feature are treated as embedded Media Player objects. That means you can go back later and edit the clip without having to reinsert it into the presentation. ■

To create a new slide containing a Video Clip Object:

1. Choose Insert, New Slide.

   The New Slide dialog box appears showing the available AutoLayouts, as shown in Figure 24.22. Two AutoLayouts include placeholders for video clips—Text & Media Clip and Media Clip & Text. The two are identical except for the positioning of the media elements. Note that you may have to scroll the AutoLayout list to view the desired type.

FIG. 24.22
The AutoLayout features makes it a snap to set up slides with embedded media elements.

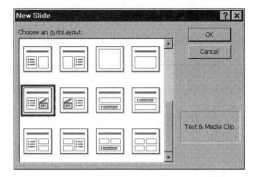

2. Choose either of the AutoLayouts that contain media clip placeholders. (The dialog box displays the type of slide you have selected.) Double-click a slide thumbnail, or click a layout and choose OK, to insert a new slide that resembles Figure 24.23.

N O T E Remember from earlier chapters that placeholders are resizable, and can be copied and pasted from other slides. Placeholders also can trigger specific applications depending on the type of object the placeholder is designed for. ■

Part
VII

Ch
24

FIG. 24.23
AutoLayout presents you with a ready-to-roll slide design.

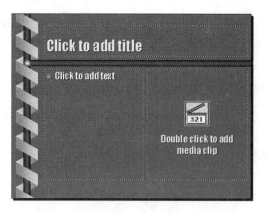

3. Double-click the media clip placeholder in the new slide to insert the video clip. The Media Player program interface now appears (see Figure 24.24).

FIG. 24.24
Double-click the media placeholder, and PowerPoint will do its chameleon act again, presenting a Media Player interface for loading a video clip.

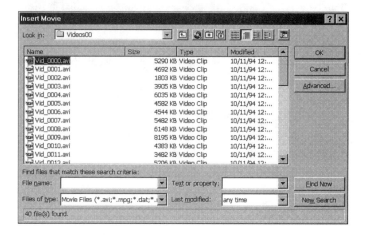

4. From the Open dialog box, locate the drive and directory that contains your video file and choose the AVI file you want to insert.

5. Choose Open or press Enter (or double-click the file name you want). The video clip is inserted directly into the placeholder.

Pasting Video Clips from Windows 95 Explorer

You can also use Windows 95 standard copy and paste functions to bring video and other media files into PowerPoint 97. There are two ways to do this: by selecting the copy and paste commands, or by using Windows 95's drag-and-drop facilities.

To copy a video file using menu commands, do the following:

1. From Windows 95's Explorer or Browser view, right-click the icon of the video file you want to import.

2. Select Copy from the Context menu and click your PowerPoint presentation.

3. In Slide view, right-click the slide and select Paste from the Context menu. The video appears on the slide as an embedded Media Player object.

To copy a video file using Windows 95 drag-and-drop, do the following:

1. Make sure you can see both Slide view of your PowerPoint presentation and the Windows 95 Explorer or Browser window showing the file you want to import.

2. From Windows 95's Explorer or Browser view, click and drag the icon of a video file onto the PowerPoint presentation and release. The video appears on the slide as an embedded Media Player object.

Part
VII

Ch
24

Using Custom Animation Controls to Control Video Playback

PowerPoint lets you control the timing and appearance of video clips using the Custom Animation controls found under the Slide Show menu. These controls not only determine when and how a video will start playing, but they also apply transition effects and other customizations.

The biggest advantage of this tool is that it lets you time video events in your slides. If you have followed the last two sections, you already know how to embed a video clip into a slide. Here's how to add some finishing touches to an embedded video within PowerPoint.

Controlling Playback of Media Objects

As mentioned earlier, PowerPoint handles video files either as embedded Media Player objects or as native PowerPoint video objects. To control embedded Media Player video clips, do the following:

1. Click the video item you want to adjust.

2. Choose Slide Show, Custom Animation to go to the Custom Animation dialog box shown in Figure 24.25.

3. Click the Play Settings tab inside the Custom Animation dialog box. You must select the Play item in the Object Action drop-down list box to display the video.

4. Select the <u>H</u>ide While Not Playing check box to make the selected video window invisible until it begins playing.

5. Click the Timing tab and click the <u>A</u>nimate radio button.

FIG. 24.25

Time your various media events using the Custom Animation dialog box.

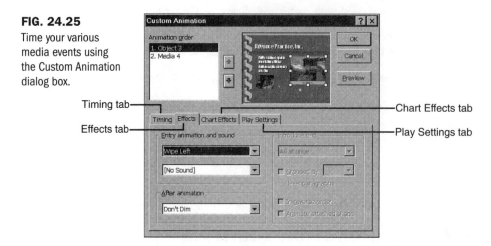

CAUTION

If the video is a media object, it does not run during a slide show unless you select Play in the Play Settings dialog box.

6. To make the video play when it is clicked during the presentation, select the On <u>M</u>ouse Click radio button. To have the video play after a specific number of seconds following another event—such as the introduction of the slide—click the A<u>u</u>tomatically radio button and enter the desired number of seconds in the spinner control box (see Figure 24.26).

N O T E If you want to time video playback against the introduction of a slide, the video item must be the top item in the Animation <u>O</u>rder list box. Otherwise, the selected video waits the specific number of seconds after the completion of the item before it in the Animation order list. ▨

7. Click OK to make your selections take effect.

FIG. 24.26
Set videos to play back on a timed schedule or when clicked during the presentation.

Controlling Playback of PowerPoint Video Objects

Native PowerPoint video objects feature many of the same controls as embedded video objects. However, native video clips add controls in the Play Settings tab of the Customize Animation dialog box.

To access the additional controls available to native video objects, do the following:

1. With the PowerPoint video object selected, click Slide Show, Custom Animation.
2. Click the Play Settings tab in the Custom Animation dialog box, and click the Play Using Animation Order check box. The items beneath the check box become active, as shown in Figure 24.27.

FIG. 24.27
Native PowerPoint media objects can be set to continue playing through several slides, among other options.

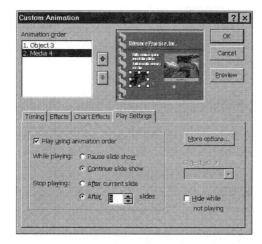

3. Use the While Playing radio buttons to determine what happens to your slide show while the selected video plays. Select the Pause Slide Show radio button to have the slide show wait until the video has finished, or select the Continue Slide Show radio button to have new slides come up with the video playing through on all the slides.

4. Use the Stop Playing section to determine what happens to the selected video as the slide show continues. Select the After Current Slide radio button to force the video clip to end when you move to the next slide, or click the After Slides radio button to set the number of slides you want the video to play for. This is particularly useful for managing video clips that loop.

5. Click the More Options button to open the Play Options dialog box, as shown in Figure 24.28.

FIG. 24.28
Set video to loop continuously and rewind when finished playing from the Play Options dialog box.

6. In the Movie and Sound Options group, click the Loop Until Stopped check box to make the selected clip play over and over.

7. Click the Rewind Movie When Done Playing check box to reset the clip to the beginning once it reaches the end. This setting is useful if you need to replay the video soon after it finishes playing.

Adding Builds and Effects to Video Objects

The Custom Animation dialog box also lets you add effects to video clips, as shown in Figure 24.29. To add some flair to a video clip, follow these steps:

1. Click the video object you want to adjust.

2. Choose Slide Show, Custom Animation to go to the Custom Animation dialog box.

3. Click the Effects tab inside the Custom Animation dialog box, and select the desired visual effect in the top drop-down list box in the Entry Animation and Sound group.

4. Click the Preview button to see how the effect will look in the slide.

5. If you want a sound to accompany the effect, select a wave audio file from the second drop-down list box. If none of the listed items appeal to you, click Other Sounds at the bottom of the list to select from other sources.

6. If you want to hide the on-screen video image or change its appearance after it has played, select the drop-down list box in the After Animation group.

7. Click OK to make your selections take effect.

FIG. 24.29
You can animate your videos so they grab attention even before playing. Use the Preview button at the right to see how an animation will look.

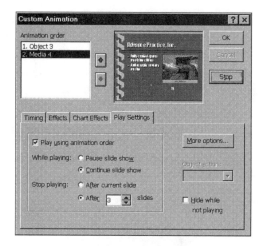

Working With Audio in Presentations

Audio is no less a challenge to work with than video. In fact, sound can make or break a presentation, whether it's simple effects that happen at slide transition, or complex musical scores designed to set tone and mood.

New to PowerPoint 97 is the ability to record narrative audio. This new feature lets you prerecord voice elements and time them to on-screen events. The result: a professional presentation that lets you bring voices of authority to bear on your pitch.

The good news is that audio clips use many of the same tools and commands as video clips. So if you've mastered the video side of things, audio should be a snap. Here are a few ways you can add audio to your presentations:

- Add audio transitions between slides
- Insert audio clips as sounds from file
- Insert audio clips as sounds from the Clip Gallery

- Insert audio clips as objects
- Insert audio clips from the Slide AutoLayout

Adding Sounds to Slide Transitions

Adding sounds to slide transitions is a simple operation. Office 97 comes with wave audio files that are perfect for transitions, including sounds like clapping hands, breaking glass, and screeching tires. To add transition sounds to your presentation, do the following:

N O T E   You can incorporate your own sounds into presentations by recording wave files in Windows 95's Sound Recorder application. Launch Sound Recorder from the Windows 95 Start button by selecting Programs, Accessories, Multimedia, Sound Recorder. In the Sound Recorder program, click the button with the red circle and begin recording your sound. Click the stop button when you are finished, and choose File, Save As to save your recorded sound to a WAV file. ■

1. From either slide or slide sorter view, choose Slide Show, Slide Transition. The Slide Transition dialog box appears as shown in Figure 24.30.

FIG. 24.30
The Slide Transition dialog box lets you add sound, motion, and timing parameters to any or all of your slide transitions.

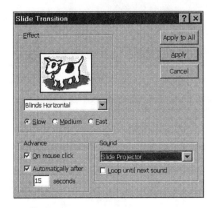

2. In the Sound drop-down list box, select the wave audio file you want to play when the slide appears.
3. Click the Loop Until Next Sound check box to make the selected sound keep playing until another wave or MIDI audio file is invoked.
4. Click the Apply button to make the selected audio file play when the selected slide opens. Click the Apply To All button to make the selected sound play when every slide opens.

Inserting Audio Clips as Sounds from File

Inserting sounds into PowerPoint 97 presentations is nearly identical to the process used to import videos. The easiest way to get audio clips into your presentations is to import sounds either from the file or from the Microsoft Clip Gallery. To insert from a file, follow these steps:

1. Choose View, Slide if you are not already in Slide view.

2. Select the slide that will contain the audio clip.

FIG. 24.31
The Insert Sound dialog box filters files to show only wave audio and MIDI file types.

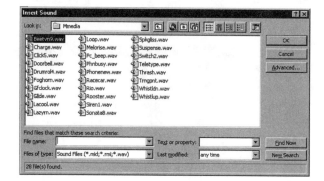

3. Choose Insert, Movies and Sounds.

4. From the spin menu, click Sound From File. The Insert Sound dialog box appears, as shown in Figure 24.31.

5. From the Look In drop-down list, choose the drive and folder in which your audio files are located. The Files of Type box at the bottom automatically shows Sound Files.

6. Double-click the desired file icon.

PowerPoint embeds the audio clip into your slide as a native PowerPoint media object.

 TIP Preview audio clips from the Insert Sound dialog box by right-clicking the desired file icon and selecting Play from the context menu. The Windows 95 Sound Recorder applet appears and plays the audio file, closing when it is finished.

Inserting Audio Clips as Sounds from the Clip Gallery

As with video files, you can also insert clips as PowerPoint sounds using the Microsoft Clip Gallery. To insert an audio clip from the Clip Gallery, do the following:

1. Choose View, Slide if you are not already in Slide view.

2. Select the slide that will contain the audio clip.

3. Choose Insert, Movies and Sounds.

4. From the spin out menu, click Sound from Gallery.

5. Click on the Sounds tab in the Microsoft Clip Gallery 3.0 dialog box.

6. Use the vertical scroll bar to view the audio files, as shown in Figure 24.32. You see the file names and the duration of the wave or MIDI files. Wave audio files are represented with speaker icons, while MIDI files are represented by an icon with a music notation symbol.

FIG. 24.32
You'll find wave audio and MIDI files on the Sounds tab in Clip Gallery's dialog box. Use the Play button to preview clips.

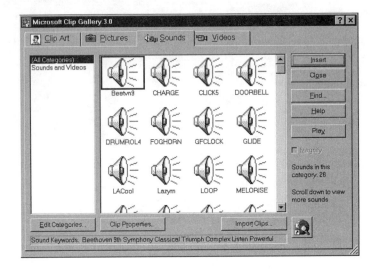

7. To insert the selected clip, click the Insert button or double-click the selected image.

PowerPoint embeds the audio clip into your slide as a PowerPoint native media object.

 TIP To preview a selected audio clip, click the Play button. To stop playing, click the button again (it toggles to Stop Playing).

Inserting Audio Clips as Objects

PowerPoint 97 also lets you insert audio clips into your presentations as embedded Media Player objects, by choosing Insert, Object. As with video clips, audio files are accessed using a Windows 95 applet, in this case the Sound Recorder. There are two ways to embed sounds as objects:

- Insert object from file
- Insert object as new

Use the insert object from file method to search for all file extensions. If you are selecting among wave audio and MIDI files, you will see the WAV and MID file extensions. To load an audio clip as an object using the Create From File method, follow these steps:

1. Choose Insert, Object. The Insert Object dialog box appears.
2. Click the Create From File radio button.
3. Choose the Browse button that appears. The Browse dialog box comes up.
4. Select the drive, folder, and file you want, and choose OK. The Insert Object dialog box reappears, displaying the name of your selected audio clip.
5. Click OK. The audio clip is inserted into your slide. You can edit or play the slide from Slide view by right-clicking the clip and selecting the appropriate command from the context menu. Or you can choose Edit, Wave Sound Object.

You can also load an audio clip as an object by using the create new option. For MIDI files (MID or RMI), do the following:

1. Choose Insert, Object. When the Insert Object dialog box appears, click the Create New radio button.
2. In the Object Type list box, select the MIDI Sequence item and click OK. The Media Player interface appears.
3. Choose Insert Clip, 1 MIDI Sequencer.
4. In the Open dialog box, select the drive and directory containing your clips from the Look In drop-down list box and click the MID or RMI file you want.

   The Media Player interface is still displayed.
5. To embed the audio object, click anywhere on the PowerPoint slide outside the clip.

For wave audio (WAV) files, do the following:

1. Choose Insert, Object. When the Insert Object dialog box appears, click the Create New radio button.
2. In the Object Type list box, select the Wave Sound item and click OK. The Sound Recorder applet appears, as shown in Figure 24.33.

FIG. 24.33

PowerPoint relies on the Windows 95 Sound Recorder to load and edit wave audio files that are inserted as objects.

Part
VII

Ch
24

3. Choose Edit, Insert File to load the wave audio file into Sound Recorder.

4. In the Open dialog box, select the drive and directory containing your clips from the Look In drop-down list box and click the WAV file you want.

   The Sound Recorder interface is still displayed.

5. To embed the audio object, choose File, Exit & Return to Document. The sound file appears as an icon in the slide.

Inserting Audio Clips with the Slide AutoLayout Feature

Inserting a sound using the Slide AutoLayout feature is identical to inserting a video, discussed earlier. Of course, audio clips inserted using the Slide AutoLayout feature are treated as embedded Media Player objects, so you can edit the clip later without having to reinsert it into the presentation.

To create a new slide containing an Audio Clip Object:

1. Choose Insert, New Slide to bring up the New Slide dialog box which displays a selection of slide templates, including those with embedded media placeholders.

2. Choose either of the AutoLayouts that contain media clip placeholders. (The dialog box displays the type of slide when you click it.) To insert a new slide, double-click a slide thumbnail, or click a layout and choose OK.

3. To insert an audio clip, double-click the media clip placeholder in the new slide. The Media Player program interface now appears.

4. Choose Insert Clip, and select either the Sound or MIDI Sequencer items.

5. From the Open dialog box, locate the drive and directory that contains your audio file and choose the WAV or MID file that you want to insert.

6. Choose Open or press Enter (or double-click the file name you want). The audio clip is inserted into the slide, with the Media Player interface still active.

Pasting Audio Clips from Windows 95 Explorer

As with video clips, you can copy and paste audio files directly into PowerPoint 97. You can either use the copy and paste commands, or simply drag and drop files into your slides.

To copy an audio file using menu commands, do the following:

1. From Windows 95's Explorer or Browser view, right-click the icon of the audio file you want to import.

2. Select Copy from the context menu and click your PowerPoint presentation.

3. In Slide view, right-click the slide and select Paste from the context menu. The audio appears on the slide as an embedded Media Player object.

To copy an audio file using Windows 95 drag-and-drop, do the following:

1. Make sure you can see both Slide view of your PowerPoint presentation and the Windows 95 Explorer or Browser window containing the file you want to import.

2. From Windows 95's Explorer or Browser view, click and drag the icon of an audio file onto the PowerPoint presentation and release. The audio clip appears as an icon on the slide, and again as an embedded Media Player object.

Using Custom Animation Controls to Control Audio Playback

PowerPoint lets you control the timing of audio clips using the Custom Animation controls found in the Slide Show menu. The timing controls are identical to those used with video files. Of course, there is no need to work with animation or other visual effects when customizing audio clips.

Here's how to customize audio elements within PowerPoint.

Controlling Playback of Media Objects

PowerPoint handles audio files either as embedded Media Player objects or as native PowerPoint audio objects. To control embedded Media Player audio clips, do the following:

1. Click the audio item you want to adjust.

2. Choose Slide Show, Custom Animation to go to the Custom Animation dialog box (see Figure 24.34).

3. Click the Play Settings tab inside the Custom Animation dialog box. You must select the Play item in the Object Action drop-down list box to display the audio.

4. Select the Timing tab and click the Animate radio button.

> **CAUTION**
>
> If the audio is a media object, it does not run during a slide show unless you select Play in the Object Action drop-down list box.

5. While you can make audio clips play when the object is clicked during a presentation (by selecting the On Mouse Click radio button), it's probably better to time audio events by entering a value in the spinner control box called Automatically. This control plays audio clips a specific number of seconds after another event—such as the introduction of the slide.

FIG. 24.34

The Custom Animation dialog box enables you to control embedded audio clips.

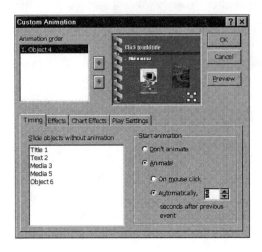

N O T E   As with video clips, to time audio playback against the introduction of a slide, the audio item must be at the top of the Animation Order list box. Otherwise, the selected audio waits the specific number of seconds after the completion of the item before it in the Animation Order list box.

6. Click OK to make your selections take effect.

Controlling Playback of PowerPoint Audio Objects

Like video files, PowerPoint handles sound files either as native PowerPoint audio objects or as embedded audio objects that are accessed via Windows 95's Media Player or Sound Recorder. Native sound clips have access to controls in the Play Settings tab of the Customize Animation dialog box, while embedded objects can be edited using the more complete editing tools provided inside Windows 95.

To access these controls, do the following:

1. With the PowerPoint audio object selected, choose Slide Show, Custom Animation.

2. Click the Play Settings tab in the Custom Animation dialog box, and click the Play Using Animation Order check box. The items beneath the check box become active, as shown in Figure 24.35.

FIG. 24.35
PowerPoint's native audio and video clips share many controls and attributes, such as timing parameters.

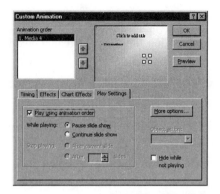

3. Select the While Playing radio buttons to determine what happens to your slide show while the selected audio clip plays. Select the Pause Slide Show radio button to have the slide show wait until the audio has finished, or select the Continue Slide Show radio button to have new slides come up with the audio playing through on all the slides.

4. Select the Stop Playing section to determine what happens to the selected audio as the slide show continues. Select the After Current Slide radio button to force the audio clip to end when you move to the next slide, or click the After Slides radio button to set the number of slides you want the audio to play for. This is particularly useful for managing audio clips that loop.

5. Click the More options button to open the Play Options dialog box.

6. In the Movie and Sound Options group, click the Loop Until Stopped check box to make the selected clip play continuously.

Using PowerPoint's Action Buttons to Add Multimedia

You can add interactive multimedia elements to you presentations using the new Action button feature. Action buttons place visible icons on your presentation screens, which perform actions when clicked or passed over with the mouse. While there are action buttons for advancing the slide show or going back to the first slide, there are two multimedia specific action buttons:

- Sound
- Movie

To add a multimedia action button, do the following:

1. Choose Slide Show, Action Buttons and from the dialog box that appears, select either the speaker icon or the video camera icon.

2. Click the slide, and drag out a box of the desired size. The Action Settings dialog box appears.

3. To invoke a video or audio file on a mouse click, make sure the Mouse Click tab is selected, and then click the Hyperlink To radio button.

4. Select Other File from the drop-down list box as shown in Figure 24.36.

FIG. 24.36

Select Other File from the Hyperlink To drop-down list.

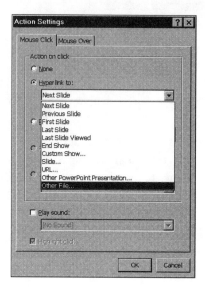

5. In the Hyperlink to Other File dialog box, select the multimedia file you want to associate with the button. Click OK.

6. If you think you will be moving your presentation files to another disk drive or directory, click the Use Relative Path for Hyperlink check box. This lets PowerPoint update the locations of media files.

7. Click OK, and the hyperlinked object appears on-screen as a simple icon, as shown in Figure 24.37.

The Sound and Movie action buttons behave no differently. The only difference is the on-screen appearance, which indicates to the user whether the icon accesses an audio or sound file.

FIG. 24.37
The hyperlinked object appears as an icon.

> **CAUTION**
> While action buttons provide useful cues for playing back media files, they do not provide the best performance. Audio and video clips can take a significant amount of time to load after the action button is pressed, halting the presentation and distracting the audience.

Adding a CD Soundtrack to Your Presentation

Another way to put compelling audio into your presentations is to use your PC's CD-ROM drive to play audio CDs. PowerPoint gives you several ways to play specific audio CD tracks in your presentation, making it easy to add familiar background music.

> **CAUTION**
> As ever, you need to be aware of copyright issues when using material like audio CDs in your presentations. To avoid the possibility of legal action, you should get explicit written permission when using a song or other copyrighted material in your presentation.

To insert a CD audio track into your presentation, do the following:

1. In Slide view, choose Insert, Movies and Sounds, Play CD Audio Track. The Play Options dialog box shown in Figure 24.38 appears.

2. In the Start section, set the Track spinner control to the number corresponding to the track number on the CD that you want to play. Then set the point within the track to begin playing by entering a time in minutes and seconds in the At item. If you want to start at the beginning of the track, leave this item at 00:00.

Part
VII

Ch
24

FIG. 24.38
PowerPoint lets you play songs and other material in your presentations directly from an audio CD.

3. In the End section, set the Track spinner control to the number corresponding to the track number on the CD that you want to stop playing. Set the end time within the track by entering a time in minutes and seconds in the At item. If you want to play one complete track, set the End Track number to one greater than the Start Track number, and leave the End At time at 00:00.

4. To make the selected CD audio play continuously until interrupted by the user, select the Loop Until Stopped check box.

5. Click OK to save the settings.

CAUTION

Remember, you must have the proper audio CD in the CD-ROM drive during your presentation. Otherwise, PowerPoint will be unable to access the tracks at runtime, and will interrupt your presentation with an error message.

Adding a Narration Track to Your Presentation

An exciting new feature to PowerPoint 97 is the ability to add narrative tracks to your presentations. To record narration for your presentation, do the following:

1. Choose Slide Show, Record Narration to display the Record Narration dialog box as shown in Figure 24.39. In the Current Recording Quality group, you see information on the currently-selected recording properties, as well as estimated available disk space and the amount of recording that will fit into the free space.

2. Click the Settings button to bring up the Multimedia Properties box. You can access recording settings here.

3. By default, narrations are recorded at CD-quality. However, if disk space is at a premium, you may want to lower audio quality by clicking the Preferred Quality drop-down list box inside the Recording group, as shown in Figure 24.40. You can select from CD Quality, Radio Quality, and Telephone Quality; or you can specify your own audio quality settings by clicking the Customize button. You can also set your recording and playback volumes using the appropriate slider bars.

FIG. 24.39

Before you get started recording narration, PowerPoint serves notice about how much space it's going to take on your hard drive.

FIG. 24.40

You can save some space—at the expense of sound quality—by setting recording fidelity to the Radio Quality setting. You can also set volume levels and create your own customized audio quality settings.

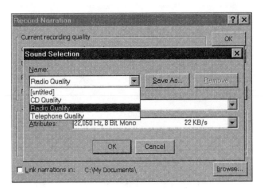

4. If you want to save your narration as a separate file linked into your presentation, select the Link Narrations In check box. Click the Browse button to save the narration to a specific directory if the default location provided is not acceptable.

5. Click the OK button to save your settings and begin narration. The presentation begins to run.

6. As the presentation runs, speak into the microphone. Note that audio elements do not play during the narration process.

7. Once you have finished narrating for a slide, you can press Enter to advance to the next slide in the presentation. If you have set your slides to advance automatically, simply wait for the next slide to appear and continue recording.

8. At the end of the show, you are prompted to save the timings along with the narration. Click Y̲es to save the timings, or click N̲o to save only the narration audio. A
sound icon now appears at the lower-right corner of all slides that include narration.

N O T E   You cannot edit your narration. You must re-record the entire sequence in order to
ensure that timings are correct. ▨

T I P   Don't need the narration track for a particular presentation? You can disable the track by
choosing Sli̲de Show, S̲et Up Show, and selecting the Show Without N̲arrations check box.

Exploring Typical Applications

by Brian Reilly

One of the most exciting things about PowerPoint 97 is its capability to truly integrate all of the Office applications into complete solutions to meet a wide variety of needs. Simple tasks like updating monthly charts can be done with minimal effort. Create presentations that can be changed daily and still look great. Create an interactive sales presentation with a host of possible presentations that can be instantly chosen depending on the circumstances that face the salesperson. All of these are a lot easier with Office 97.

Each of us has different levels of skill in each of the Office applications, depending on which one we use most frequently. So the approach to developing a solution to a specific problem may not be to learn the new application but to leverage the knowledge you already have and let the integration of the programs work for you. For instance, not everyone in your organization may be as skilled as you are in PowerPoint, but it is likely that they will be comfortable in Word or Excel. Therefore, in this chapter you explore ways to integrate the other Office 97 applications with PowerPoint to accomplish the task at hand. ■

Create stunning presentations that are easy to update using Word or Excel

Many people who need to update presentations frequently don't know PowerPoint but they do know Word or Excel. Let them use Word or Excel without sacrificing any of the features of PowerPoint.

Create presentations that summarize your data

The age-old problem with a presentation is giving the audience access to supporting data while not burying them in too much of the details. Find out how to have all the data available at the click of the mouse, yet keep it hidden if it is not needed.

Create presentations for distribution that cannot be edited

You may want to require that a presentation you distribute cannot be edited or printed. The reasons for this may vary, but the solution is actually quite simple.

Create an interactive sales presentation

You can now create interactive sales presentations so your salespeople are armed with professional presentations on almost every possible issue at the click of a button. And they don't need to be computer experts to use it.

Choosing the Best Applications for Your Tasks

Software vendors have been promising for some time that the integration of all applications will be made easier so users can focus on the document rather than the program being used to create it. Office 97 brings that promise a lot closer to reality. You can use whatever applications are best for the task at hand, and then integrate all the pieces into PowerPoint, which is the best tool for creating presentations.

Access or FoxPro can be the best tool for warehousing large databases of information, but Excel or Lotus 1-2-3 is often a better tool for analyzing that data. Word can be one of the best tools for writing thoughts about that analysis. However, PowerPoint will be the best tool to integrate all this into a coherent presentation. The following examples of real-world solutions to specific problems show how to integrate the best tool for each part of the task into the final product—that is, a PowerPoint presentation. Each example defines a specific objective, recognizes typical problems, and provides solutions to resolve those problems without compromising the quality of the final product.

Using Word to Create a Frequently Updated Presentation

Many users would like a daily, continuously-running presentation in their reception area or storefront window. The screen show might include some of the following:

Subject	Description
Information about the company	Latest sales results, earnings reports, new product introductions, new employees, new promotions, and more
A welcome message for visitors	Specific name of and message to the client visiting that day
Employee information	"Employee of the Month" or company sports team results
Lunch menus	Specials or changing items
Company-wide messages	New health care benefits or snow emergency reports

The most frequent problem is that creating a new presentation daily is often beyond the capabilities of the personnel who might be assigned to the task. They may not be very good designers, or may not know PowerPoint very well. However, chances are that they will know Word or Excel and be able to fill in some forms in either of these programs. The solution that works in this scenario is to have someone who does know PowerPoint create one master presentation that can be easily be updated by typing new data into a Word table or an Excel cell.

Setting Up the Data in Word

Here's how to create the first presentation so that it can be easily updated in Word 97. You can create the data in a Word document that a non-PowerPoint user can use to update the presentation daily:

1. Open a new Word document and create a table that is four columns wide, with the same number of rows as the number of slides that you are going to have in the PowerPoint presentation. Rows can be added or deleted later.

2. Save that Word document and note what directory you saved it in.

3. Open a new presentation in PowerPoint 97, if one is not already open, and save that file immediately to the same directory as the Word file. This will make the linking of the objects between files easier to manage.

4. Switch back to the Word table, and you are ready to begin.

One of the easiest ways to manage this solution is to think of each element of a PowerPoint page separately, and as occupying a location in a unique cell in Word. You are only going to be using one column of the table to copy and paste special with a link into PowerPoint. The other three columns are for information only, to make it easier for someone to maintain this file. Add the descriptors to the heads of the columns in the table, and you should have something that looks like Table 25.1.

N O T E You can have as many elements on a page as you need, but they should all be distinct, because each cell is copied and pasted individually into PowerPoint. I have also filled in the cells for the first three elements of page one in rows 2–4 in column 1.

Part

VII

Ch

25

Table 25.1   Word Table to Be Linked into PowerPoint

Insert Data in This Column for Updating in PowerPoint	Description	Comments
Welcome to Reilly & Associates	Page 1 Title	36-point type
Please enjoy this short welcome while you wait.	Page 1 Message	28-point type
Today is Wednesday, November 06, 1996	Today's Date	24-point type
This is clip art Standard Cat in MS ClipArt	Page 1 Picture	Company logo

Adding Clip Art to Tables   Filling in the table is easy. However, there is a trick to inserting visuals, whether they are clip art or separate picture files. In Word 97, you must first insert a text box into the cell of the table. Then you need to make sure that you can see a visual if inserted into the text box. Follow these steps:

1. Choose Tools, Options. Click the View tab and in the Show section make sure the Picture Placeholders check box is not selected.

2. Select the proper cell and choose Insert, Textbox. Your mouse point turns into a crosshair which you can use to draw the text box inside of the cell.

3. Choose Insert, Picture, and select the picture or clip art you want to insert. You could also choose WordArt or any of the other options under Insert, Picture.

Formatting the Table   Now you are ready to format the cells in the Word table so that when they are pasted into PowerPoint, they will already have the proper text size and text colors. This will make it easier to maintain the presentation and ensure that the copy that is typed into Word will not exceed the page size in PowerPoint.

To format the cell in Word, select the cell and choose Format, Font to set the size, color, and font style you want to use. You only need to apply special formatting to the cells in column 1 because those cells are the only cells you are going to import into PowerPoint. Figure 25.1 shows the formatted cells in the Word table.

FIG. 25.1
Format the cells to
Copy and Paste
Special right in the
Word table.

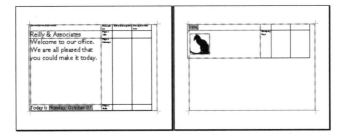

You will basically format each cell individually. Just as in PowerPoint, you can write a
short macro to format the active cell with a specific font, font size, and font color such as
the following macro which should be run after selecting the appropriate cell:

```
Sub Format_Title_Cell()
'
' Format_Title_Cell Macro
' Macro recorded 10/5/96 by Brian Reilly
'

    With Selection.Font
        .Name = "Gill Sans"
        .Size = 36
        .Bold = False
        .Italic = False
        .Underline = wdUnderlineNone
        .StrikeThrough = False
        .DoubleStrikeThrough = False
        .Outline = False
        .Emboss = False
        .Shadow = False
        .Hidden = False
        .SmallCaps = False
        .AllCaps = False
        .ColorIndex = wdBlue
        .Engrave = False
        .Superscript = False
        .Subscript = False
        .Spacing = 0
        .Scaling = 100
        .Position = 0
        .Kerning = 0
        .Animation = wdAnimationNone
    End With
End Sub


Sub Format_MessageText_Cell()
'

' Macro recorded 10/5/96 by Brian Reilly
'
```

```
With Selection.Font
    .Name = "Gill Sans"
    .Size = 30
    .Bold = False
    .Italic = False
    .Underline = wdUnderlineNone
    .StrikeThrough = False
    .DoubleStrikeThrough = False
    .Outline = False
    .Emboss = False
    .Shadow = False
    .Hidden = False
    .SmallCaps = False
    .AllCaps = False
    .ColorIndex = wdBlue
    .Engrave = False
    .Superscript = False
    .Subscript = False
    .Spacing = 0
    .Scaling = 100
    .Position = 0
    .Kerning = 0
    .Animation = wdAnimationNone
End With
End Sub
```

These two macros reside in the Visual Basic Editor in this Word document. Either one can be applied to any cell at any time just by selecting the contents of the entire cell and choosing Tools, Macro, Macros. Select the appropriate macro to run and choose Run.

TIP   You can format a cell in Word to be the exact size you need it to be in PowerPoint. That way, when you type more text in the cell than will fit, the text is stored in the cell, but is not visible and does not show up in the PowerPoint link. For example, if the cell length is exactly 330 points, only 10 lines of text will show in the cell. Formatting a cell this way adds one more safety net for you to ensure that everything in Word is properly formatted in PowerPoint. If your text won't fit into this cell, it won't fit into PowerPoint and you'll have to reduce the amount of text.

You will want to experiment with your own type size in your own document to see how many points you need for a given number of lines of type.

Linking the Word Data into PowerPoint

Now that the cells are all formatted correctly in Word, you are ready to incorporate them into the PowerPoint presentation. This is a cell-by-cell process, which may appear a bit time-consuming the first time through. However, it will make it easier to make changes to the contents of individual cells in column 1 and save the Word file. Then, when

PowerPoint is opened the next time, those changes will be automatically reflected in the PowerPoint presentation because everything has been linked to the Word document. To copy the cells contents to PowerPoint:

1. Select the cell in column 1 in the Word table and use the keystrokes Ctrl+C to copy the contents to the Clipboard.

2. Press Alt+Tab to switch to PowerPoint or click the Microsoft PowerPoint tab from the Open Program options at the bottom of the screen.

3. In PowerPoint, choose the blank page layout, because you are going to be placing these linked objects from Word and not using any text placeholders in PowerPoint.

4. In PowerPoint, choose Edit, Paste Special and click the Paste Link option.

5. Position the pasted object on the page.

6. Press Alt+Tab to switch back to Word and repeat steps 1–5 on each successive cell until you have completed the entire presentation.

You can add as many individual Word cells to a PowerPoint page as you need. If you add them as individual elements, you then can arrange them on the page to fit your design needs. Figure 25.2 shows a completed first page in this presentation.

Part
VII

Ch
25

FIG. 25.2

A PowerPoint page can have multiple cells on the same page.

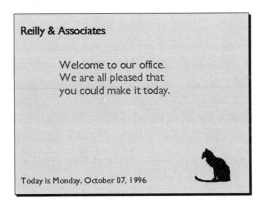

Reilly & Associates

Welcome to our office.
We are all pleased that
you could make it today.

Today is Monday, October 07, 1996

When you have transferred all the contents of your Word cells into PowerPoint, you can then go back and apply any slide transitions, slide timings, or animation effects to the presentation just as you would to a normal PowerPoint presentation. Those effects will be attached to the object on the PowerPoint page which is linked back to object in the Word cell. So whenever someone makes some simple changes to the cells in the Word document, all the same effects will still be in place with the updated linked data in PowerPoint.

N O T E Because these files are linked, they both need to be available on the computer that is showing the presentation. If the Word files are updated on one machine and the presentation is shown on another machine, then you should create the initial presentation with both the Word file and the PowerPoint file in the same directory so that when someone moves the updated file to another computer, it should be moved into the same directory as the PowerPoint file. ▦

Launching Other Applications from a Presentation

The age-old problem with 35mm slide presentations is that they are truly linear in organization. If someone in your audience wants you to cover an item in much greater detail than you have in the slide tray, you are hard-pressed to jump to supporting visuals out of sequence. Even if you are using the more flexible medium of overheads, you may still have to shuffle overheads in backup folders to find the detailed answer about the results in the Chicago market for the Rainforest shampoo brand. With PowerPoint 97, that problem no longer exists. You can hide the detail and yet have instant access to it at the click of the mouse.

The basic idea is to establish a hyperlink from the presentation page to the specific data that is summarized on that page. This will permit you to jump into the specific document that contains the data you are talking about. You can also operate that source program at the same time and manipulate the details to add extra explanations as necessary without affecting the summary level of your presentation. When you are through dealing with that specific question, a mouse click returns you to where you were in the slide show.

Let's assume that your underlying data is in an Excel PivotTable which shows net income by brand and by market. That is a lot of detail to have at your fingertips. Assume also that you are presenting the national summary by brand. Your summary report, which is a copy of the image of the summarized PivotTable, might look like Figure 25.3.

When you are asked a specific question about a specific market such as Chicago, you can immediately launch that PivotTable in Excel and then find any detail with just a few keystrokes.

FIG. 25.3
An Excel PivotTable can put a great deal of detail at your fingertips when you need it, and hide it when you don't.

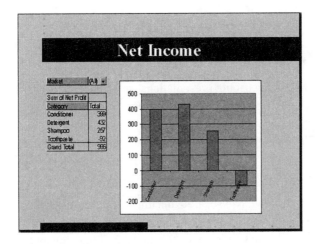

In order to launch an application or a specific file from a single click on an object in a screen show, follow these steps:

1. In this particular case, the PowerPoint object is a copy of the source PivotTable in Excel, so in Excel, select the entire range surrounding the PivotTable and choose Edit, Copy to copy it to the Clipboard.

2. Switch to PowerPoint and select the appropriate page. You may then paste the contents of the Clipboard by choosing Edit, Paste or paste it with a link by choosing Edit, Paste Special.

3. With the object selected, choose Slide Show, Custom Animation.

4. Click the Play Settings tab and set the Object Action setting pull-down to Edit.

5. Click OK to return to PowerPoint in Edit mode.

Now when you play the screen show, you can click the PivotTable object to open Excel if it is not already open or activate the Excel file that contains this PivotTable. You can then manipulate the PivotTable in Excel. You can even move around within the spreadsheet and jump from market to market if necessary. To get back to the screen show, just minimize or close the Excel sheet.

T I P This technique works with launching any application. If a particular application is much better at demonstrating a point in a dynamic environment, you can use this same technique and retain all the power of the best tool available to make your point without losing the power of PowerPoint to control the overall presentation.

Part
VII

Ch
25

Protecting a Presentation from Editing or Printing

Many users want to distribute presentations with a lock on them, so the presentation cannot be edited or printed. There may be legal or pricing issues involved, or the user may not want the viewer to be able to see the steps used to create an effect. PowerPoint 97 still has no file protection feature, but there is a workaround that is quite easy to implement invisibly. It's not 100 percent foolproof, but it will protect your presentation from most PowerPoint users.

The solution is to create two separate documents. In this case, it will be two presentations. The first presentation is the one you want to protect. Let's call that Protectme.ppt. The second file is called Container.ppt and contains the Protectme.ppt file and shields it from being edited. The Container.ppt file need not be any longer than one page. To insert (and protect) the Protectme.ppt file:

1. Make sure Protectme.ppt is saved and closed.

2. Open Container.ppt, if it is not already open, and go to the page on which you want to embed the Protectme.ppt file.

3. Choose Insert, Object.

4. From the Object Type scroll bar, choose Microsoft PowerPoint Presentation, and then click Create From File.

5. Next, use the Browse button to locate the Protectme.ppt file.

6. Make sure the Link check box is not checked, and click OK. You return to PowerPoint and see an image of the first page of the Protectme.ppt file on the page.

7. Size it as you see fit. The shape and position of the Protectme.ppt object have no significant effect on the ability to show that presentation.

8. Choose Slide Show, Custom Animation. (The Protectme.ppt object was automatically selected when you came out of the Insert Object dialog boxes.)

9. You can then set the custom effects you want for this embedded presentation. For example, by switching among the various tabs, you can set the timing for the presentation to play and whether you want it to start automatically or only on a mouse click. Be sure in Play Settings to set the option to Show and check the Hide While Not Playing check box if you want it invisible until the presentation starts.

You can also embed PowerPoint presentations into Word and Excel documents and have them play from there. You just need to be sure that the host machine has PowerPoint installed if you are running it from inside of Excel or Word.

Creating an Interactive Presentation Complete with Branching

Salespeople never know what to expect in client presentations. But they have to be ready for it anyway. The best salespeople have always been able to handle the hard questions with their own verbal skills and knowledge. However, unless they were using expensive and difficult programs like Director, they never had the audio-visual tools to support what they were saying. Now they do. With PowerPoint 97, they can jump around from item to item in a sales presentation quite easily, even if they're computer neophytes. And preparing, modifying, and updating the presentation is just as easy.

Note that branching generally differs from jumping. *Branching* can be thought of as a side trip to another presentation and then returning to exactly where you branched from. *Jumping* is literally a move to a new presentation without the connection to return back to your departure point.

Let's take a look at the structure of a simple interactive sales presentation that permits the salesperson to cover any number of subjects in random order. Figure 25.4 shows an schematic diagram of part of this presentation. I focus only on the possibilities that are shown connected with the solid lines. There could easily be additional branches possible for much more detail from any of the other options that show no additional detail.

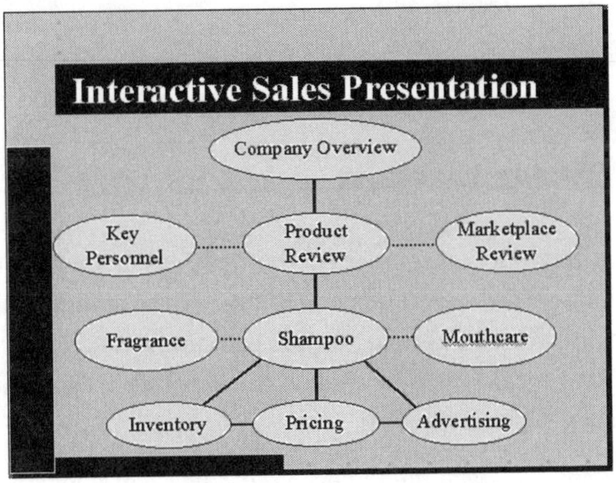

Part
VII
Ch
25

FIG. 25.4
You focus on Company Overview, Product Review, Shampoo, and Inventory, Pricing, and Advertising.

The presentation can be assembled in a variety of ways. The two simplest ways are:

- As one presentation with all pages in each section in sequential order.
- As a separate presentation for each section with each page within a section in sequential order.

While the choice is yours, you might strongly consider the second choice, because updates to a specific section may be easier to update and distribute to each of the sales people. That is the option that you explore in this example.

Let's focus on the structure of the presentation rather than how to create any specific page. The structure of the presentation dictates the path the salesperson will be able to take at any point in time. You can build as much flexibility into your presentation as you like, but if you plan to jump only one level at a time, the graphic design will look less cluttered.

Take a look at Figure 25.5 to see what might be the first slide of the Company Overview section. In fact, no matter what page in this section, each page can have these same hyperlink buttons so that the salesperson could jump to the following level from any page in this section.

FIG. 25.5
The left-hand bar has three hyperlink buttons that permit you to jump to either of the next three options on the following level.

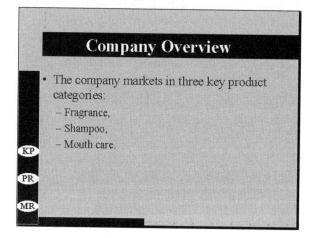

The three ellipses that function as the hyperlink buttons are just that—ellipses drawn with the Drawing tool. They have a text box added to serve as an unintrusive menu for the salesperson. Because you are focusing on the path to the next level to Product Review in this case, look at how to add the hyperlink to the separate presentation named Product Review.ppt. To establish the hyperlink:

1. Select the object to attach the hyperlink, in this case, select the ellipse that says PR.

2. Right-click and choose Action Settings from the shortcut menu.

3. From the dialog box that appears, select the Mouse Click or Mouse Over tab, depending on whether you want to activate the hyperlink based on a mouse click or just by passing the mouse over the button.

4. Click the Hyperlink To button and select Other PowerPoint Presentation as shown in Figure 25.6.

5. Browse to select the presentation Product Review.ppt and click OK.

6. At this point, you see a list of all the slides in the selected presentation. You have the choice of establishing a hyperlink to any of the slides in that presentation by clicking a slide in Slide title. In this case, you can establish the link to slide 1.

7. Click OK to return to the previous dialog box. Click OK again to accept the setting and return to Edit mode in PowerPoint.

FIG. 25.6

Set the hyperlink to Other PowerPoint Presentation.

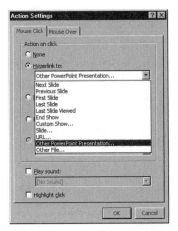

Part

VII

Ch

25

Follow the same steps to set the hyperlinks for the two other buttons on this page but choose the file Key Personnel.ppt or Marketplace Review.ppt, depending on which button you are using for the hyperlink.

If you run the slide show and click the PR button on this page, PowerPoint automatically opens Product Review.ppt in Slide Show view on the page number you have selected.

If you want to place these same hyperlink buttons on every page in this Company Overview section, you don't need to repeat these steps on each page. If you have completed the other pages and want to assign the hyperlink buttons to each page, there is a quick easy way once you have set the first set of hyperlinks. To copy the hyperlink buttons and the hyperlink assignments from this first page to each following page in this section:

1. Hold down the Shift key and click each of the three buttons to select them all.

2. Press Ctrl+C to copy the buttons and the assigned hyperlink code to the Clipboard.

3. Press the Page Down key to advance one page and press Ctrl+V to paste the buttons into the exact same location on that page.

4. Press the Page Down key again to advance to the next page and press Ctrl+V to paste the buttons again to that page.

5. Repeat step 4 until you are finished with every page in the section.

The nice part about copying and pasting objects from one page to another is that PowerPoint automatically pastes the object into exactly the same location on the page, and it also copies all properties associated with that object, such as the hyperlink code in this case.

You could now repeat this process with each separate file in the presentation. Open the Product Review file and create ellipses—or any shape for that matter—and hyperlinks to the next level of the presentation using the same technique. In a case like this example, you may want to add a fourth and a fifth ellipse with a hyperlink pointing upward in the presentation rather than downward. You can move up one level with one of these hyperlink buttons and return home to the very top of the presentation with the other.

Hyperlinks are a very powerful technique to use to jump to another location, either within a presentation or another presentation. You can even select which slide in a presentation to which you want to jump.

 While this example permitted the salesperson to jump only one level at a time, you may want to create a master opening page that has more options and permits them to jump multiple levels immediately. For example, this same presentation could be used with an existing customer, and the salesperson may want to jump immediately to Pricing to cover new pricing on existing products.

TROUBLESHOOTING

The hyperlinks worked fine on my computer, but when I moved the presentations to the salesperson's computer, some of the hyperlinks didn't work. What am I doing wrong?
Hyperlinks are very sensitive to the path of the linked files. If you created the presentation on a computer and linked to files in different directories, the path to those directories are recorded invisibly, so the hyperlink button knows where to go and open the linked file. When the presentation was moved to a second computer, the files were probably put into different relative locations. If you are going to move presentations with hyperlinks to other computers, it is wise to create all the links to files in the same directory. That way, when the hyperlink button tries to find the linked file, it says, "I will look for that file in the same directory that I'm in." If the file is there, the link will work.

You have learned about several different ways to develop solutions to specific problems that are common in real life. There are many more that could be addressed using the same kinds of approaches presented here. Find the best application to solve the specific task at hand, and use the power of integration to let PowerPoint 97 assemble the elements for you from whatever application solves the problem best for you. ●

Part
VII

Ch
25

CHAPTER 26

Building Your Own Custom Presentation

by Brian Reilly

Microsoft has finally implemented its plan to integrate a common programming language in all of the Office 97 products. Now, with the addition of Visual Basic for Applications (VBA) to PowerPoint, Word, Project, and Access, you can create very nice looking custom presentations that use elements from all of these sources, choosing the best source for each task.

For example, while Access is the workhorse at storing and manipulating a very large database, you might prefer Excel to analyze that database. Word is still the best place to create tables and to write about the analysis done in Excel. PowerPoint, though weak in the area of analysis, is the thoroughbred of the group at assembling all of the others into easily understood and easily navigated graphic presentations.

With VBA, you can integrate all of these products and create custom presentations in seconds. ▪

Create custom presentations that show or hide key information, such as a customer's name, throughout the entire presentation

You can make a simple 15-second change and have that reflected in an entire presentation immediately.

Create custom presentations that let you change the underlying data immediately during the presentation without leaving Slide Show view

Whether you need to change languages during a presentation to explain a particularly complex concept in a different language or change the categories you want to examine during a budget review, you can do this at the click of a button.

The Foundation of a Custom Presentation

Many companies give essentially the same presentation to many customers and would like to customize their presentations to each specific customer. Until now, this could have been a fairly time-consuming project. However, with PowerPoint 97, the task is much easier.

Imagine that you are presenting a market analysis of sales results to a customer. What will vary from market to market is the list of products and the list of retailers in that marketplace. However, the structure of the tables and charts will remain constant. The trick then is to manipulate the underlying data in Excel and create all your tables and charts in Excel. Then using VBA in PowerPoint 97, you can control the manipulation of the data in Excel so that all your charts and tables are re-created from code and then instantly updated in PowerPoint.

Let's look at some specific examples of what you can do to customize your presentation.

Customizing Data in Presentations

A host of opportunities enable you to customize data in presentations. I have seen requests to hide all customer names in a chart except for the name of the particular customer being presented. There are also situations where the names of customers will vary by market—for example, when presenting to a retailer. A frequent request is for the ability to create a presentation that can be instantly switched into a different language.

Customizing Names to Hide in Charts

The ability of Excel to manipulate data is frequently a key to customizing the data in a presentation. If you want to hide all the customer names except the name of your particular audience's company, you can do that in an easy step if you prepare your tables and charts correctly in the first place. Figure 26.1 shows a worksheet in Excel with a list of customer names from Customer1 to Customer4.

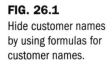
FIG. 26.1
Hide customer names
by using formulas for
customer names.

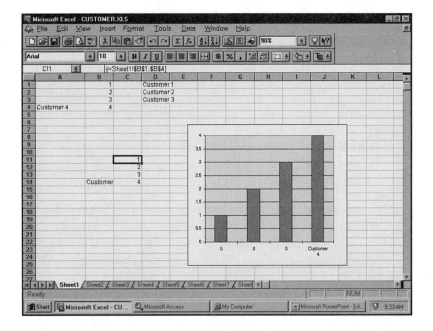

The chart shown is created from the range B10:C14. However, the customer names in
B10:B14 are formulas referring to the actual text in the range A1:A4. If you were to create
all your charts like this one with the customer names being formulas referring to cells
A1:A4, you could just drag the customer names you want to hide into another location
such as column D, and they disappear from all charts immediately.

Each chart created in Excel should then be copied and pasted into PowerPoint by choosing Edit, Paste Special, Paste Link.

Switching Languages During a Presentation

With the continuing globalization of the economy, you may find yourself presenting to
audiences whose native language may be different from yours. Sometimes complex concepts are better understood when explained in the native language of a particular audience. You could carry multiple copies of the same presentation, but if you found yourself
in the middle of a presentation and wanted to switch languages, it would be somewhat
distracting to both the presenter and the audience to open another presentation and find
your place in the new version.

Part
VII

Ch
26

You can now do this instantly with the use of VBA. If you have created your presentation by typing the text into individual cells in Excel, you could attach macro commands to change the text from one language to another instantly.

However, in this case you are going to place the contents of the Excel cells directly into the Title placeholder or the Click Here placeholder on each PowerPoint page and let the PowerPoint master apply the formatting.

Let's look at that in more detail. There are several steps to setting up this presentation and a little bit of VBA code to be written to make the language change at any point during the presentation.

Type some of the text into Excel cells and add the translation to the adjacent column. Figure 26.2 shows a section of a spreadsheet with the text for page 1. Column A is used as a description to make it easier to keep track of what text will go where. Column B contains the English text. Column C contains the French text.

FIG. 26.2

Using the first column to describe where the cell contents will go will be helpful later.

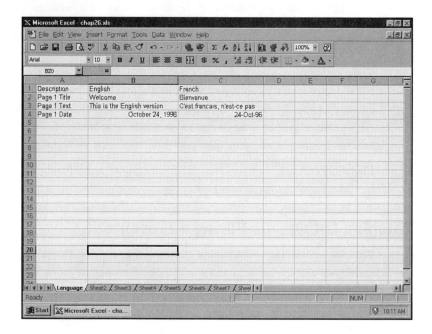

The next step is to add two option buttons to a PowerPoint page, because you will want to be able to choose only one language to show at a time.

The other choice that you might have made would be to use check boxes to get user input with a mouse click. However, check boxes are used in situations where you can make multiple selections. The Properties dialog box is a two-column table. The first column lists the description of the property and cannot be modified. The second column shows the setting of that property and this is where you modify the settings. To add the two option buttons to the PowerPoint page:

1. Switch back to the PowerPoint presentation or open a new presentation.
2. If the Control Toolbox is not visible, make it visible by choosing View, Toolbars and clicking in the check box next to Control Toolbox. See Figure 26.3 to view the Control Toolbox toolbar.

FIG. 26.3
The Control Toolbox is new to PowerPoint.

3. Click the option button to select that tool.
4. Drag the mouse on the page to draw the option button. This is very similar to adding a shape with one of the drawing tools. You see the option button, and if you made the button large enough you can see the text OptionButton1 on the button face. Repeat steps 3 and 4 to add a second option button. That button is automatically named OptionButton2.
5. Size both buttons, just like a drawing object, and place them into the desired position on the page (see Figure 26.4).

FIG. 26.4
These option buttons permit you to make choices of a language during a slide show.

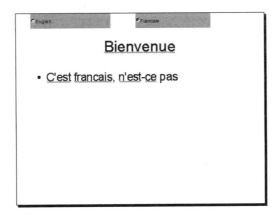

Part
VII

Ch
26

At this point, you have added the buttons to control the presentation language during the slide show. There are several options that can change the interface, and they all relate to the Properties of the OptionButtons.

Change the caption property to be more descriptive than OptionButton1 or OptionButton2. It really would not be a very user-friendly application if the descriptions on buttons contained generic text. Fortunately, you can change not only the name on the button, but also other properties of the button such as the font type, color, and size.

You can also change the color of the button. If you right-click the mouse on the option button, you see the menu shown in Figure 26.5. Click the Properties choice to access the Properties dialog box. To change the caption on the button, just type your new description in the box to the right of Caption on the Alphabetic tab in the Properties dialog box.

FIG. 26.5

Right-clicking the option button brings up these choices.

You can add pictures to the Button face so the buttons can now become a significant design element that you can use. For example, assume that in this example of choosing a different language, you had two pictures of flags that you have saved as USFLAG.BMP and FRFLAG.BMP. You can consider using these flag images on the buttons rather than using text. You need to assign a macro to the button later in this process, but first you can place the flag images on the two buttons.

To place a picture on the button, select the row in the Properties dialog box for Picture; initially, it says None. You are presented with a drop-down button in the right-hand column of the row. Figure 26.6 shows much of the Properties dialog box. You can then just browse your directories to find the correct picture to insert on the button. This process is very similar to inserting a picture into a PowerPoint page, but it is done within the confines of the Properties dialog box.

FIG. 26.6

Properties are
changed in the
Properties dialog box.

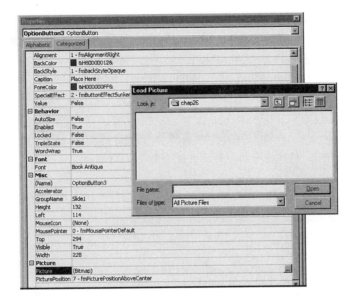

 T I P When making changes to the properties of a variety of objects, you can use the pull-down box at
the top of the Properties dialog box to switch immediately to another object and view those
properties.

You are now ready to write several different macros to handle the actual changing of text
on the slide. This process involves several steps, so the first thing you should do is to list
the steps such as the following:

1. Clear the existing text on a page by deleting the existing text in each placeholder.
2. Activate Excel and open the spreadsheet that is the container for all of the language
   versions.
3. Copy the correct range of Excel cells to the Clipboard.
4. Activate PowerPoint, select the correct text placeholder, and paste the contents of
   the Clipboard.
5. Repeat steps 3 and 4 for each range in the Excel sheet that needs to be changed.

 T I P If you are copying several bullet points from Excel, you can select the multiple cell range and copy
it to the Clipboard. When the range is pasted into a bullet placeholder, PowerPoint recognizes
each cell as a different bullet.

Part
VII

Ch
26

Listing 26.1 shows the way to accomplish each step for changing the text from English into French. Similar code would reverse the process. Note that the lines of code that begin with an apostrophe are not executed by the macro and are comments to explain what the next line of code accomplishes. The macro in Listing 26.1 clears the present text values of the Title and bullet placeholders on this slide.

Listing 26.1   Clearing Present Text Values of Title and Bullet Placeholders

```
Sub Clear_Title_and_Bullet_Placeholder_Text()
'
' Macro recorded 10/22/96 by Brian Reilly
' This selects the active slide and the Title Text placeholder
    ActiveWindow.Selection.SlideRange.Shapes("Rectangle 2").Select
' This selects all the text in the placeholder
    ActiveWindow.Selection.ShapeRange.TextFrame.TextRange.Select
    ActiveWindow.Selection.ShapeRange.TextFrame.TextRange.Characters(Start:=1,
➥Length:=0).Select
' This sets the contents of the placeholder to nothing
    With ActiveWindow.Selection.TextRange
        .Text = " "
'this With/End With section is not necessary because the master page controls
'the formatting, but if you use the macro recorder you will see this code.
        With .Font
            .Name = "Times New Roman"
            .Size = 44
            .Bold = msoFalse
            .Italic = msoFalse
            .Underline = msoFalse
            .Shadow = msoFalse
            .Emboss = msoFalse
            .BaselineOffset = 0
            .AutoRotateNumbers = msoFalse
            .Color.SchemeColor = ppTitle
        End With
'This End with closes the With from the With ActiveWindow.Selection.TextRange
'        .Text = " " line of code
    End With
'This unselects the Title Text placeholder and is not necessary
    ActiveWindow.Selection.Unselect
'This line selects ("Rectangle 5") which is the Bullet Placeholder
    ActiveWindow.Selection.SlideRange.Shapes("Rectangle 5").Select
    ActiveWindow.Selection.ShapeRange.TextFrame.TextRange.Select
'This sets the text in the bullet placeholder to nothing
    ActiveWindow.Selection.ShapeRange.TextFrame.TextRange.Characters(Start:=1,
Length:=4).Select
    ActiveWindow.Selection.TextRange.Text = " "
    ActiveWindow.Selection.Unselect
End Sub
```

The next task is to open Excel and copy the appropriate range to the Clipboard. Because you will be performing several copy and paste actions between Excel and PowerPoint, it is wise to separate these into separate tasks:

1. Open Excel and open the file containing the language translations.
2. Copy the first range to the Clipboard.
3. Use the Alt+Tab keys to switch back to PowerPoint and paste the contents of the Clipboard into the correct placeholder in PowerPoint.
4. Copy the second range to the Clipboard in Excel.
5. Paste the contents of the Clipboard into the correct placeholder in PowerPoint.
6. Close the Excel application and do not save the Excel file because no changes were made.

The macro in Listing 26.2 opens Excel and the correct file.

Listing 26.2 Opening Excel and the Correct File

```
'Option Explicit means we have to declare all variables.
Option Explicit
' Dim declares the variable xlapp as an object. It could be called anything, but
¦xlapp is 'somewhat descriptive and will help you remember that it refers to
¦the xl application.

Sub Open_xl_langfile()
'This sets the variable xlapp equal to the Excel.exe file to open Excel
Set xlapp = CreateObject("Excel.Application.8")
'The next choice is whether to run Excel visibly or invisibly
'For debugging purposes, set visible = True so you can follow the steps
'Then when all is working change Visible = True to = False and it will not show
'up on the screen
xlapp.Visible = False
'Next you open the correct file. Use the correct path name or it will not work.
Xlapp.Workbooks.Open "c:\MyDocuments\langfile.xls"

End sub
```

Now the Excel file would be open and running invisibly behind the PowerPoint screen show. The next task you want to do is copy the appropriate cells from Excel and paste them into the appropriate placeholders in PowerPoint. The macro in Listing 26.3 does just that.

Listing 26.3   Copying Excel Cells and Pasting into PowerPoint Placeholders

```
Sub Copy_Paste_Page1_French()
'If xlapp is still declared as a variable and this code is in the same module as
¦the previous code, you do not have to re-declare it.
' copies cell C2 to the clipboard
Xlapp.Range("C2").Copy

' You should probably break the following code into several more macros that
¦would be called from this point, but in this case to simplify the logic it is
¦continued in this macro.
'This selects the Title placeholder
ActiveWindow.Selection.SlideRange.Shapes("Rectangle 2").Select
    ActiveWindow.Selection.ShapeRange.TextFrame.TextRange.Select
'This selects the first character in the Title placeholder which is empty in
this case.
    ActiveWindow.Selection.ShapeRange.TextFrame.TextRange.Characters(Start:=1,
Length:=0).Select
'This pastes the contents of the Clipboard into the Placeholder
    With ActiveWindow.Selection.TextRange
        .Paste
End With

'This copies Cell C3 in Excel to Clipboard
Xlapp.Range("C3").Copy
'This selects the bullet placeholder
ActiveWindow.Selection.SlideRange.Shapes("Rectangle 5").Select
    ActiveWindow.Selection.ShapeRange.TextFrame.TextRange.Select
'This selects the first character in the bullet placeholder which is empty in
¦this case.
    ActiveWindow.Selection.ShapeRange.TextFrame.TextRange.Characters(Start:=1,
Length:=0).Select
'This pastes the contents of the Clipboard into the Placeholder
    With ActiveWindow.Selection.TextRange
        .Paste
End With
End sub
```

Now that these macros are written, it is time to combine them into one macro that calls each macro in sequence and makes the language change. That way, you can assign only one macro to the OptionButton2 for the French flag. When you write the similar code to change the contents of the placeholders to English, you can reuse some of these macros such as the one that opens the correct Excel file. To call other macros from a macro, just type the name of the macro in the correct sequence to execute, but do not include the Sub or () part of the macro name. The macro to change the language from English to French is shown in Listing 26.4.

Listing 26.4   Changing the Language from English to French

```
Sub Change_To_French()

Clear_Title_and_Bullet_Placeholder_Text
Open_xl_langfile
Copy_Paste_Page1_French
End sub
```

This macro changes the text in both placeholders on the page. Making the appropriate changes to these macros to change the presentation text back to English is now a very quick and easy task to accomplish. Because the Excel file is still running invisibly in the background, you don't need to re-open Excel. But you do have to change the macro to copy cells B2 and B3, instead of C2 and C3. Just copy the entire macro `Copy_Paste_Page1_French` and paste it into a module (see Listing 26.5). Then you only have three simple changes you have to make along with two other changes that won't affect the code. All of the changes to be made are:

1. Change the name to say `English` instead of `French`.

2. Change C2 to B2.

3. Change C3 to B3.

4. Optionally, change the comment for C2 to B2.

5. Optionally, change the comment for C3 to B3.

Listing 26.5   Copying and Pasting the Macro into a Module

```
Sub Copy_Paste_Page1_English()
'If xlapp is still declared as a variable and this code is in the same module as
¦the previous code, you do not have to re-declare it.
' copies cell B2 to the Clipboard
Xlapp.Range("B2").Copy

' You should probably break the following code into several more macros that
¦would be called from this point, but in this case to simplify the logic it is
¦continued in this macro.
'This selects the Title placeholder
ActiveWindow.Selection.SlideRange.Shapes("Rectangle 2").Select
    ActiveWindow.Selection.ShapeRange.TextFrame.TextRange.Select
'This selects the first character in the Title placeholder which is empty in
¦this case.
    ActiveWindow.Selection.ShapeRange.TextFrame.TextRange.Characters(Start:=1,
Length:=0).Select
'This pastes the contents of the Clipboard into the Placeholder
    With ActiveWindow.Selection.TextRange
        .Paste
End With
```

continues

Part
VII

Ch
26

Listing 26.5   Continued

```
'This copies Cell B3 in Excel to Clipboard
Xlapp.Range("B3").Copy
'This selects the bullet placeholder
ActiveWindow.Selection.SlideRange.Shapes("Rectangle 5").Select
     ActiveWindow.Selection.ShapeRange.TextFrame.TextRange.Select
'This selects the first character in the bullet placeholder which is empty in
¦this case.
     ActiveWindow.Selection.ShapeRange.TextFrame.TextRange.Characters(Start:=1,
Length:=0).Select
'This pastes the contents of the Clipboard into the Placeholder
     With ActiveWindow.Selection.TextRange
          .Paste
End With
End sub
```

N O T E   If you want to close Excel instead of keeping it running in the background, you need to
add another macro with the following single line:

```
xlapp.Quit
```

Or, just add it as a last line when you are finished copying and pasting from Excel. ■

The last thing to do so that all this works is to assign the macro to change the language to the correct OptionButton on the page. This is done by calling the macro—for example,

```
Sub Change_To_French()
```

from the OptionButton2 code. Return to the PowerPoint page and right-click the OptionButton2 which should have the French flag on the button face. Choose View Code. That will show you the code for OptionButton2 which is empty at the moment. Type the command to call the Change_To_French macro into the second line as follows:

```
Private Sub OptionButton2_Click()
Change_To_French
End Sub
```

That's all there is to it. While this example dealt with changing languages, it could also easily have changed charts or ranges that reflect different budgets in spreadsheets or budgets that reflect different divisions. The OptionButtons that let you navigate the presentation don't have to be included on every page. You may choose to create multiple presentations such as one for each division each month. Depending on what your specific needs are if you take some time to set up the spreadsheets carefully, you can create multiple presentations every month with the click of a few buttons, instead of spending all the late nights performing these repetitive tasks. ●

P A R T

VIII

Appendixes

Resources

by Nancy Stevenson

Several resources can help you create PowerPoint
presentations, from slide bureaus that can generate
your 35mm slides to companies that produce
collections of clip media. ■

Microsoft Resources

What follows are just a few representative resources to get you started. They are organized by category so you can find them easily. Many have a page on the World Wide Web, and that address, as well as a phone number, is given, where available.

PowerPoint Home Page

http://www.microsoft.com/mspowerpoint/

Here you can get information on new releases of the product, add-on products from third-party software vendors, and tips on using PowerPoint.

PowerPoint 32-Bit Viewer

http://www.microsoft.com/powerpoint/Internet/Viewer/default.htm

Go to this site to download the PowerPoint 32-bit Viewer, which enables those without PowerPoint installed on their computer to view PowerPoint presentations.

PowerPoint Animation Player

http://www.microsoft.com/mspowerpoint/internet/player/default.htm

Using this player, you can create Web pages with PowerPoint and browser extensions.

Microsoft Support

http://www.microsoft.com/powerpoint/ps_ppt.htm

Send messages to Microsoft Technical Support from this page. You can also reach them through PowerPoint. Select Help, Microsoft on the Web to connect.

Slide Bureaus

Slide bureaus are used to generate 35mm slides from your PowerPoint files. They are usually set up to receive your file online with an online order form. Turnaround can take as little as a day or two, with overnight express shipping costing you extra; however, be alert to rush charges, which can be very high. Here are some slide bureaus to check into.

Genigraphics is the service bureau for which Microsoft has integrated ordering procedures in PowerPoint. For more about this company, look in PowerPoint's Help topic index under the term Genigraphics. You can contact them at 1-714-553-1101.

Here's a list of other companies:

Company	Location	Web/Internet Address	Phone Number
Konold Kreations	Columbus, OH	Slides@aol.com	1-614-866-4376
S & L Professional Imaging	Tampa, FL	http://www. allworld.com/ s-l-imaging/	1-813-980-1400
Slide Express	Boston, MA		1-800-472-7449
Slidemaker	Eureka, CA	http://www. slidemaker.com/ index.html	1-310-396-4421
Slides R Us	New York, NY		1-800-707-0681
Slides Unlimited		slidesun@ slidesunlimited.com	1-818-705-1084
RDP	Cincinnati, OH	104047.2314@ compuserve.com	1-513-621-9136

Font Collections

You may want to get additional typefaces for use in your presentations. You can buy collections of fonts on CD-ROM or online and download them as you go. Here are a couple of suggested resources.

Adobe Systems, Inc.

http://www.adobe.com

Adobe produces the Adobe Type Library, Adobe Type Manager to fine-tune your type, and Adobe Type On Call CD-ROM. The latter allows you to call a number, order, and download new typefaces as you need them.

Jerry's World

CompuServe: **74431,225**

This online store has a wide variety of typefaces, clip art, photos, and sound effects for sale.

Clip Art and Graphics

If you like PowerPoint's ability to place pictures, photographs, videos, and sound in a presentation, you might want to expand your collection of clip media by contacting some of these vendors. Remember, you can add as much media as you like to Microsoft's Clip Gallery within the various categories.

The Clip Art Connection

http://www.acy.digexnet/%7Einfomart/clipart/index.html

This is a great source for clip art collections in various styles; they're constantly adding new art, so you might want to check in frequently.

Three D Graphics

http://www.threedgraphics.com/compadre; 1-800-913-0008

Try this service for additional textures, backgrounds, and action buttons for your presentations.

desktopPublishing

http://www.desktoppublishing.com/cliplist.html

desktopPublishing handles a wide variety of clip art, as well as photos.

Jerry's World

CompuServe: **74431,225**

This online store sells clip art collections, typefaces, photos, and sound effects.

Metro Creative Graphics, New York, NY

Metro produces a popular line of clip art on CD-ROM called ClipMASTERPRO. You can contact them at 1-212-947-5100.

PrePress Solutions, East Hanover, NJ

This company sells a large selection of photo CDs and graphics hardware. You can contact them at 1-800-631-8134, ext. 2.

Publications

Publications are available that keep you up-to-date on the latest technologies for presentations, including projection hardware, clip media, animation, and sound. Graphics- and desktop publishing-oriented publications can also be useful for finding advertisements for clip media products, projection systems, or articles on page design which can be applicable to PowerPoint slides.

Inside Microsoft PowerPoint

http://www.cobb.com/ipp/free1001.htm

This monthly newsletter is published by The Cobb Group. It's full of tips and techniques for the PowerPoint user, for $39 per year. You can get a free copy of the newsletter from their World Wide Web site.

PC World Multimedia Edition Online

http://www.multimedia.com

Formerly *Multimedia World Magazine*, this helpful publication was gobbled by *PC World* and is now known by the aforementioned name. This is their online location, where you can search for articles in the category of presenting.

Software

Some products are available that can either build elements, such as animations, which can be used in PowerPoint presentations, or that work as add-on products to make PowerPoint easier to use. Here are a few you might want to explore. You might also want to check into shareware products by cruising around multimedia or graphics forums on your online service or the Internet.

N O T E The release of versions of these products that support PowerPoint 97 may lag slightly behind the release of PowerPoint itself. However, these software products have supported PowerPoint in the past and are likely to offer compatible versions in the near future. Check for availability. ■

AddImpact!

Gold Disk, 1-800 465-3375

This product adds a new toolbar to PowerPoint that makes it easier to add voice, animation, and sound effects.

Animation Works

Gold Disk, 1-800 465-3375

Build your own animations for use in PowerPoint presentations by using this set of tools from Gold Disk.

PointPlus Maker

Net-Scene, **http://www.net-scene.com**

PointPlus Maker allows you view PowerPoint presentations embedded in HTML pages. Using this software, you can publish PowerPoint presentations as Web-compressed files.

WalkThrough

Virtus Corporation, 1-800 847-8871

WalkThrough is a 3-D drawing program you can use to build animations for use in PowerPoint presentations. ●

Glossary

16-bit   In Windows, refers to the way memory is accessed. 16-bit applications access memory in 16-bit "chunks" (2 bytes). Most pre-Windows 95 applications are 16-bit.

32-bit   In Windows, refers to the way memory is accessed. 32-bit applications access memory in 32-bit "chunks" (4 bytes). Large portions of Windows 95 and many of its new applications are 32-bit applications, and may run faster because it has become more efficient to access chunks of memory.

A

accelerator key   A keyboard shortcut for a command. For example, Shift+Delete is an accelerator command for the Edit, Cut command.

action buttons   Pre-drawn button icons that can be placed on a PowerPoint slide and associated with an animation effect.

activate   To bring a window to the front and make it active.

active printer   The printer that will be used by programs.

active window   The window that is currently being used. Active windows show the "active window color" in their title bar (settable through the Control Panel). Other windows are inactive. To activate an inactive window, you must click somewhere in the inactive window or use the taskbar to select the window (see *taskbar*). On the taskbar, the active window looks like a pressed button; inactive windows are represented by unpressed buttons.

add-ins   Supplemental programs that can be loaded and used to add commands and features to a program such as PowerPoint.

address book   A list of persons, phone numbers, and other information used by various Windows 95 programs, including Microsoft Office and its various programs.

Adobe Type Manager (ATM)   An Adobe program that enables you to work with PostScript fonts in Windows 95.

airbrush   In "paint" and graphics programs, a tool that "sprays" dots in a randomized pattern around the point indicated by the user. In most programs, the output of the airbrush can be configured to modify the color, pattern, and density of the dot pattern.

alert message   A critical warning, confirmational, or informational message appearing in a dialog box.

alignment   The spatial arrangement of text or objects on your screen; elements can be aligned along the left edge of a slide, the right edge, or centered between the two.

animation   A set of images, pictures, or drawings displayed in sequence to imply movement. Computer animation files can be inserted in programs such as PowerPoint and run by the speaker or viewer.

annotate   To add notes. For example, you can add your own notes to Windows Help.

ANSI   A standard for ordering characters within a font.

anti-aliasing   A graphics technique used to hide the diagonal edges and sharp color changes (*jaggies*) in a graphic or font. Because a computer screen possesses limited resolution, such changes highlight the pixels on the screen and don't look smooth. Using anti-aliasing smoothes out the changes and makes them appear more attractive.

Anti Virus   A program included with Windows 95 that helps eradicate viruses (see *virus*) from your hard drive or floppy disks.

API   See *Application Programming Interface.*

APPC   See *Advanced Program-to-Program Communications.*

applet   A small application unable to run by itself. When you purchase PowerPoint or another application, it may come with additional applets. For example, PowerPoint comes with applets for manipulating fonts (WordArt), drawing graphs (Microsoft Graph), and creating graphics (Microsoft Draw).

application   A computer program.

Application Programming Interface (API)   A set of interface functions available for applications.

ASCII characters   A subset of the ANSI character standard.

ASCII file   A file consisting of alphanumeric characters only. Although virtually every file can be converted to an ASCII file, all formatting (for example, bold, italics, underline, font size, and so on) will be lost in the ASCII file.

associate   Linking a document with the program that created it so that both can be opened with a single command. For example, double-clicking a Word table embedded in a PowerPoint slide opens Word for Windows and loads the selected document.

AT command set   A set of commands originally developed by Hayes for modems. Its name originates from the fact that each command starts with "AT" (attention). Today, most modems support the AT command set, enabling Microsoft to supply the Unimodem driver with Windows 95.

ATM   Asynchronous Transfer Mode: a high-speed, but expensive, networking solution. ATM networks reach speeds of 155M/s.

attribute   A property or characteristic.

auto arrange (Explorer)   In Explorer, organizes the visible icons into a regular grid pattern.

AutoClipArt   A feature that scans a PowerPoint presentation; by matching keywords with the presentation content, AutoClipArt suggests clip art images that might be appropriate to add to the slides.

AutoContent Wizard   A PowerPoint wizard that steps you through the creation of a new presentation.

AutoLayout   In PowerPoint, applied to each slide in a presentation displaying various types of placeholders used for entering slide content. Placeholders include title, bulleted lists, clip art, charts, organization charts, and multimedia clips.

App
B

AutoShape   A menu on the PowerPoint Drawing toolbar that contains a variety of common shapes (also called *AutoShapes*) which can be drawn automatically by clicking and dragging the cursor across a slide.

B

background   The colors, patterns, and gradients that fill the interior of objects or the PowerPoint slide area itself.

background operation   A job performed by a program when another program is in the active window. For example, printing or creating a backup can be performed by Windows 95 as a background operation.

Backup   A program that comes with Windows 95 and enables the user to back up the files from a hard disk to a floppy disk, tape drive, or another computer on a network.

backup set   The set of duplicate files and folders created by a backup program (see *Backup*). This set is stored on tapes, disks, or other storage media that can be removed and stored safely away from your computer. See *Full System Backup*.

batch program   A text file that instructs Window 95 to perform one or more tasks sequentially. Used for automating the loading or execution of programs. Batch files have a BAT or CMD extension.

Bézier curve   A mathematically constructed curve, such as the one used in drawing programs.

bi-directional printer port   Bi-directional Printer Communications sends print files to your printer and listens for a response. Windows quickly identifies a printer that is unable to accept a print file.

binary file transfer   A data transfer in which files aren't converted. Typically used with a modem to send programs or complex documents from computer to computer.

binary transfer protocol   When using a communications program to transmit binary files, it is very important to ensure that errors are not introduced into the data stream. Various binary transfer protocols check for matches between the data transmitted and the data received. The most common protocols are Xmodem, Ymodem, and Zmodem.

bitmap   A screen page in memory. Most bitmaps represent some sort of viewable graphics. You can use a "paint" program to edit graphic bitmaps and make modifications to them. However, although objects such as rectangles and circles may appear in a graphic bitmap, these objects cannot be edited as objects. You must modify these objects one bit at a time using the paint tools in the program.

bits per second (bps)   A measurement of data transmission speed, usually over a serial data link. Roughly equivalent to baud rate. A single character requires approximately 10 bits, so a transfer rate of 9600 baud results in about 960 characters per second (cps) being transferred. This speed, however, varies depending on the make of your modem.

black and white   A setting for displaying or printing PowerPoint presentations where only black and white, and no shades of gray, are represented.

browse   To search through or examine a directory tree of files, directories, disks, workstations, workgroups, or domains. Often done via a Browse button in a dialog box.

bullet   A text symbol, often a small solid circle, used to set off the items on a list with no sequential order.

Bulletin Board System (BBS)   An electronic service that can be accessed via a modem. A BBS typically includes collections of files, notes from other computer users, and many other services. Examples of commercial BBSes include CompuServe, Prodigy, Delphi, GEnie, and America Online (AOL). Information about Windows 95 and Windows 95 applications can be found on all these BBSes.

bus network   One of various network topologies. A bus network is one in which all of the computers on the network are connected to the main wire of the network.

C

Calculator   A program that comes with Windows 95 and enables you to perform standard or scientific calculations.

callout   A text label placed relative to a drawing or other object to draw the reader's attention to a specific point or element.

Cardfile   A program that comes with Window 95 and enables you to record information cards and sort through them by using their index lines.

cascade (Windows)   To arrange all the windows so that they are neatly stacked; only their title bars show behind the active window.

cascading menu   A submenu that appears (usually to the left or right of the main menu item) when a menu selection is made.

CD-ROM drive   Uses discs (not "disks") as the storage media. These discs look much like audio CDs, but can store about 600M of data on a single disc. They can only be read by a normal CD-ROM drive (hence the Read-Only Memory portion of the device's name), and take special equipment to create (write) them. CD-ROM drives are rated in multiples of the original (1x) drives that transfer data at the same rate as audio CD players (150K/s). Today, 1x drives no longer exist, and 2x drives (300-330K/s) are cheap. 3x (450K/s), 4x (600K/s) and even 6x (900K/s) drives are available. 4x drives fulfill basic requirements needed to achieve decent performance when playing animations from a CD-ROM.

CD Audio Track   A portion of a CD which can be associated with a PowerPoint presentation and played back continuously as slides display.

CD Player   A program packaged with Windows 95. CD Player lets you play audio CDs from your CD drive in the background while you are working in another application. It offers many of the controls found in stand-alone audio CD players. As a result, it looks and operates in a similar fashion. In addition, it allows you to edit your playlist. Thus, the tracks play in the order you want.

character-based   Usually used when referring to non-Windows applications. Character-based applications display information using the ASCII character set, or characters normally found on the keyboard. Also known as *text-based*.

character formatting   In word processing, this refers to formatting that is applied to individual characters. This type of formatting includes font, effects, size, and color.

chat room   A place on The Microsoft Network where you can have a live conversation with other MSN members. They see your comments immediately.

check box   A square dialog box item that takes an off or on value. Clicking in a check box adds or removes an X in the box, indicating whether the setting is on (checked) or off (unchecked).

choose   A term used in many instructions in this book. Usually means opening a menu and clicking a command. Also can refer to dialog box items, such as "Choose Basic Shapes from the drop-down list."

clear   Typically refers to turning off the X in an option or check box.

click   Quickly pressing and releasing the mouse button. Also, PowerPoint placeholders use a click to add function or contents to a presentation.

client As opposed to *server*, a workstation that connects to another computer's resources. A client also can include the server, and doesn't necessarily have to be another workstation. Basically, a client is just another application or workstation that uses resources from another process.

client application In OLE context, a program that uses an object (such as a graphic) supplied by another application (the *server* application).

client/server networking As opposed to *peer-to-peer* networking, an arrangement in which central computers called *servers* supply data and peripherals for use by *client* computers (workstations). Typically, a server contains a large, hard disk that supplies not only data, but also programs. It even executes programs. A server might also supply printers and modems for clients to use on the network. In other words, client/server refers to an architecture for distributed processing wherein subtasks can be distributed between services, CPUs, or even networked computers for more efficient execution.

clip art A collection of images you can use in your documents. Clip art is often distributed on CD-ROM in large collections (thousands of clip art pieces) organized into categories. Various clip art formats are sold, and the most popular are CGM, WMF, BMP, and GIF format files. PowerPoint comes with a set a clip art contained in the Clip Gallery 3.0.

Clipboard A temporary storage area in all versions of Windows used for storing various types of data (for example, text, graphics, sound, and video). The Clipboard can hold one piece of information at a time for use in a program or to pass information between programs.

Clipboard Viewer A Windows 95 program enabling you to store and save more than the single item that the Clipboard can hold.

clock An area at the far right edge of the taskbar that displays the time (and date if you leave the mouse pointer over the time). You can configure the taskbar to show or hide the clock.

close button A button in the upper-right corner of a window with an X in it. When clicked, it closes the program running in the current window.

Collapse A function of PowerPoint's Outline view that allows you to temporarily hide all text except for slide titles. See *Expand*.

collapse folders To hide additional directory (folder) levels below the selected directory (folder) levels. In Explorer, you can collapse the view of a folder to hide the folders stored within by double-clicking the folder in the left pane (tree view) of Explorer. When a folder contains no additional folders, a minus sign (–) appears next to the folder.

color palette   A display consisting of various color blocks; you can select a color fill to add to an object or slide from a color palette.

color pattern   A color selection made up of two other colors.

color rendering intent   Provides the best ICM settings for three of the major uses of color printing—for example, presentations, photographs, and true color screen display printing.

color scheme   A selection of colors that PowerPoint uses for screen display of applications, dialog boxes, and so forth. The color scheme is set from the template on which a presentation is based.

COM   Refers to the serial port, usually to attach a mouse and/or a modem to the computer. Most computers have two serial ports, labeled COM1 and COM2. The serial port transmits data in a single-bit stream. This serial transmission of bits gives the port its name.

command   Usually an option from an application's menus. Also refers to commands typed in from a command-prompt session or from the Run dialog box from the Start menu. In essence, it's a way of telling an application or Window 95 to perform a major chore, such as running an application or utility program.

command button   A dialog box item that causes an action when clicked.

comment   While viewing a PowerPoint presentation, notes objects called *comments* can be added directly to slides and are contained in *comment* boxes.

complex document   See *compound document*.

component   A portion of a program. When installing PowerPoint, you have the option of installing (or not) various components. For example, you might choose to not install certain graphic translators. Later, you can go back and add/remove components using the original install disks or CD-ROM.

compound document   A document (created using OLE) that includes multiple types of data. For example, a PowerPoint document that includes a Paint picture and a WordArt object is a compound document.

conference   A PowerPoint presentation with several users connected over a network or online service such as the Internet. See also *Presentation Conference*.

connection (HyperTerminal)   In HyperTerminal, a connection sets and saves all the configuration parameters for one party you want to contact.

connection (network)   A communication session established between a server and a workstation.

connector   A category of AutoShape object used to connect two or more objects. Connectors typically have arrowheads at one or both ends to indicate flow or direction.

container object   An object that contains another object or several objects. For example, a PowerPoint presentation might be the container object that holds the Excel object. See also *compound document*.

control menu   A menu that exists in every window and enables you to modify its parameters or take global actions, such as closing or moving the window.

Control Panel   A program that comes with Windows 95 that enables you to make settings for many Windows 95 actions, such as changing network, keyboard, printer, and regional settings. Some programs (including many video card drivers) may add sections to the control panel for you to use to configure that program.

conventional memory   Memory located in the first 640K.

cross-linked file   A disk error (which can be found using ScanDisk) in which at least two files are linked to data in the same cluster.

current directory   The directory that activates if you log onto the drive at the command prompt by typing the drive letter and pressing Enter. When you switch drives, the operating system remembers the directory that was current when you switched away. It will still be the active/current directory when you switch back; it becomes the default directory. Applications will store or look for files on that drive if they're not specifically told which directory to use. This concept also works in Explorer—when you switch back to a drive, the last active directory (or folder) is still the active one.

current window   The window that you are using. It appears in front of all other open windows. See also *active window*.

cursor   The representation of the mouse on-screen. It may take many different shapes.

Custom Animation   A feature in PowerPoint that allows you to set special effects and the sequence of slides in an on-screen presentation.

Custom Shows   A feature in PowerPoint that allows you to save different subsets of slides in a presentation to create different versions of the show from the same set of slides.

App
B

D

dash style   A line style using broken segments in various patterns.

database   A file or group of related files that are designed to hold recurring data types as if the files were lists.

data bits   The number of bits used to transmit a piece of information, usually 7 or 8.

DCI   Drive Control Interface; a display driver interface that allows fast, direct access to the video frame buffer in Windows. Also, it allows games and video to take advantage of special hardware support in video devices, which improves the performance and quality of video.

DDE   See *Dynamic Data Exchange*.

DEC printer utility   Adds features to the standard Windows 95 print window and updated printer drivers. The utility includes a very detailed help file for configuring both local and network printers. Additionally, it creates an enhanced set of property menus for configuring DEC printers.

default button   The command button in a dialog box that activates when you press the Enter key. This button is indicated by a dark border.

default printer   The printer, which is established using the Printer settings, to which documents will be sent if the user doesn't specify another printer.

deferred printing   Enables people with laptop computers to print even though their laptops are not in docking stations. Once connected in a docking station, it will automatically print. Also refers to computers whose only printer access is to a network printer, and the computer is temporarily disconnected from the network. When the network connection is reestablished, the print job starts.

density   A brightness control that lightens or darkens a printout to more closely reflect its screen appearance and to compensate for deficiencies in toner or paper quality.

design   The visual elements of a slide. When changing presentation templates in PowerPoint, the Apply Design command is used. A template contains various design elements for slides such as graphic objects and a color scheme.

desktop   The screen area on which the windows are displayed.

desktop pattern   A bitmap decorating your desktop. You can select one of Windows 95's patterns or create one of your own.

destination document   The document into which a linked or embedded document is placed.

device driver   A program that provides the operating system with the information it needs to work with a specific device, such as a printer.

Dial-up Networking   Dialing into a network from a remote site by using a modem.

dialog box   An on-screen message box that conveys or requests information from the user.

distribute   To arrange elements on a slide relative to each other horizontally (from left to right) or vertically (top to bottom).

dither pattern   A pattern of dots used to simulate an unavailable color or gray scale in a printout or graphic. Most frequently used when specifying a printout of a color graphic on a monochrome printer or simulating more colors in a graphic than are available in the current graphics mode.

docking station   For a portable computer, an external device that provides additional resources such as speakers, CD-ROM, keyboard, empty card slots, and so on. A docking station is typically plugged into a portable computer using the port replicator connection.

document   A file created using an application. For example, you might create a text document using a word processing application (such as WordPad) or a presentation document using a graphic application (such as PowerPoint).

document formatting   In word processing, refers to formatting that is applied to a whole document. Document formatting includes margins, headers and footers, and paper size.

document window   The window in which a document appears.

DOS   A term used to refer to any variation of the Disk Operating System (for example, MS-DOS and PC-DOS).

double buffering   The process of displaying the screen currently in the frame buffer while painting the next screen in another portion of RAM. Then the new screen is quickly copied to the frame buffer. This makes video playback and animation appear much smoother.

double-click   To press the mouse button twice in rapid succession while keeping the mouse pointer motionless between clicks.

download   Retrieving a file from a remote computer or BBS (see *upload*).

drag   To move an object on the screen from one place to another by clicking it with the mouse, holding the mouse button down, and pulling it to where you want it to be.

drag and drop   A particular action you can make with the mouse. Click an object such as a folder, then hold down the mouse button as you drag the object to a new location. You drop the object by releasing the mouse button.

drop-down list   A dialog box item showing only one entry until its drop-down arrow is clicked.

Dynamic Data Exchange (DDE)   A feature of Windows 95 that allows programs to communicate and actively pass information and commands.

E

editable fax   A file transfer between computers, with the additional option of a cover page. Once received, the editable fax can be edited in the application that created it—or another application capable of reading that file type. For example, if you send a document created in Microsoft PowerPoint for Windows, the recipient can open it in PowerPoint, PowerPoint Viewer, or Lotus Freelance, using import filters if necessary.

ellipsis   Three dots (...). An ellipsis after a menu item or button text indicates that selecting the menu or clicking the button will display an additional dialog box or window from which you can choose options or enter data.

e-mail   Electronic mail; a message file that can be sent electronically through a phone line using a modem and either a network or online service, such as the Internet.

embedded object   Data stored in a document that originated from another application. Differing from a linked object, this type of object doesn't have its own file on the disk. However, it runs its source application for editing when you double-click it. For example, a Word table embedded in a PowerPoint presentation.

embossed   A shadow effect that can be applied to text to make the letters appear raised from the background.

Encapsulated PostScript (EPS) file   A file format for storing PostScript-style images that allow a PostScript printer or program capable of importing such files to print a file in the highest resolution equipped by the printer.

engraved   A shadow effect that can be applied to text to make it appear to be carved into the background.

Enhanced Meta File (EMF)   The process of converting generic Spooling print instructions to the instruction set "understood" best by a particular printer. This conversion has the capability to create faster printouts of better quality.

escape codes   A set of codes that appear in a text string on a terminal (see *terminal emulation*). Although these escape codes (which provide formatting information) aren't visible in terminal emulation, they will show up as non-text characters if you capture the text to the screen or printer. In fact, some escape codes may cause the printed output to skip pages, switch into bold mode, and other undesirable effects because the codes may conflict with printer command codes.

exit   When you are finished running Windows applications and Windows, you must not turn off the computer until you correctly exit Windows. Windows stores some data in memory and does not write it to your hard disk until you choose the Exit command. If you turn off the computer without correctly exiting, this data may be lost.

Expand   A function in Outline view of PowerPoint that allows you to open up all the lines of an outline to display all the detail points. See *Collapse*.

expand folders   Views the structure of folders that are stored inside other folders. In Explorer, you can expand the view of a folder that has a plus sign (+) next to it to see the folders stored within by double-clicking the folder in the left pane (tree view) of Explorer. When a folder does not contain any additional folders, a minus sign (–) appears next to the folder.

expanded memory   Memory that conforms to the LIM 4.0 standard for memory access. Windows 95 has the capability of converting extended memory (see *extended memory*) to expanded memory (using EMM386.EXE) for programs that require it. However, most modern programs no longer use expanded memory.

Explorer   A program in Windows 95 that helps you view and manage your files.

export   To send a copy of a file from one program to another program. You can export a PowerPoint outline to Microsoft Word, for example.

extended memory   Memory that can be accessed by Windows 95 beyond the first megabyte of memory in your system.

F

file allocation table (FAT)   The native DOS file system that uses a table, called the file allocation table, to store information about the sizes, locations, and properties of files stored on the disk.

file converter   Takes the file format and transforms it to a format that the application can read. During a file conversion, text enhancements, font selections, and other elements are usually preserved. Sometimes, however, these elements are converted to a similar format, and then converted to ASCII format.

file name   The name that a file system or operating system gives to a file when it's stored on disk. File names in Window 95's file system can be 256 characters long. Additionally, Windows 95 assigns a file name compatible with older DOS (eight characters with a three-character extension) naming conventions.

filename extension   The three-character extension that you can add to a file name—either the standard eight characters of DOS and Windows 3.1, or the long file names of Windows 95. The filename extension is only visible in Explorer if you enable the appropriate option. Otherwise, the extension is hidden. Nevertheless, the extension is still part of the file name, even when you can't see it — it is this extension that Windows 95 (as well as earlier Windows) uses to associate a document with the application that created it.

file utility   A program that can directly manipulate the information available on the disk that defines where files are found, sized, and other attributes. It is important to not use file utilities that were designed for earlier versions of Windows, as Windows 95 stores some file information in different places — and earlier file utilities could scramble the file information, destroying the file.

fixed-space font   Fonts that have a fixed amount of space between the characters in the font.

folder   Represents directories on your drives. Folders can contain files, programs, and even other folders.

folder window   A window in Explorer that displays the contents of a folder.

font   A description of how to display a set of characters. The description includes the shape of the characters, spacing between characters, effects (for example, bold, italics, and underline), and the size of the characters.

foreground operation   The program in the active window.

format   To apply certain characteristics to text or an object, such as size or color.

forum   On The Microsoft Network, a folder with a collection of related documents and subfolders.

frame   Using a drawn object such as a square as a border around another object on a slide.

freeform   A drawing style and drawing object type that provides no preset definition to the object. Freeform drawing is similar to drawing on paper with a pencil and no ruler or guides to direct the line.

free rotate   A PowerPoint function that allows you to turn an object in any direction, 360 degrees.

full system backup   A backup set (see *backup set*) that contains all the files on your hard drive, including Windows 95 system files, the Registry, and all other files necessary to completely restore your system configuration on a new hard drive.

G

GIF   The Graphics Interchange Format (a graphics file format).

Genigraphics   A slide service bureau for which PowerPoint provides a built-in preparation wizard.

gradient   A subtle shading from lighter to darker in a background of one or two colors giving the effect of a light source from the selected direction.

graphic   A visual element which can be added to a slide, such as a line drawing, shape or picture.

graphic format   The protocol used to save a graphic file, such as EMF, GIF, or EPS.

grid   A background pattern that defines regular intervals — for example, a 1/4-inch grid displays dots in the background every quarter inch in a rectangular pattern. Many graphics programs make a grid available. Even when turned on, a grid won't print. When you "snap to grid," your graphic endpoints are constrained to fall on a grid point.

group   To associate two or more objects so that any action—formatting, moving, copying or resizing, for example—is applied to all the objects as if they were one object.

guide   A set of two moveable, intersecting lines that can be displayed on PowerPoint slides to enable you to place objects precisely.

App

B

H

handouts   Printed output of PowerPoint presentations containing miniature versions of two, three, or six slides. Audience handouts are intended to be distributed to presentation viewers to help them follow a presentation.

header information   Data sent to a printer to define aspects of the printout and prepare the printer prior to printing. PostScript documents include header information.

Help   A program that gives you information about how to run Windows 95 and its programs, including how to use the Help program.

hidden file   A characteristic of a file that indicates that the file is not visible in Explorer under normal circumstances. However, by selecting the View option to view all files, hidden files will still be visible.

hidden object   Slide or element on slide that temporarily doesn't appear on-screen and is not included in printed output of a PowerPoint presentation.

hierarchical   A way of displaying text or graphics in a structure. In a hierarchical structure, items closer to the top of the structure are considered *parents* of items connected to them, but which are lower down in the structure. The tree structure of Powerpoint's Outline view is an example of a hierarchical structure.

home page   A document on the World Wide Web dedicated to a particular subject. From a home page, you can use hyperlinks to jump to other home pages to gain more information.

HP JetAdmin   A tool that can be used to install and configure networked Hewlett-Packard printers using the HP JetDirect network interface. The HP JetAdmin utility appears as a substitute for the Windows standard Printer window. This utility can also be used to interface printers connected to a NetWare LAN.

HTTP   Hypertext Transport Protocol; used to designate a site on the World Wide Web. PowerPoint presentations can be opened at HTTP sites.

hue   The numerical representation of the colors of a color wheel. It is almost always seen with saturation and brightness.

hyperlink   A link in a document that, when activated (often by clicking it), links—or jumps to—another document or graphic.

HyperTerminal   A program included with Windows 95 that enables you to easily connect to a remote computer, a bulletin board, or an online service. It replaces Terminal from Windows 3.1.

Hypertext Markup Language (HTML)   A hypertext language used to create the hypertext documents that make up the World Wide Web.

I

I-beam   The shape the cursor takes in the area of a window where text can be entered.

icon   A small graphic symbol used to represent a folder, program, shortcut, resource, or document.

Image Color Matching (ICM)   A technology developed by Kodak that creates an image environment that treats color from the screen to the printed page. Microsoft licensed ICM from Kodak to be able to repeatedly and consistently reproduce color matched images from source to destination.

import   An OLE term. In Object Packager, you can import a file into a package and later embed it into a destination document.

inactive   An open window that is not currently in use. On the taskbar, the active window looks like a pressed button; inactive windows are represented by unpressed buttons.

Inbox   Holds incoming and outgoing messages and faxes that are sent or received over Microsoft Outlook.

indent   In the PowerPoint outline structure, to demote or make a line of text subservient to another line.

Industry Standard Architecture (ISA)   The design of the 8/16-bit AT bus (sometimes called the *classic bus*) developed by IBM in the original IBM PC.

in-place editing   A feature of OLE 2. With in-place editing, you may edit an embedded or linked object without that object being placed into an additional window (the way it was in OLE 1.0). Instead of creating an additional window, the tools for the object you want to edit appear in the toolbar for the container object (see *container object*). Also, the menus for the object you want to edit replace the menus of the container object. In-place editing is less disruptive; it is much simpler to ensure that the changes you make to an embedded or linked object are updated to the original complex document.

insertion point   A flashing, vertical line showing where text will be inserted.

Integrated Services Digital Network (ISDN)   A special phone line that supports modem speeds up to 64Kbps. However, these phone lines can be quite expensive to acquire. Many ISDN adapters support two-channel access.

Intellimouse   A Microsoft pointing device.

interactive   A PowerPoint or other multimedia presentation is interactive when the viewer is able to make selections as to how the presentation runs or what is displayed, in effect interacting with the presentation itself.

interface   The visible layer enabling a user to communicate with a computer. In DOS, the interface consists largely of typed commands and character-based feedback. Windows 95 is an entirely graphical interface, using a mouse, menus, windows, and icons to allow the user to communicate his instructions and requirements to the computer.

interframe compression   A technique that achieves compression of a video file by eliminating redundant data between successive compressed frames.

Internet   A "network of networks;" a global linkage of millions of computers, containing vast amounts of information, much of it available for free to anyone with a modem and the right software. The Internet is an aggregation of high-speed networks, supported by the NSF (National Science Foundation) and almost 6,000 federal, state, and local systems, as well as university and commercial networks. There are links to networks in Canada, South America, Europe, Australia, and Asia, and more than 30 million users.

Internet Assistant   A programmed series of steps a PowerPoint user can invoke to create a folder of presentation files to be moved to an Internet server.

Internet Explorer   A Web browser bundled with the Windows 95 Plus! kit. It takes advantage of features in Windows 95, such as shortcuts and long file names.

Internet Protocol (IP)   A network protocol that provides routing services across multiple LANs and WANs that is used in the TCP/IP protocol stack. IP packet format is used to address packets of data from ultimate source and destination nodes (host) located on any LAN or WAN networked with TCP/IP protocol. IP provides routing services in conjunction with IP routers, which are incorporated into many computer systems and most versions of UNIX. IP Packet format is supported in NetWare 3.11 and 4.0 operating systems, and is used throughout the Department of Defense Internet—a network of thousands of computers internetworked worldwide.

interoperability   Compatibility, or the capability for equipment to work together. Industry standards are agreed upon or used by vendors to make their equipment work with other vendor's equipment.

interrupt request line (IRQ)   A line (conductor) on the internal bus of the computer (typically on the motherboard) over which a device such as a port, disk controller, or modem can get the attention of the CPU to process some data.

intraframe compression   A technique that compresses the video by removing redundancy from individual video images.

I/O address   Input/Output address. Many I/O devices, such as COM ports, network cards, printer ports, and modem cards, are mapped to an I/O address. This address allows the computer and operating system to locate the device, and thus send and receive data. Such I/O addresses don't tie up system memory RAM space. However, there are a limited number of I/O addresses. You can access an I/O port in one of two ways: either map it into the 64K I/O address space, or map it as a memory-mapped device in the system's RAM space.

IPX   Internetwork Packet Exchange; a network protocol developed by Novell to address packets of data from ultimate source and destination nodes located on any LAN networked with NetWare. IPX also provides routing services in conjunction NetWare and third-party routers. An IPX packet has information fields that identify the network address, node address, and socket address of both the source and destination, and provides the same functionality of the OSI Network layer in the OSI model.

J

Journal   A Microsoft Outlook feature that tracks documents created in Office programs, such as PowerPoint.

JPEG   Joint Photograph Experts Group graphics file format.

K

keyboard buffer   Memory set aside to store keystrokes as they're entered from the keyboard. Once it's stored, the keystroke data waits for the CPU to pick up the data and respond accordingly.

keyboard equivalent   See *keyboard shortcut*.

keyboard shortcut   A combination of keystrokes that initiates a menu command without dropping the menu down, or activates a button in a dialog box without clicking the button.

kiosk   A booth or display area where an on-screen computer presentation may be set up for use by those visiting the area. An example of a kiosk would be an information counter in a shopping mall or booth at a trade show.

App
B

L

landscape　The orientation of a print page of output with the longer side of the page running across the top of the document.

layering　In PowerPoint, the process of placing objects one on top of another on your slide to give the appearance of a stack of objects. Objects can be brought forward to appear to be placed at the top of the stack, or sent back to any of the layers behind the first object.

layout　In PowerPoint, layouts (also called AutoLayouts) are applied to each slide in a presentation displaying various types of placeholders used for entering slide content. Placeholders include title, bulleted lists, clip art, charts, organization charts, and multimedia clips.

license　Refers to the agreement you are assumed to have acceded to when you purchased Windows 95. As with much other computer software, you don't own your copy of Windows 95, but instead just license the use of it. As such, there is a long list of legalese-type things you supposedly agree to when you open the envelope containing your copy of PowerPoint. These legal agreements are part of the license.

line style　A choice of predesigned formatting effects that can be applied to selected line objects.

linked object　In OLE terminology, data stored in a document that originated from another application. Unlike an embedded object, this type of object has its own file on the disk. The source application is run for editing when you double-click it—for example, a Paint drawing linked to a PowerPoint presentation. Linking saves space over embedding when a particular object must be included in more than one other document, because the data does not have to be stored multiple times. Additionally, you can directly edit a linked file, and all the documents that link to the file update automatically.

list box　A dialog box item that shows all available options.

local area network (LAN)　A limited-distance, multipoint physical connectivity medium consisting of network interface cards, media, and repeating devices designed to transport frames of data between host computers at high speeds with low error rates. A LAN is a subsystem that is part of a network.

local printer　A printer connected directly to your computer.

local reboot   The ability of Windows 95 to close down a single misbehaving application. When you use the Alt+Ctrl+Delete key sequence, Windows 95 queries you for the application to shut down. In this way, you can close down only the application you want, without affecting other running applications.

logical drive   A drive that isn't a physical drive, as in the floppy drive A or B. Instead, a logical drive is a drive created on a subpartition of an extended partition and given an arbitrary letter such as C, D, or E.

long file name   A reference to Windows 95's ability to use file names up to 256 characters long.

App
B

looping   To set up a PowerPoint presentation to repeat until stopped. Looped presentations are useful when a speaker is not present, such as at a trade show booth.

LPT   The parallel port used for printing. Most computers have a single parallel port (labeled LPT1), but some may have two. The parallel port transmits data one byte (8 bits) at a time. This parallel transmission of all 8 bits gives the port its name.

luminosity   When working with colors, indicates the brightness of the color.

M

macro   A sequence of keyboard strokes and mouse actions that can be recorded so that their playback can be activated by a single keystroke, keystroke combination, or mouse click. Unlike Windows 3.1 and Windows for Workgroups, Windows 95 does not come with a macro recorder. In PowerPoint, macros can be attached to toolbar buttons.

mailing list (Internet)   An e-mail discussion group focused on one or more topics. The mailing list is made up of members who subscribe to that mailing list.

manual timing   Determining the timing of slide transitions with the click of a mouse or keystroke, rather than assigning preset time increments.

master   A feature in PowerPoint that contains certain formatting settings. Additional formatting or objects placed in these views automatically appear in every corresponding location. There are four types of masters in PowerPoint: Title, Slide, Handout, and Notes.

maximize button   A button in the upper-right corner of a window with a square in it. When clicked, it enlarges the window to its maximum size. When the window is already at its maximum size, the maximize button switches to the restore button, which returns the window to its previous size.

media control interface (MCI)   A standard interface for all multimedia devices, devised by the MPC counsel, that allows multimedia applications to control any number of MPC-compliant devices, from sound cards to MIDI-based lighting controllers.

Meeting Minder   A PowerPoint feature used to coordinate the running of a presentation conference and take meeting minutes.

Meeting Minutes   The feature in PowerPoint which allows you to keep a record of discussion topics which come up during the presentation and record action items.

menu   A list of available command options.

menu bar   Located under the title bar, displays the names of all available menu lists.

menu command   A word or phrase in a menu that, when selected, enables you to view all the commands.

metafile   A Windows graphics file format.

microprocessor   A miniaturized processor. Previous processors were built in integrated circuit boards with many large components. Most processors today use high-tech, silicon-based technology that improves performance, reduces heat generation, and increases efficiency.

Microsoft Client for NetWare Networks   Allows users to connect to new or existing NetWare servers. It permits you to browse and queue print jobs using either the Windows 95 network user interface or existing Novell NetWare utilities. The Microsoft Client for NetWare interfaces equally well with both NetWare 3.x and 4.x servers.

Microsoft Fax   A program included with Windows 95 that enables you to send and receive faxes directly within Powerpoint.

Microsoft on the Web   A feature of the PowerPoint Help system that allows you to access Microsoft's home page, Web tutorial, product news, and technical support from the Help menu.

Microsoft Network, The (MSN)   An online service run by Microsoft. With The Microsoft Network, you can exchange messages with people around the world; read the latest news, sports, weather, and financial information; find answers to your technical questions; download from thousands of useful programs; and connect to the Internet.

MIDI   Musical Instrument Digital Interface; originally a means of connecting electronic instruments (synthesizers) and letting them communicate with one another. Computers then came into the MIDI landscape and were used to control the synthesizers. PowerPoint can play MIDI files.

minimize button   The button in the upper-right corner of the window that has a line in it. When clicked, it reduces the window to display the taskbar only.

mirror image   An exact duplication of an object, flipped 180 degrees.

App
B

mission-critical application   An application program considered indispensable to the operation of a business, government, or other operation. Often, these applications are transaction-based, such as for point-of-sale, reservations, or real-time stock, security, or money trading.

modem   A device, usually attached to a computer through a serial port or present as an internal card. A modem makes it possible to use ordinary phone lines to transfer computer data. In addition to a modem, a communications program is required. *Modem* is short for *modulator/demodulator* — the processes whereby a digital stream of data is converted to sound for transmission through a phone system originally designed only for sound (modulator) and the conversion of received sound signals back into digital data (demodulator).

motion JPEG   Developed by the Joint Photographic Experts Group, a compression/ decompression scheme (codec) for video files. It is a variation on JPEG, this group's codec for compressing still pictures. It uses only intraframe lossy compression (see *intraframe compression, lossy compression*), but offers a tradeoff between compression ratio and quality.

mouse pointer   The symbol that displays where your next mouse click will occur. The mouse pointer symbol changes according to the context of the window or the dialog box in which it appears.

MPEG   Created by the Motion Picture Experts Group, a specification for compressing and decompressing animation or "movie" files, which are typically very large. Although extremely efficient at reducing the size of such a file, MPEG is also very processor-intensive.

MS-DOS-based application   An application that normally runs on a DOS machine and doesn't require Windows 95. Many MS-DOS-based applications will run in Windows 95's DOS box, but some will not.

multimedia   A combination of various types of media, including (but not necessarily limited to) sound, animation, and graphics. Due to the generally large size of "multimedia" files, a CD-ROM is usually necessary to store files. Of course, a sound card and speakers are also necessary.

multitasking   The capability of an operating system to handle multiple processing tasks, apparently, at the same time.

My Computer   An icon present on the Windows 95 desktop that enables you to view drives, folders, and files.

N

narration   A recorded verbal description that can be saved with a PowerPoint presentation and played back in sync with the slides as they are displayed.

NetWare   A trademarked brand name for the networking operating systems and other networking products developed and sold by Novell.

network   A group of computers connected by a communications link that enables any device to interact with any other on the network. The word *network* is derived from the term "network architecture," which describes an entire system of hosts, workstations, terminals, and other devices.

Network Interface card (NIC)   Also called a network adapter, an interface card placed in the bus of a computer (or other LAN device) to interface to a LAN. Each NIC represents a node, which is a source and destination for LAN frames, which in turn carry data between the NICs on the LAN.

non-Windows program   A program not designed to be used specifically in Windows. Most non-Windows applications or programs are character-based in nature (for example, DOS programs).

Note   Also called Notes Pages. This feature allows you to add comments to individual PowerPoint slides to assist a speaker in making a presentation. A comment with background information or reminders that can be added to each slide in a PowerPoint presentation to aide a speaker in making the presentation.

Notepad   A program that comes with Windows 95 and enables you to view and edit text files.

nudge   To move a drawing object on a slide by a very small, preset increment.

O

object   Any item that is or can be linked into another Windows application, such as a sound, graphics, piece of text, or portion of a spreadsheet. Must be from an application that supports object linking and embedding (OLE).

object linking and embedding   See *OLE*.

OEM fonts   Provided to support older installed products. The term OEM refers to Original Equipment Manufacturers. This font family includes a character set designed to be compatible with older equipment and software applications.

Office Art   A collection of media clips including clip art, animation, and sound, that comes with all Microsoft Office products.

Office Assistant   A Help system feature that allows you to enter questions about an Office product in a natural language format (such as by typing a simple English sentence, rather than a keyword).

offline   A device that is not ready to accept input. For example, if your printer is offline, it will not accept data from the computer, and attempting to print will generate an error.

offset shadows   A shadow effect that is set slightly apart from the object assumed to be casting the shadow. An offset shadow effect can seem to add depth to an object.

OLE   Object linking and embedding; a data-sharing scheme that allows dissimilar applications to create single, complex documents by cooperating in the creation of the document. The documents consist of material that a single application couldn't have created on its own. In OLE, version 1, double-clicking an embedded or linked object (see *embedded object* and *linked object*) launches the application that created the object in a separate window. In OLE version 2, double-clicking an embedded or linked object makes the menus and tools of the creating application available in the middle of the parent document. The destination document (contains the linked or embedded object) must be created by an application that is an OLE client, and the linked or embedded object must be created in an application that is an OLE server.

OLE automation   Refers to the capability of a server application to make available (known as *exposing*) its own objects for use in another application's macro language.

online   Indicates that a system is working and connected. For example, if your printer is online, it is ready to accept information to turn into a printed output.

option button   A dialog box item that enables you to choose only one of a group of choices.

Organization chart   A chart object that can be placed in a PowerPoint presentation representing the hierarchical structure of an organization, such as a corporation.

orientation   For printer paper, indicates whether the document is to be printed normally (for example, in Portrait mode) or sideways (in Landscape mode).

Outline view   The view in PowerPoint where you can enter presentation content and reorganize it according to a standard outline hierarchy.

overlapping objects   Elements on a slide which appear to be stacked so that one is "behind" the other.

P

Pack and Go Wizard   A wizard used to prepare a PowerPoint file for presentation at a remote location.

Paint   A program that comes with Windows 95 and enables you to view and edit various formats of bit maps.

palette   A collection of tools. For example, in PowerPoint, there is a color palette that displays the 48 colors available for use in creating a graphic.

pane   Some windows, such as the window for Explorer, show two or more distinct *areas* (Explorer's window shows two such areas). These areas are referred to as *panes*.

Panose   A Windows internal description that represents a font by assigning each font a PANOSE ID number. Windows uses several internal descriptions to categorize fonts. The PANOSE information registers a font class and determines similarity between fonts.

paragraph formatting   In a word processing program, formatting that can be applied to an entire paragraph, including alignment (left, center, right), indentation, and spacing before and after the paragraph.

parallel port   A port (usually used for printing) that transmits data 8 bits at a time. This parallel transmission of 8 bits at a time gives the port its name.

partition   A portion of a physical hard drive that behaves as a separate disk (logical drive), even though it isn't.

path   The location of a file in the directory tree.

pattern   An arrangement of lines or dots that can be used to fill the internal area of an object, such as a drawing.

PC Cards   Formerly called PCMCIA cards, small (usually only slightly larger than a credit card) cards that plug into special slots provided in notebook computers. PC Cards can provide functionality for additional memory, modems, sound, networking, hard drives, and so on. PC Cards normally identify themselves to the computer, making configuring them quite simple.

PCMCIA   The old name for PC Cards (see *PC Cards*).

pen   While showing a PowerPoint on-screen presentation, you can draw on the slides themselves with an electronic pen. Pen colors can be determined while setting up the presentation.

personal information store   Outlook's term for the file that contains the structure of folders that make up your Inbox, Outbox, sent files, deleted files, and any other personal folders you may choose to create.

Phone Dialer   A program that is included with Windows 95 that enables you to place telephone calls from your computer by using a modem or another Windows telephony device. You can store a list of phone numbers you use frequently, and dial the number quickly from your computer.

picon   Small, bitmapped images of the first frame of your video clip. They can be used to represent the in and out source of your video segments.

PICT   A Macintosh picture file format.

PIF   A file that provides Windows 95 with the information it needs to know in order to run a non-Windows program. Unlike earlier versions of Windows, there is no PIF editor in Windows 95. Instead, you set up a PIF file from the properties for the file. Access the file properties by right-clicking the file from My Computer.

placeholder   Part of a PowerPoint layout that provides a shortcut to entering presentation content by allowing the user to enter various types of information into a presentation with a one-click interface.

play list   In CD Player, a list of tracks from an audio CD that you want to play.

Plug and Play   An industry-wide specification supported by Windows 95 that makes it easy to install new hardware. Plug and Play enables the computer to correctly identify hardware components (including plug-in cards) and ensures that different cards don't conflict in their requirements for IRQs, I/O addresses, DMA channels, and memory addresses. In order to fully implement Plug and Play, you need an operating system that supports it (as stated, Windows 95 does), a BIOS that supports it (most computers manufactured since early 1995 do) and cards that identify themselves to the system (information from these cards is stored in the Windows Registry). If you have hardware, such as modems that aren't Plug and Play (so-called *legacy hardware*), then Windows 95 will prompt you for the information necessary for setup, and store such information in the Registry.

pointer   The on-screen symbol controlled by the mouse. As you move the mouse on the desk, the pointer moves on-screen. The pointer changes shape to indicate the current status and the type of functions and selections available.

point size   The unit used to measure the size of a font in increments of 1/72 of an inch.

polygon   A multisided shape, in which each side is a straight line.

port   A connection or socket for connecting devices to a computer (see *I/O address*).

port replicator   On portable computers, a bus connection that makes all bus lines available externally. The port replicator can be used to plug in devices which, in a desktop computer, would be handled as cards. Port replicators are also the connection used to connect a portable computer to its docking station.

portrait   An output orientation that places the top of a document along the shorter side of the paper.

postproduction editing   The steps of adding special effects, animated overlays,and more to a "production" video.

PostScript   A special description language, invented by Adobe. This language is used to accurately describe fonts and graphics. Printers that can directly read this language and print the results are termed *PostScript printers*.

PowerPoint Animation Player   An add-in program that works with a Web browser to play animated PowerPoint presentations on the Internet.

PowerPoint Central   An online magazine with articles and advice on using PowerPoint. *PowerPoint Central* also contains links to the Office 97 ValuPack and various Internet sites for downloading additional media clips.

PowerPoint Viewer   A program that allows someone to view a PowerPoint presentation on a computer without having PowerPoint itself loaded.

presentation   A term for a set of PowerPoint slides. A PowerPoint presentation can be a stand-alone unit with recorded narration and interactive capabilities, or used in conjunction with a live speaker.

presentation conference   The ability to have several people at different locations view a PowerPoint presentation over a network or the Internet.

printer driver   A Windows 95 program that tells programs how to format data for a particular type of printer.

printer fonts   Fonts stored in the printer's ROM.

printer settings   A window that displays all the printers for which there are drivers present. You can select the default printer from the installed printers, as well as configure each printer using the shortcut menu and the Options dialog box.

printer window   For each installed printer, you can view the printer window. The printer window displays the status of each print job in the queue, and enables you to pause, restart, and delete the print job.

App
B

processor   The controlling device in a computer that interprets and executes instructions and performs computations, and otherwise controls the major functions of the computer. This book discusses Intel 80x86-series processors, which are miniaturized single-chip "microprocessors" containing thousands to millions of transistors in a silicon-based, multilayered, integrated circuit design.

program file   A program that runs an application directly (not via an association) when you click it.

program window   A window that contains a program and its documents.

promote   In PowerPoint outlines, to place a line of text at a higher level of detail in the outline hierarchy.

property sheet   A dialog box that displays (and sometimes enables you to change) the properties of an object in Windows 95. To access a property sheet, right-click the object to view the shortcut menu, and select Properties from the shortcut menu. Property sheets vary considerably between different objects.

proportional   To keep the relative relationships between the measurements of elements in an object. Objects can be resized proportionally, retaining their original relative proportions (a square stays a square), or disproportionally (a square becomes a rectangle).

proportional-spaced fonts   Adjust the intercharacter space based on the shape of the individual characters. An example of a proportional-spaced font is Arial. The width of a character is varied based on its shape. Adjusting intercharacter spacing is really a function of kerning, which is similar but not exactly the same. For instance, the letter A and the letter V are typically stored in each font as a kerning pair, which means they will be spaced differently when appearing next to each other. In a monospace font versus a proportional font you will see a difference in the width of the letter i.

protocol   Rules of communication. In networks, several layers of protocols exist. Each layer of protocol only needs to physically hand-off or receive data from the immediate layer above and beneath it, whereas virtual communications occur with the corresponding layer on another host computer.

Q

queue   Documents lined up and waiting to be printed, or commands lined up and waiting to be serviced. Use the Printer window to view the print queue for a printer.

Quick View   A program included with Windows 95 that enables you to view files stored in 30 different file formats without needing to open the application that created the file. Quick View is available from the File menu of Explorer if a viewer is available for the selected file type.

QuickTime   Developed by Apple, a compression and decompression (codec) scheme for animation files. It is unique in that versions are available for both Windows and Macintosh, enabling software designers to provide their data in a format compatible for both platforms.

R

RAM   Random Access Memory; physical memory chips located in the computer. Typically, Windows 95 machines have 16 million bytes (16M) of RAM or more. However, Windows 95 will run on machines with 8M of RAM.

raster font   A font in which characters are stored as pixels.

read-only   Characteristic of a file indicating that the file can be read from, but not written to, by an application. Note however, that a "read-only" file can be deleted in Explorer, although you will get a warning (beyond the normal "are you sure" you normally get when you try to delete a file) if the file is read-only.

Recycle Bin   An icon that appears on the Windows 95 desktop. To discard a file, you drag the file from Explorer, My Computer, or any other file handler to the Recycle Bin. This action hides the file—but doesn't actually erase it from the disk. You can "undelete" the file by dragging it from the Recycle Bin back to a folder. To actually delete the file, select the Recycle Bin menu selection to empty the Recycle Bin.

registering a program   The act of linking a document with the program that created it so that both can be opened with a single command. For example, double-clicking a DOC file opens Word for Windows and loads the selected document.

Registry   A database of configuration information central to Windows 95 operations. This file contains program settings, associations between file types and the applications that created them, as well as information about the types of OLE objects a program can create and hardware detail information.

Registry Editor   Ships with Windows 95 and enables you to fine-tune Windows 95 performance by adjusting or adding settings to key system information. Because Windows 95 has placed WIN.INI and SYSTEM.INI file settings in the Registry, the ability to remotely edit these parameters is an extremely powerful tool. Warning: you can totally destroy a workstation using this tool!

App

B

rehearse   To run through the slides of a PowerPoint presentation while recording the time that each slide remains on-screen.

resize button   A button located in the lower-left corner of a non-maximized window. When the mouse pointer is over this button, it turns into a two-headed arrow. You can click and drag to resize the window horizontally and vertically.

restore button   A button in the upper-right corner of a window that has two squares in it. When clicked, it returns the window to its previous size. When the window is at its previous size, the restore button switches to the maximize button, which returns the window to its maximum size.

restore files   Copies one or more files from your backup set to the hard disk or to another floppy.

revision tracking   A feature of Microsoft Office products used to keep a record of any changes made to a document.

rich text format (RTF)   Compatible with several word processors and includes fonts, tabs, and character formatting.

ROM (Read-Only Memory)   A type of chip capable of permanently storing data without the aid of an electric current source to maintain it, as in RAM. The data in ROM chips is sometimes called *firmware*. Without special equipment, it is not possible to alter the contents of read-only memory chips—thus the name. ROMs are found in many types of computer add-in boards, as well as on motherboards. CPUs often have an internal section of ROM as well.

rotate   To move an object to any point in a 360-degree range.

ruler   A horizontal or vertical measuring device that can be displayed on the PowerPoint screen in Slide view to assist in positioning objects precisely on a slide.

S

saturation   When working with colors, indicates the purity of a color; lower values of saturation have more gray in them.

scaling   A method of reducing or enlarging an object by entering horizontal and vertical measurements, or a percentage increase or decrease.

ScanDisk   A program used to check for, diagnose, and repair damage on a hard disk. Part of your routine, hard disk maintenance (along with defragmenting your hard disk) should include a periodic run of ScanDisk to keep your hard disk in good repair. In its standard test, ScanDisk checks the files and folders on a disk for *logical errors*, and if you ask it to, automatically corrects any errors it finds. ScanDisk checks for *crosslinked files*, which occur when two or more files have data stored in the same *cluster* (a storage unit on a disk). The data in the cluster is likely to be correct for only one of the files, and may not be correct for any of them. ScanDisk also checks for *lost file fragments*, which are pieces of data that have become disassociated with their files.

scanned art   Any artwork that has been placed in a file in electronic format using a digital scanner.

screen fonts   Font files used to show type styles on the screen. These are different from the files used by Windows to print the fonts. The screen fonts must match the printer fonts in order for Windows to give an accurate screen portrayal of the final printed output.

screen resolution   The number of picture elements (or *pixels*) that can be displayed on the screen. Screen resolution is a function of the monitor and graphics card. Higher resolutions display more information at a smaller size, and also may slow screen performance. Screen resolution is expressed in the number of pixels across the screen by the number of pixels down the screen. Standard VGA has a resolution of 640×480, although most modern monitors can display 1024×768, and even higher (larger monitors can usually display a higher resolution than smaller ones).

screen saver   A varying pattern or graphic that appears on the screen when the mouse and keyboard have been idle for a user-definable period of time. Originally used to prevent a static background from being "burned into" the screen phosphors, this is rarely a problem with modern monitors. Many screen savers (including those that come with Windows

95) can be used with a password—you must enter the correct password to turn off the screen saver and return to the screen. However, someone could simply reboot the machine, so a screen saver password is not very sophisticated protection.

Scribble tool   A freeform drawing tool.

scroll arrow   Located at either end of a scroll bar, can be clicked to scroll up or down (vertical scroll bar) or left or right (horizontal scroll bar). Clicking the scroll arrow will move your window in that direction.

scroll bar   Allow you to select a value within a range, such as what part of a document to see, or what value to set the Red, Green, and Blue components of a color to.

scroll box   A small box located in the scroll bar that shows where the visible window is located in relation to the entire document, menu, or list. You can click and drag the scroll box to make other portions of the document, menu, or list visible.

select   To specify a section of text or graphics for initiating an action. To select also can mean to choose an option in a dialog box.

selection handles   Small, black boxes indicating that a graphic object has been selected. With some Windows applications, you can click and drag a selection handle to resize the selected object.

serif fonts   Serif fonts have projections (serifs) that extend the upper and lower strokes of the set's characters beyond their normal boundaries—for example, Courier. Sans-serif fonts do not have these projections; an example is Arial.

server   A centrally administered network computer, which contains resources that are shared with "client" machines on the network.

server application   In OLE terminology, an application that supplies an object (such as a drawing) to a client application (such as a word processing program) for inclusion in a complex document.

service bureau   A company that takes computer files and generates 35mm slides.

shading   Using a fill color in an object.

shadow   A perspective effect that makes it appear as though an object is casting a shadow; this adds depth to the object.

shareware   A method of distributing software, often including downloading the software from a BBS or The Microsoft Network. With shareware, you get to use the software before deciding to pay for it. By paying for the software and registering it, you usually receive a manual, perhaps the most up-to-date version (which may include additional functionality). Shareware versions of software often include intrusive reminders to register—the registered versions do not include these reminders.

shortcut   A pointer to a file, document, or printer in Windows 95. A shortcut is represented by an icon in Explorer, on the desktop, or as an entry in the Start menu. Selecting the program shortcut icon or menu entry runs the program to which the shortcut "points." Selecting a document shortcut runs the application that created the document (provided the document type is associated with a program). Dragging and dropping a document onto a printer shortcut prints the document. Note that a shortcut does *not* create a copy of the program or document itself.

shortcut keys   A keystroke or key combination that enables you to activate a command without having to enter a menu or click a button.

shortcut menu   A popup menu that appears when you right-click an object for which a menu is appropriate. The shortcut menu displays only those options which make sense for the object you select and current conditions.

slide   The term for the working desktop area in Slide view of PowerPoint, as well as for each page of output of a PowerPoint presentation.

slide show   A term for a PowerPoint presentation.

Slide Sorter   A view in PowerPoint that shows miniatures of all slides in a presentation.

Small Computer System Interface (SCSI)   An ANSI standard bus design. SCSI host adapters are used to adapt an ISA, EISA, MCI, PCI, or VLB (VESA Local Bus) bus to a SCSI bus so that SCSI devices (such as disk drives, CD-ROMs, tape backups, and other devices) can be interfaced. A SCSI bus accommodates up to eight devices; however, the bus adapter is considered one device, thereby enabling seven usable devices to be interfaced to each SCSI adapter. SCSI devices are intelligent devices. SCSI disk drives have embedded controllers and interface to a SCSI bus adapter. A SCSI interface card is therefore a "bus adapter," not a "controller."

snap   To control the location of objects on a PowerPoint slide by pulling them to an invisible measurement—for example, snapping them to a grid or the location of another object.

soft fonts   Depending on your printing hardware, may be downloaded to your printer. Downloading fonts reduces the time taken by the printer to process printouts. Although downloading soft fonts is done only once (per session), benefits are realized through subsequent printing.

Soundblaster An extremely popular family of sound boards, developed and marketed by Creative Labs. Because of the popularity and large market share of this product family, most sound boards advertise themselves as "Soundblaster-compatible," meaning that drivers provided in Windows, Windows 95, and programs such as games will work with these boards. However, some boards' compatibility is not perfect.

source document In OLE, the document that contains the information you want to link into (to appear in) another document (the destination document).

splitting A method of breaking up text on slides with too much information on them into a series of slides.

spool A temporary holding area for the data you want to print. When printing a document, it can take some time (depending on the length of the document and the speed of your printer) for the document to come off your printer. By spooling the data, you may continue using your computer while the document is printing, because the computer "feeds" the spool contents to the printer as fast as the printer can handle it. When the print job is completed, the spool file is automatically deleted.

Start menu A menu located at the left end of the taskbar. Clicking the button marked "Start" opens a popup menu that makes Help, the Run command, settings, find, shutdown, a list of programs (actually, program shortcuts), and a list of recently accessed documents available for you to run with a single click. For some items (such as the Documents item), a submenu opens to the side of the main item to display the list of choices. You can configure the Start menu to specify which programs are available to run from it.

Startup folder A folder that contains any programs that you want Windows 95 to run whenever you start up. You can drag and drop program shortcuts into the Startup folder to add them to the list of programs to run.

static object In OLE, where some objects have a "hot link" to their original application, static objects are simply pasted into a destination document using the Clipboard. These objects are not updated if the original object is updated. This is the simple "pasting" that most Windows users use on a daily basis.

Style Checker A feature of PowerPoint that checks for consistency in grammar and style in the text of slides.

stroke font A font that can have its size greatly altered without distortion.

submenu A related set of options that appear when you select a menu item (see *cascading menu*).

subtitle A secondary heading on a slide.

summary slide   A slide that can be automatically generated containing the title text from each slide in a PowerPoint presentation.

system disk   The disk containing the operating system, or at least enough of it to start the system and then look on another disk for the support files.

system fonts   Used by Windows to draw menus, controls, and operate specialized control text in Windows. System fonts are proportional fonts that can be sized and manipulated quickly.

T

tab (dialog boxes)   In dialog boxes, there may be multiple panels of information. Each panel has an extension at the top that names the panel. This small extension is called a *tab*.

TAPI   Telephony Applications Programming Interface; provides a method for programs to work with modems, independent of dealing directly with the modem hardware. All the information you give Windows during the modem configuration is used for TAPI to set up its interface. Communications programs that are written specifically for Windows 95 will talk to TAPI, which will then issue appropriate commands to the modem. This is called *device independence*.

taskbar   An area that runs across the bottom of the Windows 95 desktop. The Start button (see *Start menu*) is at the left end of the taskbar, and the clock can be displayed at the right end of the taskbar. Running applications are represented as buttons on the taskbar, the current window is shown as a depressed button, and all other applications are displayed as raised buttons. Clicking the button for an inactive application activates that application and displays its window as the current window.

task list   A list of currently running applications. You can switch tasks by clicking an item in the task list. The task list is accessed by pressing Alt+Tab on the keyboard.

template   A file containing certain graphic elements, text, or formatting styles that can be applied to any document.

text-based   See *character-based*.

text box   A drawing object that allows you to enter text within it.

text file   A file containing only text characters.

text object   An object consisting of letters and numbers, as opposed to graphic elements.

textured background   A background design that emulates a texture such as wood or marble.

thumbnail   A miniature rendition of a graphic file. A thumbnail gives an idea of what the full-size graphic looks like, and is usually used as a gateway to view the full-size graphic.

TIFF   Tagged Image File Format.

tile   To reduce and move windows so that they can all be seen at once.

timing   The automatic settings applied to an on-screen slide show that control how long each slide is displayed.

time-out   A time period after which a device or driver might signal the operating system and cease trying to perform its duty. If a printer is turned off, for example, when you try to print, the driver waits for a predetermined period of time, then issues an error message. In computer terminology, the driver has *timed out*.

title bar   The bar at the top of a program or document window that shows you what its title is. The control menu, maximize, minimize, restore, and taskbar buttons can be accessed in the title bar.

toolbar   A collection of buttons that typically make the more common tools for an application easily accessible. Although often grouped in a line under the menus, a toolbar can be located on the left or right side of the working area — or even be relocated to any area of the screen the user wants. In some applications (for example, MS Office applications such as Word), the toolbar is user-configurable — the user can display different toolbars, and add or remove tool buttons from the bar.

transition   The change from one slide to another in a slide show; transition effects can make the new slide appear to fly in from the side of the screen or rain down from the top of the screen, for example.

transparency   A clear film printed with images and text and used with an overhead projector to display a presentation.

transparent background   A background effect that allows any objects behind the transparent object to show through.

TrueType fonts   A font technology developed by Microsoft in response to Adobe's success in the scaleable font business with its own Type 1 and Type 3 PostScript fonts. Used as a simple means for all Windows applications to have access to a wide selection of fonts for screen and printer output. TrueType fonts greatly simplify using fonts on a Windows

App

B

computer. The same fonts can be used on Windows 3.1, Windows NT, Windows 95, and other Windows products, such as Windows for Workgroups. Consisting of two files (one for screen and one for printer), hundreds of TrueType fonts are available from a variety of manufacturers. Depending on your printer, the TrueType font manager internal to Windows, in conjunction with the printer driver, generates either bitmapped or downloadable soft fonts.

U

ungrouping   The act of disassociating objects which have been grouped together to function as a single object.

unimodem driver   A universal modem driver supplied by Microsoft as part of Windows 95. The modem driver assumes that the modem supports the Hayes AT command set (most do).

uninstalling applications   When you install an application in Windows 95, places the necessary files in many different places on your hard drive. You can't remove all of a program by simply erasing the contents of its main subdirectory. To uninstall the application—and remove all the files it placed on your hard drive — you must run a special program that should have been included with the application. Many applications do not include the uninstaller program, although, to be certified under Windows 95, the uninstaller program must be included.

unprintable area   The area, usually around the extreme edges of the paper, in which the printer is incapable of printing. For example, a laser printer cannot print in the 1/4 inch at the left and right edges of the paper. It is important to know the unprintable area, since graphics or text you place in this area will be cut off when printed.

upload   The act of sending a file to a remote computer (see *download*).

URL   Uniform Resource Locator; a string that identifies a specific location on the Internet.

V

ValuPack   A set of multimedia files and applications that come with Microsoft Office programs and can be run from the program CD.

vector fonts   A set of lines that connect points to form characters.

vertical alignment The relative measurement of an object from elements above and beneath it.

video clip A file containing a video sequence.

video for windows A set of utilities and protocols for implementing full-motion video in Windows 95.

view Different displays in PowerPoint that allow you to see the information in your presentation from different perspectives and use different tools and menu commands.

App
B

virtual memory The use of permanent media (for example, a hard drive) to simulate additional RAM (see *swap file*). This allows large applications to run in less physical RAM than they normally would require. When RAM runs low, the operating system uses a virtual memory manager program to temporarily store data on the hard disk like it was in RAM, which makes RAM free for data manipulation. When needed, the data is read back from the disk and reloaded into RAM.

virus A computer program written to interrupt or destroy your work. A virus may do something as innocuous as display a message, or something as destructive as reformatting your hard drive—or almost anything in between. Your computer can *catch* a virus from a floppy disk, or even from a file downloaded from a remote source, such as a BBS. Once your computer has become *infected*, the virus may spread via connections on a network or floppy disks you share with others. A variety of virus-detecting software exists, (including one packaged with Windows 95).

volume Disk partition(s) formatted and available for use by the operating system.

volume label The identifier for a volume (see *volume*) or disk. This is specified when formatting the volume or disk.

W

wallpaper A backdrop for the Windows desktop, made up of a graphics files. The graphics can be either *centered*, appearing only once in the center of the desktop, or *tiled*, repeating as many times as the graphic will fit.

WAV files Named for the three-character extension WAV (for sound wave), a file containing a digitized sound. Depending on the sampling rate and resolution, the sound recorded in the WAV file seems realistic (provided you have the sound card and speakers to hear it). These files can be quite large, running into the multi-megabyte range for high-quality recordings.

Web browser   A software program that enables you to view home pages and retrieve information from the Internet.

wizard   Microsoft's name for a step-by-step set of instructions that guide you through a particular task. For example, there are many wizards included with Windows 95 for installing new hardware, configuring the Start menu, and changing other aspects of the environment.

WordArt   An applet that comes with PowerPoint which allows you to create text enhancement effects.

WordPad   A program included with Windows 95 that enables you to do basic word processing and save the results in plain text format, Word 6 format, or rich text format.

word wrap   In word processing, this refers to words that cannot be completed on one line automatically "wrapping" to the beginning of the next line. Most word processors use word wrap automatically — an exception is Notepad, where you must turn on word wrap.

workgroup   A collection of networked PCs grouped to facilitate work that users of the computers tend to do together. The machines are not necessarily in the same room or office.

World Wide Web   The fastest growing part of the Internet, the Web or WWW is a collection of hypertext documents. It provides access to images and sounds from thousands of different Web sites, via a special programming language called HyperText Markup Language, or HTML. This language is used to create "hypertext" documents, which include embedded commands.

WYSIWYG   Short for "What you see is what you get," this term refers to the ability of an application to display an accurate representation of the printed output on the screen.

X

x coordinate   The position of an item relative to the left side of the screen. Values increase as you move to the right.

Xmodem   An error-correction protocol (see *binary transfer protocol*) used by the DOS application XMODEM and many other communications programs. Xmodem uses CRC (cyclical redundancy check), a means of detecting errors in transmissions between modems or across wired serial links.

Y

y coordinate   The position of an item relative to the bottom of the screen. Values increase as you move down the screen.

Ymodem   Another form of Xmodem that allows batch transfers of files and (in Ymodem G) hardware error control.

Z

Zmodem   A fully functional streaming protocol where Xmodem is a send and acknowledge protocol that causes delays in the transfer equal to twice the modem lag on a connection. Zmodem is the preferred way of exchanging data because it is reliable, quick, and relatively easy to implement.

zooming   A feature used to change the size of the display on your screen by percentages.

Index

Broaden Your Mind
And Your Business
With Que

The *Special Edition Using* series remains the most-often recommended product line for computer users who want detailed reference information. With thorough explanations, troubleshooting advice, and special expert tips, these books are the perfect all-in-one resource.

Special Edition Using Microsoft Office 97 Professional
- ISBN: 0-7897-0896-5
- $39.99 USA
- Pub Date: 12/96

Special Edition Using Windows 95
- ISBN: 1-56529-921-3
- $39.99 USA
- Pub Date: 8/95

Special Edition Using Microsoft Word 97
- ISBN: 0-7897-0962-7
- $34.99 USA
- Pub Date: 12/96

For more information on these and other Que products, visit your local book retailer or call 1-800-772-0477.

que

QUE'S MICROSOFT® OFFICE 97 RESOURCE CENTER

For the most up-to-date information about all the Microsoft Office 97 products, visit Que's Web Resource Center at

http://www.mcp.com/que/msoffice

The web site extends the reach of this Que book by offering you a rich selection of supplementary content.

You'll find information about Que books as well as additional content about these new **Office 97 topics**:

- **Word**
- **Excel**
- **PowerPoint®**
- **Visual Basic® for Applications**
- **Access**
- **Outlook™**
- **FrontPage™**

Visit Que's web site regularly for a variety of new and updated Office 97 information.

The best resources and tips for getting things done with Office 97!

Complete and Return this Card
for a *FREE* Computer Book Catalog

Thank you for purchasing this book! You have purchased a superior computer book written expressly for your needs. To continue to provide the kind of up-to-date, pertinent coverage you've come to expect from us, we need to hear from you. Please take a minute to complete and return this self-addressed, postage-paid form. In return, we'll send you a free catalog of all our computer books on topics ranging from word processing to programming and the internet.

☐   Mrs. ☐   Ms. ☐   Dr. ☐

me (first) ☐☐☐☐☐☐☐☐☐☐   (M.I.) ☐   (last) ☐☐☐☐☐☐☐☐☐☐☐☐☐☐☐☐☐

dress ☐☐☐☐☐☐☐☐☐☐☐☐☐☐☐☐☐☐☐☐☐☐☐☐☐☐☐☐☐☐☐☐☐

☐☐☐☐☐☐☐☐☐☐☐☐☐☐☐☐☐☐☐☐☐☐☐☐☐☐☐☐☐☐☐☐☐

ty ☐☐☐☐☐☐☐☐☐☐☐☐☐☐☐☐☐   State ☐☐   Zip ☐☐☐☐☐   ☐☐☐☐

one ☐☐☐   ☐☐☐   ☐☐☐☐   Fax ☐☐☐   ☐☐☐   ☐☐☐☐

mpany Name ☐☐☐☐☐☐☐☐☐☐☐☐☐☐☐☐☐☐☐☐☐☐☐☐☐☐☐☐☐

mail address ☐☐☐☐☐☐☐☐☐☐☐☐☐☐☐☐☐☐☐☐☐☐☐☐☐☐☐☐☐

Please check at least (3) influencing factors for purchasing this book.

ont or back cover information on book .... ☐
ecial approach to the content .... ☐
mpleteness of content .... ☐
uthor's reputation .... ☐
blisher's reputation .... ☐
ok cover design or layout .... ☐
dex or table of contents of book .... ☐
ice of book .... ☐
ecial effects, graphics, illustrations .... ☐
ther (Please specify): _____ ☐

How did you first learn about this book?

w in Macmillan Computer Publishing catalog .... ☐
ecommended by store personnel .... ☐
w the book on bookshelf at store .... ☐
ecommended by a friend .... ☐
eceived advertisement in the mail .... ☐
w an advertisement in: _____ ☐
ead book review in: _____ ☐
ther (Please specify): _____ ☐

How many computer books have you purchased in the last six months?

his book only .... ☐   3 to 5 books .... ☐
books .... ☐   More than 5 .... ☐

4. Where did you purchase this book?

Bookstore .... ☐
Computer Store .... ☐
Consumer Electronics Store .... ☐
Department Store .... ☐
Office Club .... ☐
Warehouse Club .... ☐
Mail Order .... ☐
Direct from Publisher .... ☐
Internet site .... ☐
Other (Please specify): _____ ☐

5. How long have you been using a computer?

☐ Less than 6 months   ☐ 6 months to a year
☐ 1 to 3 years   ☐ More than 3 years

6. What is your level of experience with personal computers and with the subject of this book?

	With PCs	With subject of book
New	☐	☐
Casual	☐	☐
Accomplished	☐	☐
Expert	☐	☐

Source Code ISBN: 0-7897-0961-9

7. Which of the following best describes your job title?

Administrative Assistant .... ☐
Coordinator .... ☐
Manager/Supervisor .... ☐
Director .... ☐
Vice President .... ☐
President/CEO/COO .... ☐
Lawyer/Doctor/Medical Professional .... ☐
Teacher/Educator/Trainer .... ☐
Engineer/Technician .... ☐
Consultant .... ☐
Not employed/Student/Retired .... ☐
Other (Please specify): _____ ☐

8. Which of the following best describes the area of the company your job title falls under?

Accounting .... ☐
Engineering .... ☐
Manufacturing .... ☐
Operations .... ☐
Marketing .... ☐
Sales .... ☐
Other (Please specify): _____ ☐

9. What is your age?

Under 20 ....
21-29 ....
30-39 ....
40-49 ....
50-59 ....
60-over ....

10. Are you:

Male ....
Female ....

11. Which computer publications do you read regularly? (Please list)

_____
_____
_____
_____
_____
_____
_____
_____
_____

Comments: _____
_____
_____

Fold here and scotch-tape